PRAISE FOR *The New Chinese Empire*

"Mr. Terrill has written a fascinating book, filled with historical lore and contemporary observations, about the red dragon."
—*The Washington Times*

"There is much food for thought in this comprehensive study of China's view of the world. The author has carefully examined the roots of China's view as well as its trends. Any serious student of China and officials engaged in China policy would benefit from its conclusions and analysis."
—James Lilley, former U.S. Ambassador to China and Director of the American Institute in Taiwan

"Terrill has produced another engaging book, and anyone interested in China, especially in the relationship between the U.S. and China, would do well to study it."
—*The Christian Science Monitor*

"Outstanding.... Ross Terrill's The New Chinese Empire puts the U.S.–China relationship into the vast context of China's millennia-old imperial Weltanschauung and the strategic thought it has engendered."
—*Journal of International Security Affairs*

"This is China with an edge, as incisively described by an old hand who for the past four decades has been there, done it. Terrill's China veers from possible implosion to possible explosion as it strives to maintain a self-proclaimed economic and political dominance in Asia. It is a China not fully understood by America."
—Seymour M. Hersh

"I hope that Terrill's book will find a place on State Department reading lists.... He masterfully describes the full nature of Chinese ambitions, their deep historical roots, and the coming developments that will thwart them.... [The New Chinese Empire has] many keen insights and memorable phrases."
—*The American Enterprise*

"The author backs up his intriguing reflections and insightful prognosis with a wealth of historical background…. For those who are uneasy about China's role in the stability and fortune of the U.S., this is an excellent tutorial."
—*The Asian Reporter*

"By looking at China's past, Terrill has provided an excellent road map for understanding its future."
—*Business Week*

"Ross Terrill shows how China's Communist rulers have re-imagined the empire as a nation, essentializing a rich and ambiguous history as an imperial project. This bold and broad-ranging work offers a powerful challenge to those with a too-sanguine vision of China's future and the impact of that China on our peace and prosperity."
—Prof. Edward Friedman, U. Wisconsin–Madison, author of *Chinese Village, Socialist State*

"The New Chinese Empire is an ambitious effort to penetrate the mystery of the Chinese state. With provocative commentary that boldly blends ancient history with current events, Ross Terrill examines not only the complexity of Chinese politics, but the fear, awe, and even reverence it inspires worldwide."
—Iris Chang, author of *The Rape of Nanking*

"To long-standing China-watcher and journalist Ross Terrill's credit, he reminds us in his new book The New Chinese Empire: 'Repeatedly, American and other officials, commentators, and scholars skip over the fundamentals of the authoritarian Chinese state.'"
—*The Weekly Standard*

"Ross Terrill lays out, expertly and lucidly, the most likely scenarios for the development of China as it stands poised at a new crossroad. His extensive personal experience combined with penetrating historical perspectives have yielded an engrossing portrait of China in transition which provides the critical insights we need to gauge its future impact on our society."
—Seymour Topping, Professor Emeritus of International Journalism, Columbia University, former managing editor, *The New York Times*

CHINA AND ITS FOURTEEN NEIGHBORS

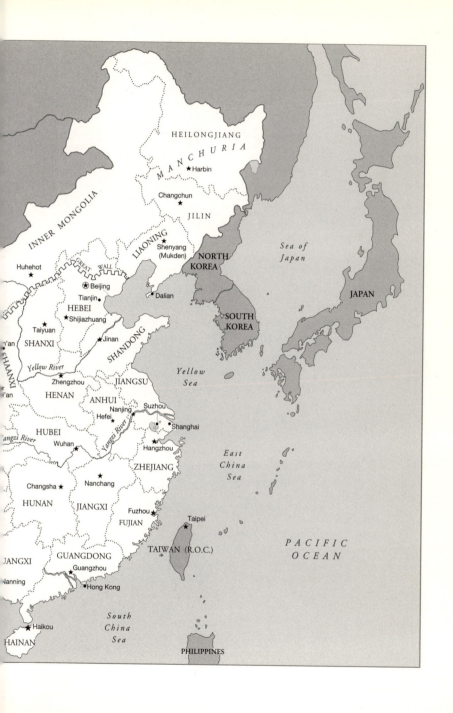

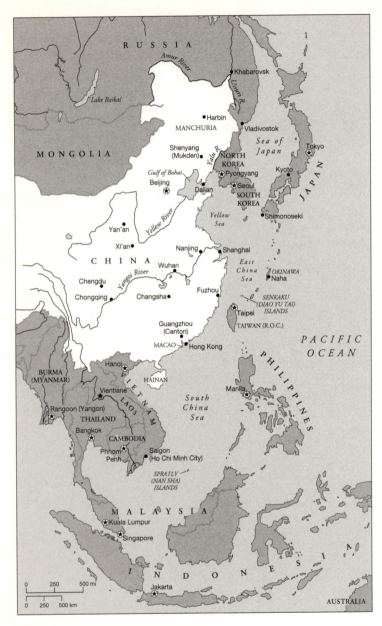

CHINA'S MARITIME FLANK

CHINA'S INNER ASIAN FLANK

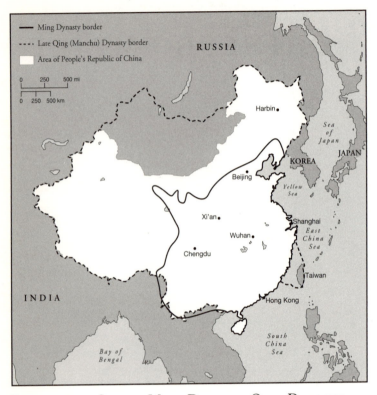

COMPARATIVE SIZE OF MING DYNASTY, QING DYNASTY, AND PRC.

THE NEW
CHINESE EMPIRE

*And What It Means for
the United States*

ROSS TERRILL

*In Rebecca -
All best,
Ross Terrill*

A Member of the Perseus Books Group

 A CORNELIA AND MICHAEL BESSIE BOOK

Jian wang zhi lai

"Know the Future in the Mirror of the Past"

—CHINESE SAYING

 A CORNELIA AND MICHAEL BESSIE BOOK

Published by Basic Books,
A Member of the Perseus Books Group

Hardback first published in 2003 by Basic Books
Paperback first published in 2004 by Basic Books

Books published by Basic Books are available at special discounts for bulk purchases in
the United States by corporations, institutions, and other organizations. For more information, please contact the Special Markets Department at the Perseus Books Group, 11
Cambridge Center, Cambridge MA 02142, or call (617) 252–5298, (800) 255–1514, or
e-mail special.markets@perseusbooks.com.

Library of Congress Cataloging-in-Publication Data
Terrill, Ross.
    The new Chinese empire - and what it means for the United States /
by Ross Terrill.
        p. cm.
    ISBN-10 0-465-08412-5 (hardcover) ISBN-10 0-465-08413-3 (pbk)
    ISBN-13 978-0-465-08412-8 (hardcover) ISBN-13 978-0-465-08413-5 (pbk)
    1. China—History—1976- I. Title.

DS779.2 .T47 2003
951.05—dc21
                                                                    2002152575

EBA   06 07 08 / 15 14 13 12 11 10 9 8 7 6 5

CONTENTS

ACKNOWLEDGMENTS

The first books I wrote on China were a reportage, *800,000,000: The Real China,* and a study of five cities, *Flowers on an Iron Tree.* Later, as I understood that personality counted in the politics of Mao's China in inverse proportion to Beijing's assertion that not individuals but only the "socialist line" counted, I mostly turned to biography, with *Mao* and *Madame Mao* as the results. Recently, I have focused on the power and peculiarity of the Chinese state.

In the aftermath of the tragic night of June 3–4, 1989, in Beijing, which I spent in and around Tiananmen Square, a young Chinese friend reflected on the democracy movement and its crushing. He had seen a soldier shoot a pro-democracy demonstrator dead; in the darkness he grabbed a cook's metal stirring rod and hit the soldier on the head. "I had never seen anyone die before my eyes before," said the 26-year-old during the days of tears and fear that followed the massacre. "A Westerner could not believe the current situation in Beijing. The power of the state in China is just overwhelming."

Three years later another participant in the democracy movement, who fled China in the aftermath of June 4 and became a student at Boston University, returned to China and was nabbed in the middle of the night at his mother's house. He had "undermined the state" with wrong political ideas. I was in Beijing and had met up with this student; I, too, was grabbed by the Chinese police. A knock on the door of my hotel room shortly after midnight signified my expulsion from China. "Public Security" men, inspecting my belongings inch by inch and finding documents with "bourgeois ideas," declared that I had "hurt the feelings of the Chinese people" by sympathizing with a young Chinese who wanted elections in his country.

These two experiences helped propel me to write this book. My aim is to show that fundamental features of the Chinese party-state, which combines Leninism with Chinese autocratic tradition, explain much of the domestic and foreign policies of China today. This state does not lack a much-tested rationale. Had the French not given us the phrase *raison d'état*, Chinese philosophers of state power from 2,000 years ago offer rich equivalents. But today the Chinese state is an anachronism.

Portions of the book in draft benefited from the sage advice of colleagues and friends in China studies: Lucian Pye, Edward Friedman, Richard J. Smith, James Millward, Paul Ropp, Gordon Bennett, John Schrecker, Tim Connor, Frank Langfitt, and Alan Wachman. With Chinese materials, I was helped by Huang Lei, Kuan Hung-Chang, and Sui Jun. Harvard's Fairbank Center for East Asian Research, with Wilt Idema as director, and Harvard's Modern Asia Center, under Dwight Perkins, are my intellectual home for China studies, and are enormously appreciated. Each spring, the University of Texas at Austin offers welcome and stimulus. At the Fairbank Center library, Nancy Hearst was indispensable, the staff at Harvard's Yenching library solved problems courteously, and John C. Thomas's careful copy-editing eye staved off error. Simon Michael Bessie, my first and beloved editor (he published my *Mao* in 1980 at Harper & Row; it is still in print around the world in many tongues) first saw the potential of this book. He eased my writing task and improved its outcome.

CHINA'S PRINCIPAL DYNASTIES

Shang	16th–11th centuries B.C.
Zhou	1045–256 B.C.
Qin	221–206 B.C.
Han	202 B.C.–A.D. 220
Sui	581–618
Tang	618–907
Song	960–1279
Yuan (Mongol)	1279–1368
Ming	1368–1644
Qing (Manchu)	1644–1912

ONE

THE PROBLEM OF CHINA

CHINESE CIVILIZATION is one of the greatest our globe has known. China boasts a political governance over its core territory longer than that of any other nation. The Chinese people have displayed conspicuous talent and industry when given the opportunity. Until the time of the French Revolution, the Chinese empire was probably unmatched among all communities for scope, populousness, bureaucratic sophistication, wealth, and, as any gallery or library can attest, for arts, crafts, and literature. At the dawn of the twentieth century, the Chinese boldly toppled a monarchy that had stood intermittently for ten times as long as U.S. history. Many remarkable products, taken for granted today, originated in China, including gunpowder, printing, and the compass. Chinese paved the way in astronomy, strategies of warfare, and theories of hard-nosed statecraft.

But the nineteenth and twentieth centuries were poor ones for Chinese politics. John Paton Davies exaggerated only somewhat in his 1972 memoir *Dragon by the Tail* in calling China since the fall of the monarchy in 1911–1912 a disappointment to just about everyone. Wrote the American diplomat with his long experience of pre-1949 China: "The Western businessmen, missionaries and educators who had tried to modernize and Christianize it failed. The Japanese militarists who tried to conquer it failed. The American government, which tried to democratize and unify it, failed. The Soviet rulers who tried to insinuate control over it failed." More regrettable, China's own political experiments disappointed. "Chiang [Kai-shek] failed," Davies went on. "Mao failed."[1] After five decades under the rule of Mao Zedong, Deng Xiaoping, and Jiang Zemin, the People's Republic of China (PRC) stands as the most contradictory of the major nations. The Chinese state hovers between a set of unsustainable authoritarian traditions-cum-myths and an elusive modern political form to match its now-transformed society and economy.

Since the collapse in 1911–1912 of a 2,500-year-old Confucian-Legalist monarchy—vividly portrayed in Bernardo Bertolucci's film *The Last Emperor*—China has neither established a worthy and just political system nor adapted to being a nation-state. From the struggle between idealistic nationalists and regional generals (usually known in English as "warlords") of the early twentieth century, to the confrontation between Leninists and a student democracy movement at Tiananmen Square in 1989, China flirted with freedom but generally opted for repression when it perceived any threat of disorder. "China today is more certain of what it does not want," observes Gordon Bennett of Chinese politics, "than of what it does want."[2]

The failure to find a respected, modern replacement for monarchical rule is connected with Communist Beijing's clinging to the ways of empire. The Chinese state at the start of the twenty-first century is a misfit on the chessboard of major power relations. China remains a "civilization pretending to be a nation,"[3] in the phrase of Lucian Pye. It condescends to its own people, as we shall see in Chapters 5 and 6. It is not yet comfortable as one country among others in an ever-shifting international balance of power.

Former empires fill the trash can of history, but the case of China is far from typical. An imperial structure fell with the end of the Qing Dynasty in 1911–1912, yet its components did not totally disappear. An empire is not merely a large and far-flung realm. As a political construction, it is by nature repressive, because it requires mechanisms and/or myths to hold together diverse cultures. A modern democratic nation is different. It is a

[1]Davies, 1972, 429.
[2]Prof. Gordon Bennett to the author, University of Texas at Austin, July 4, 2002.
[3]Pye, 1990, 58.

political organism, the open-ended sum of its parts, which are the citizens whose expressed will determines the nation's direction. (To be sure, between the pure types of empire and modern democratic nation there are numerous gradations.) In truth, the nation *is* the modern nation, or what Anthony Smith calls the "citizen-nation." The ancient polities were ethnic states, but not nations, for a nation requires a public culture. There are "pre-modern elements within many nations," including location, myths, and memories, but nations did not exist before the eighteenth century.[4]

By this definition of empire, the PRC, an autocratic Chinese state ruling a land nearly half of which was historically inhabited by non-Chinese people, is indeed an empire of our time, as out of place as fish in trees. In basic respects it lacks the traits of a nation and does not behave like a nation. It consistently uses the techniques of the autocratic side of Chinese imperial tradition and its goals partake of imperial goals. Historically, China - not known as such until modern times - was a fluid entity, now ruling foreign peoples, on occasion ruled by foreign peoples. The final dynasty, the Qing (Manchu), took form by military conquest, and it is this China that the Chinese Communists control today.

That the PRC is imperial does not mean China is about to eclipse the United States and dominate the world. On the contrary, I believe the Beijing regime is quite powerful at home but rather weak on the global stage. The PRC is *not* an empire in the sense of trying to communize or otherwise control the world (as the Soviet Union, arguably, aimed to do). Its imperial behavior is mostly limited to its own (extensive) neighborhoods of Northeast Asia, Southeast Asia, and Central Asia. But the PRC *is* an empire in that it appropriates an imperial idea of China, reinventing a 2,500-year-old autocracy to control its populace and hector non-Chinese neighboring peoples.

The PRC regime, as a result, is dysfunctional in the world of nation-states. It is attached to an idea of unity that does not befit the jumping reality of a modernizing China, and is probably antithetical to unity under modern conditions. From 1949 on, Marxist universalism strengthened China's neo-imperial pretension. Was socialism, which

---

[4]Anthony Smith, 1991, 44, 46, 70.

Beijing trumpeted, not the destiny of all peoples? Would the socialist East not "bury" the capitalist West? The fading of Marxism since the 1980s has seen the Chinese Communist Party (CCP) return to a version of pre-modern Chinese universalism, the idea of *Da yitong* ("Great Systemic Whole"),[5] a political-moral monolith that occupies all available philosophic space. Still, as Beijing twists history and uses false maps of China's periphery as weapons, autocracy is reinforced, the imperial sense vindicated, and the contradiction with a loosened society and freer economy intensified.

As long as the idea of a Great Systemic Whole is retained, the Chinese will remain "burdened by their history," as Harald Bøckman observes, "victims of their historical success." Yet, unlike Bøckman, I see the claim to Han-Communist-led universalism as doomed. Increasing numbers of Chinese individuals, in their actual lives and their mentality, no longer support the suffocatingly statist *Da yitong* idea, which they see to be imperial, top-down, a fusion of doctrine and power.

DESPITE BEING a misfit in the late twentieth and early twenty-first centuries, the Chinese Communist state has often been successful in turning weakness into strength. From stale crusts it has thrown a banquet. Since 1949 the PRC has huffed and puffed its way to respect in many a surprising quarter. In the early 1970s, it persuaded dozens of nations that "One China" meant the separate island community of Taiwan was part of the PRC; just as its rival, Chiang Kai-shek's Republic of China (ROC), in retreat on Taiwan, insisted that the Mainland belonged under the ROC. In the late 1970s, Beijing formed what was widely seen as a global strategic triangle with the United States and the USSR. By switching its weight from the Soviet side to the American side, it changed the face of international relations, even though China was far weaker than the United States and considerably weaker than the USSR.

In 1991 the USSR disappeared and China faced a shrunken strategic future. Yet in the eight years of the Clinton presidency, China, even with

---

[5]Bøckman, 1998, 332.

a weak hand, consistently set the agenda for its relations with the United States, which had the colossally strong hand of being the world's sole superpower, dominant alike in economics, culture, and military affairs. "China is a second-rank middle power," wrote Gerald Segal in his last article before an untimely death in 1999, "that has mastered the art of diplomatic theater: it has us willingly suspending our disbelief in its strength."[6] The PRC leaders enjoyed the spectacle of Henry Kissinger, a hard-boiled man, gush about Zhou Enlai's letter agreeing to Kissinger's secret visit to Beijing in 1971. "This is the most important communication that has come to an American president since the end of World War Two," Kissinger said. He also called "the opening to China the country's greatest watershed since the Civil War."

In 1972, when President Nixon first sat down with Zhou, the initial topic was the need for secrecy. Nixon spoke as if bathed in the glow of the Chinese state's sense of itself, almost entirely forgetful of America's freedoms. He told Zhou that only he, Nixon, had seen the transcript of Kissinger's prior talks in Beijing and only he, Nixon, would see the transcript of the conversation about to begin. "The interpreter is yours," Nixon went on, eager to acknowledge his capitulation. He explained to Zhou that U.S. officials "have a problem keeping secrets."

Said Kissinger later to Nixon, "with the exception of the UK, the PRC might well be the closest to us in its global perceptions. No other world leaders have the sweep and imagination of Mao and Zhou, nor the capacity and will to pursue a long range policy." After another talk with Mao, Kissinger noted: "[He] radiates authority and deep wisdom. . . . I was even more impressed by the grandeur of the Chairman this time than last." The awe in which the Washington leaders held the Beijing court led to a policy position different from that revealed to the American public. "[I]n plain terms," Kissinger wrote to Nixon, "we have now become tacit allies."[7] Yet the Nixon administration did not speak this way to the American people.

Certainly there were valid, important reasons for Nixon's opening to China. Granted, too, some of Kissinger's high claims for China's

[6]Segal, 1999, 24.
[7](All Kissinger and Nixon quotes) Mann, 1999, 29, 41, 60, 61, 63.

importance were a calculated effort to gain support for Nixon's policy in the Republican Party and elsewhere. Nevertheless, for Beijing, the rhetoric from Washington was a striking diplomatic success for a second-rank power. The American leaders had "gone to China and become Sinified" (*lai hua*). This Chinese phrase could be translated as "come and be shaped into a Chinese." It had long been used by the Confucian-influenced monarchy to signify China's capacity to civilize lesser peoples, overlooking China's practical borrowing from others.

China–U.S. relations was not the only arena in which Mao and Zhou turned weakness into a kind of strength. They also did it with the USSR and others. Mao bamboozled Nikita Khrushchev by techniques of hospitality like scheduling a summit meeting at a swimming pool (Khrushchev could not swim and did not enjoy sitting with Mao in a bathing suit) and serving him endless cups of tea (Khrushchev did not like tea). From time to time Mao would slip into the pool, leaving Khrushchev stiff and self-conscious in his poolside chair. Khrushchev never touched the Chinese tea, but each full cup was periodically taken away and replaced with another.

Such techniques soon helped Beijing play the "American card" against the Soviet Union under Khrushchev's successor, Leonid Brezhnev. The Chinese made bold to insult Moscow, on paper its ally, during the 1960s and 1970s, with language that, read today, seems unbelievable. From being the junior partner of the Soviet Union in the Communist bloc, Beijing, for most of the time between Nixon's first visit to China in 1972 and the Soviet Union's demise in 1991 (which China's defection from the socialist bloc helped to bring about), assailed and defied a power far mightier than itself. Of course, lesser powers do sometimes bait superior powers with impunity, but the Chinese case stands out in the twentieth century.

In 1971 I saw the ingenuity of the Chinese state firsthand. On a visit to China during the period of early rapprochement between Beijing and the United States, Australia, and other countries, I was given good treatment and some of my activities were reported in the Chinese media. The reason was that I had been an intermediary between an Australian political leader and the Chinese government, with the

French ambassador in Beijing also involved, in a maneuver that promised to transform relations between the PRC and Australia.[8] On the 1971 trip, I was called a "guest" who had been "invited to China." This was inaccurate. I was on a tourist visa. I did stay in some "guest houses," but mostly I paid the bill. Yet the combined flattery and condescension of the term "guest" was a clever flourish of dramatization. An invited guest could hopefully be controlled, as a private citizen could not be. If he was also labeled a "friend of China," as I was, expectations were created that he was under pressure to fulfill.

One day on that 1971 trip, Zhou Nan, then a foreign ministry aide and, years later, Beijing's chief in Hong Kong, together with a colleague, invited me to a talk at the International Club in the old Legation Quarter. I soon found out that the meeting had a concrete purpose. Since I knew Henry Kissinger slightly, and I was a captive friend in Beijing, I was expected to supply a full picture of the man and his views on international relations. Perhaps the fact that I was an Australian citizen, not an American, made me a more readily exploitable resource.

Zhou Nan pressed me about the national security advisor's aversion to the Soviet Union. It happened that Kissinger had not long before spoken to me of Moscow's inconstancy. Decisions are suddenly reversed, he had complained in his White House office, "as if there were a Government A and a Government B tugging away in opposite directions." I passed on this point of view to the two Chinese diplomats. Writing it all down, obviously pleased, Zhou Nan said this Russian style reminded him of a saying dating from the Warring States period (403–202 B.C.): "In the morning for Qin, in the evening for Chu." Zhou swept on with his inquiry: "Now tell us how Kissinger views Japan. . . ."

On another occasion, Zhou Nan drew me aside to advise him on which Australian journalists were most sympathetic to China. Beijing was preparing to issue visas ("invitations") to some Australian press to cover an upcoming visit by the Australian Leader of the Opposition, the nation's alternative prime minister. Chinese officials wanted advice

---

[8]Whitlam, 1985, 55; Manac'h, 1980, 382-383, 405, 408, 419-420; Terrill, 1992, 94ff.

on the best choices, and so turned to their guest-of-the-moment for help. On this matter the guest could not oblige.

When opposition leader Gough Whitlam arrived from Sydney, a summons reached him one hot rainy July evening to go to the Great Hall of the People on Tiananmen Square. I was among those accompanying him. Premier Zhou Enlai was waiting. To Whitlam's surprise the session was to be an open one in front of the half-dozen Australian journalists to whom Zhou Nan had issued visas. By this means, Premier Zhou put the Australian leader under considerable pressure. Whitlam's promises, in particular to ditch Taiwan for Beijing, would be written in stone. Indeed the Chinese premier made his imperial expectations crystal clear: "So far this is only words," he said in a stentorian tone at the end of the session. "When you return to Australia and become prime minister you will be able to carry out actions." All of these techniques were borrowed from the Chinese imperial tradition, given an edge by Marxist self-entitlement.

———

AMERICA AT PRESENT, in its sweet and sour relations with China, is dealing with an increasingly modern Chinese economy and society, yet simultaneously with a Leninist state that utilizes techniques of a creakingly old-fashioned Chinese state. This authoritarian state builds selectively and opportunistically on a more than 2000-years-old tradition of imperial rule. Many countries have an autocratic past, but no ancient empire survived into the twentieth century as China's did. The dynastic Chinese state saw itself as a moral agent, the guardian of a higher doctrine. Mandated by heaven itself, the state's jurisdiction was coterminus with the civilized world. The Chinese imperial state was a civilizer of peripheral peoples not yet blessed with the Chinese emperor's direct rule. Within China proper, it was a paternal force comparable to a father guiding a household.

Both democratic nations and empires can be multicultural, but in different ways. The multicultural character of American society is mediated to the level of government by the votes of individuals. In an empire, the "natives" (British empire style) or "minorities" (USSR or

PRC empire styles) are *building blocks* within a higher design conjured up by the imperial center. It is the authoritarian rule of an empire that keeps the multiple cultures of its realm obedient to a single center.

The United States and the former Soviet Union can both be seen as multicultural societies; but whereas Moscow held onto the Ukraine, Uzbekistan, and other republics in a fashion redolent of empire, Washington holds the Hispanics and other non-Anglo-Saxons of the United States within a free constitutional form. The Ukraine was a building block in the edifice of the Soviet Union. Mexicans who gain U.S. citizenship are Hispanic-American individuals who relate to state and federal government pretty much as white and black Americans do, voting as individuals, leading their (culturally different) lives within the rule of law.

The PRC is the last remaining major multicultural empire. The previous one of these to fall was the Soviet Union. As a multicultural empire, with the ethnic Chinese (Han) in charge, China is comparable to the Soviet Union as a multicultural empire, except that Han are 92% of the PRC population, whereas Russians were about half of the Soviet population. The manner of Beijing's hold over Tibet resembles Moscow's hold over Estonia, Latvia, and Lithuania prior to the Gorbachev era. In his authoritative study of Tibet, Tsering Shakya says Chinese nationalism has implemented "a policy of integrating Tibet within the greater polity of China, a perspective which sees Tibet as a prior part of China and does not, therefore, allow for consideration of the views or wishes of Tibetans."[9] Likewise, the Uighurs, a Turkic people alien to Chinese culture who preceded the Han people in what is now the western Chinese "autonomous area" of Xinjiang, are treated less as citizens with rights than as a designated "minority" under the collective tutelage of the Han majority.

Within America we welcome manifestations of China without a second thought. The Chinatowns of New York and San Francisco are not a threat to us because the United States is a free country in which individuals of all races make their way as permitted under the rule of

---

[9]Shakya, 2000, 447.

law established by democratic procedures. By contrast, being a non-Chinese within the new Chinese empire can be a very self-conscious experience. Western books or plays in China are vulnerable to sudden denunciation as "bourgeois liberal" by the ever-jumpy Communist Party. Muslims in Xinjiang and Buddhists in Lhasa are suspect in the eyes of the autocratic Han state. Even American scholars of Chinese ancestry were arrested in China during 2001 and confronted with absurd charges of "spying for Taiwan."

This defensive posture cannot be attributed to Chinese culture, nor to the attitudes of most Chinese people. "Disappointment with China," writes Lucian Pye, "is of a [particularly] troublesome sort. . . . [O]utsiders often have an easy time establishing comfortable, even warm relations with individual Chinese. Problems almost invariably arise out of the actions of the government."[10] At issue is the nature of the Chinese state. It is a state that is oppressive, yet also afraid of its own people.

Many Americans who are informed about China, whether in business, government, arts, or education, find themselves uncertain or sharply divided about the fundamental condition and intentions of the PRC. Some say China is becoming an economic superpower that soon will buy and sell its neighbors at will. Others expect it to fragment into pieces. Is China nationalistic and on the march? Does it remain a Communist dinosaur? Is it already a billion-citizen unit of the global village? Is it, as the Clinton administration claimed, a "strategic partner" of the United States? Or is it, as President Bush said in distancing himself from Clinton, a "strategic rival"?

Reports on China abound in our newspapers, but it is not easy to agglomerate them into a coherent picture. One reason for our uncertainty about China's future is that grassroots and elite levels seem to inhabit different realms. Substantial parts of Chinese society purr with satisfaction at increased economic freedom and respite from the zealous politics of the Mao era, which tapered off after the demigod's death in 1976. But the ruling Communist Party seems far from satisfied. It is

---

[10]Pye, 1990, 57.

fearful of much around it, smoldering with historical grievances, and frustrated by the gap between China's goals and its capacities. This dualism is incomprehensible without unpacking the ingenious riddle of the Beijing party-state.

Is the true nature of the Chinese state not well known? Is it not apparent in Beijing and Shanghai that political authority has stepped aside to allow Chinese society to focus full throttle on making money? Well, not really. Some analysts describe the Chinese government as a "normal, Third World authoritarian regime." Others say that China is a transitional (from communism) state. Or a case of "market Leninism," or post-totalitarianism, or a "stable inhibited center." There *is* confusion about the nature of the Chinese state.

Repeatedly, American and other officials, commentators, and scholars skip over the fundamentals of the authoritarian Chinese state. Often there is a plausible reason: *culture* is destiny, or *economics* is destiny, worthy analysts believe; politics will take care of itself as society evolves. The culturalists tend to be cautious, feeling that both Marxism and democracy are unrecognizable in a Chinese context. The economics-first analysts tend to be optimistic, confident that a commercialized society will painlessly throw up a modernized politics. In the long run, one or other of these views may be vindicated. But, for the coming years, *politics* is destiny for the PRC. In the 1990s, the U.S. president on three occasions spoke as if Communist authoritarianism were a thing of the past in China. On the third occasion, shortly before his 1998 trip to Beijing, President Clinton said: "Russia and China, where the shackles of state socialism once choked off enterprise, are moving to join the thriving community of free democracies."[11] It is not a trivial distinction that Russia is an emerging democracy and China a Leninist system, albeit one flavored by Chinese autocratic tradition and presiding over a loosened-up society and commercialized economy.

Today's Chinese party-state has selected a Chinese past to suit its authoritarian purposes. Chinese history is rich and complex, and Chinese regimes regularly mythologized it in order to cling to office and

---

[11]*New York Times,* May 19, 1998.

pacify the people. The common picture of an old and unchanged China—united, orderly, matching the ideal and the real, haughtily passive before its neighbors, with a recorded history second to none—partakes of some clever fiction. Chinese history books are a concoction of tales and norms, regularly distorted for power purposes. The Chinese polity has had a tumultuous history, now an operating force, now a kingdom of the imagination. China's centrality and unity was at times a post hoc rationalization for the grabbing of other people's territory. Effectively, the CCP has essentialized a rich, ambiguous historical legacy to fuel its neo-imperial project.

No country, not China, nor Japan, nor Russia, is imperial by nature. Between the 1930s and the 1960s, Japan changed from a hard-edged, dissatisfied empire to a well-behaved, prospering democratic nation. Tokyo's subjugation of Asia in the name of a "Greater East Asian Co-prosperity Sphere" during the 1930s and 1940s was brief but violent; for its duration Japanese domestic politics was militarized. Yet, since World War Two, not only has Japan's foreign policy been a model of conciliatoriness, but its domestic politics have been pluralist and its press free.

During the 1990s, Russia turned away from its former imperial path and by 2002, under Vladimir Putin, was substantially democratic and pro-Western. By 2001, Moscow had essentially joined NATO, and the Russian economy, following a rocky decade in which an imperial, militarist, autocratic state was dismantled, had grown 5% for the year. "Never in the four and a half centuries of the modern Russia state," wrote Leon Aron in 2002, "has there been a Russia less imperialist, less militarized, and less threatening to its neighbors and the world than the one forged in the 1990s."[12] All this without being beaten in war and occupied by war victors. The new policy orientation in Moscow came because the *Russian state had changed.* Elections and the coming of the market were the tools that produced this new Russia. The elected Putin noted in September 2001 that for the first time in history Russia was spending more on education than on the military.

---

[12]Leon Aron, "Putin's Progress," *The Weekly Standard*, March 11, 2002, 21.

SINCE THE DEATH of Mao, the first neo-emperor of the PRC dynasty, China has been hurtling down one road in economics and limping down a different road in politics. This second, political road is an extension of the imperial way trodden by (some of) the emperors. The resulting contradiction between economics and politics runs through fundamental areas in the governance of the China that Jiang Zemin tentatively handed over to Hu Jintao at the 16th CCP Congress in 2002: rights of the citizen, ideology, and how China behaves in the world.

Consider some episodes from turn-of-the-century China, and their significance for our theme. In these three recent incidents, we see naked imperial nationalism, its fleshless bones protruding from a worn body politic. History and reality are left in the dust; myth takes over.

The first incident occurred in 1995, when Lee Teng-hui, then president of Taiwan, traveled to Cornell University to deliver an address. He had taken a Ph.D. at Cornell years before; his 1995 trip did not take him to Washington or include contact with the Clinton administration. But Beijing erupted in fury that President Lee should travel internationally and be seen—a correct perception!—as elected leader of the 22 million Taiwan people who live in all essential respects as a sovereign nation.

U.S.–China relations were buffeted as Beijing said Washington should have refused President Lee entry to the United States. True, the situation was not aided by the fact that Clinton had led Beijing to believe Lee would *not* be granted a visa, then changed his mind as virtually the entire Congress objected. Still, President Jiang Zemin, who had never been elected to anything by the Chinese people, was telling the elected leaders of the United States and Taiwan what they may and may not do in their bilateral relationship. It seemed absurd—yet it was entirely logical within Beijing's raison d'état.

The next year a repeat performance ensued. The Taiwan presidential election was held in March 1996, and just before it Beijing tested missiles close to the coastal fringes of Taiwan. This startling action was intended to demonstrate Beijing's nonacceptance of the reality of Taiwan's separateness and its preference for the fiction that Taiwan belongs to the PRC. The pretentious leaders in Beijing also felt they could scare millions of Taiwan voters into voting, not for Lee Teng-hui, who had resisted the Beijing version of "One China," but for an opponent more inclined to compromise with PRC demands.

Lee won the election by a margin larger than expected. The gap between the reality of Taiwan's situation and the new Chinese empire's view of Taiwan widened even more. You might think Beijing would feel embarrassed that democracy had come to Taiwan, while in the PRC it was not even acceptable, or legal, to propose a pro-democracy political party. You might imagine the Chinese Communist leaders would hesitate in the late twentieth century to use missiles to influence a neighbor's election campaign.

But Beijing does not draw from these contrasts the conclusions that readers of this book might find logical, because it is not interested in the *view from below* on fundamental political issues. The Chinese Communist dictatorship, like the Chinese dynastic polity, is an imposition from above. Lee Teng-hui represented a heterodox idea—democracy—that conflicted with the orthodoxy Beijing felt should stem from it alone. The Chinese Communist Party, self-deluded by its imagined version of Chinese history, in the name of a Great Systemic Whole, presumed to tell the 22 million people of Taiwan who should, and who should not, lead them, and indeed whether they should have their own government at all.

During the 1990s a similar dispute arose between Beijing and the then British-governed colony of Hong Kong. For his role in giving some limited democracy to Hong Kong in preparation for the agreed handover by Britain of Hong Kong to the PRC in 1997, Governor Chris Patten was called by the official Beijing media "the whore of the East." He was treated to a vituperation reserved for the heterodox that, historically, marked the Chinese court's insults toward Barbarians (non-Chinese) and, in our own time, flavored the political theater of Mao's Cultural Revolution of the 1960s. Beijing, peering down the long corridor of time, called the British governor a "criminal who would be condemned for a thousand generations."[13]

---

[13]Patten, 1999, 57.

The real issue, in Hong Kong as in Taiwan, was the incompatibility between the CCP imperial view of sovereignty as a mandate of heaven (adapted by the Communist Party to be a mandate of *history*) and the democratic view that sovereignty is formed by popular will from below. Toward Lee Teng-hui and Governor Patten, the Pretentious State of the new Chinese empire, with frightening sincerity, displayed its ideology and asserted its prerogatives. Happily, Clinton burst the bubble of Beijing's pretension toward Lee by sending an aircraft carrier task force to the Taiwan area in March 1996.

In our second incident, during May 1999, NATO bombers mistook the Chinese embassy in Belgrade for another structure and wrecked the compound, killing three Chinese. The Chinese public was angry, and justifiably so. China had relatively few interests in southeastern Europe, other than commercial ones (not a bonanza in Yugoslavia), and China's stake in the Belgrade situation did not seem to warrant the risk, bad luck, or malice of such a tragedy.

Moreover, the Chinese public was angry because for weeks before the bombing of the embassy, Chinese readers and viewers had been told of "American imperialism's" vicious assault on innocent Serbia. An April 9 cartoon in the *China Daily* showed Serbia as a ram giving shelter to a lamb that was Kosovo, as wolves and tigers labeled "NATO" circled round with bared teeth. No other view of the Kosovo conflict was presented in any media outlet in the PRC.

Who could be surprised that crowds descended on the U.S. embassy in Beijing, and other American sites in China, hurling missives and shouting denunciations of the "deliberate attack by American imperialism on the property and lives of People's China"? A typical slogan written on the fence of the embassy, within which Ambassador James Sasser cowered in fear of his life, ran "Get Out of China, American Butchers." These butchers, however, bought more than a quarter of China's total exports, an essential contribution to China's current economic health.

In fact, the anger of many Chinese people at the tragedy was but a puppet show. The real drama was the Beijing Opera mounted by what we might call "The Wronged State." The Chinese students demonstrating against the United States were bussed to their appointed sites by Chinese government organizations, perhaps to obviate them marching through the city and venting anger at buildings of the Beijing party-state. As with the preceding weeks of media bias, so with a climactic weekend of breathtaking media selectivity following the bombing of the Chinese embassy in Belgrade. Promptly, President Clinton made a televised apology to Beijing for the assault, and NATO headquarters also apologized to China. A full enquiry was announced. No hint of Clinton's words or of the other apologies was given to the Chinese public during the weekend of rage and rocks. The Chinese media continued to present the bombing as a calculated attack on China; how could Chinese readers, viewers, and demonstrators conclude otherwise? Contrary to an impression given by some eager optimists, middle China does not get its news from the Internet. The official media, which saturates China, likened the United States to Nazi Germany.[14]

It was immensely revealing that after four days the Chinese government changed its tune. The Clinton and NATO apologies were finally conveyed (in brief) to the Chinese public. Mysteriously—except to those who knew how the "spontaneous" demonstrations arose—the angry crowds dispersed and the attacks on American and other Western facilities ceased. The Wronged State's imperial self-indulgence had been both satisfying and useful to the state—up to a point. "Patriots versus imperialists" is an irresistible motif for the CCP, especially when it feels frustrated (the NATO operation, of course, excluded China) or trapped in a corner. But China, after all, is headed in the direction of being a modern nation. Its government is well-informed, fairly rational, and knows a good market when it sees one. The bout of imperial self-indulgence contradicted Beijing's policy of expanding trade and seeking investment and technology from the United States.

During this same spring of 1999, a major concern of the office of Zhu Rongji, premier at the time, was to secure American agreement for the PRC's attempt to enter the World Trade Organization. It was in part for this reason that the anti-American demonstrations, turned on

---

[14]*Renmin ribao*, May 15, 1999.

like a hose, were also turned off like a hose in less than a week. Popular anger was real, but it was channeled and de-channeled by the CCP. The dualism revealed that for the new Chinese empire, the United States was at once a necessary enemy and a key to China's ongoing economic growth. The Wronged State had erupted, but it had also seen a cost to the luxury of a theatrical victimhood.

Our third incident, in April 1999, saw 10,000 followers of *Falungong* (Wheel of Law), a Buddhist-influenced movement centered on the philosophy and breathing techniques of *qi gong*, teaching compassion, benevolence, and kindness, plus some weird ideas about an apocalypse, gather in Tiananmen Square in a silent bid to be recognized as a legitimate entity in PRC society. Mostly from Tianjin, they were hurt at being described in an academic article as crazy people. Shocking the CCP, they appeared out of nowhere, and Beijing had on its hands, in part through its own fault, the largest illegal demonstration since the Tiananmen democracy movement of 1989.

The *Falungong* adherents, who perform smooth, flowing exercises that enhance the circulation of energy in the body, were dispersed. Many were arrested and some later died in detention. A state-led onslaught on the credibility, sincerity, and even sanity of *Falungong* members began; by July the association had been banned. The Fearful State in Beijing had transformed *Falungong* from a harmless, health-promoting lifestyle choice of millions of mostly older Chinese into a menace to the "stability and unity" of the Red Middle Kingdom.

That loyal and quite senior members of the CCP, some in the army, police, and air force, were among the *Falungong* membership did not undermine the imperative to stamp out a potential, if unwitting, philosophic challenge to the state.[15] "Stability and unity" is a mantra, to be sure. Yet it does not lack a profound meaning: It is a code phrase for the uncompromisable interests of the fused power-and-doctrine (*zhengjiao heyi*) of the Chinese Communist Party-state. These same interests explained why Beijing took the extraordinary risk of denouncing a movement based on 2,000 years of Chinese tradition, in the name

---

[15]Vermander, 2001, 9, 1-7.

of Marxist-Leninist principles imported a mere century ago from Germany and Russia.

Said the state that sees itself as the pinnacle of a Great Systemic Whole: "*Falungong* is a heterodox religion." The "materialism" of Communist thought was being denied by the "idealism" emanating from the lips of Li Hongzhi, the leader of *Falungong*. It was a stunning revelation of the fragility of Beijing's imperial myth; for the bewildered meditationists of *Falungong* were being erected, *mutatis mutandis*, into a philosophic counterpart, and challenge, to the glorious Communist Party of China!

There has come into existence, it is said, a new and normal China since the death of Mao. That indeed is true of aspects of society and the economy. But it is not true of the state. The campaign against *Falungong* was cut from the same cloth as the ideological drives of the Mao years. No matter that Maoism now has a mixed reputation even within the CCP. If *Falungong* was "bad for the health" of its members, it might be remembered that Mao's Great Leap Forward in 1958–1959 was very bad indeed for the health of millions of Chinese farmers; some 30 million of them died from starvation because of the folly of its utopianism. In 2000, Beijing TV showed footage from inside mental asylums that "proved" that *Falungong* had driven some of its adherents insane (just as in the Mao years "class enemies" were sometimes "proved" to be insane on no medical evidence). Wrote Elizabeth Perry after observing the repression of *Falungong* firsthand: "Not since the Suppression of Counterrevolutionaries Campaign in the early 1950s have we seen such sustained national attention directed to the threat of sectarian resistance, and *never before have we witnessed an attack of this kind on but a single target.*"[16]

Indeed, the pedigree of the drive against *Falungong* went farther even than the rule of Mao, for the impossibility of compromise between orthodoxy and heterodoxy was a classic position of the Chinese monarchical state. Truth of a political nature could not be various. Philosophic difference was generally a threat to the state. *Falungong*

---

[16]Perry, 2000, 69 (emphasis added).

was "unregistered," said the CCP government, so it could not be permitted to meet or speak. Actually, the original *Falungong* gathering of 10,000 in April 1999 was precisely for the purpose of seeking a registered status. Why was the organization blamed for not possessing what it had peacefully sought but been refused?

The central point was that the mightiest state bureaucracy on earth was *afraid* of the elderly Buddhists with their rhythmical exercises and their apocalyptic visions. Anyone with a systematic philosophy outside the parameters of Marxism was to be feared by a CCP that can never cease to be conscious that it won power by the gun alone. All the more so, as with *Falungong,* when an organization extended nationwide, used the Internet, had tens of millions of adherents outside China as well as tens of millions inside, and a leader who had been living in New York. The very mandate of heaven was at stake. The Fearful State gave the world a glimpse of its soft underbelly of self-doubt.

In these three episodes—Beijing's response to democracy in Taiwan and steps toward democracy in Hong Kong, the reaction to the bombing of the Chinese embassy in Belgrade, and the clash between the CCP and a Buddhist spiritual-health association—the Chinese state showed itself to be, respectively, Pretentious, Aggrieved, and Fearful. The PRC was uncomfortably caught between the compromises and mutual influences of an interdependent international existence and the unilateral, condescending, ideological pronunciamentos of an imperial state.

Yet there is another angle to the story. The Chinese imperial state has a long history, and powerful reasons lie behind its hopes and fears. China in the twentieth century was not the total failure that John Paton Davies portrayed. In many realms of society, economy, and foreign policy, China saw transformation and improvement. Still, in political terms much of the twentieth century was a series of false starts, with regular bursts of political tragedy that seem a poor match for the historical greatness of Chinese civilization.

With all its contradictions, Communist Beijing has enjoyed some success at home and abroad. If that should be reversed, the likely concrete outcomes, for Beijing's relation to its restive non-Chinese areas, and for Beijing's ambitions as a world power, would be substantial. Meanwhile, Americans, in facing China, must figure out whether they are dealing with a tottering dinosaur or an ingenious blend of tradition and modernity.

———————

IT IS DIFFICULT for we non-Chinese to appreciate the problems of governance faced by Beijing. The PRC is home to a fifth of the world's people, more than four times the populace of the United States. It borders no less than fourteen other nations, to the north, west, and south, grimly holding on to the disparate lands of Tibet, the Muslim territory of Xinjiang, and part of Mongolia. It is in size, language, and culture a rough equivalent to the whole of Europe. No wonder the Chinese called World War One the "European civil war"; for China possesses a "France" and a "Germany" and an "Italy" and more, all within the confines of its sprawling realm. A Westerner visiting Tibet could be excused for doubting she was in China; the same Westerner, visiting Singapore, or parts of Bangkok, could be excused for thinking she *was* in China. We are reminded that China is primarily a civilization, and only tentatively, and by dint of concocted history and repressive politics, a state.

The CCP's response to hefty problems of governance is to put "stability and unity" in top priority; in a word, to repress any activity or thought that is heterodox to the self-image of the Chinese state. Hence the assault on the meditationists in *Falungong*, the denunciation of the Dalai Lama as a "splittist," and the judgment that the mosques of Islamic west China are bastions of "separatism." But a government that pursues stability as its paramount goal is probably in trouble.

In the manner of past dynasties, the Communist rulers also have employed ideology as a mystification to hold recalcitrant elements, and far-flung pieces of Chinese or semi-Chinese civilization, together in one polity. Periodically, Marxism is dusted off and wielded as a rusty weapon to cut away any possible alternative to the Communist party-state. "This cult denies the fundamental truth of Marxism-Leninism," boomed the official Beijing media of the quasi-Buddhist *Falungong*. "The splittists [Uighur nationalists in Xinjiang]," said the official radio in Urumqi in 1997, "are enemies of Mao Zedong Thought." Few believe this talk, and yet it continues.

Like the age-old dynastic court, the CCP views itself as the enlightened ruler of fringe peoples and the guardian of an unassailable doctrine. It stamps out variant political ideas, and scorns compromises urged upon it by foreigners or tough rules devised by international institutions. When the Taiwan presidential election of 2000 brought to power Vice President Annette Lu, who sees Taiwan and the Mainland as two very different societies, Beijing declared this neighboring political leader of Chinese descent "the scum of the Chinese race." So much for the norms of civil discourse in contemporary international relations.

Almost half the world's governments are democratic. Most of the world's large countries are federations. China, the giant of the globe, is neither democratic nor a federation. This sprawling realm, in size and complexity comparable to Europe, as it modernizes, cannot continue to be governed as a unitary state in no way answerable to its populace. Jiang Zemin, beaming in a dark Western suit, attended Asia–Pacific Economic Cooperation (APEC) and other international conferences and sat beside heads of government who have mostly been elected to office, and Hu Jintao begins to do the same. But a Chinese leader's smile and business suit cannot hide the fact that he comes to the conference with no popular mandate behind him. President Clinton, at the end of his 1998 visit to China, while in Hong Kong, said of the Chinese Communist leadership: "What I would like to see is the present government, headed by this president and this premier, who are clearly committed to reform, ride the wave of change and take China fully into the 21st century."[17] The Chinese people have never been given a say on that.

Leaving aside Clinton's dubious tendency to see Jiang as a Gorbachev (bridge to post-communism) rather than a Brezhnev (gatekeeper of Leninism), which during the 1990s gave Beijing something of a free ride, simple prudence requires the United States and the rest of the world to prepare for drastic political discontinuity within China. It was a historic change when, starting in 1979, economic reforms were

---

[17] *New York Times,* July 4, 1998.

courageously mounted by Deng Xiaoping, the second neo-emperor of the PRC dynasty. Deng's commercialization of China in the 1980s and 1990s was the best policy development in Beijing for years, as will soon be explained. Yet, in a fascinating way, the reforms gradually drew a veil away from China's political problem. The aging Deng turned into a Mao-like colossus, almost above criticism and reigning until he died, like the emperors. In addition, a major stress on economics is a two-edged sword for the future unity of a realm of 1.3 billion people. The return to family farming, the rise of private entrepreneurs, and a huge growth in trade have together produced a marked devolution of certain kinds of power away from Beijing.

Provinces now do deals with other provinces, bypassing the national capital. In 2001, Guangdong, the southern commercial bastion, several times ignored Beijing's laws and regulations in making huge business deals with Jiangsu, the Lower Yangzi province, and with the city-province of Shanghai. "A set of 'feudal economies,' each of which is answerable only to itself, has formed," wrote two Chinese scholars. "Each forms a complete, self-contained system that closes off regions and sets up trade barriers."[18] In addition, more than one hundred million ex-village dwellers "float" around the country; Beijing does not control them and can offer them no urban jobs that would allow it to control them.[19] During 2001–2002 the number of "floaters" probably increased by *ten million*.

A changed pattern of state revenue and the piecemeal way foreign money is spliced into the economy are the key reasons for the devolution away from the center. "The revenue of the state is the state," wrote Edmund Burke in his *Reflections on the Revolution in France,* and China in the first years of the twenty-first century proves the point. Beijing's formal government structure receives an ever smaller slice of the Chinese state revenue pie. In a "dysfunctional fiscal system," accrued revenue fails to find its way into the government budget available for public services and the rest. "Off-budget revenue" is directed to dubious

---

[18]Wang and Hu, 2001, 14.
[19]Solinger, 2001, 182.

projects and into slush funds for officials.[20] Meanwhile, in southeast China wealth and (potential) power accumulate.

In Guangdong Province many people refer to themselves not as *Han ren,* the usual phrase for "a Chinese person," but as *Tang ren,* another term for being a Chinese that harks back to southern-flavored dynasties. This sense of the south as the heartland of China echoes some past chapters in dynastic history. Viewed historically, the Open Policy of Deng and his colleagues has become a nod in the direction of a southern maritime tradition. John K. Fairbank, in *The Great Chinese Revolution* and other works, delineated the divide between hinterland China and coastal China and showed how different the mentality of the two could be. Now, as in earlier centuries, a northern bureaucratic mind-set finds itself in tension with a southern ocean-oriented cosmopolitan mind-set.[21]

President Jiang Zemin was the third neo-emperor of the PRC dynasty. Mao led the revolution and secured power for the CCP. Deng led a reform era whose economic and social policies amounted to a dismantling of Maoism, allowing the Chinese genius for business to unfold. Jiang represented a fresh generation that possessed no revolutionary merit from past heroic struggles. The challenge before him was to institutionalize the Deng era's priority on economics and the resulting devolution of power to the provinces. This he largely failed to do, preferring to be a mere balancer, leaning this way or that to maintain "unity and stability."

Yet Jiang understood some of the implications for politics of the economic changes of the 1980s and 1990s. He sometimes spoke as if the phenomenon of provinces "going their own way" threatened the very unity of China. The situation is actually more complex than that, as we shall see. Certainly the new commercialism threatens the Communist version of a party-state. Repression that is resented bids fair to undermine the very "unity and stability" that the Mandarins of the new Chinese empire seek to preserve. This may be one reason why Jiang, in a

---

[20]Pei, 2002, 105-106.
[21]Friedman, 1995, 3-5, chap. 5.

dozen years in power, did not institutionalize a single major policy initiative. His achievement was to keep *dis*-unity and *in*-stability at bay—and unshackle the Chinese economy, with excellent results.

This book does not conclude that devolution will necessarily lead to a breakup of the PRC. At some point the CCP may become alarmed at the threat to Beijing's authority and seek to reverse the devolution, at whatever economic cost, in order to save its own political skin. One should also acknowledge that the devolution of power to some regions of China has seen economic successes and human benefits (as distinct from benefits for the long-term interests of the Chinese imperial state), and there are good reasons for it to continue. The internal market of China is huge, and the slack to be taken up after the austere Mao years was great; stimulated by decentralized decision-making, twenty-five years of economic reforms have brought great advances to many areas of the nation.

Few parts of the "inner PRC" display separatist instincts. Should any of them turn separatist, it would not be of their own volition, but because disorder arose due to Beijing losing its grip over "outer PRC," the heavily non-Han western part of China. Yet Beijing today faces specific problems from within the Han areas that were not faced by the Qing Dynasty (1644–1912) until its dying phase. Taiwan and Hong Kong, the richest and most modernized parts of the total Chinese realm, in their different ways reject control from Beijing. Their vigor and anxiety could be one of the matches that ignites the powder keg of the PRC's pretensions to be an empire.

Beyond the Han areas—whether part of the inner PRC, like Guangdong, or merely coveted by the PRC, like Taiwan—live the so-called "minority peoples" of the outer PRC. It is here in the west (Moslem Xinjiang), the southwest (Tibet), and the north (Inner Mongolia) that discontent with Beijing's imperial ways has the potential to unravel the PRC.

To understand Beijing's policies on its western and northern fringes, one must understand the influence of traditional Chinese world order thinking. Most dynasties tottered or collapsed when faced with the terrible twins of *neiluan* (disorder within) and *waihuan* (external threat).[22] This is what Beijing fears today. The new Chinese empire is peculiarly vulnerable to such double trouble because of the burgeoning new society and economy of parts of the PRC, the brittleness of centralized Leninist rule, and the anachronism of being a multicultural empire in the twenty-first century.

"I HATE OUR CHINA POLICY," President Clinton burst out at a White House staff meeting in 1996. "I mean . . . we give them the [trade privileges] and change our commercial policy and what has it [actually] changed?"[23] After the Hainan Island airplane collision of 2001, President Bush found himself facing a petulant and obfuscating Chinese state.[24] A future U.S. president may feel a similar frustration with China's deceptive behavior in the World Trade Organization, as Beijing gives assurances to Geneva but allows key provinces to flout them. Ultimately, the reason for Beijing's intractability is that the party-state habitually rewrites history and prettifies reality to preserve its power and protect an imperial agenda. This imperial agenda results in several behavioral traits. The CCP is obsessed with doctrine, even as the populace yawns at the emptiness of the doctrine. Give and take with various nations does not come naturally to the party-state. History, in the CCP view, has bestowed on the party-state a destiny hidden to the outside eye.

At times the problem China presents to America and to its neighbors is misstated because China represents a type of imperial challenge to which the twentieth century was not accustomed. Britain from the eighteenth century to World War Two mounted a formal empire of police, flag, courts, and schools. The Soviet Union (1917–1991) kept its "colonies," from Bulgaria to Cuba, in line with Marxist doctrine and

---

[22]Fairbank, 1968, 3.
[23]*Washington Post,* June 21, 1998.
[24]Ross Terrill, "A Crisis That Beijing Really Needed," *Los Angeles Times,* April 15, 2001.

military muscle. Today, America's global preeminence rests on the unconscious triumph of its technology, investment, and popular culture; military interventions start and stop, but this tripod of indirect influences is constant.

The new Chinese empire is different. At once more modest and more arrogant, it is an empire of theater and presumption. It is a construct both of domestic repression and of international aspiration. Its arsenal of weapons includes secrecy, deception, and a sense of history that enables it to take a long view of China's interests and ambitions. The essential traits of the new Chinese empire are three: Its driving force comes from above, not below; it sees itself as the guardian of truth; and any compromises it makes with other great powers are tactical in nature, not based on an acceptance of moral comparability between China and the world of sovereign states.

The U.S.–PRC rivalry is less tangible, except in the Taiwan Strait, than the Cold War rivalry between the Soviet Union and the United States. The problem of China is not its economic rise, or that it militarily threatens us and half the world, the way the Soviet Union did, but that an imperial-Leninist dictatorship rules this rising China. Nixon said to Mao in 1972, when the Soviet Union was a common problem for Beijing and Washington: "What is important is not a nation's internal political philosophy," but rather "its policy toward the rest of the world and toward us."[25] Yet today in U.S.–China relations, internal political philosophy *is* important. As the authors of *The Coming Conflict with China* put it: "Beijing's rulers will risk war with America not because it is in their country's interest but because it is in the interests of the governing clique."[26]

Federalism would seem an apt constitutional form for the burgeoning China of the post-Mao boom. No nation of even a quarter China's size and population has been ruled with good results in modern times *without* some sort of federalism. For a century, leading Chinese minds

---

[25]Nixon, 1978, 562 (paperback edition, 1979, vol. 2).
[26]Bernstein and Munro, 1997, 11.

have proposed federalism for their country; but when the unity of China depends on the sword, federalism cannot be on the agenda.[27] Nor is federalism a concept that comes easily in a political tradition that stresses unity and the center (*zhongyang*). In the Chinese language, the term *lianbang* is used alike for federations, as in Australian Federation (*Audaliya lianbang*), and for some international entities, as in British Commonwealth (*Yingguo lianbang*). To say the least, this suggests an ambiguity on the part of Beijing about sovereignty in a nation-state system.[28]

Certainly, federalism is to a Leninist party as a hot sun is to ice cream. Federalism is about the division of power under law. Leninism (like empire) is about the centralization of power in the hands of a self-appointed elite. The Chinese Communist Party fundamentally denies the authority of law by claiming a mandate to rule based on the Marxist theory of historical stages. The decentralization of recent decades is better than the prior form of centralization; still, it is no substitute for law-based federalism.

Jittery and defensive, Beijing grasps rule *by* law as a means of staving off rule *of* law. It allows no fundamental political dissent. It declines to institutionalize the leakage of power from Beijing to distant provinces that economic reform has wrought. Beijing even seeks to *expand* its territory to include Taiwan, repeating like a mantra that Taiwan is one of its provinces, even though the PRC has never ruled Taiwan for a single day.

One day a liberalized China will shed its imperial role, as the Soviet Union began to do under Mikhail Gorbachev, and Russia largely had to do after the Soviet Union collapsed. As it stands, the Beijing regime is overstretched on its western and southeastern flanks, deeply corrupt, politically unstable, yet extremely ambitious. Dynastic China was in theory and practice an empire and could not be called a nation-state. The China that Jiang Zemin in form handed

---

[27]Yan, 1992, 5, 18.
[28]Bøckman, 1998, 345, n.84.

over to Hu Jintao in 2002–2003 has reached a point halfway between empire and nation-state. Resolution of this contradiction cannot be far away. How a Chinese civilization still afflicted with repressive imperial rule adjusts to its new economic strength, a growing middle class of independent producers and avid consumers, and a world of nation-states will affect every American and also every East Asian and Central Asian who lives on China's borders.

HOW THE CHINESE
IMPERIAL STATE
WAS FORMED

One could say that in China, the state is all. History explains this. The
state was not an organism which . . . was obliged to make a place for
itself among other powers, as was the case in the West, where the state
had to impose itself on the independent powers of the Church, of
feudalism and of the nobility, come to terms with the merchants, and
seek the support of the financiers. In China the state was an established reality from the beginning, or in any case from the time when
the formula was worked out in the state of Qin [pre–221 B.C.].

—*Jacques Gernet*[1]

TODAY, AS CHAPTER 1 has suggested, the Chinese state is distinctive for its sense of destiny, didacticism, distance from its people, and pronounced awkwardness in international relations. These are
in good part handicaps. Yet the Chinese Communist state has avoided,
so far, the fate of its once-senior partner, the Soviet Union. It has
shown a capacity to "box above its weight" by an ingenious use of political theater.

Nevertheless, the Chinese state seems riven with contradictions. It
seeks to be modern and international, as displayed in its push to enter
the World Trade Organization in 2000–2001. Yet it struts and poses,
lecturing the world, especially the United States, as if it were addressing, not other nations, but recalcitrant elements within its own domain.

---

[1]Gernet, 1985, xxxii.

It is capable of simultaneously mouthing out-of-date doctrine yet acting with Machiavellian realism. All of this stems both from Stalinism and from selected remnants of the imperial past.

Recent political science in the United States has little place for the Soviet-style state or the central state as it has existed in China intermittently for millennia. Typically, an interest-group approach to the state is taken, in which the government "is seen as a cash register that totals up and then averages the preferences and political power of societal actors."[2] This state is far removed from mythology, paternalism, expansionism, ritual, and massive coercive power, all of which marked the maximal Chinese empire. Morton H. Fried, in an influential essay on the state as an institution, dismisses Louis XIV's *L'etat, c'est moi* as having no "utility" for our understanding of the state, yet the remark is apt for both imperial rule and Maoist rule in China.[3] It would be easy to draw the conclusion that democratic and authoritarian states cannot be studied as if they form one genus.

Gabriel Almond attributes our piecemeal American view of the state to the "enormous political mobilization that took place in the Western world in the nineteenth and twentieth centuries and the proliferation of new political institutions—political parties, pressure groups, the mass media, and the like—that accompanied it."[4] In a word, the wave of pluralism and democracy led us to a relaxed view of the state. David Ciepley finds that "the state was *dropped from American social science*" as part of a reaction to the rise of totalitarianism in the 1920s and 1930s.[5] To some Europeans, who say "the state is force," to which many Chinese would nod in agreement, American political analysis, at least since Arthur Bentley's *The Process of Government* a century ago, has "dissociated the study of political phenomena" from any reflection on the state.[6] Bentley called "the idea of the state" just one of "the intellectual amusements of the past."[7] David Easton in *The Political System* in 1953 said

---

[2]Krasner, 1984, 227.
[3]Fried, 1968, 143.
[4]Almond, 1988, 855.
[5]Ciepley, 2000, 157 (emphasis added).
[6]D'Entrèves, 1967, 4, 59, 60.

the very word "state" should be avoided by political scientists.[8]

Within the United States, today, only in "area studies," where "quantitative methods" are not all, and culture gets a look in, is the strong state now and then encountered and the *origins* of the state probed. Alfred Stepan, studying Latin America, is a rare voice who gives attention to the state other than as a dependent variable, actually describing the state rather than just society. As a result, the topic of the Chinese state, in some ways the most formidable state the world has seen, is left to historians of China, some of whom are innocent of political theory. European sinologists who experienced twentieth-century totalitarianism firsthand often had an instinctive feel for the nature of the Chinese state. "We can understand only what we already know," wrote Balazs, Hungarian-born and a refugee from totalitarianism, "and, what is more, we can become genuinely interested only in something that touches us personally."[9]

Chinese of the twentieth century whose roots were in dynastic China, whether the revolutionary nationalist, Sun Yat-sen (born 1866), the conservative nationalist, Chiang Kai-shek (born 1887), or the Communist nationalist, Mao Zedong (born 1893), all displayed or grappled with the Chinese state's character and sense of itself. When Sun, who played a major role in the fall of China's last dynasty, heard about Communist doctrines from the representative of Moscow in China, he declared there was "nothing new in Marxism. It had all been said 2000 years ago in the Chinese [Confucian] Classics."[10] When Mao, just after the fall of the Qing Dynasty, saw a map of the world on a wall in the Hunan Province Library, it was the first time in his life he had seen China depicted as one nation with others around it, rather than as its own world with a dim periphery shaded in.[11]

---

[7]D'Entrèves, 1967, 62.
[8]D'Entrèves, 1967, 63.
[9]Balazs, 1964, 14.
[10]Short, 1999, 136. Sun may have been thinking of the "soft socialism" of *Datong* ("Great Community").
[11]Snow, 1961, 141.

Beyond the limitations of Western theories of the state to handle the Chinese case, it is pointless to compare the Chinese state with that of "new nations" in the Third World merely on the ground that the state in both cases refers to a land, a people, and a government. The Indonesian state, for example, only came into existence when the Dutch left in the 1940s and a series of islands formed an indigenous polity for the first time. We cannot speak of the Chinese state in the same breath as this upstart Indonesian state.

"The way in which [states] were built," said S. E. Finer in his exhaustive history of government, "usually has most important consequences for the way they come to be governed."[12] The U.S. state was built from the grassroots aspirations of idealist refugees newly arrived from troubled countries across the sea; hence, Americans have readily equated American values and universal values. In Britain, dissident forces murdered a ruling monarch in the pre-modern era; hence, to this day, the British have been able to retain a decorative monarch who does not actually rule. Australia began as a prison settlement, in which the government ran everything; hence, Australians came to have a mentality of depending on the government that is rarely found in a democracy. The Chinese polity had sharply different origins from these and virtually all other polities.

The Chinese governmental system is old, but the recorded history of government on our planet began not in East Asia but in the Middle East. The Sumerian city-states appeared in southern Mesopotamia around 3500 B.C., and the Egyptian polity emerged in the Nile Valley in 2850 B.C. Only in the sixteenth century B.C., with the establishment of the Shang Dynasty, known for fine bronze technology, horse-drawn chariots, and maturation of the Chinese writing system,[13] did a coherent Chinese polity take root. By the Zhou Dynasty (1045–256 B.C.), which was formed from "country cousin" frontiersmen of the Shang world,[14] the polity displayed features—unity as a creed, a king with a

---

[12]Finer, 1997, 4.
[13]Hucker, 1975, 28.
[14]Hucker, 1975, 41.

doctrine, a claim to rule by virtue, strict hierarchy, an assumption of being at the center of the world—that continued to mark the Chinese polity until our own time.

In the last period of the Zhou, Confucius and Mencius supplied Chinese civilization with its most influential public philosophy, later to be known as Confucianism. Some of this philosophy was vague, some was pie-in-the-sky. Not everyone would see profundity in Mencius's oft-quoted words: "There is a way to win the empire; win the people. There is a way to win their hearts; supply them with what they want."[15] But Confucianism did have the virtue of binding government and people together in a comprehensive ethic.

The Qin Dynasty (221–206 B.C.) set up an iron dictatorship. Emperor Qin Shihuang, popularly known today for Mao Zedong's praise of him and for the terra-cotta soldiers from his tomb near the city of Xi'an, established a centralized rule that scoffed at virtue and ruled by tough laws and the sword. Religion played a smaller role than under the Zhou. The Qin court may have been rustic and racially dubious, but it knew how to seize and wield power. It knocked out five competing states and set up a totalitarian regime two millennia before the English word was uttered. Qin Shihuang's policy was not to appeal for good behavior from the people, but to employ measures that stopped bad behavior. "Anyone engaging in political or philosophic talk will be put to death," ran one of his edicts, "and his body exposed in public."[16] To a degree Qin Shihuang created the Chinese state, just as Machiavelli in Europe, confronting a world of vying polities not totally unlike pre–Qin Shihuang China, introduced the term "state" in its modern Western sense.[17]

Against Qin's cruel but effective *realpolitik*, there came a reaction during the pivotal Han Dynasty (202 B.C.–A.D. 220). A compromise was reached between rule by virtue and rule by the sword. A Confucian-flavored monarchy, pulling together the agricultural life of the

---

[15] Schrecker, 1991, 20 (translation adjusted).
[16] *Shiji*, juan 87.
[17] Machiavelli, 1960, chap. 1; Sabine, 1968, 328.

central China plain into a territory two-thirds the size of the United States, with some 60 million people, built a formidable bureaucracy that also made use of moral suasion. From this dynasty derived *Han ren,* a common term today for "Chinese person." Following the Han Dynasty came an interlude of chaos and contention (not the first or last in Chinese history). Only with the tough-minded Sui Dynasty (581–618) did unity return.

After less than four decades of the Sui, the brilliant Tang Dynasty (618–907) began to reinvent the Chinese polity, building a complex legal structure. This dynasty's capital, today's Xi'an, boasted 2 million people, which made it the world's largest city. (Even centuries later, European cities were tiny compared with the big cities of East Asia and the Middle East; Venice at its height had about 5% the population of Xi'an in the Tang.) Poetry reached a new height during the Tang, as did Buddhist sculpture. The court boasted an imperial library of 200,000 volumes (scrolls) and there existed grand private libraries possessing twenty or thirty thousand scrolls.[18] The governmental system, inherited from the Han Dynasty and refined, had such appeal that neighboring Japan borrowed it holus-bolus in the seventh century. The tax base grew, which advanced urbanization. An examination system for select-ing officials on the basis of grasp of Confucian Classics came into full flower. This was of enormous importance in later Chinese history in reinforcing Confucian doctrine. Beyond China, the Tang, whose ruling clan had often intermarried with non-Chinese nobility, attacked and regained control of Korea, and parts of Persia and Vietnam. The Tang Dynasty, whose artifacts may be viewed to this day at the Shaanxi His-tory Museum in Xi'an, is one of many reasons why one should not underestimate Chinese civilization, or any Chinese person's pride in its tenacious course.

Yet the Tang Dynasty came crashing down after being fatally weak-ened by the massive An Lushan rebellion that lasted from 755 to 763. Following this rebellion, imperial authority dissipated and both social and economic power shifted to the provinces. Widespread farmer

---

[18]Schafer, 1963, 271–272.

revolts at the end of the ninth century clinched the Tang's demise. Like the end of the Han Dynasty, the Tang's fall produced an era of turmoil, albeit a much shorter one of sixty years. Still, with the achievements of the Tang, the Chinese polity had become a major entry in the annals of governance across the globe. This monarchy-plus-bureaucracy, deceptive in its mixture of strength and weakness, administration and psychology, the gun and sheer bluff, was henceforth a leading model of how a community could arrange itself in contradistinction to other "states." It could be called civilizational-rule, a brilliant device that nonetheless sometimes misaligned China's state and China's territory.[19]

IT IS NOT ONLY the contemporary Chinese state that stands out among the major powers. The Chinese state was also unusual in the world of a thousand years ago, and in that of two thousand years ago. Indeed, to utter the word "state" may be to misconstrue the way governance and "Chineseness" have interrelated. China's sense of itself as a civilization mattered as much for the effectiveness of the polity as did the nuts and bolts of China's government. Certainly, the state as seen in the West since feudalism passed away in Europe 400–500 years ago was alien to Chinese theory and practice until dynastic China entered a King Lear phase in the late nineteenth century.

To be sure, during the earliest phase of the history of government in the world, China's civilizational-rule was not particularly distinctive. In Egypt, Mesopotamia, and elsewhere there existed kingships comparable to China's of the Zhou Dynasty. But, after the time of Jesus Christ, no ancient polity came in and out of existence for two millennia the way the Chinese polity did. The Chinese mode of civilizational-rule lived on to astonish foreigners in the reign of the Empress Dowager (1835–1908), as the last dynasty sank. Echoes of it complicate U.S.–China relations to this day.

Writes the historian Wang Gungwu of early books on foreign relations with which the Song (960–1279) and later dynasties sought to

---

[19]Tu, 1991, 15–16, uses a similar term, "civilization-state."

align their own foreign policies: "Of what other country in the world can it be said that writings on its foreign relations of two thousand, or even one thousand, years ago seem so compellingly alive today?"[20] Much that we recognize in China's policies today was invented and tested long before Europe counted for much in the world. According to a Tang Dynasty notion, China had to show "that no one was left out"; every known kingdom and community should have a status of one kind or another in the Chinese scheme of things. Ran a maxim about foreign countries in the *Song shi* (Song Dynasty History): "When they came, they were not rejected; when they went, they were not pursued."[21] This was the ideal form of the "tribute system," of which we will hear more, whereby neighboring polities sent missions to the Chinese court to pay deference as an insurance policy against being attacked. Almost every dynasty followed the essentially pragmatic dual policy of "a hard core of *wei* (force) surrounded by a soft pulp of *de* (virtue)," the iron fist tucked into the velvet glove.[22] The option of invasion was held in readiness, in case the moral claim to Chinese primacy fell on deaf ears.

All these themes are found in Beijing's foreign policy today. Plucking autocratic elements from the diverse Chinese past, the CCP perpetuates an imperial tradition, alas, often the most repressive, least humanistic aspect of it. One may paraphrase Finer's point: The nature of a polity, *especially in the Chinese case, because of its longevity*, hinges on how it arose and grew.

WHAT IS A STATE? In ancient times it meant a slice of mankind living on a particular territory and regulated by a common authority. Specialized personnel and a military force gave shape and muscle to this authority. Each slice of mankind with its common authority saw itself as separate from other "states," and was seen as distinct by them.[23] Such

---

[20]Wang Gungwu, 1968, 61.
[21]*Song shi*, juan 485.
[22]Wang Gungwu, 1968, 47, 49, 53, 55; Fletcher, 1968, 207.
[23]Finer, 1997, 2–3.

a state, following Finer's definition, mostly omitted our modern idea of a state as exhibiting a community of feeling and allowing participation from below.[24] Certainly it knew nothing of the common authority being determined by the will of the people.

The first of these traits of the ancient state did not apply to the Chinese polity. China's territory ebbed and flowed. To say boundaries were vague would be the understatement of a millennia. For a long time the Chinese simply did not accept the idea of boundaries. An edict of the Tang Dynasty declared: "The height of the emperor is as great as that of Heaven, his width is as huge as the Earth. His radiance matches that of the Moon and Sun, his honesty and faithfulness is equal to that of the four seasons."[25] Of what import were "state borders" in such a cosmology? We find a line from the Han Dynasty that makes the point clear: "The virtuous power of the Han [Chinese] has no borders."[26] It was culture, way of life, and a cosmological way of thinking, not lines on a map, that set the Chinese apart from nearby peoples. Even in much later dynasties, maps drawn by officials were ambiguous as to "where a map of 'China' ends and a map of 'the world' begins."[27] To be sure, the Chinese polity observed boundaries when it was convenient to do so, but it also preserved a sense of infinite jurisdiction.

In Europe, of course, there was a period when political allegiance and territoriality were divorced from each other. During the age of feudalism, which amounted to a breakdown of the state, the question of allegiance was "Whose man are you?" It was not, "What country do you live in?" The Chinese tradition does not quite fit either. Perhaps the real question in the China realm was "How do you live?" China's borders were ever-changing and often deliberately ambiguous. But *being a Chinese* came to be slow-changing and very clear. If you were Chinese, you practiced certain rituals, knew some Chinese characters, paid taxes, had a surname, cultivated the fields, ate with chopsticks, and were a child of the emperor. If you weren't quite Chinese, the empire

---

[24]Nettl, 1968, 565–566.
[25]*Tang da zhaoling ji*, juan 13, 77.
[26]Wang Guowei, 1984, 1150.
[27]Richard J. Smith, 1996 ("Mapping . . . "), 53.

might nevertheless conquer and "Sinify" you; your Chineseness would then be taken for granted. Despite Mencius's view that only a government that respected the people was a just government, legitimation of authority in China never stemmed from sovereignty of the people.

The Chinese polity came into existence over such a long time that no one can say without fear of contradiction when "China" commenced. Certainly "China" did not exist as a term in the Zhou Dynasty. As for the Shang Dynasty, which preceded the Zhou—and the Xia prior to the Shang—one can only say they were small pieces of what later became China. The Chinese terms for "Chinese person" (*Zhongguo ren*) and "Chinese race" (*Han zu*) are very modern phrases.[28] Enormous discontinuity and variation are to be found over the millennia. The early pre-Zhou "dynasties" had priest-kings, but the final thousand years of the imperial system saw negligible theocracy. The Shang Dynasty (sixteenth to eleventh centuries B.C.) was not in important respects the same polity and civilization as the succeeding Zhou Dynasty. The meritocratic examination system, selecting bureaucrats by their grasp of the Confucian classics, was not developed until the Tang Dynasty. The key southern province of Guangdong was only Sinicised in the Tang. Fujian and Jiangxi, in the southeast, became recognizably Chinese much later, in the Song. Only in the Ming (which fell, in 1644, after the founding of Harvard University, in 1636) did Yunnan and Guizhou start to be ruled by the Chinese court and adopt the Chinese way of life.[29] Manchuria, today's northeast China, was only Sinicized much later still, during the maturation and decline of the Qing Dynasty.

Finer's second trait of the state did indeed apply to the Chinese polity: A civil service and a military were on duty to arrange and defend, as in Egypt, Rome, and the rest. But the third trait of the state was absent from the Chinese case: The Chinese polity did not see itself as one among comparable others. True, the Jewish kingdoms of Israel and Judah (1025–598 B.C.) were also in their own view "a nation apart."

---

[28]Wilkinson, 2000, 96.
[29]Ting, 1931, 11; Ma, 1987, 142–143.

But the Chinese emperor was more than "apart" from all others: He was the *only* ruler representing heaven itself. Consider the hauteur of Emperor Tai Zong, pondering his achievements in the comparatively modest Song Dynasty (960–1279): "Our state has worked a transforming influence on China and Barbarians, our favors have even spread to animals and plants."[30]

What, then, was "China" in Zhou, Han, and Tang times, if not a state like the Greek *polis*, or Assyria, or early Japan? The Chinese polity took form, first, as an "Us-and-Them" system, developed to control the agricultural society, principally around the Yellow River, of people who spoke some form of Chinese. By the middle of the second millennium B.C., this primitive society, taxed in kind by local lords, developed an identity. But prior to the seventh century B.C., a "burn and clear agriculture"[31] existed. There were no permanent fields and property was not bought and sold. During the Zhou Dynasty (eleventh to third centuries B.C.), the Chinese *wang* (king) began to call himself Son of Heaven, establishing a wider, "international," indeed unlimited jurisdiction.

In a basically two-class pattern, a cultivated elite developed techniques of rule and myths of legitimation to impose order on farming communities. Ritual demarcated the world of the Son of Heaven-plus-bureaucracy from that of the common folk, who were simply the objects of paternalistic rule. The words "freedom" and "equality" were virtually absent from Chinese political writing; these leading concepts of Western political thought were incompatible with the centrality of *duties* and *hierarchy* in the emerging Chinese realm. Even the emperor had an upward duty—to his ancestors. To be sure, respect for ancestors was inseparable from duty to care for all the people descended from the ancestors.

The Chinese polity had formidable strengths. The absence of a strong hereditary aristocracy after the Tang gave the system authority, staying power, and a certain rationality. The ethical doctrines of hierarchy and duty of Confucius and Mencius, as interpreted by power-holders, provided a sophisticated justification for an imposed political order. In this optic, as Perelomov and Martynov write, "the world consisted

---

[30] *Song huiyao jigao,* ce 7, 6874.
[31] Elvin, 1973, 23.

of two parts—their [the cultivated elite's] own, a realm of civilization, and that of others [Chinese farmers and non-Chinese peoples], a realm of chaos."[32] Arrogant as this may seem, it proved an enduring formula. As we shall see, there is a connecting line, albeit with a thousand curves, between this dualism and the paternalism of the Chinese state at least through the Mao era.

Going to China first in 1964, and frequently in the 1970s, I was struck by the gulf that yawned between the all-knowing Mao state and a populace expected to gaze up at it. At schools and colleges I would ask young people what they would like to do after graduation. The answer was so uniform I have never forgotten it: "The state will decide [*guojia yao jueding*]." Likewise, visiting a commune, the combined economic and political unit intended to catapult China to a shining socialist future ahead of the USSR, I would ask about plans for future cropping. "That's up to the state," came the reply. Of course these replies were not always honest. But the norm, to which almost everyone in Mao's China bowed a knee, in public, was to subjugate decisions about career, farming priorities, even technical issues—not to speak of anything pertaining to values—to the cadres of the Communist party-state. These cadres, half political machine boss and half village priest, strongly resembled the "father and mother of the people [*min zhi fumu*]" officials of the imperial state. Such officials were the linchpin of the Chinese dynastic system. Heaven had made rulers "parents of the people."[33] Gazing upward at the state became part of what it meant to be Chinese, especially in the rulers' view.

The main difference was that the PRC party-state, fortified by Leninism, became more repressive than the dynastic state. "The state will decide" was not a cry on many lips in old China. For Mencius, one should never disobey parents, but a bad ruler could be overthrown. For the Mao era CCP, the authority of the Communist cadres was a given *no less* than the authority of parents. No wonder the CCP called Mencius "reactionary," a swearword of choice.

---

[32]Perelomov and Martynov, 1983, 101.
[33]Mei, 1929, 44.

A SECOND, MAJOR STEP in the shaping of the Chinese polity occurred as the Us-and-Them system was extended to Chinese dealings with non-Chinese communities, notably the largely horseback peoples who impinged from the north and the west as early as the Shang Dynasty. For dealing with the nomads, who were less numerous than the Chinese, good in battle, and much in need of tea, silk, and other products of agricultural China, the Chinese polity developed the odious but enduring concept of *hua–yi*, a sharp distinction between Chinese and Barbarians. The cosmos itself, it was claimed, designated the former (Chinese) as the natural rulers and the latter (Barbarians) as lesser breeds. Confucian scholars saw lesser peoples as redeemable by education, but Legalist power-holders did not.

By the Tang Dynasty, we find the phrase *tian di zhi dao*, which means, in its context, "Approach the Barbarians from the positions of Heaven and Earth." Benevolence toward the non-Chinese people should be practiced. "Any creatures, so long as they exist in this world," were to receive the emperor's nurture. As long as they did not resist the Chinese emperor, they could not be rejected. The emperor, in a word, was Heaven and Earth alike to his own people and the Barbarians.[34] Advisors to Emperor Gao Zu during the Tang appeared to put Koreans into the category of Barbarians ("lesser peoples" could be another rendition). "Us-and-Them," meaning the elite and the farmers making up Chinese society, had also become "Ourselves-and-the-Others," meaning Chinese and surrounding races. "China is to the lesser peoples," advisors said to Emperor Gao Zu in reference to Koreans and other non-Chinese, "as the Sun is to the stars."[35]

Lamentably, the Chinese sometimes likened the Barbarians to animals, whose highest hope could only be to find a niche in the Chinese-arranged realm of all-under-heaven (*tian xia*). The racism was undeniable. The *Shanhai jing* ("Classic of Mountains and Seas"), written two millennia ago and still cited in the Qing Dynasty, describes a southern non-Chinese people as having human bodies and faces, but birdlike

---

[34] *Jiu Tangshu*, juan 194, 5162.
[35] *Xin Tangshu*, juan 220, 6187.

wings and beaks, and a western people with human faces but the bodies of snakes.[36] Said a close advisor to Emperor Tai Zong in the seventh century, of the Huns, or Xiongnu: "The Hsiung-nu [Xiongnu] with their human faces and animal hearts are not of our kind. When strong, they are certain to rob and pillage; when weak, they come to submit. But their nature is such that they have no sense of gratitude or righteousness."[37] Said the Ming Emperor Jia Qing of non-Chinese on the southern border: "The *yi* and *di*, like birds and beasts, are without human morality."[38] Alastair Iain Johnston, in his study of Ming memorials on foreign policy, found only one memorialist among 120 who acknowledged that Mongols, "like humans . . . could reason and understand costs and benefits." Even this one writer judged the Mongols to be "by nature dogs and sheep."[39] In late imperial documents, Westerners, too, were portrayed as animal-like.[40]

The historian Yang Lien-sheng, in a learned essay making the strongest possible claim that (some) Chinese *did* have a sense of the "foreign," and did *not* equate China with the civilized world, nevertheless acknowledged that Barbarians were likened to animals. "Racism," Yang concluded sagely, "is particularly difficult to reform if the habit was formed in . . . the early historical period of a society."[41] We will be reminded of this in the story of African students in the People's Republic of China, protesting the condescension they experienced from Chinese officials and Chinese students: "It was enough for a [Chinese] girl to be seen walking with an African for her doom to be sealed," wrote Emmanuel Hevi of the experiences of African students in Beijing in the 1960s.[42]

All states, to be sure, not least the United States, go into the world with preconceptions. But in the case of China, the worldview it carried

---

[36]Richard J. Smith, 1996, 17–18; Richard J. Smith, 1996 ("Mapping . . . "), 68, 95.

[37]Rossabi, 1983, 48–49.

[38]*Ming Shi Zong shilu,* juan 199, 6b–7b.

[39]Johnston, 1995, 188, n.17.

[40]Richard J. Smith, 1996 ("Mapping . . . "), 88.

[41]Yang, 1968, 28.

[42]Hevi, 1963, 132, 134–135; Sautman, 1994, 414–415, 424–425, 429–436.

into "international relations" was baked into the Chinese soul over a very long evolution, and the worldview gained unshakable power from being intertwined with China's domestic institutions. "Us-and-Them" within China gave extra potence to Us-and-Them, Chinese and Barbarians.

Harmony between Chinese and Barbarian could be maintained when the Barbarians were willing to *gui shun* ("follow the [emperor's] way"), as did the nomadic Kalmyks in 1771. The Qing emperor Qian Long (reigned 1736–1796), with a pat on the head, declared that the Kalmyks, a Mongol people, believers in Tibetan Buddhism, who came from an area on Russia's southeast, had indeed attained *gui shun*. To gain this status the Kalmyks, and other Barbarians, had to express *cheng*, a rich term for which "sincerity" is not an adequate rendition. The usage had a cosmological ring to it. The Barbarians were "sincere" if they adhered to the "proper course of things," which meant if they followed the Chinese emperor's way. To say the sincere Barbarian was one who conformed to Heaven (*ge shang tian*) meant more than the antonym of hypocrisy. Barbarian abjectness before the glitter of the Chinese world was made clear by the use of the additional term *hua*, "transformation." *Hua* was linked with *cheng*. The good Barbarian would "implement sincerity and position himself for transformation" (*tou cheng xiang hua*).[43] As a Russian Sinologist team has put it, "*cheng* was both the effect and the cause of 'transformation' (*hua*)."[44]

There was an opposite label supplied by the Chinese polity for the Barbarian who had his *own* notion of "heaven," his *own* values. Such Barbarians—Turkic peoples were a recurrent case—were said by the Chinese court to "resist Heaven" (*ni ming*). These nonperforming Barbarians, as a result, were simply attacked by the Chinese. If defeated, the deflated Barbarians were then put into the next-best category of *gui xiang*, "submitting to the Way through surrender."

The didacticism was taken one step further. A defeated recalcitrant who later improved his ways could be rewarded with an upgrade! His

---

[43] Qi, 1884, juan 15. We encountered *lai hua,* "come to China and be Sinified," in discussing Nixon and Kissinger in Chapter 1, and will do so again in Chapter 8.
[44] Perelomov and Martynov, 1983, 118.

category *gui xiang* could be amended to *gui shun,* the preferred response of adhering to the (Chinese) proper course of things. The same Qing period emperor Qian Long who praised the northern Kalmyks in 1771, in the case of the southern Nepalese, two decades later, declared them to be resisting Heaven, and thereupon conquered Nepal. This put the Nepalese king into the category of *gui xiang,* submitting to the Way only by virtue of surrender. But Emperor Qian Long later discerned "profound and sincere repentance" from the direction of Katmandu. He took away the label *gui xiang* and put Nepal into the category of *gui shun.* The cosmos was in good order again.[45] One way or another, sooner or later, the Chinese court would secure submission of lesser peoples.

———

A NEW CHINESE DYNASTY typically set about four world-arranging tasks that were concentric in the territory of their implementation. The four tasks shaded imperceptibly from domestic policy to foreign policy, from affirming Us-and-Them among Chinese, to securing "Ourselves-and-the-Others" between Chinese and lesser peoples. First, the new ruler applied a firm rein to the territory of inner China. Fiscal, doctrinal, and organizational control was secured beyond any risk of shortfalls, heterodoxy, or disorder.

In a second zone, somewhat equivalent to today's "outer China" (discussed in Chapter 7), the new dynasty did whatever was necessary to neutralize the regions of military danger in the north and west, base of the nomadic peoples. This often included parts of Mongolia, Tibet, and Turkistan. Use of force was frequent in the second zone.

Third, the dynasty buttressed its political influence in outlying regions where a general political hegemony was assumed. Today's Korea and Vietnam were the most important of these. A Ming emperor, on hearing that a Korean king was showing an interest in Buddhism, scolded him as a father might scold a son. This same Ming

———

[45]Qi, 1884, juan 15.

Dynasty did not find it easy to evoke the necessary respect from a Vietnam that had breathed the air of independence from China for several centuries starting in 939. A variety of methods was employed. In 1405 an Imperial Denunciation was tossed at Vietnam. When this did not work, troops were sent.

Yet the Ming court clung to its "reign of virtue" doctrine with one hand, even as it punched Vietnam with the other hand. An Imperial manifesto issued at the very time China invaded Vietnam declared: "The people of Annam [northern Vietnam] are all my little children." The emperor blamed the Chinese military intervention on a recalcitrant Vietnamese leader: "He has oppressed the people of the country and the people hate him to the marrow of their bones. The spirits of Heaven and Earth are unable to tolerate this." The emperor said to the departing Chinese troops: "You are proceeding there [Vietnam] to relieve [the people] of their suffering and must not be tardy in this."[46] Hundreds of thousands of Vietnamese were probably killed. Still, China was unable to resume formal rule over Vietnam.

PRC historians still write of Vietnam, and Yunnan Province in the southwest, having been "punished" or "pacified" by various emperors, suggesting the tenacity of the legacy of condescension.[47] Worse, PRC cultural officials speak of Vietnam as part of China until the coming of the French in the nineteenth century, confusing tributary ties with possession. "Vietnam," read a caption in the Shaanxi History Museum in Xi'an in 2002, "until 200 years ago was part of China, and still today in the homes of Vietnam people you can see Chinese characters." The last phrase overlooks the distinction between Vietnamese and Chinese residents of Vietnam. Unsurprisingly, Chinese youth have no idea of China's long record of invasion, slaughter, and control in dealing with Vietnam and other neighbors.

The fourth world-arranging task of an incoming dynasty was to find some theoretical place in the cosmological scheme of things for "remote lands" of which China knew little. These were sometimes

[46]*Ming Shi Zong shilu,* juan 197–200.
[47]Wade, 2000, 43; Ma, 1987, 143–155.

called "south seas" or "western ocean" territories. Included were some Southeast Asian islands and also Europe. Such lands were considered no threat, and China had few ambitions toward them. But the Chinese emperor would not be the Son of Heaven unless he found a niche for them in the planetary order.

Said the Ming emperor Zhu Yuanzhang in a manifesto of 1372: "Countries of the western ocean are rightly called distant regions. They come [to us] across the seas, and it is difficult for them to calculate the year and month [of arrival]. Regardless of their numbers, we can treat them [on the principle of] 'those who come modestly are sent off generously.'"[48] We shall see the resemblance to Beijing's lofty approach to the Third World, Africa in particular, in the 1950s.

Generally, early in a dynasty, these four world-arranging tasks of a concentric nature were accomplished more or less successfully. Almost invariably, later in the dynasty, the arrangements fell apart, and it will be important, in the following chapter, to see why. The struggle to cope with the gap between theory and practice was recurrent. The difference in way of life between Chinese and Barbarian was intractable.

ARGUMENTS OFTEN flew within the Chinese court over how to deal with the Xiongnu, a nomadic people rooted in northern Mongolia. The Xiongnu, who overlapped with the Huns, were Altaic-speaking, believers in shamanism, and the inventors of trousers and cavalry. Regularly, during the final centuries B.C., they were equal in physical power to China. During the reign of Maodun, a Xiongnu chief, censor Cheng Jing pleaded with the Chinese emperor: "One must not [move against them]. The Xiongnu, by their nature, gather [in packs] like beasts and disperse like birds; to chase them is like trying to catch one's own shadow. If you attack the Xiongnu now, I fear that despite your lofty virtues, you will only court danger."[49] In the Qin–Han periods,

---

[48]Perelomov and Martynov, 1983, 184.
[49]Perelomov and Martynov, 1983, 57.

such arguments often were rejected, not always with good results. Lofty virtue unaided could bring disaster.

Sometimes, in relations with Muslims, Tibetans, and other westerly peoples, marriage arrangements, whereby a Chinese dynasty would be linked with another kingdom through intermarriage, were resorted to by the Chinese to fend off a war they felt they could not afford. But the Chinese did not favor matrimonial pacts, since these bespoke equality, which was anathema to the Son of Heaven. Today, PRC historians tend to deny that equality, or even an "international" relationship, ever existed between China and peripheral non-Chinese peoples. "Matrimonial pacts," writes Xiao Zhixing, "furthered the solidarity *of brotherly nationalities within our country.*" Citing a Tang history on how marriage pacts enhanced harmony "as in a family," he argues that the pacts "promoted the unification of the country."[50]

A study of the Tang period shows how the Chinese court wriggled out of marriage agreements it could not explicitly refuse, at a time when the Tibetans and the Uighurs were strong. Out of twenty-one Chinese princesses given in marriage to non-Chinese rulers, only three were truly the daughters of the emperor—the rest were fake.[51] In 658, Tibet asked China for a fresh matrimonial union. For decades the Chinese court dragged its feet. In 702, Empress Wu (the sole female to ascend the Chinese throne, of whom we will hear more) agreed in principle. But only after further Tibetan pressure did the Chinese, in 706, pick a bride. The Tibetans were told the girl was a daughter of a grandson of Emperor Gao Zong. The emperor himself had brought the child up, said the Chinese side. None of this was true. Still, the Chinese staged a tearful farewell ceremony between the emperor and the departing maiden, with court poets on hand to catch the moment in verse.[52]

---

[50]Xiao Zhixing, "Han-Tang de 'heqin' zujinle woguo lishishang geminzu de youhao tuanjie," *Guangming ribao*, Dec. 9, 1978 (emphasis added).
[51]Guang, 1935, 49–50, 52–53, 53–56, 65 (table of all marriage pacts).
[52]Demieville, 1952, 1–5.

To a degree, there was a tendency to say virtue could rule the Chinese and toughness was necessary to control the lesser peoples. In fact the Confucian classic *Zuozhuan* says as much: "By virtue, the people of the Middle Kingdom are taken care of; by punishments, the wild tribes on all sides are dealt with."[53] Matrimonial pacts, suggesting rules and equality, were an uncomfortable middle path between rule by virtue and rule by the sword. The surrounding nationalities were ultimately viewed as part of the realm of China.

The Chinese "world-arranging" function was until the Qin Dynasty the king's alone. But from the Han Dynasty, the sense of superiority, and therefore the right to rule, spread from just the emperor to a qualified Confucian elite. The learned *jun zi* ("virtuous one") could share in the world-arranging role. Thus did a more formidable wall arise between *hua* (Chinese) and *yi* (Barbarian). Virtue emanated by definition from those steeped in the Chinese Confucian classics. It followed—at least to the Chinese mind—that the Barbarians could only look up to the (Chinese) Son of Heaven, and that a Barbarian state could never be more than a vassal in relation to the Chinese court.

We see at once that this structure does not resemble any known *international relations* pattern. The emerging Chinese world view ruled out, in theory, the existence of any polity stronger than the Chinese, indeed of any other polity that stood equal to the Chinese; perhaps of any polity that we would think of as an independent state. It is important to our line of argument that, as Perelomov and Martynov sum up, "the *hua–yi* dichotomy sprang not from the experience of contacts with neighbors, but from the structure of the Chinese state."[54]

To a substantial degree at least, the Chinese court was not practicing foreign policy, but an extension of its paternalistic domestic policy.[55] Within the Chinese realm, the Us-and-Them dualism was comparable to the distinction, in Europe, between royalty-plus-aristocracy and commoners. Toward non-Chinese peoples, the condescension was still sharper. Of course, China at times lost out to a stronger political force,

[53] *Zuozhuan*, Xigong, ershiwu nian.
[54] Perelomov and Martynov, 1983, 187.
[55] Tikhvinsky and Perelomov, 1981, 26.

for instance the Mongols, but they never ceded cultural superiority to any non-Chinese entity.

What, in practice, was "wrong" with the Barbarians? Their steppe location counted against them in the eyes of a Chinese polity that assumed cultivation was the normal relation of human beings to land. In Chinese documents, the Barbarians were alluded to as whimsical and arbitrary. This may have meant they simply did not share the Chinese worldview. I am tempted to add that the trouble with the Barbarians, for the Chinese, was simply their existence—a common syndrome in the history of Chinese paternalism, because of the close analogy between state and family. If you were not a "child" of the mother-father state, you were a potential problem; at best, you did not belong to the family.

A sense of middle and periphery was deeply rooted in early Chinese public philosophy. This high self-consciousness was comparable to the Roman polity's sense of its own centrality. But the nomadic peoples of the northwest, who were a grave problem for the Chinese from about 1000 B.C., did not think of the world in terms of a middle (us) and a periphery (them). Their notion of governance stemmed from a mobile view of the world. Compromise between Chinese and nomad was difficult. The Chinese could never extend their way of life onto the steppe for a sustained period. And the nomadic peoples could never *both* conquer China proper and avoid co-option by Chinese civilization.

THE FLAVOR OF MISSIONS of tribute by lesser states to the Chinese court, a custom reaching its height in the Ming and Qing, is suggested by the case of the Ryukyu Islands during the Qing Dynasty.[56] The small island kingdom (today's Okinawa in part) sent a mission by ship each year from its chief port of Naha to Fujian Province on the southeastern coast. For some five hundred years (1372–1879), from the early Ming to the late Qing, this tributary relationship continued with stiff ceremony, unending subtlety, and remarkable stability.

---

[56]Ch'en, 1968, 136–163.

There were political, commercial, and cultural goals on both sides. According to Qing statutes, when a new ruler attained the throne in Ryukyu, the Chinese emperor was required to invest him. It was mainly on these occasions that the Chinese stirred themselves to send an envoy *to* the Ryukyu Islands. Otherwise they "received," grandly and generously, displaying condescension and very little curiosity about events within Ryukyu.

For an investiture, Ryukyu first sent an envoy to China to "report the death" of the previous king. Some years later a second mission arrived to formally "request the investiture." Beijing would graciously agree. A third mission would be sent from Shuri, the Ryukyu capital, to "meet the investiture envoys" whom China had chosen to go to Ryukyu. After the Chinese mission to Shuri for the investiture, Ryukyu sent a fourth mission to China to "express gratitude for the emperor's grace."

The first three missions were invited only to Fujian, the province opposite Taiwan. The last alone was permitted to travel to the holy ground of Beijing. Meanwhile, the new king of Ryukyu was not allowed to call himself such—only "heir apparent"—until the completion of all the trips back and forth between vassal state and imperial court.

A Chinese mission to Ryukyu might consist of 500 persons, including a staff of scribes, gong-beaters, cooks, sedan-chair bearers, tailors, and barbers, plus a military force of 200 to protect the 500 from pirates in the East China Sea. Sometimes the mission took hoes and ploughs, in case a storm at sea should bring shipwreck, leaving the travelers stranded on an island, and making return to China impossible. Even coffins were taken for this eventuality. The Chinese stayed some five months in Naha and Shuri, which required Ryukyu to scratch for funds to house, entertain, and bestow gifts on the imperial team. Only after a blizzard of ceremonies, during which the Ryukyu king would each time perform a full kowtow, with nine prostrations, was the investiture complete. The heir apparent, finally, became a real king.

I think of the Chinese empire as analogous to the Chinese character. Chinese writing is perhaps the most difficult in the world, and most Chinese for most of Chinese history could not read it, though literacy fluctuated with the presence or absence of social order. Moreover, the Chinese characters were *pronounced differently* in the various regions of China. Today, as spoken and written Chinese still are not aligned, this leads people new to China to ask, "Which [Chinese] language do you speak—Cantonese, Mandarin?" Yet the Chinese character, in part because of its very limitations, was and is a crucial instrument of rule, crystallizing the dominance of the (powerful) cultivated elite over the (powerless) common folk. Owen Lattimore put the dualism starkly: "The 'typical' Chinese, therefore, was two quite different people—a peasant whose functions were little higher than those of a draught animal, and a scholar whose long fingernails were the proof that he did no hard work."[57]

The character also took—and takes—the power of China beyond inner China. A Chinese character (however pronounced) carried—and carries—similar meaning whether read in Japan, Ryukyu, Korea, or Vietnam, wherever the elite absorbed Chinese high culture.

Chinese characters exemplified the subtlety of imperial control. Just as the logograms endured even though most people could not understand them, and if they did understand the characters, spoke them in varying sounds according to where they lived (whether by the Yellow River, say, or in northern Vietnam), so the empire came in and out of existence for untold centuries, against all odds, even though the far-flung peoples often were not actually ruled. Many people subject to the Son of Heaven "pronounced" their fealty differently, as it were, and remained "illiterate" in the hallowed classics—and the Son of Heaven lived with the ambiguities.

The character, beyond analogy, actually embodied three key elements of the Chinese empire. It was a classic tool for the Us-and-Them division. It both united and divided. "The written word has played a much greater role in China than in any other civilization," writes Jacques Gernet.[58] As early as 1310, a 136,000-character *Treatise on Agriculture* was published, bought, and read by an elite across the empire.[59] Yet, as Wittfogel observed, Chinese writing "separated social classes but united regions."[60]

---

[57]Lattimore, 1962, 144, 149.
[58]Gernet, 1985, xxvii.
[59]Elvin, 1973, 116.
[60]Wittfogel, 1935, 54.

Second, the elusiveness of the Chinese characters highlighted the "superficiality" that Fairbank ascribed to Chinese rule.[61] An aphorism from on high gave the long-gowned officials at the center a *sense* that they were ordering the realm, but a far-flung province may or may not jump to the aphorism. "Rule by writing," as we may call it, created a kingdom of the imagination. Mark Edward Lewis, in his study of how the written word commanded assent and obedience in the Warring States period (475–221 B.C.), concludes that "the Chinese empire . . . was based on an imaginary realm created within texts."[62]

Third, the Chinese characters were an epitome of the smoke-and-mirrors method of the Chinese polity. They cried out ambiguity and mystification. Leopold von Ranke's definition of history as "what actually happened" was the last thing history meant to the Chinese power-holders who paid so much heed to history. Distilling tales from the sage kings of the Shang and Zhou Dynasties, they were concerned with norms that would secure obedience.

After the fall of the Han in A.D. 220, "the textual dream at last swallowed up the political reality," writes Lewis. "Dynasties with their administrative codes and population registers came and went, but the Chinese empire survived them all in the form of a set of texts." Armed with these texts, rejuvenated elites "would re-establish a new dynasty in the rubble of the old."[63] Chinese history itself became an instrument of rule. "Chinese historiography," wrote Balazs, "is the most massive monument ever raised to glorify a particular social class."[64] At the same time, the smoke-and-mirrors of Chinese rule sometimes resulted in miscalculation. The "powerless" rebelled, a dynasty fell, and the intricate game had to begin again.

Despite periods of disunity, and other periods of introspection, and no matter where its vaguely defined borders lay at any point of time, China, deep in its bones, was long an empire; and one purpose of this book is to show that Beijing has not relinquished all the modes of

---

[61]Fairbank, 1968, 8.
[62]Lewis, 1999, 1, 4.
[63]Lewis, 1999, 10, 11.
[64]Balazs, 1964, 23–24.

empire. An empire is a big and dominating state that likely attained its dimensions through military conquest. It is a peculiarity of China that it became an empire, in the sense of the Roman *imperium*, even before, or without, its attempted domination over northern and western Barbarians, and over Vietnamese, Koreans, and others in the Confucian culture zone. The modes of civilizational-rule were developed within the relatively narrow bounds of inner China, and later extended to an outer China that intermittently included the steppe lands, the Confucian culture area, and, in a looser way, more distant peoples.

The Us-and-Them model by which the Chinese sought to keep the lesser peoples at bay was, by global standards, out of date by the Middle Ages. In the ancient world, the model could be seen as "an illustration of the manner in which the mentality of the ancient man developed as he assimilated inhabited space." By virtue of this "imaginary cosmic plan," there was (our) Middle and (their) Periphery. But, "neither the [later] spread of man across the earth's surface nor the diversity of the world's political picture were in the least reflected in the *hua–yi* (China–Barbarians) model."[65] The view of the non-Chinese world held by the Chinese polity became steadily more anachronistic.

Yet that worldview, seductive to some, an annoyance to others, always adapting, was never abandoned. The last two dynasties, the Ming and the Qing, regularly resorted to force, at home and abroad. At the same time, the Ming and the Qing not only retained the Confucian notion of virtue as the key to government policy, at home and abroad, but strengthened and institutionalized it. The Chinese polity grew in pomp and pride even as, in the late Qing, it became less masterful. Dissenting Confucian views—as against Ming emperor Tai Zu's tyranny—were often present but seldom powerful.

To the end, as Manchu interacted with Chinese, the political system remained a work in progress. Chinese civilization and the Chinese polity changed and adjusted greatly over time, and only quite late coalesced into what we recognize as the country and state of "China." Only in the nineteenth century did the Chinese term *Zhongguo* ("China")

---

[65] Perelomov and Martynov, 1983, 186.

emerge as the name of the country. Much of "Chinese" food as understood in 2003 is post–Tang Dynasty fare.[66] It was less a case of an established China encountering Barbarians and other lesser peoples, than of China and its neighbors shaping each other's character as interaction proceeded. The notion of China as old, unchanging, united, and consistent is a myth.

"Racial nationalism," writes Barry Sautman, "holds that each of us can trace our identities to a discrete community of biology and culture whose 'essence' has been maintained through time."[67] This false idea, which buttresses a polity of a Great Systemic Whole, runs rampant in China today. The longevity of China and the coherence of the Han race are constantly exaggerated by the Communist party-state, to further autocracy and the idea of "One China." Still, later distortions to one side, the Chinese state, regardless of who was its custodian, stood intermittently for thousands of years and heavily defined Chinese identity. To be Chinese came to mean being a child of the Chinese state. The culture has yet to disentangle itself from that paternal straitjacket.

[66]Wilkinson, 2000, xviii, 132, 625, 636; Hostetler, 2001, 27.
[67]Sautman, 2001, 95.

WE ARE THE WORLD

An Imperial Tradition Both Defensive and Superior

China had a very high opinion of its own achievements and had nothing but disdain for other countries. This became a habit and was considered altogether natural.

—Sun Yat-sen[1]

THE MATURE CHINESE EMPIRE was singular in ways echoed by the Chinese state today. It possessed a sense of superiority that was spectacular in world history, at least until the twentieth century brought Soviet-style and fascist regimes upon the scene. Beyond any *measurement* of military, economic, or political prowess, imperial China's sense of superiority was all-round, fundamental, a cosmological given. The Chinese world seemed "as self-contained as a billiard ball."[2] Everyone who dealt with the Chinese court—Korean envoy, Russian trader, the Muslim conqueror Tamerlane himself—remarked on the Chinese sense of superiority. The Chinese elite gave voice to it themselves. Even in the relatively cosmopolitan Tang Dynasty, if a foreigner resident in China took a Chinese wife or concubine, he was not allowed to leave China. It was out of the question to take the Chinese woman out of the bounds of civilization to a lesser realm.[3]

---

[1]Sun, 1956, 188.
[2]Peyrefitte, 1989, ix.
[3]Schafer, 1963, 25.

The doctrine behind this confidence was cosmological, hierarchical, and based on a social ethic, yet with a dose of *realpolitik*. The components of the social ethic of Confucianism included an optimistic humanism, the centrality of the family, high priority to education for those judged worthy of it, and a tight bond (if only by analogy) between the family and the wider Chinese community. A pattern of duties—no real rights—was the basis for achieving these ideals. The emperor linked each village to the sky itself by virtue of being a father to the people *and* the Son of Heaven. The deep genuflection (kowtow) of officials before the emperor "echoed the ritual kowtows of children in front of their parents."[4] The emperor alone made sacrifices to Heaven and Earth, on behalf of all. There was only one Son of Heaven and his Way was in tune with the universe, or supposed to be. When this ideal faltered, there was always the law and the sword. Chinese maps, from early times and also in the Ming and Qing Dynasties, included not only earth, with China central, but also heaven, with the sun depicted at the top and the moon at the bottom.[5] Many ancient polities considered themselves as the "center," but none took on and sustained China's sense of superiority over all others.

Emperor Yong Le of the next to last dynasty, the Ming (1368–1644), set out the pretension of the Chinese throne very plainly: "Reverently we hold the mandate of Heaven to rule both China and foreigners."[6] This goes back to the *Shijing* (Book of Odes)—*Bu tian zhi xia, mo fei wang tu* ("There is no land that is not the emperor's"). No neighboring state with any self-respect or desire to be independent could stomach such condescension unless necessity or profit required it. This was a superiority that had no need of effort or proof. A Manchu leader stated succinctly the objection any non-Chinese inevitably had to the cosmological arrogance of the Son of Heaven: "The only ruler of all the countries under Heaven is Heaven itself."

The American distinction between "what works" and "what is right" was absent in this Chinese worldview. National power was simply the

[4]Rawski, 1998, 297.
[5]Richard J. Smith, 1996, 3, 37–38.
[6]Fletcher, 1968, 206.

expression of national virtue. "Right made might," Mark Mancall points out. Might never had to make right. The American self-consciousness at the gulf between the two did not exist. "[T]he use of might was justified by its very existence, because, without right, there would have been no might in the first place."[7]

A Ming emperor explained his military drive against non-Chinese people in the area of today's Burma this way: "At first I did not wish to send troops to eliminate [this bandit leader]," said Emperor Ying Zong. "I warned him, but he did not correct his evil. Instead, he became ever more greedy." Ying Zong sadly concluded that tougher methods were unavoidable: "[The bandit's behavior] is unbearable to Heaven and Earth and the spirits; I have ordered the regional commander to advance troops to eliminate him."[8] When China attacked a neighbor, it was considered almost a favor to that lesser people. Heaven, through the instrumentality of the Chinese emperor, was reestablishing a proper order of things.

At times, non-Chinese regimes profited from fitting into this Chinese worldview. The case of Burma illustrates the high price the Chinese court could pay for the burnishment of its imperial self-image. Lucian Pye points out that the first Burmese tributary mission to China took only cheap gifts, but the Chinese plied the visitors with costly gifts. Burma, happy with a surplus, suggested to China that tributary missions be an annual affair. China demurred and said every five years would suffice. The two countries split the difference. The Burmese felt satisfied that, in return for prostration of the head to the floor in the presence of the Chinese emperor every two or three years, they came away with prized booty. "The Burmese showed how much could be got," observes Pye, "in return for flattery about China's greatness."[9] But if a foreign land failed to pay tribute as China expected, displeasure or worse resulted. Emperor Yang Di of the Sui Dynasty complained that he extended his largesse to the various countries of the "Western regions," but two, India and Byzantine, did not respond with

[7]Mancall, 1963, 18.
[8]*Ming Ying Zong shilu*, juan 76, 7b–8a.
[9]Lucian Pye, communication to the author, July 23, 2002.

a tribute mission to China. Yang Di vented his anger at India; still, India was distant enough to escape invasion.[10]

A second peculiarity of the Chinese empire would seem to fit ill with its effortless superiority. The Son of Heaven frequently administered his realm with a light touch. A special phrase, *jimi,* "loose rein," from the time of the Han Dynasty came to apply to the preferred mode of rule. It could apply within or beyond the assumed frontiers of China, but its linguistic sense implies a nasty comparison between the "lesser people" and cattle. The "loose rein" policy was explicitly contrasted with "repression" (*bu zhuanzhi*). The peripheral peoples were to be "bridled," not dominated.

By the Tang Dynasty, an institutionalization of the loose-rein policy was in place. The center accepted that the chief of a frontier prefecture should be, not a Chinese, but an "ethnic" local. He was not required to report to the center at Xi'an on population or finances, like the areas of inner China. It was a relationship not unlike that of frontier Hong Kong to Beijing in 2002. The Qing Dynasty, writes a Beijing historian, ruled border peoples by "being flexible according to the region concerned (*yindi zhiyi*)" and "controlling according to the customs pertaining (*yin su er zhi*)."[11]

To be sure, there were many periods of exception, most famously in the emperorship of Qin Shihuang, whose every instinct ran against the "loose rein" idea. But experience kept teaching the Chinese court that a light touch was for the most part better than the alternative, which was frequent strife.

Confucian doctrine did carry a bias toward rule by moral modes, rather than by law and/or brute force. Frequently, in periods when China was an unmatched empire and not a part of a plurality of states, that empire was not as centralized in practice as the Roman Empire or Byzantium. It was perhaps nearer to the Persian and Ottoman polities, where neither the laws nor the values of the center always prevailed throughout the empire. Chinese rule was frequently a comparatively

[10] *Xin Tangshu,* juan 221 (1).
[11] Li Shiyu, 2000, 22–23.

relaxed rule. By the peak of the Qing Dynasty, the economy in particular was by no means micromanaged by the state, even within the "eighteen provinces" of China proper; markets flourished and there was considerable social mobility.

A further, structural factor buttressed the limits on the center's grip. The emperor and his vast bureaucracy were not always in harmony. Mandarins could drag their feet in implementing policies they did not agree with. An emperor could restrain the bureaucracy by setting one part of it against another. Discussing the Song Dynasty, Wang Ruilai writes of emperor and officials "checking each other," of a mutual balancing of "those above and those lower down, of the heavy-weights and the light ones."[12] The early Qing emperors happened to be strong, warrior figures; they tightly controlled the bureaucracy and army. The late Qing emperors were mostly the opposite; their grip was feebler. In general, the earlier dynasties saw less dominance by the emperor over his court officials than the later dynasties.[13]

Chinese bureaucracy was not quite what it seemed. Max Weber's traits of bureaucracy were a system of rules, impersonality, hierarchy, and specialization. But this model was drastically modified by the impact of Chinese *society.* The Chinese social order was marked by stress on the primary group with its networks of personal relations, Confucian moral teachings, and self-sufficiency at the local level. In effect, Chinese bureaucracy, famous as it became for its rationality, had to operate within a social order that undermined bureaucracy. Some scholars feel the indirect, localized rule during some dynasties even calls in question the term "state" to describe it.[14]

C. K. Yang says China's social order "could operate by itself, with a minimum of assistance from the formal political structure." The existence of this broader world "may actually have given the bureaucratic structure an elasticity which helped it to revive after each breakdown."[15] Hence a paradox: One reason for the persistence of the Chinese polity,

---

[12]Wang Ruilai, 1985, 107.
[13]Fu, 1993, 65.
[14]Grimm, 1985, 49–50.
[15]Yang, 1959, 134–135, 164.

its alternation between rules and custom, also made it liable to inefficiency and periodic collapse.

———————

SURPRISINGLY, the loose rein and the sense of superiority were not
deeply contradictory, especially in dealings with the culturally alien
people of the steppe. The conceit that made the Chinese court feel
superior to the Barbarians inclined the court to keep its distance from
people of whom Emperor Tai Zong said, with distaste: "These people go
about with flowing hair, and it is their habit to eat food uncooked."[16] At
times Chinese supremacy was maintained by a stunningly unusual policy: the "defense" against an attack from the Barbarians was a *cultural
policy* of Sinicizing, or pretending to Sinicize, the Barbarian attackers.

Chinese dealings with the "Sinic zone," including Vietnam and
Korea, where Chinese language and philosophy had put its stamp and
the agricultural way of life resembled that in inner China, showed a
similar indirection. China's strong influence on Korea was sometimes
achieved by military means, other times by a moral suasion at once
light-handed and arrogant. Vietnam's ties with China were not very
different. A degree of seduction of the Vietnamese elite by Chinese
culture occurred. But physical attack was periodically resorted to and
China once occupied Vietnam for a thousand years (from the Han
Dynasty until 939). Sometimes, a Vietnam king who opposed the Chinese, in periods when Vietnam was independent, had to come to China
afterward to ask for pardon.[17]

When the court was sure of itself and Barbarians were not rebelling,
largesse was displayed toward peripheral peoples. Emperor Tai Zong of
the Tang Dynasty declared in 647: "From antiquity all rulers showed
great concern for China and contempt for Barbarians. But, myself, I
love both Chinese and Barbarian equally. That is why all tribes and
peoples have submitted to me as they would to their father and
mother."[18] Yet, largesse could turn to a snarl if proper deference was not

———————

[16] *Song huiyao jigao*, ce 7, 6874.
[17] Lam, 1968, 174.
[18] *Zizhi tongjian*, juan 198.

shown, and/or if the Chinese court was harried by multiple problems. When the Sui emperor, Yang Di, could not elicit the required respect from Korea, he angrily denounced the Koreans as "little freaks" (*xiao chou*). The northeastern neighbors had "not only failed to defer to my court, but joined with another tribe to invade China." Tossing aside the rule book of etiquette and ritual, Emperor Yang Di sent a huge military force to deal with the "vicious" Koreans.[19]

It has often been remarked that China did not extend itself by founding formal colonies, even during the Ming Dynasty, when it possessed the sea power to traverse the Indian Ocean and reach Africa. Of course, the Chinese were preoccupied with the Inner Asian, not the maritime, frontier. But the China–Barbarians model employed toward the peoples of the steppe itself seemed curiously uncreative. Although China often used military force against the lesser peoples, it never succeeded in extending the Chinese way of life far into the steppe. "A few dynasties, such as the Han and the Tang," writes Morris Rossabi, "sought to and sometimes did conquer the adjacent nomadic peoples, but their gains were short lived."[20] Typically, as the dynasty matured and declined, the Chinese retreated to "China." The Chinese polity "had to find a different way of dealing with these potentially powerful and dangerous adversaries," who rode horses, drank milk, and ate raw flesh—not Chinese practices.

Perhaps China's geography lent itself to passive centrality. Wrote Benjamin Schwartz: "China was not challenged in its immediate vicinity by the emergence of any universal state whose claims it felt obliged to take seriously in cultural terms."[21] Other states of the ancient world were far smaller than the Chinese realm. Egypt, for example, was a thin ribbon by the Nile, and other kingdoms lay not far away. Unlike the Mesopotamian *oikos*, where the economy was basically the palace, the Chinese realm was far-flung. Its outer fringes were at times a thousand or more miles from the capital. China gained little experience of dealing with an equal. As the scholar-of-all-talents during the early twen-

---

[19] *Sui shu*, juan 4.
[20] Rossabi, 1983, 2.
[21] Schwartz, 1968, 281.

tieth century, Ding [Ting] Wenjiang, wrote, "China had no Athens or
Alexandria [formidable neighboring civilizations] to serve as a stimu-
lant to Imperial Rome [China]."[22]

By the standards of most empires, China's treatment of the small
kingdom of Ryukyu (also part of the Sinic zone), during the Ming and
Qing Dynasties, while condescending, was far from heavy-handed.
Beijing's policies could be said to illustrate the philosopher Lao Zi's
comment that a large realm—East Asia in this case—should be run as
if cooking a small fish: stir as little as you can. Arrogance certainly was
present. As we have seen, a Ryukyu king had to be invested by the Chinese emperor. He was referred to in Beijing as "a subordinate subject of
the Celestial Court."

Yet Ryukyu gained undoubted cultural benefits from the relationship. In trade, it haggled over prices in a way that did not suggest it was
being trampled on by the Chinese. All the while, China did not object
with any vigor to Ryukyu being simultaneously close to Japan. When
control over the Ryukyu Islands became an issue between China and
Japan in 1873, Ryukyu officials tactfully wrote the Japan Foreign Ministry that the Ryukyu Islands regarded China as father and Japan as
mother.[23] In a word, China wanted and got respect from Ryukyu, but
the "small fish" was not crushed or severely burned.

In its dealings with peripheral peoples, China quite often knew when
to stop. Its grip was seldom so tight that the aim of respect and influence was lost in a storm of destruction. As John Fairbank said, the
superficiality of Chinese rule was a secret of its success. When punishments grew more draconian, this did not necessarily mean the Chinese
empire was at its peak. More often it was a sign of fear and desperation.

Defensiveness and arrogance, indeed, were two sides of a single coin.
The Chinese were defending the alleged purity of their Way. In
China's relations with the tribes of the steppe, give and take, intercourse, and agreements on an equal basis, would seem to have been an
option. These were impossible, however (except to a degree during the

---

[22]Ting, 1931, 10.
[23]Sakai, 1968, 114.

Song Dynasty),[24] given the sense of superiority that prevailed within the Chinese court. Such a mentality might be called, in modern parlance, confident isolationism.

———————

A FURTHER STRIKING TRAIT of the Chinese empire was that doctrine was sometimes honored only in the breach. Although the Son of Heaven possessed an all-encompassing and ambitious doctrine, in dealings with non-Chinese peoples a hostile environment regularly forced him to act contrary to the optimistic norms of Confucianism, in a word, to be pragmatic. The Chinese court compromised with Tibet and the Turki Khanate in the west, and with the Khitan and Jurchen states in the north, without admitting it in the official histories. Yet, despite setting doctrine aside in actual policy, the Chinese did not feel it necessary to abandon or even revise that doctrine.

Instead, Chinese rulers devised a cornucopia of fictions to disguise their departures from doctrine. A famous Qing Dynasty work on China and non-Chinese peoples and places says Italy presented tribute to China in 1667, which it did not, and even that the Pope once brought tribute personally to the Chinese court, which never occurred.[25] "The Barbarians covet Chinese products," runs the official history of the Ming Dynasty, "and make enormous profits by trade and the roads are packed with them."[26] Sometimes this was true, and the Ming and Qing Dynasties generally looked beyond trade to questions of control, stability, and respect. But at other times the Chinese desperately coveted the horses that only the Barbarians could supply. We shall see a similar bending of reality in Beijing's current effort to make the world believe the United States needs China more than China needs the United States.

The Chinese also did not like to admit their regular resort to force against the Barbarians. They preferred the fiction that the Barbarians accepted the reign of virtue. In fact many foreigners felt contempt for

———————

[24]Xie, 1935, 52–53; Tikhvinsky and Perelomov, 1981, 10.
[25]Richard J. Smith, 1996 ("Mapping . . . "), 84.
[26]Mancall, 1968, 70.

the Chinese. An eighth-century Turkic khan, Koltegin, said the Chinese "always had sweet speech and luxurious treasures, and, seducing us with this sweet speech and luxurious treasure, they so strongly attracted faraway peoples to themselves, who settled close by, and then absorbed their evil practices."[27] The Moslem leader who succeeded Tamerlane sent a Ming emperor a letter in Arabic, and another in Persian, advising him to put aside his infidel ways and adopt Islam.[28] He got back a letter that, unlike some Tamerlane had received from Beijing, was written monarch-to-monarch to the Turkic kingdom, accepting gifts as gifts, rather than as tribute. China had backed down, though the Chinese histories never tell us so.

War was generally more costly and damaging for China, with its agricultural economy, than for the peoples to the north and west. Nevertheless, force played at least as big a role as moral control in the relations between inner China and the adjacent peoples of Tibet, Mongolia, and Manchuria. Yet the doctrine of rule by virtue was never abandoned. Said the founding emperor of the Ming Dynasty: "Ever since the earliest emperors ruled all-under-heaven, China has controlled the Barbarians from within while the Barbarians have respectfully looked to China from without."[29] This was untrue, but it helped the Ming claim they were restoring a long-established and flawless polity.

With an eye to the import of all this for today's China, the reader may well enquire: Was dynastic China a dominating empire, or was it a vacillating player in a wider game with other serious protagonists? Over its 3,000-year duration, from the Zhou Dynasty to the fall of the Qing Dynasty in 1911–1912, the Chinese polity was both. Often it was an unmatched empire; sometimes it was hardly more than one kingdom among others. Mostly, the prosaic factor of balance of power between China and nearby states determined the Chinese court's oscillation between hauteur and humility, between loudly proclaiming its doctrine and quietly counting the numbers.

---

[27]Mancall, 1968, 70.
[28]Fletcher, 1968, 211.
[29]Wang Gungwu, 1968, 34.

In the eighth century, when Tibet was strong compared with the Tang Dynasty—and Lhasa controlled much of today's Xinjiang, Gansu, and Qinghai provinces—the Tibetans refused to accept the condescension involved in the custom of the "broken fish." The Chinese court was in the habit of manufacturing a bronze fish—fish being a token of abundance—to be shared as an insignia of authenticity between China and a tributary state. The fish was in two parts, which fitted perfectly together. One part was kept at the Chinese court, the other was brought by the non-Chinese envoy on tributary missions. The fish was carried in a purse attached to the girdle of a ceremonial robe that the Chinese emperor gave to the foreign envoy. The Chinese required that a vassal state possess twelve of these bronze fish, one for each month of the year, and on arriving at the imperial court the vassal envoy had to present the one appropriate to the date of his journey. When the envoy arrived and the metal fish was made whole, this was proof that the tributary envoy was bona fide and all was well with the world.[30]

But in 730, when Tibet was in semi-equal negotiation with China, after intermittent warfare between the two kingdoms since 670, the Tibetan officials refused to play this game with the metal fish. The Tibet envoy, visiting the Tang capital, today's Xi'an, said this ornament was not known in Tibet and he could not possibly accept such a rare gift. The whole idea of the bronze fish seemed to him, as indeed it was, a piece of political theater designed to cement vassalage. The Chinese side had no choice but to accept the Tibetan position.[31] In much later history, Tibet lost its power to maneuver with the Chinese and was controlled.[32]

Quite often, strength and weakness could be found within the span of a few decades. Soon after unifying various contending states and creating "China" in 221 B.C., Emperor Qin Shihuang sent half a million troops to attack Vietnam. Yet a decade or so later his dynasty col-

[30]Schafer, 1963, 26.
[31]Richardson, 1970; Des Rotours, 1952, 63.
[32]Courant, 1912, chap. VII.

lapsed. The Song Dynasty in its first years maintained "international" but paternalistic relations with various southern neighbors. As long as the Southern Tang, the Southern Han, and the Kingdom of Wuyue paid tribute, as vassals were required to do, the Song court let them be. Later, when the Song grew stronger, it eliminated these three separate polities.

In the north, however, the Song never dominated and was required to participate in a system of quasi-international relations.[33] The Song had to deal on equal terms with the Khitan, a nomadic people from grasslands east of Mongolia, who formed the Liao Dynasty (916–1125), and later with the Jurchen, a people stemming from the Amur River valley, who formed the Jin Dynasty (1115–1234). The Liao and Jin both at one time or another asked tribute from the Chinese court![34] The flux of power determined the mix at any time between arrogance and humility, between implementing the imperial doctrine and plugging holes in the dike by whatever means lay to hand.

SAY WHAT ONE MAY about the Chinese empire, no system of government in the world lasted so long. What were the reasons for its remarkable longevity? I leave aside for the moment that it was longevity in a rather technical sense; for substantial periods, the polity departed from the Way, fell and gave way to fragmentation, or lost control to non-Chinese rulers. From the collapse of the Tang Dynasty in 907, until the final curtain came down on the Chinese monarchical polity in 1911–1912, for a total of 700 years non-Chinese ruled over much of Chinese civilization. Either the whole of the Chinese realm, as with the Yuan and Manchu Dynasties, or northern portions of it, as with rule by the neighboring Jurchens and Khitans (916–1234). Only for some 300 years of this millennium was the full Chinese realm in Chinese hands.

---

[33]Tikhvinsky and Perelomov, 1981, 128; Xie, 1935, 19, 34, 38–39.
[34]Rossabi, 1983, 10.

One might say the Chinese were lucky. They had a free ride on the eastern and southern flanks virtually until the nineteenth century. The story of the Chinese system's long survival is inseparable from the *absence of pressure from the maritime side.* A set of challenges from the seacoast, similar in scale to those from the steppe, would no doubt have cut short the Chinese empire. Still, more than the luck of isolation was involved. Of course, toward Inner Asia the Chinese experienced great vicissitudes and ended with a mixed record. Yet the Chinese polity was never toppled, or replaced by a fresh, enduring polity, by an assault from Inner Asia.

A major reason for the resilience of the Chinese system was the symbiosis between Confucianism and Legalism, the two leading public philosophies. Amidst the turmoil of the late Zhou, a quest arose, not for ultimate truth, but for an improved society.[35] Confucius, a somewhat disgruntled teacher who upheld a durable humanism, focused on this endeavor. To Confucians, the cosmos was an inseparable, ultimately mysterious bundle of Heaven, Earth, and Man. Earlier, in the Shang Dynasty, Chinese had believed in God with a human personality (*Shang-di*). But, by the end of the Zhou Dynasty, an anthropomorphic God was replaced by Heaven as a vague but vital force hovering over all.

In the Confucian optic, Heaven was well-disposed toward people but it had its imperatives. Virtue among human beings, expressed in filial, respectful, obedient conduct, was related to cosmic harmony. Mencius was more egalitarian than Confucius; he tossed the term "people" around in a seemingly populist fashion. Neither Confucius nor Mencius put store in technical knowledge, military valor, or theories of an afterlife. Both men's philosophies eventually overlapped with more religious views, on one side, and law-and-order Legalism, on the other. Many ordinary Chinese constructed their worldview as a kind of insurance policy, with a careful nod to the Gods and the emperor as well as to the immediate superiors of father or husband.

---

[35]Hucker, 1975, 70–84.

By itself, if successful, the Confucian moral scheme, stressing education, decorum, restraint, and treating others as you would wish them to treat you, would call only for a night-watchman state. If people behave well, a strong state is hardly necessary. Yet, quite often, the Confucian moral scheme was a cry in the wilderness. "Why is it that morality is still difficult to make clear," an examination question in the reign of Emperor Hui Zong of the Song Dynasty asked plaintively, "and social customs are not unified?"[36]

Human nature being what it is, Chinese rule was sometimes draconian, and the realms of family and education were, in such circumstances, manipulated by power-holders. In the history of Chinese governance, Confucianism won its role only in symbiosis with its nemesis, the *realpolitik* philosophy of Legalism. The result was a brilliant tradition of statecraft.

Chinese Legalism is as Western as Thomas Hobbes, as modern as Hu Jintao. It speaks the universal and timeless language of law and order. The past does not matter, state power is to be maximized, politics has nothing to do with morality, intellectual endeavor is suspect, virtue is rare, violence is indispensable, and little can be expected from the rank and file except an appreciation of force.

We see the doctrines of Legalism in the pages of Han Fei (280–233 B.C.). His advice to his own ruler having being disregarded, Han Fei wrote down his philosophy. Since no norms could be handed down from the past, he said, political arrangements must follow economic conditions and the bleak realities of human nature (people are "stupid and slovenly," their minds are "as undependable as a babe's"). Han Fei pointed out that the same people who, during a famine, do not even feed "the little boys of the family," in a year of abundance will go so far as to feed "casual visitors." The variable is not the human heart, but "the difference in the amount of food to be had."

The interests of the government and the governed are not mutually harmonious, in Han Fei's view. Authority is everything. "Superior and inferior fight a hundred battles a day," he cites the legendary Yellow

---

[36]Bol, 2001, 18.

Emperor as saying. When Han Fei heard of a soldier running away from battle because he feared that, if he were killed, he would no longer be able to serve his father, the Legalist philosopher coolly riposted: "A filial son to his father can be a traitorous subject to his ruler."[37] Lord Shang, Han Fei's fellow Legalist, offered a sharp measure of a well-governed state and its opposite: "An effective state employs seven punishments to three rewards; a weak state employs five punishments to five rewards."[38] Today, if asked the "root causes of crime," Han Fei would probably say every crime has a single cause: the failure to deter.

Han Fei was sarcastic about Confucianism. "Using public funds to make gifts to the poor is called being benevolent. To subvert the laws in order to protect one's own family is called having principles. To pass out favors and gain a mass following is called winning the people."[39]

Han Fei's doctrines, together with those of Lord Shang (385–338 B.C.) and Li Si (280–208 B.C.), were put into practice by Emperor Qin Shihuang. All four had no time for Confucianism. Lord Shang understood the techniques of a totalitarian bureaucratic state. "The people are to be organized into groups of fives and tens," in his formula. "They must practice mutual supervision. They are to be punished for any crime committed by other members of their group. Those who fail to inform against a crime will be cut in half at the waist. Those who inform against a crime are to be rewarded equal to the merit of having killed an enemy. Those who protect an enemy will be punished as if they had surrendered to the enemy."[40]

It is often said that Chinese political history exhibits a tussle between the antithetical public philosophies of Confucianism and Legalism, but the keystone of the Chinese polity and a major reason for its longevity was an uneasy *marriage* of Confucianism and Legalism. In the end Legalism needed Confucianism, as Confucianism needed Legalism. The Legalists were concerned with a science of rule;

---

[37]Han Fei words based on Watson, 1964, 95, 128, 98, 40, 106, 107, with translation adjusted by reference to Chen Qiyu, 1958.
[38]*Shangjun shu*, juan 1.
[39]Hsiao, 1979, 387.
[40]*Shiji*, juan 68.

their doctrine told the emperor "why and how the monarchs should rule." The Confucianists offered a complement; their doctrine instructed the people on "why and how subjects should obey rulers,"[41] or, *in extremis,* on the need to overthrow the ruler.

The early Confucian scholar Dong Zhongshu (195–115 B.C.) gave an important explanation of the Three Bonds—subject obeys ruler, son obeys father, female obeys male. Making the Confucianism–Legalism symbiosis stark, Dong said the three bonds were all based on the *yin–yang* dualism. This is a cosmic concept. *Yin* is "moon," and by extension female, subordinate. *Yang* is "sun," and by extension male, assertive. Hence the Chinese ruler was seen as a cosmic, absolute force. Said scholar Dong: "The ruler holds the position of life and death over men; together with Heaven he holds the power of change and transformation."[42] Here is not merely moral authority, but the crack of the whip.

The codes of the Han (202 B.C.–A.D. 220) and Tang (618–907) Dynasties hardly suggest the perfumed world of Confucian ideals! The Han code listed 409 offenses that would draw the death penalty. This legal maze is "rather like a cross between the U.S. Government Manual and a telephone directory," Finer remarks.[43] And indeed, "the very notion of a public code with fixed penalties for the various types of offences is unConfucian." Yet the Han Dynasty (along with the Ming) is known as a particularly "Confucian" dynasty.

The point is Confucianism came to terms with Legalism. In the process it was tamed; it was selectively absorbed by the power-maximizers. Ideology tended to be manipulated for the securing of law and order. Already the Tang code was both severely penal, in Legalist fashion, and also mindful of the centrality of the family, in Confucian fashion; the penalty for striking a parent was death. "Heaven is my father and earth is my mother," wrote the Song Confucian Zhang Zai. "The emperor is the eldest son of my parents." Perhaps meant as an ideal,

---

this sentiment could nevertheless be used to buttress hierarchical authority.[44] The Us-and-Them, two-class character of Chinese society was a product of the Confucianism–Legalism interaction. Superior men were also authoritarian men. Regrettable as this may be from a modern Western point of view, the Confucian–Legalism dualism lent stability to the Chinese polity.

Etienne Balazs attacked the idea of traditional China as a picture of Confucian harmony, but he also saw truth to it. By implication, he detected the symbiosis between Confucian harmony and Legalist toughness. Balazs rejected the idea of a "calm, unchanging, smiling land suddenly transformed into a blazing inferno by the flaming torch of twentieth century social and nationalist revolutions; of China as an amiable giant, torn from three thousand years of somnolence amidst gracious works of art, sophisticated customs, and mystical wisdom, by the shrill call to arms of foreign emissaries and agitators."

Yet Balazs hinted at a major secret behind the smoke-and-mirrors of Chinese continuity. The idealized picture was not "pure invention," he said. "The force of inertia in a social mechanism whose driving power is generated by conflicting pulls," he wrote in a brilliant insight, "easily gives the impression of a pre-established harmony. Tensions are kept under control by force, and thus tend to cancel each other out, so that the internal dynamic force appears to be in a state of constant equilibrium."[45] We shall see how in the PRC, too, tensions are kept under control by force.

The long-running story of the Chinese empire was only possible because of Qin Shihuang. Confucianism could not have been a philosophy of government, absent Legalism and the institutions it set up. Writes Steven Sage of Confucianism, which stemmed from the central plains: "This philosophy may occupy the very core of Chinese identity but it could not unify the lands we know as China. Unity derived from Qin. . . . The rulers of Qin did not subscribe to the same visions as cen-

---

[44]Schrecker, 1991, 47.
[45]Balazs, 1964, 152.

tral plains philosophers. . . . In Qin the state ruled supreme, remolding society via legal statute and backed by force."[46]

To be sure, it can be argued that in the Ming Dynasty a *Confucian state* came into existence, with power and doctrine quite closely aligned. Also that by the late Qing, this Confucian state showed traits, including a lack of enthusiasm for commerce, that were not typical of the Chinese state in the many periods when Confucianism was sidelined, including the *early* Qing Dynasty. And I will argue that updates of Confucianism and Legalism have each played a role in the post-1949 Communist dictatorship.

But, at root, Legalism was the iron scaffolding of the Chinese empire; Confucianism was its silken costume. Qin Shihuang himself saw fit to add Confucian flourishes to his ideas. Sometimes it sounded as if he ruled the entire world: "Under all the vast Heaven [he] won the hearts of [men] and concerted their endeavors," ran an official document, referring to the emperor's awesome power. Yet Qin Shihuang was quite aware of the distinction between the boundaries of his own kingdom and the "four cardinal directions of the Earth," which he grandly spoke of blessing. He played both sides of the street: (Legalist) science of power, and (Confucian) doctrine to keep the people pliable.

Without Qin Shihuang there would have been no Mao Zedong. An ingenious alternation, or blend, of Confucianism and Legalism has lasted off and on for more than 2,000 years. The Ming, although known as one of China's more defensive dynasties, nevertheless fought 308 external wars in its three centuries of existence.[47] The Confucianism–Legalism dualism extended all the way from the Han Dynasty to Mao, who essayed the reign of virtue, but kept the sword at hand. It continued to arm Deng Xiaoping and Jiang Zemin, both of whom gave verbal obeisance to the reign of virtue, but acted as neo-Legalists.

A SECOND REASON for the persistence of the Chinese polity is that the Son of Heaven was not a fanatic. His interest lay in statecraft, not

---

[46]Sage, 1992, 195.
[47]Johnston, 1995, 184.

the supernatural. This set China apart from all other major empires of ancient and medieval times, except Persia. The more religious empires did not possess the staying power of the nonreligious Chinese empire. In most early empires—but rarely in the Chinese empire—issues of faith and politics became explosive, the rise of new faiths was destabilizing, and clashing religious schools interfered with state policies.

It is true that Confucianism was sometimes a functional equivalent to a religion. The intellectual bureaucrats of China could be compared with the priests of Christian Europe or the imams of the Caliphate. By the time of Ming and Qing, Chinese society was Confucian in the way some Western societies are Christian. Yet the Chinese empire, post-Qin Dynasty, was never a theocracy, as was Byzantium, with its cry of "One God, One Empire, One Religion."

Confucianism was fundamentally an ethics. It was not dualistic, as were the great religions, offering a realm of nature and a second, supernatural realm. Being an ethical system, with no apocalyptic overtones, Confucianism did not lend itself to the persecution of nonbelievers or rival faiths as did the Caliphate or the Christian Roman Empire. Indeed it came to overlap with Buddhism, Daoism, and, in a different sphere, Legalism. "Confucianism could be many things to many men," it has been said with only slight exaggeration. "Christianity had to be one thing to all men."

The Chinese empire did not stand or fall with its (Confucian) doctrine, as did Egypt with its faith. When Christianity destroyed the religion of ancient Egypt, "it destroyed the entire Pharaonic culture as well." Finer makes a second comparison: "Whereas the Jewish prophets, the Christian Church, and Islam had come into existence outside the state form (indeed *against* the state), and claimed a supernatural sanction, the Confucian establishment had been called into being by the state itself, and its doctrines were man-made things."[48]

The this-worldly orientation of Confucianism implied a respect for history, a stance that is conservative and stability-minded. Awe for those who went before probably aided the survival of the system. The

---

[48]Finer, 1997, 821.

tradition of ancestor worship, writes Harald Bøckman, "created a pull towards the past that promoted a sense of common origin and destiny that has no equivalent in Western civilization. This created a horizontal orientation towards the past instead of a vertical orientation toward a personal God."[49]

Confucianism as an ethics allowed some give and take with rival worldviews, which made the Chinese empire less brittle than most others. As early as the Warring States epoch (475–221 B.C.), there was philosophical diversity in the underpinnings available for public policy. Daoism favored a retreat to the private and the whimsical, in the bosom of nature, with no attempt to repair the organized world. Confucianism proposed recovering a past Golden Age by following the precepts of the Zhou Dynasty kings. Legalism had no taste for the past or the otherworldly, pursuing instead a science of power.

To be sure, this philosophical diversity did not imply freedom for the individual. Few Chinese, educated or not, felt free to propose an alternative to the orthodoxy of the moment. Some did, for instance the brilliant Ming statesman-philosopher Wang Yangming (1472–1529), but it was always risky. Yet, in the longer perspective, variety existed. From century to century, the possibility of choice lent some resilience, some "room to move," to the Chinese system. Peter Bol has shown the sharp change from idealism to empiricism after the abdication of the twelfth-century emperor Hui Zong. The examination question for would-be officials in 1124 assumed that antiquity, and the cosmos, offered "the grounds for a style of governing that would transform the world." But the examination question of 1128 saluted concrete study of grassroots conditions: "Investigate the situation of the populace," ran its premise.[50]

Viewed from another angle, the Chinese empire endured because it cultivated the secrets of stability. It was by no means an effortless stability; the Chinese court continually engaged in battles to maintain stability. Emperors and their advisors put stability above visions and schemes, most of the time. The frequently favored doctrine, Confu-

---

[49]Bøckman, 1998, 314.
[50]Bol, 2001, 25.

cianism, was not immune to influence from rival ideas or religions. To a degree from the Han Dynasty, and certainly from the Tang and Song Dynasties, there existed a pull and tug between a strong (or weak) emperor and a weak (or strong) bureaucracy. This, like the philosophical diversity, gave the system resilience. A usefully elusive Way seemed to define a mythical center of gravity for the Chinese polity.

In dealings with non-Chinese peoples, a continuum of methods was employed, from accepting tribute and exchange of gifts, at the soft end of the spectrum, to warfare, at the hard end of the spectrum. In between lay rhetorical crossfire, trade disputes, and raids. A smoke-and-mirrors theatrical politics allowed alternation between principle and pragmatism. The same political method sustained the myth of Chinese unity. In today's terms, the myth is known as "One China." When defeat occurred, it was touched up as victory. This was another trick inherited by the Communist Party.

MANY A VISITOR to China today comes home wondering why she did not see more of the Chinese past. The answer is that it burned down or rotted away. For the Chinese built less in stone than in wood. The superb Temple of Heaven in Beijing, not an ancient building but a rare survivor from the grand structures of the Ming Dynasty, does not hold within its wooden beams a single nail or stone. Most of its wood-built contemporaries have long since turned to dust. Edward Gibbon tells us he was inspired to write his *History of the Roman Empire* by contemplating the remaining pieces—still there for the eye to see—of Imperial Rome.[51] But the cities of China offer little of the Han Dynasty compared with the legacy of Imperial Rome offered by today's Rome.

Perhaps the Chinese elite esteemed the Way far above monuments to the Way. Monuments are explicit. The Way of the Chinese empire was implicit. The writings of Confucius and Mencius, subject to a hundred interpretations, have endured. The dwellings of the emperors,

---

[51]Gibbon, 1932 (1787), vol. 3, 880.

warriors, and philosophers, less open to interpretation, are not available for our inspection. Confucius, "without any attribute of kingship acted as a ruler in the parallel realm of writing."[52] The Chinese empire was—and is—in substantial part an empire of the imagination.

The stones of Paris offer the visitor an actual presence of the medieval era. But the contemporary French polity reflects little or nothing of the political system of Philip Augustus (ruled 1180–1223) or Louis IX (ruled 1226–1270). With China the converse is true. The edifices of the past are little to be found. But the Way—of ruling, thinking, behaving—still lives. It has endured in part because it was implicit, flexible, and honored as much in the breach as in the letter. Also, because the Chinese Communist Party appropriated the more autocratic elements of the Way for its own social engineering purposes.

One sniffs a connection between putting the Way above monuments to the Way and cosmic pretension. Here, we may contrast the Roman emperor with the Chinese, in two interrelated points. The Roman office possessed less cosmic significance than the Chinese imperial office, and the Roman emperor was a more public figure than the Chinese. The Chinese emperor, who seldom showed his face to the public, unlike the Roman emperor, seemed to be implying that his doctrine was more important than his outstretched arm. The same contrast could be made between the Chinese emperor and the ruler of the Greek states. We do not find the Son of Heaven opening a sporting event, as the Greek king inaugurated the Olympic Games in 776 B.C.

DESPITE THE STRENGTHS of the Chinese polity, each dynasty eventually puttered and ended. Within a certain overall survival of the Chinese system from the Zhou Dynasty to 1911–1912, there occurred extraordinary variation and periodic turmoil. It will be instructive to ask why, and the fall of the Han and Tang Dynasties, together with adaptations that followed both collapses, suggests some answers.

---

[52]Lewis, 1999, 364, 365.

The Roman Empire and the Han Dynasty had traits in common, including their time slot and the way they declined. Barbarians from the north threatened the regime, powerful families created division, and farmers rebelled. A new religion came upon the land, and there was a shakeout of the economy. The last phase of the Han brought a hair-raising string of troubles. Tax evasion, floods, locusts, apocalyptic cults, all fed into rebellions by the Yellow Turbans and, in the southwest, the Five Pecks of Rice Band. Within the Han court, intrigue, bungling, and massacres. But there was more finality to the fall of the Roman Empire than to the fall of the Han Dynasty. The Roman Empire tradition died as a living form, and feudalism soon spread across the area formerly ruled by Rome. But the essential system of the Han (202 B.C.–A.D. 220) was eventually rebuilt as the Tang Dynasty.

Even before that, during some 350 years when China lacked a united political system, intriguing adaptations were foreshadowed in the overall Chinese polity. A differentiation between south and north occurred, with the Yangzi River as the marker, and this was to continue, now slight, now sharp, into our own era. Buddhism and Daoism spread at the grassroots and Confucianism was required to share China's philosophic space with these transcendental worldviews. Sinicization, sometimes involuntary, other times tactical, also occurred. Contending kingdoms of non-Chinese origin won control of the Chinese polity. Yet they came to speak Chinese (to make their rule more efficient), eat Chinese food, and govern in the Chinese style. The Way was preserved, even as it was adapted; and with the Tang Dynasty, it experienced a formidable reconstruction.

Yet like the Han Dynasty, and for substantially the same reasons, the Tang after some three centuries collapsed. The tolerance and prosperity of the Tang at its height gave way to narrowness, scratching for revenue, and violence. When the Tang fell in 907, north China saw five dynasties in quick succession in half a century, and south China split into separate states. In both the Han and Tang cases, and in others too, the great fall was caused by two flaws, plus two factors that were mixed strengths-and-weaknesses of the Chinese polity. Legitimacy and succession problems were the two fundamental problems of the Chinese polity.

Which was prior, the mandate of heaven or the quality of the ruler who acquired the mandate of heaven? If the mandate of heaven was real, and an absolute qualification for the exercise of power, the very imprimatur of the cosmos on the emperor, how could power struggle and even usurpation recur? If the emperor's legitimacy came from heaven, how could it be challenged from earth?

No abiding answers existed to these questions. It hardly helped to list, after the fall of an emperor, the floods, droughts, and earthquakes that had occurred under his rule. To an unbelieving eye these could be viewed as bad luck, rather than bad management on the ruler's part. How are we to evaluate a rebel's relationship to heaven? One moment, as he challenged entrenched power, he was violating heaven's mandate bestowed upon another. Next moment, as he grabbed power for himself, success made him heaven's new choice!

Rebellion by farmers and others occurred repeatedly, but despite Mencius's teaching that a bad ruler could be overthrown, the mandate of heaven provided absolutely no guidance in advance as to who should be supported and who opposed. It may have been the case in China, as seems to have been true of Egypt, that a two-stage process was at work: In the pursuit of power, everything depended on the qualifications and skill of the aspirant; after he had gained office, the throne helped make this person a real emperor.

Which brings us to the related issue of the succession. Leaving heaven aside, the reality of imperial succession was frequently maneuver, factions, plots, and murder. Sex was never far from the surface. This was true not only in the Chinese empire, but in the Caliphate, Persia, Rome, Egypt, and elsewhere. Indispensable currency for the power struggles over succession at the Chinese court were concubines, wives, and teen-aged princesses.

In between heaven and earthly mayhem, there was supposed to be a hereditary pattern of succession. A son of the emperor would succeed him. But which son?—for in China there was no strict rule that it should be the eldest. The cloud of females in the emperor's life, most of them concubines, meant there often was a large pool of sons available to succeed. At times a revolving door existed between the harem and the post of empress. This effectively negated the fixed succession procedure. In the Qing Dynasty, twenty sons of Emperor Kang Xi battled for the mantle of their father's power. Even in the relatively well-ordered court of the early Tang Dynasty, we find an emperor impaled on the "which son?" issue. "I have already appointed my eldest son Crown Prince," said Emperor Tai Zong in 642, "but the fact that his brothers and the sons of my concubines number almost forty is a constant source of worry to me."[53]

At the other extreme, occasionally no son existed, or the putative heir was a child. In these cases, maneuver, plotting, and murder were virtually unavoidable. Forging an emperor's "last will" was a recurrent scheme. The second emperor of the Qin Dynasty reached the throne by forging Qin Shihuang's will and murdering the crown prince. Such methods of solving the dilemma of the succession in an autocracy were duplicated by Communist Party contenders to succeed Mao, more than two thousand years after their first use in the Chinese polity. The CCP learned from Stalin, certainly, but also from Chinese autocratic tradition.

GREAT AS THE Tang Dynasty was in some respects, the climb to power of the long-reigning monarch, Empress Wu, was a nightmare of deceit, sex, and violence.[54] Wu, as a concubine of Emperor Tai Zong, began her rise with a play for the emperor's son. One day the Crown Prince left the emperor's presence for the bathroom. As he emerged into the antechamber, concubine Wu stepped forward with a smile and a golden dish of water. A few minutes later, the heir to the Chinese throne was writhing on a silken couch with his father's favorite concubine.

Emperor Tai Zong soon died, and Wu, together with other concubines, was sent as a Buddhist nun to a convent. But the Crown Prince, now Emperor Gao Zong, did not forget his experience on the silken couch. He already had an empress at his side, Lady Wang, but he found an excuse to visit Wu's convent and bring the beauty back to the court

[53]Wright and Twitchett, 1973, 249.
[54]Qu, 1963, 67–76; Fitzgerald, 1968, 15–19, 147–148; Chou, 1971, 27–28.

in a minor post. Wu's next step was to frame Lady Wang by suffocating Wang's own infant in its bed and persuading Emperor Gao Zong that the empress had done the deed.

Concubine Wu supplanted Lady Wang as empress. Soon the mother of two sons by the emperor, Wu accrued enough power to eliminate elder statesmen who objected to a strong woman's influence over the sex-crazed Gao Zong. Wu took into her own hands many affairs of state, including a war against Korea.

When Emperor Gao Zong died in 683, Wu, then 55 years old, should have become empress dowager and folded her hands in genteel retirement. But after fierce struggle, during which Wu disposed of two crown princes, her own sons, she declared herself in 690 the Son (Daughter) of Heaven, the first woman to ascend the Chinese throne. Her rule (in an interregnum dynasty named Zhou) lasted twenty-six years from the death of Emperor Gao Zong. As a result of seduction, murder, and conspiracy, she had managed to get to the top of the Chinese polity and essentially run the empire for half a century.

Not every emperor's death was followed by the plots that followed the demise of Emperor Tai Zong, but, in sum, each dynasty wrestled unsuccessfully with problems of legitimacy and succession. The collapse of a dynasty led to the rise of a new dynasty that gradually failed, in its turn, to find solutions. Still today, in the People's Republic of China, the Chinese autocracy is without an answer to the challenges—made more acute by an international environment that is increasingly democratic—of legitimacy and succession. In truth, legitimacy and succession must always be time bombs in a dictatorship.

———————

TWO FURTHER reasons for strife in the Chinese empire stemmed from mixed strengths-and-weaknesses of the polity: The loose grip the center often held over the fringes of the empire; and the gap between imperial doctrine and imperial practice. Both factors contributed to the stability and longevity of the Chinese empire, but only up to a point.

"What emerges," writes Lyman Miller of recent work on the Qing, "is a picture of imperial power severely limited by the practical realities and complexities of elite politics. Emperors in the late imperial era reigned far more frequently than they ruled."[55] The shaky grip of the center over far-flung provinces, and problems of securing revenue for the center's prosecution of wars and other purposes, made farmer rebellion a danger always present on the horizon. Farmer uprising was a far greater factor in the Chinese empire than in the Roman Empire or most other systems. A number of major dynasties—Han, Tang, Yuan, Ming—fell in the context of rural rebellion. The Qing Dynasty, in its final century, experienced six large rebellions of which farmers were the core.

The gap between doctrine and practice was obscured by clever fictions. These were efficacious unless the fictions became self-delusions that veiled the court from reality. Three fictions convey the idea. The sense of superiority could be deployed against an inexperienced non-Chinese counterpart, but it could be counterproductive if it led the Son of Heaven to underestimate the strength of a potential foe. This indeed happened with the Koreans in the seventh century, when, after a string of military setbacks, the Chinese had to accept the independence of the Korean state of Shilla. Overconfidence toward Koreans as a lesser breed contributed to the setback. A similar miscalculation was to occur with the British in south China in the 1840s. Recently, the Beijing party-state may well have deceived itself over public opinion in Taiwan, wrongly imagining that the island would "change color" were it to receive the magic touch of the socialist motherland.

Likewise, the distorted accounts of past events in the official histories were a two-edged sword. When the Ming wrote the history of the Yuan, or Mongol Dynasty (1279–1368), a delay of nearly seventy years was required to cope with the heterodoxy of Mongol rule; when the Manchus wrote Ming history, a delay of ninety years ensued to get it right! Doctored history comforted the court with a pretty picture of the recent past, so important to confidence in the present. "History is a maiden," runs a Chinese saying, "and you can dress her up however you please." But to believe something was true, because it was written

---

[55]Miller, 2000, 29; also Kuhn, 2002, 22.

down, could also be dangerous. Chinese documents asserted, and perhaps the Chinese court believed, that King George III presented tributary gifts to the Jia Qing emperor in 1804. In fact he did not.[56] Four decades later the "humble tributaries" from London dealt a stinging military defeat to a surprised Qing Dynasty.

Ming Dynasty records stated that Tamerlane, the Muslim leader whose base was the jewel city of Samarkand, in today's Uzbekistan, offered to the Chinese court a tribute of 200 horses and a letter of submission. In 1395 the Ming emperor, evidently believing this account, based on Chinese bureaucrats' reports of visits by Tamerlane's envoys to Beijing, sent a "return embassy" to thank the Muslim leader for his submission. But Tamerlane had not paid tribute. The missions from Samarkand to Beijing had been purely commercial. With the arrival in Central Asia of the 1,500-man Chinese "return" embassy, Tamerlane discovered that China considered him a vassal. The Muslim chief locked up the Chinese ambassador and vowed to avenge the insult with a military attack on China.

Fortunately for the Ming Dynasty, affairs in India and elsewhere for the moment preoccupied Tamerlane. But in 1402, a new emperor, Yong Le, came to the Ming throne. Astonishingly, Emperor Yong Le evidently did not know of the Muslim's fury. He sent a fresh embassy to Samarkand, accompanied by a trade caravan of 800 camels, to ask why Tamerlane had not paid his annual tribute for seven years. Tamerlane seized the caravan of 800 camels, denounced the Chinese emperor, and prepared an expedition to destroy the Ming Dynasty and *convert China to Islam.*

Again fortunately for the Chinese, Tamerlane died while on his away to Beijing in 1405. Throughout these rocky dealings, a few shrewd Chinese officials declined to pass on to their emperor certain explosive truths, such as Tamerlane's recommendation that the Chinese emperor embrace the Muslim faith. "The Ming court had no conception of the dangers it faced," wrote Rossabi.[57] Of course, many bizarre

---

[56]Feuerwerker, 1974, 4.
[57]Rossabi, 1976, 16, passim.

minor regimes over the centuries have deceived their people, but China, while arguably the leading civilization and polity on earth, massively deceived its people and even its own Son of Heaven.

A third ingenious fiction with implications of disaster was the assertion of a cause-and-effect relation between enlightened rule and cosmological harmony. Under a virtuous emperor, the weather would be equable and the harvest abundant. Occasionally, there was empirical truth to the connection. The risk, of course, was that a non-man-made flood, or even the fall of a few meteors, could provide an argument that the emperor lacked virtue. Opponents thus had ammunition delivered into their hands. All three of these clever fictions of imperial rule by smoke-and-mirrors, fraught with political danger, have been on display in the twentieth-century history of China, including, as we shall see, the eras of Mao, Deng, and Jiang.

LATE IN CHINESE dynastic history, the British, leaders of European expansionism in the wake of the industrial revolution, arrived in China via the maritime flank. As Britons developed a taste for silk, porcelain, lacquerware, and especially for tea, trade arose with China. The British side consisted mainly of the nongovernmental East India Company. The Qing Dynasty, in conformity with its policy of limiting foreigners to the outer fringes of the empire, licensed some *hong* (firms) to handle the British in Canton (Guangzhou), 1,500 miles south from sacred Beijing.

Seeking to eliminate frictions that had developed at Canton, and also to extend the trade, the British government in 1793 dispatched an elaborate mission to talk directly to Emperor Qian Long in Beijing. Its head, Lord Macartney, was a friend of Edmund Burke and an experienced member of the British foreign policy-cum-trade elite. On his obligatory "grand tour" of the Continent early in his career, Macartney met Voltaire in Paris. "How can you, sir, at your age," said Voltaire to the young man, "have got [sic] so much knowledge on so many subjects?"[58] Postings in Saint Petersburg, the Caribbean, and Madras all

---

[58]De Beer, 1967, sec. 45, 57.

involved commercial issues. In 1793 Macartney was instructed to seek from China a trade agreement, access to additional ports, and a permanent mission at Beijing.

Even before Macartney and his entourage of 700 arrived, the Chinese court had prepared a draft edict rejecting all the British requests. "We have never valued ingenious articles," ran the edict that was eventually passed to King George III, who had occupied the British throne since 1760, "nor do we have the slightest need of your country's manufactures."[59] Essentially, Qian Long repeated the rejection of trade overtures that the Ming and Qing had earlier dealt to Portuguese, Dutch, and Russians.

A number of traits of late imperial Chinese political culture were illustrated in the encounter between Macartney and the court of Qian Long. The Chinese polity displayed its hierarchical approach to "international" relations. "Although your country, O King, lies in the far oceans," ran Emperor Qian Long's edict, "yet, inclining your heart towards civilization, you have specially sent an envoy respectfully to present a state message, and sailing the seas he has come to our Court to kowtow."[60] Actually, Macartney refused to kowtow. The Chinese empire was comforting itself with one of its signature fictions. Two centuries later, Jiang Zemin, in the wake of his summit meetings with President Clinton, in party documents and through the Chinese media's reports to the Chinese people, also comforted himself with touched-up history.

The edict's argument against permitting a resident British mission at Beijing reflected the concocted "rules" of the Chinese imperial court. The British envoy would not be able to speak Chinese and his clothing would be unsuitable! Should he wish to "enter the imperial service," of course, he would be ordered to adapt to Chinese ways. "However, we have never wished to force on others what is difficult to do."[61]

---

[59]Macartney, 1963, 340.
[60]Macartney, 1963, 337; the elaborate prostration of the kowtow was more abject in the chair-level culture of nineteenth-century China than it had been in the mat-level culture of pre-Tang China (Wilkinson, 2000, 106).
[61]Macartney, 1963, 338, 339.

The dualism of defensiveness and superiority was richly in evidence. Qian Long showed no inclination to meddle with Britain, or go against its national interest strictly defined. It was the British who knocked on Beijing's door, not the Chinese who knocked on London's door. Yet Qian Long undeniably looked down on Macartney and his mission. "By perpetual submission to our Throne," he wrote to King George, "you may secure peace and prosperity for your country thereafter." Beneath the dualism of arrogance and defensiveness lay a fundamental lack of curiosity about lands far from China.

The edict addressed to King George, in rejecting diplomatic missions, made an egregiously wrong assumption: "Besides, if the Celestial Empire desired to send someone permanently to reside in your country, surely you would not be able to agree to it?"[62] London would have welcomed a Chinese ambassador. But China, which called its officials traveling on missions abroad "Heavenly Envoys" (*tian shi*), had no concept of exchanging resident missions on an equal basis.

The Chinese court's ignorance and complacency cost China little as long as Beijing could remain undisturbed in equating its imperial dream with reality. But, as it happened, 1793 was a peak of Qing power. Mostly the dynasty went downhill from then on. Had Qian Long truly listened to Macartney he might have caught wind of the dangers facing the Qing. For a materially superior West was about to show up the rigidity and uninventiveness of nineteenth-century China. The Chinese court saw itself as Number One, but it did not have the guns to prove itself Number One.

Within Britain, the Macartney mission dispelled illusions. "If China remained closed," wrote Peyrefitte of reaction in London, "then the doors would have to be battered down."[63] Within a few decades, China, shocked, weakened, galvanized, would see its different personae juggled before its own eyes. The Chinese court saw its realm as a civilization, *the* civilization, rather than as a state like the Greek *polis* or the Mesopotamian city-state. Yet the Qing Dynasty was also an empire,

---

[62]Macartney, 1963, 339.
[63]Peyrefitte, 1989, xxii.

Han and Barbarian together in one polity, China defining itself in the course of its struggles with Inner Asia. Was the realm of China also going to turn itself into a modern nation, the better to fend off the new maritime Barbarian challenge?

It is to the fall of the Qing Dynasty that we now turn. What happened in 1911; and what did not happen? A century later, China is still a cocktail of civilization, empire, and nation.

FOUR

"THE KING IS DEAD; LONG LIVE THE KING"

The Post-Dynastic Quest for a New Political Order

Could another central principle take the place [of the emperor system], or would the imperial role, by whatever name, turn out to be an ineluctable feature of the Chinese political order?

—*Ernest Young*[1]

[I]n spite of all the changes that have taken place in the world, the bureaucratic society of an empire that lasted for two thousand years is still with us as an extremely active force.

—*Etienne Balazs, 1957*[2]

CERTAIN FEATURES of the current China scene jump out: Quick economic growth and social change. Absence of faith in the official ideology. A regime bent on "reform," but without altering the fundamental state system. Pain that the West and Japan have a higher standard of living than China. Fear in certain quarters that the West, though it has supplied inspiration for China's development, wishes to hold China back. A widespread view, expressed quietly in

---

[1]Young, 2000, 196.
[2]Balazs, 1964, 27.

China and loudly by Chinese abroad, that the political system might have to be replaced in order to "save the nation." Am I speaking only of China today, or also of China in the last years of the nineteenth century? In truth, these features apply to both periods.

By the nineteenth century, the high self-esteem and low performance of the Chinese empire were on display in battles with newly expanding powers, especially Britain, whose imperial reach touched China from the sea. The Qing Dynasty, so masterful in establishing its own land empire, showed formidable pride but comic misjudgment in dealing with the fresh wave of maritime Barbarians. Chinese accounts of the West prior to the Opium War displayed "superficiality and confusion." The great scholar Gu Yanwu in 1662 located Portugal "south of Java" and said one of its interests in China was "buying small children to cook and eat."[3] Unfortunately for China's progress, the Manchu–Chinese elite was blinded by its feeling of superiority toward remote lands. "The self-confidence of the Chinese is incomprehensible to the mind," noted the diary of a traveler from Russia, which also encroached on China, in the north and west. "He never praises anything that is not Chinese."[4]

In 1839, when the British trade chief in south China urged the Viceroy of Canton to settle differences between the "two nations" peacefully, the Qing official mistook "two nations" to mean England and the United States.[5] China could not be one of two nations! The Qing elite were unaware of the danger to their political system, indeed their way of life, in the burgeoning contacts between the Celestial Kingdom and the West. Otherwise, Qian Long would have engaged with Macartney, if only to defend China's interests in a new era.

Why China was in danger is a complex question that is viewed differently today from a hundred years ago—yet still without consensus. Early in the twentieth century many Chinese intellectuals saw China's traditional culture as poverty-stricken and worthy only for the trash can

---

[3]Richard J. Smith, 1996, 21, 56.
[4]Paine, 1996, 17.
[5]Hsu, 1960, 13.

of history. Later, some in China and abroad asserted that the West was in no fundamental way more "advanced" than China of the Qing, but merely more violent and aggressive.

Today, in the West, there is debate between a school that asserts China had come to "lag" in the world power stakes, for clearly identifiable reasons, and was vulnerable to be knocked off its perch by a masterful West; and a second school that maintains Qing China was in no all-round sense "behind" the West, but merely taking a different road, poor at some things and excellent at others. To the economic historian David Landes, Portugal changed the world in the fifteenth century when Vasco da Gama, while in India, discovered that European ships and guns were superior to Asian ones. By the fifteenth century, says Landes, "China had lost its lead in navigation and gunpowder." Landes concludes that "the Chinese were lousy learners; the Europeans were excellent learners." Much followed from this, including, ultimately, the collapse of the Chinese monarchy in 1911–12.

To the younger historian Peter Perdue, on the other hand, "China and Europe were until the 18th century about equal economically." He asserted, in a debate with Landes and others in Cambridge, Mass., that China displayed a take-it-or-leave-it attitude to the West because there was in fact "no great wealth to be found, for China, in the West." Such a position has been taken in one or other form by a number of recent scholars, many of them from California.[6]

In this debate middle ground exists. Historian Peter Bol warns, "Be careful of Chinese imperial rhetoric." As we have seen in the previous chapter, there was frequently a gap between China's theory and China's practice. The Chinese court sounded more loftily complacent than it sometimes was. Economist Dwight Perkins points to a long list of Chinese scientific breakthroughs, but observes that they were "not clustered, like those of the West on the eve of the industrial revolution," and hence had less impact on China's socioeconomic development.[7]

---

[6]Pomeranz, 2000.
[7]Landes, Bol, Perdue, and Perkins quotes from a seminar at the Fairbank Center, Harvard University, Nov. 8, 2000.

The picture of a stagnant, changeless, isolated China was certainly overdrawn during the twentieth century, in part because the West's view of China crystallized in the dying years of the Qing Dynasty. Landes argues that three unique traits of European civilization fed the West's economic growth: science as an autonomous force; Max Weber's point that Europeans valued work, initiative, and investment; and European skill in step-by-step learning.[8] These are powerful factors, but it may be better to view them as having been present in modern Europe as a result of world circumstances, rather than inherent in Europe alone. It is obvious that some cultures at some periods in time, like part of the Arab world today, are stagnant, failing to learn from others, and without innovation. This last observation is not necessarily a value judgment on Islam, for the same Arab lands were once in the vanguard of world development. Andre Gunder Frank's remark, "Europeans did not do anything—let alone modernize—by themselves," has some truth to it.[9]

China was by no means an inferior civilization simply traveling with less speed and success on the same road as Western civilization. In the thirteenth century, Chinese agriculture was almost certainly "ahead" of that in any other society. This at a time when China was "the most urbanized society in the world."[10] Europe at times manifested its share of obscurantism, division, and incompetence. Nothing *inherent* in European civilization made it superior to China in the nineteenth century. Paul Ropp points out: "The social and economic systems, artistic and literary values, political structures, and philosophic assumptions that we take for granted in the Western world . . . simply did not exist as recently as three or four centuries ago. They did not exist in the West or anywhere else."[11]

The traits of civilizations are not immune to circumstance. Look at the success of Chinese entrepreneurialism in Southeast Asia at the very time—the Mao era—that it was nowhere to be seen within China.

---

[8]Landes, 1998, 523.
[9]Frank, 1998, 259; see also pp. 4, 5, 33, 37, 258, 344, 355, 356.
[10]Elvin, 1973, 129.
[11]Ropp, 1990, x; see also Hostetler, 2001, 10, 21.

Compare the performance of Overseas Chinese in California with that of Overseas Chinese in the different circumstances of Communist East Europe. Given the chance, Chinese certainly can be as industrious, thrifty, and entrepreneurial as Europeans. As for openness, Chinese history sometimes displayed it and sometimes did not. The Tang and the Song showed the capacity to "learn from others," which Landes praises in Europeans; the Ming and the Qing showed less.

A bottom line is that we cannot deny the force of the widespread judgment of Chinese political and cultural leaders by the dawn of the twentieth century that China had "lost its way" and urgently needed a "way out" from what had become an all-round crisis. Liang Qichao, perhaps the most prominent political analyst of the last years of the Qing Dynasty, said in 1900 that it was urgent "to challenge the erroneous ideas and beliefs of a tradition that has lasted 2000 years."[12] It was not just a few Westerners, but leading Chinese minds and tens of millions of ordinary Chinese, who felt China needed a major change of direction.

China, after all, failed to work its will in dealing with the West in the nineteenth century, while the West often succeeded in working its will on China. This is a fundamental fact about the encounter between stability-minded Chinese and thrusting Westerners on the China coast. Within less than a century, China lost battles to Britain, France, Germany, and Japan. The reasons for China's nineteenth-century failure were three.

Geographically, China for many centuries had neither faced nor expected any challenge from its maritime flank. The Qing Dynasty's muscles of readiness were in poor shape to respond to the seafaring West. Jared Diamond's point that Europe's long set of coastlines was a stimulus is persuasive; the Europeans, being plural, had to compete with each other, whereas China, a centralized land empire, stood in solitary eminence.[13]

Second, despite the revisionist labors of some excellent historians in recent years, the record indicates that China *in the late Qing Dynasty*

---

[12]Tang, 1996, 42.
[13]Diamond, 1997, 412–416.

did have a mentality of narrowness and condescension toward the non-Chinese world; for this it paid a price. Emperor Kang Xi (reigned 1662–1722) was curious about the foreign world; his grandson, Emperor Qian Long (reigned 1736–1796), was not.[14] One need only recall Emperor Qian Long's remark that he wanted maps of China's borders that would be "handed down for all eternity," as if a map was a religious dogma, rather than a reflection of historical evolution.[15] In the end, as Endymion Wilkinson writes, the Qing "saw more literary purges, more people imprisoned, and more books proscribed and burned than any other dynasty in Chinese history."[16] Third, internally, the Chinese system, flexible and inventive in some earlier phases, had become rigid and unenterprising by the nineteenth century. By the last phase of the Qing, *children* sat on the throne.

The combined result of these three points was a Chinese political culture that was attached to balance, not eager to stride ahead; a political elite that honored precedent, accepted limits, and seldom tried to operate out of the box. Donald Munro writes of the "imperial style" of thought: "Beliefs that exalt a mind supposedly already in possession of totalistic knowledge obstruct acquaintance with any new kind of knowledge."[17] Elvin concludes in his study of the textile industry that China came to suffer from a "weakening of those economic and intellectual forces which make for invention and innovation."[18] The conclusion of Balazs holds for the late Qing and some other key periods of Chinese history: "It was the state that killed technological invention in China."[19]

China by the late nineteenth century, then, for various reasons, some clear and some in contention, was as vulnerable, militarily, politically, and culturally, to the challenge of another powerful civilization as ever in its history. An important contributing factor was the pressure of

---

[14]Hostetler, 2001, 39.
[15]Perdue, 1998, 275.
[16]Wilkinson, 2000, 274.
[17]Munro, 1996, 6.
[18]Elvin, 1973, 199.
[19]Balazs, 1964, 11; also pp. 15, 18.

population on land; China had some 200 million people in 1580 and 410 million by 1850. Few once-great polities ever appeared as pathetic in the face of other encroaching powers as China did in the reign of the Empress Dowager (the lady did not lack ability; she just lacked curiosity and a policy). The Qing Dynasty fell not for one reason but for a hundred, so bankrupt of vision and strategy had it become. The West *did* have knowledge and goods from which the Qing Dynasty could have benefited.

FOR THE ARGUMENT of this book, the salient point about the end of the Qing Dynasty was that a gap opened up between saving the age-old Chinese monarchical polity and saving the nation. Who could have imagined, during the Han Dynasty, or even the Tang, that the community of Chinese people would, in the name of self-preservation, seek to pull down the very political structure that had seemed to define them as Chinese?

A mood of excitement and anxiety at rapid change existed in China at the turn of the century. A bizarre social movement in 1899–1900, apocalyptic, violent, and anti-Western, based on secret-society tradition, crystallized the Chinese court's contradictory situation. This movement, *Yihetuan* ("militia united in righteousness"), known as Boxers in English, quickly won adherents in northern China. The Empress Dowager quietly encouraged the Boxer Rebellion's antimodern excesses, as its zealots assaulted Western missionaries and diplomats. But eight nations attacked Boxer-infested Beijing, a two-month war roiled north China, and China had to pay a huge indemnity to the foreign powers. The Boxer fiasco, from which south China stood aside, nerved many reformers, inside and outside the Qing court, to change the system in a do-or-die spirit. Mary Wright sums up numerous foreign accounts of the Chinese scene in 1900: "This is not the China we have known; 'New China' has arrived and is gathering momentum."[20]

---

[20]Wright, 1968, 3.

"New China" seemed willing to toss out the whole box and dice of Chinese monarchy, for the higher good of advancing the Chinese race.

In 1900, Chinese identity was expressed in a fashion unique among the major powers, as well as threatening to the long-standing Chinese polity. Chinese found themselves with a strong sense of who they were, but a weak sense of what the Chinese state should be. Writes historian Arthur Waldron: "China did not face anything like the problems that nationalism usually addresses. There was no need to carve a 'China' out of some larger polity or to assemble it, à la Cavour or Bismarck, out of a lot of small pieces. The map as already drawn would do: A republic regime could succeed an imperial house relatively easily, in the same capital, and rule the same provinces, through many of the same people." The community was strong, but the polity was weak.

Contrary to the European norm, the various cultural identities within the realm of China were "both prior to and stronger than the state."[21] That fact, a consequence of long gestation, was the conundrum of China early in the twentieth century, and, in a different way, it remains a conundrum of China early in the twenty-first century. "The breakaway movements of the post-1911 period," writes Evelyn Rawski, "are testimony to the fact that we cannot simply equate the Qing empire with a nation-state called China."[22] The "China" that the Qing bequeathed the twentieth century was not a nation, *tout simple*. Yet Yuan Shikai, and, later, Chiang Kai-shek, and, equally, Mao Zedong, did not want to call it an empire.

When today's Communist party-state falls, as the Confucian dynastic state fell before it, both collapses will be seen as initially ending a *jurisdiction* and a *style of rule*. Preceding the institutional change, in both crises, there will be discerned a steady, irreversible erosion of a worldview. In both cases, new political forces will be seen to jettison a petrified doctrine in the name of the interests of the nation. Marxism-Leninism will be thrown overboard to "save China," just as the Confucian monarchy was discarded to "save China."

---

[21]Waldron, 1995, 271.
[22]Rawski, 1998, 301.

"[T]he treaty system in its early decades from the 1840s to the 1880s," wrote Fairbank, "was not merely a Western device for bringing China into the Western world; it may equally well be viewed as a Qing device for accommodating the West and giving it a place within the Chinese world." In short, there was a synergy between China and the Western powers of that time. The Qing could see that the West was powerful, but it did not intend to embrace Western law; just as the Han and other earlier dynasties knew the nomadic Xiongnu were powerful, but this did not shake the Chinese court's values.

The China–West synergy of the nineteenth century was not a success. Fairbank gives part of the explanation: "The invading Westerners could and did participate in the Qing power structure but were quite incapable of taking on Chinese culture as previous Barbarian invaders had done."[23] In the later nineteenth century, the international trade and the customs administration of China became joint ventures between China and foreign powers. But no "joint venture" occurred between the political cultures of China and the West. Probably, China could only be ruled "as a combined state-and-culture." But the West was not interested in ruling China in Chinese cultural style, as the Mongols and Manchus did. Hence the abortive nature of the nineteenth-century synergy. Chinese political culture did not synergize with Western political culture (as Japanese and Western political cultures synergized from the Meiji era), but collided with it.

From its side, the late Qing Dynasty misread the synergy. It thought it could contain the West within its own world-arranging structures, while drawing technical benefits from the West. Chinese accounts of the period have Western envoys trembling before the emperor, dropping their papers in their nervousness; the masterful Chinese court always called the shots. Yet Western accounts have a Niagara of souls falling into the arms of Jesus, China's millions abandoning chopsticks for the knife and fork, and a cotton shirt on every Chinese back quickly paving the streets of Manchester with gold. Everyone was disappointed, but the most devastating miscalculation was the Qing's.

---

[23]Fairbank, 1968, 259, 273.

THE STORY OF 1911–1912 is at once dramatic and anticlimactic. As revolutions go, the Xinhai Revolution (named after its date on the Chinese calendar) was a peculiar one. It broke out when a bomb accidentally exploded at a revolutionary hideout in Wuhan, in the province of Hubei, in central China. Parallel rebellions in other provinces singed Qing authority, but there was little unity among the anti-Qing forces.

Sun Yat-sen, the best-known revolutionary, looked to the grassroots secret societies as a constituency. Other revolutionaries saw provincial military forces, collectively called the New Army, as the best tool to topple the Qing. Sun complained that the Qing had held the West at arm's length and thus hindered China's progress. Other equally revolutionary figures saw the Qing as supine toward the West. At times only a coating of racial varnish made the revolutionaries look the same. Was the Manchu race not smothering the Han race? Well, not really. The Manchu elite had been substantially Sinicized by the late nineteenth century. What, then, was the 1911 revolution really about?

The first act of the political drama of 1911 was the divorce of the center by a number of provinces. Starting on October 10, one by one, seventeen provinces declared independence from the Qing Dynasty. But the diverse and sometimes abstract reasons offered by revolutionaries in various parts of the country for opposing the old order suggested that China was not going to change much. No new political force existed that could transform Chinese society. The revolutionaries enjoyed more immediate success than they could follow up with a constructive agenda. The basic point was the political, intellectual, and financial bankruptcy of the Qing court.

Choice was limited by the Han–Manchu tension. "China could not go the route of a constitutional monarchy," Pye points out, "as Japan did during the Meiji Restoration, or as Britain did earlier, because its last imperial household, the Manchus, was an alien one and thus not able to represent Chinese nationalism." To jump directly to a republic, without a transition from traditional authority to modern institution, "was too demanding."[24] Sun Yat-sen, with tactical skill, played the anti-

---

[24]Lucian Pye, communication to the author, July 23, 2002.

Manchu card to lay the foundation for a modern Han imperial chauvinism that was unlikely to bring democracy.

In 1911, "constitutionalism" was embraced by gentry, military officers, and others, with varying motives. No national mass uprising
occurred. Part of the struggle was about money; who would receive the
revenue from railroads: the Qing government, drained of funds by war
and resulting indemnities, including a $330 million Boxer Indemnity,
or private interests?

The second act of the political drama of 1911 came when the self-
proclaimed independent provinces, for the purpose of negotiating an
end to the emperor system, joined together in a federation. A world
away, while riding a train in Colorado, Sun Yat-sen read in a Chinese
newspaper of the explosion in Hubei Province that triggered the revolution. He hurried back to China, to replace fund-raising abroad with
dynasty-busting at home. The revolutionary provinces chose Sun as
provisional revolutionary president. In the early weeks of 1912, Yuan
Shikai, a reform-minded Qing military figure, like Sun of Han race,
negotiated with Sun the apparent end to a Chinese polity whose roots
went back thousands of years. A bizarre package of agreements
emerged in February 1912.

The emperor, a Manchu boy of six named Puyi, abdicated, but was
to remain in his palace on the government payroll. A republic was
declared, but its initial head was to be the Qing official Yuan Shikai.
Sun, ostensibly the leader of the revolution, resigned as chief of the revolutionary government. By April 1912, Yuan was ruling from Beijing
under a constitution penned by Sun's forces. Soon most of the revolutionary program evaporated into pretty talk. Yuan was a centralizer. He
even contemplated eliminating provinces as administrative units.[25]

A new Nationalist Party, the Guomindang, or KMT, which grew out
of Sun's United Alliance,[26] founded in Tokyo in 1905, was harassed by
Yuan's regime. When it won China's first general election, held on a

---

[25]Cohen, 1988, 522.
[26]Sun's organization, *Tongmenghui*, is sometimes translated as "The Revolutionary
Alliance." But, as Esherick points out (1976, 54), Sun Yat-sen's proposal to put *geming*
(revolution) in the title was explicitly rejected. So it "seems inadvisable for translators to put
it back in."

very limited franchise, in February 1913, Yuan's reaction was to arrange the murder of the Nationalist Party leader, Song Jiaoren, at the Shanghai railroad station. Fairbank, seeing Yuan Shikai as a traditionalist, and later, in the 1930s, experiencing first-hand some of the disappointments of the Nationalist era, wrote toward the end of the twentieth century: "This [murder] demonstrated a principle (that the ruler is above the law) and a tactic (that opponents can best be checked by eliminating their leader) which have strangled democracy in China ever since."[27]

As if confirming that the abolition of the monarchy was merely a technical change that did not transform the soul of China, Yuan explained that China could not do without an emperor, and that he himself would sit on the Dragon Throne. The imperial system was back! To Yuan, talk of elections was tantamount to the promotion of disorder. The idea of a parliament was a recipe for disunity. An opposition party was simple disloyalty.[28] A cabinet responsible to a parliament reversed the traditional idea of ministers looking *upward* to the emperor.

Within a year, Yuan was ruling as a dictator, Confucian ceremonies returned as state ritual, and Beijing embraced the old cosmology of "Heaven" as its legitimation. In all this, Yuan was helped by British support—ironic, given the missed opportunity for China's modernization of the Macartney mission of 1793. Foreign money, a hangover of imperial political thought, and abundant armaments were perhaps Yuan's three chief assets. Fairbank saw a certain logic to Yuan's grab for the throne: "Once the Son of Heaven vanished from the scene, China's political life inevitably deteriorated because the chief of state now lacked the customary ideological sanction for the exercise of final authority."[29] No doubt Yuan felt this to be true.

But too much had changed in China during the nineteenth century for the Yuan reign to stick. Yuan could not secure adequate revenue from the provinces to run a strong center. The provinces rebelled once

[27]Fairbank, 1983, 222.
[28]Zhang and Li, 1990, 33, 35.
[29]Fairbank, 1983, 220.

more against Beijing. Yuan, facing the possibility that he might have to flee China, mercifully died in 1916. But China still could not stand up as a republic. "China's storied talent for order and political management," writes Young, "was reduced to the maneuvers and escapades of devious if clever generals."[30] In a dozen years following the death of Yuan Shikai, China had nine changes of government, twenty-four cabinet reshuffles, and twenty-six prime ministers.

The years following the collapse of the Qing Dynasty looked, so far, not unlike the years of disorder following the collapse of the Han Dynasty in 220 and the Tang Dynasty in 907. Since the fall of the last Qing emperor, there had always been rival claimants to political legitimacy in the realm of China. So there would continue to be throughout the twentieth century.

———————

IN HUNAN PROVINCE, a young man born on a farm just a century after Lord Macartney's mission to Emperor Qian Long contemplated China's disunity with dismay. Down the long corridor of Chinese history, the fall of the Confucian-Legalist monarchy in 1912 is not far back in time from today. Mao Zedong was an 18-year-old, already married (against his will), when the revolution occurred. He had one foot in dynastic China, yet he lived on to transform Chinese society in the 1950s, and, shaking hands with Richard Nixon, alter the international balance of power in the 1970s.

In 1920 Mao Zedong wrestled with his loyalty to Hunan Province, which had declared its independence from the Qing Dynasty in 1911, on the one hand, and his patriotic feeling for China on the other. Urging a period of independence for Hunan, the 26-year-old Mao spoke of his home province "joining hands directly with the nations of the world endowed with consciousness."

Mao's ultimate goal was a revitalized China. But his key concern in 1920 was what kind of governance China should have. He said of the unity of China: "I would give my support if there were a thorough and

———————

[30]Young, 2000, 200.

general revolution in China, but this is not possible. . . . Therefore . . . we cannot start with the whole, but must start with the parts." And on another occasion: "I propose not talking about the politics of the central government for twenty years."[31] The price of unity, not for the first or last time in Chinese history, was a period of disunity.[32]

Mao envisioned Hunan becoming a Switzerland of the East (an aspiration not unlike the current impulse of some coastal provinces of China to avoid the center's suffocations by establishing international links). Mao's vision, alas, was only a fleeting one. The political party he would come to lead, the Chinese Communist Party, like its Nationalist Party rival, saw strong central power as the necessary tool for China's advancement. Soon provincial autonomy and federalism were dismissed with the dirty labels "warlord" and "feudalism."[33]

The significance of Mao's "Hunan independence" phase was its demonstration that Chinese identity as a civilization was not in question in the multiple crises of China in the late nineteenth and early twentieth centuries. In question was a new political form to replace the age-old monarchy.

IN THE EARLY twentieth century, a number of blows were dealt to the spirit and flesh of the imperial Chinese polity. The emperor himself disappeared (yet, in a pathetic twist, the Japanese invaders would resurrect Puyi, by then grown to an adult of 26, in 1932, to be emperor of a separate kingdom in Manchuria). The nexus between culture and power was severed. Chief symbolic act of that rupture was the abolition in 1905 of the imperial examination, a highbrow affair that had been the pathway to power of a Confucian-educated elite. Soon China actively sought, for a time and to a degree, to become part of the West-

---

[31]Schram, 1992, xxxix, 547; McDonald, 1976, 771ff.
[32]Bøckman, 1998, 329.
[33]Young, 2000, 201; Yan, 1992, 12. The regional military figures were really *dujun*, the term for the traditional province military commander, but the more dramatic term *junfa*, from the Japanese "warlord," took over in the 1920s (Bøckman, 1998, 344).

ern-derived nation-state system, signing bilateral and multilateral agreements that implied China was one nation among others. These were all stunning departures from a long-established imperial mechanism and imperial mentality.

Yet a number of important things that might have been expected to happen did not happen in 1911–1912. The revolution "succeeded"—a monarchy fell—but it also "failed"—a modern national political structure did not emerge. In fact, far from the will of the people being unleashed, provincial and local authoritarianism was enhanced by the collapse of the imperial center. Joseph Esherick writes of "the two faces" of 1911: "A progressive republicanism . . . to some extent masked a regressive 'feudalism.'"[34] A durable new form did not emerge, so could the old form really be dead?[35]

The "feudalism" was partly new and substantially a continuation of Qing localism. Railroads, a badge of the new, Western-influenced China of the 1880s and 1890s, were a foundation for the regional military leadership that rendered 1911 a national dream unfulfilled. The hope for parliaments and constitutionalism sank in the marshes of territorial skirmishes. Railroad control was at once the tool and the prize; a warlord who controlled a line of railroad possessed his own kingdom.

The railroads were mostly the fruit of foreign capital, a fresh phenomenon in China, yet the kingdoms were an older, home-grown story. The devolution of power from the center in the last decades of the Qing, in part a necessity to help the dynasty beat back the fearsome Taiping Rebellion (1851–1864), left a legacy of tenacious regionalism that was one root of 1920s military regionalism. "In the absence of either a dynastic succession or a party election," aptly inquired Fairbank, "how was an administration to be legitimized?"[36] In early twentieth-century China there was a costly, if ultimately understandable, failure to reconstruct the political center after the formal disappearance of the imperial polity.

---

[34]Esherick, 1976, 8–9.
[35]Yan, 1987, 84.
[36]Fairbank, 1983, 220–221.

In some far-flung parts of the realm, the revolution brought no change. Owen Lattimore made a firsthand observation of "Chinese Turkistan," as the Moslem area of Xinjiang was often called by foreigners: "It went through the Revolution of 1911 with scarcely a change," he wrote, "the real power being seized by an experienced official of the civil service, who flew the flag of the republic but ruled the province for himself until his assassination in 1928."[37] By the late 1930s, Xinjiang became "a virtual territorial extension of the Soviet Union."[38] Between Xinjiang and China proper, the provinces of Gansu, Qinghai, and Ningxia were essentially ruled by the Ma clan of Muslims. Yunnan was a semi-independent fiefdom of the Yi people. Tibet was effectively independent.[39] The law of balance of power, which had been a determinant of control on the frontiers of the Chinese empire through most dynasties, was still at work, regardless of events in Hubei Province and Beijing.

CHINA DURING THE EARLY twentieth century was caught up in three currents. One was the familiar trauma of dynastic collapse; it had struck more than a dozen times before. Another was the threat and lure of the West. This was entirely new. Non-Chinese challenges had never before blended force with cultural appeal. The Barbarians from Inner Asia possessed little to attract China, except for their magnificent horses. A final current was a fervent sense of Chineseness; new in its explicitness, this "nationalism" arose as a consequence of the West's threat-lure.

These three currents interacted in a quick dance of confusion, making the outcome of the actual dynastic collapse less clear-cut than the revolutions of 1789 in France and 1917 in Russia. Rapidly, various jarring events rearranged the currents into fresh patterns, which themselves were to prove transient. In retrospect, less was at stake in the fall

---

[37]Lattimore, 1962, 187.
[38]Forbes, 1986, 157.
[39]Eberhard, 1982, 154–155.

of the Qing Dynasty than in the terminal crises of the all-or-nothing French and Russian monarchies.

Two years after the "end" of the Confucian monarchy, Yuan Shikai, as we have seen, declared himself emperor of China. The next year World War One broke out. If Europe were truly "advanced," why was it tearing itself apart in war? In 1917, the Bolshevik Revolution ditched the Russian monarchy, offering some Chinese a new angle of vision on their post-Qing future. Barely had World War One finished than an emotional political demonstration led by a new strata, college students, stir-fried the three ingredients afresh.

On the spring day of May 4, 1919, several thousand students from thirteen colleges in Beijing demonstrated against the decision, by the Versailles Peace Conference, to grant the former German concessions in China to Japan, which had acquired them during battles of World War One. The students torched the home of a pro-Japanese cabinet minister and seized and maltreated the Chinese envoy to Japan.

The young intellectuals (and their teachers) assailed the Chinese government's acquiescence in Japan's encroachment into China. Beyond that, they blamed Chinese Confucian culture for the current weakness of the nation, and called for the emancipation of the individual, Western-style, as a step toward a stronger China. They scoffed at the authoritarianism of the Chinese family, declared Chinese classical writing a hindrance to progress (as Latin came to be considered in Europe), avowed that knowledge is only valuable if it solves problems, and embraced science and democracy as panaceas.

May Fourth's take on China's quest for a new political form was to reject Chinese tradition and look to the West, despite the horrors of World War One, while being nationalistic at the same time. The May Fourth enthusiasts overlooked the fact that China had lost territory (Tibet, Outer Mongolia) since the fall of the Qing, and forgot that nationalism cannot do without roots in the nation. As we shall see, the CCP today has chosen to reverse May Fourth's verdict on Confucianism, coyly resurrecting it in the service of an updated autocracy.

May Fourth turned out a mixed blessing for the rest of the twentieth century. Young remarks: "There was never any single, authentic

Chinese nationalism."[40] In the late Qing three different terms were used for aspects of "nationalism," revealing the *problematik* of the term in a Chinese context: *guojia*, which carried the idea of "state," though it was and is widely used in the sense of "country"; *aiguo*, which is close to "patriotism"; and *minzu*, which one may translate as "people," as in "the Japanese people," or "nationality," as in "the Korean nationality." Certainly Chinese nationalism was ambiguous as to its political direction (and has remained so ever since). It could be liberal (admiring of the West) or radical (any stick to beat the West). For much of the past century, there has been a sharp divide between the idea of nationalism as attachment "to home, to family, to mother tongue,"[41] and nationalism as expressed in hard-line high state policy.

May Fourth enthusiasts did not pause to find a way to relate the value of the individual to the value of the nation. Corruptly, they wielded individualism only as a method (to bolster China), and never embraced individualism as an end in itself (the self-fulfillment of each person). Fatally, they saw Confucian tradition as a holistic entity. In this respect the iconoclasts of May Fourth drank from the cup of an ancient Chinese conservatism. Their "monistic and holistic attitude to tradition," writes Huang Chang-Ling, "was affected by the long-term historical Chinese disposition to interlace the cultural core with the sociopolitical core."[42]

China, like other parts of Asia, Africa, and the Middle East, faced a discomforting reality. The chief cradles of advanced governance for millennia were overtaken by the European nation-state, which grew dominant and spread its power across the globe. This changed the course of nearly everyone else's history. The Western nation became the model *as a territorial secular nation-state proclaiming democracy* for most of the world's development in the twentieth century.[43]

As China writhed under that pressure, part of its intelligentsia gulped down Marxism as an antidote to the lure of the West, greatly

---

[40]Young, 2000, 184–185.
[41]Waldron, 1995, 279.
[42]Huang, 2000, 136.
[43]Finer, 1997, 94.

complicating its efforts to find a new political form. Mao Zedong, in Hunan Province, added some Marx and Lenin to the anarchism, nationalism, and individualism in the ragbag of his political ideas. The May Fourth Movement split in two, a left wing jumping to collectivism and a right wing sticking with individualism. Fertilized by the left wing of May Fourth, a Chinese Communist Party was founded in 1921 in Shanghai, with the tall, shy Mao in attendance as a delegate from Hunan.

Bolshevism seemed to offer Chinese political intellectuals a release for two emotions. One was resentment against the gunboat aspect of the West because it had revealed China's crisis; for a Chinese to be a Leninist was to be progressive and anti-Western at the same time. The other was the attraction of quick solutions inspired by the impact of the spiritual aspect of the West on China; the Russian Revolution of 1917 seemed to be carrying the idea of Western linear history (as opposed to Chinese cyclical history) to an exciting high point.

The West fascinated the Chinese elite, but it did not offer an immediate remedy for China's ills; liberal democracy lacked a sufficient Chinese constituency. Soon, part of the pro-Westernism of May Fourth was dissolved in a surge of Chinese nationalism (in the 1920s) and a surge of military-mindedness (as a major war hit in the 1930s). The Bolshevik revolutionary model, too, lost steam in the new arena of China. Its notion of an uprising of urban workers seizing power and building socialism fell victim, with Mao calling the shots, to the weight and traditionalism of China's numberless villages; once more, Barbarians from the north, or at least their ideas, succumbed to a Chinese way of life.[44]

Chinese traditions were quietly reclaimed and embraced, albeit in adjusted forms. This process was often obscured by a combination of territorial limitations (at no point between 1911 and 1949 was more than half the empire under central control), foreign influences (German, Soviet, American, British), recurrent political turmoil, and the overwhelming distraction of the Japanese attack from 1931. All these

---

[44]This parallel is suggested by Lattimore, 1962, 204.

made it less clear than it would otherwise have been that the imperial state, or at least the imperial style, was not dead.

Compared with China, Japan handled the challenge from Europe and the United States with institutional smoothness. Declining to attack its own past, less attracted to Marxism, Japan calmly took from the West what it desired and packaged it as Japanese. Japan did not abolish its emperor, experience a violent revolution, plunge into civil war, or produce a Mao Zedong. It did, however, invade its neighbors, which China did not do in the first half of the twentieth century.

IN THE PERSON of Sun Yat-sen, the three currents in which China was caught up during the early twentieth century interacted. Sun was born in 1866 to a farming family in the south China province of Guangdong. As a young man, he was a personal project in synergy between China and the West. He went to an Anglican boys school in Hawaii and to medical school in Hong Kong. His United Alliance was founded, not in China, but in Japan. Funds for it he sought mainly among Chinese living in Southeast Asia, the United States, Australia, and elsewhere.

Sun Yat-sen's ideas were a mélange of ancient and modern, left and right, Chinese and foreign, authoritarianism and freedom. He managed to be pro-West and, in a quick change of clothes in 1922, pro-Bolshevik, proving how unstable were the underpinnings of much Chinese political thought in the early twentieth century. He believed in democracy, but not right away (which recalls Saint Augustine's prayer, "Lord, make me chaste, but not quite yet"). He was a statist. In Europe, the nation now transcended the state. In China the nation still was defined by the state.

In the struggles of Sun with the Qing court, and later with Yuan Shikai and others, we see a version of the well-entrenched dichotomy between Chinese idealism and Chinese *realpolitik*. Historically, this dichotomy often took the form of Confucianism versus Legalism. Philosophically, it pitted optimists about human nature against pessimists about human nature. Face to face with Yuan, Sun clutched a constitution while Yuan deployed an army.

Sun possessed liberal ideas, but they shared a bed with the Us-and-Them mentality of Chinese autocratic tradition. He stepped out from the ranks of the reformers, in the 1890s, to guide a scattered cloud of revolutionaries. The difference between the two could not be seen in goals; both reformers and revolutionaries sought to save, strengthen, and modernize China. Rather, it was a difference on methods (gradualism or shock treatment, persuasion or force), and on how intensely one disliked the status quo (was the Qing Dynasty redeemable).

The final element in the political thought of Sun Yat-sen was a magician's trick involving the concept of the Chinese race. Sun made a fiction of the Han race for political purposes. The better to play the race card, he declared the realm of China to be composed of five races: Han, Tibetan, Manchu, Mongol, and Hui (Muslims). This bestowed on the Han a unity that it did not possess. Increasingly, archaeological finds call in question the origin of a single Han race in the area of the Yellow River. The southern tradition, as revealed in tombs in Sichuan Province, seems also a valid root of Chinese identity. The Han is really a diverse collection of peoples with a variety of origins, traditions, and dialects.[45] Even today, within the Han there are eight mutually unintelligible languages spoken.[46]

Sun's nationalism made the lines of division between Chinese and Manchu explicit. He pulled the veil off the clever but risky notion that China was secure even when Chinese were not in charge. Later, Sun's Han nationalism used anti-Manchu sentiment to reembrace a version of the Qing Dynasty empire on behalf of a hoped-for new Chinese republic.

We noticed in the previous chapter that parts of Chinese history are not terribly Chinese. The Mongol, Manchu, and other foreign dynasties could be said to be in synergy with Chinese civilization. Like two drugs whose combined effect differs from each part, foreign and Chinese culture together produced a novel outcome. The first synergy of

---

[45]See Wang Guanghao, 1988, chap. 1, 461–463, on the complex development of the *chuzu* (Chu people).

[46]Information from Dr. Dru Gladney, to the author, at the Association for Asian Studies annual meeting, Boston, 1999.

the post–Qing Dynasty era was Sun Yat-sen's attempted blend of Chinese traditional political thinking and modern political thinking from various foreign sources.

In his final years, Sun stirred the three currents that played upon his revolutionary career into a novel brew with a military-authoritarian flavor. Disillusioned with the Western parliamentary path, he turned to Moscow and restructured the Nationalist Party (Guomindang) on Leninist lines. His idealism wilted; his taste for *realpolitik* grew; he reached for the gun as a way to unify China.

In 1917 he went to Guangzhou, with part of the Chinese navy, and played the warlord game. In 1920 he joined the Guangdong Province boss in fighting the equivalent boss in Guangxi Province. He opposed the movement toward a federal China. He seemed to have given up on a political system built from below, unable to detach himself from the top-down ways of traditional China. The idea of "One Sun in Heaven, One Ruler on Earth" was strong indeed. With great passion and some skill, Sun helped dismantle the Chinese dynastic polity. But when he died, in 1925, it was not clear what he and others had replaced it with. Sun himself said it was all rather like tearing down one's old house before building a new one.[47]

LIKE SUN, his mentor, Chiang Kai-shek synthesized a variety of views into an opaque political philosophy. Born in Zhejiang Province in 1887, Chiang grew up in a commercial, cosmopolitan setting. He studied for several months in the Soviet Union, and for two years in Japan. Left-wing theories did not attract him, though he imbibed Leninist organizational ideas in Moscow. He was by instinct a military politician. One of his heroes was Zeng Guofan (1811–1872), the Qing Dynasty military politician who did most to crush the Taiping Rebellion. Christianity, in the form of Methodism, was among the Western ingredients in his moral-military worldview.

---

[47]Brødsgaard and Strand, 1998, 5.

After Sun Yat-sen died, Chiang boldly began a military drive to defeat the warlords who ruled northern China and hence unify the country. Arthur Waldron observes: "Modern China, like nearly every other state, has been formed chiefly by war."[48] War led to the downfall of the northern warlord regime and to the "National Revolution" that brought Chiang to quasi-national power in 1927. Likewise with the gun, Chiang Kai-shek crushed labor unions where the left was strong and outmaneuvered the left wing of the Nationalist Party, pulling the party to the right. His "northern expedition" led to the establishment of a Nationalist government in 1927 at Nanjing, on the Yangzi River 300 kilometers inland from Shanghai.

Unlike Sun, Chiang wielded supreme power for long enough to put his views into practice. The result was a semitraditional military dictatorship, which integrated the Nationalist Party with a state apparatus devised by Sun from the dynastic polity. By the 1930s, elements of fascism, a result of the German military's close relations with Nanjing, made Chiang's political thought even more eclectic.

Chiang took up where the Qing Dynasty self-strengtheners left off. Zeng Guofan sought to build up the nation the better to defeat enemies within (the Taiping Rebellion) and without (the British and French). Chiang set up a developmental state, with increasing party-state control of economic life, the better to eliminate the Western grip on China's coast and repulse the Japanese military machine.

After fifteen years in power, more than half the industry in Chiang's realm was state owned.[49] Some of the Nanjing regime's modern features were inspired by Moscow. Both Sun and Chiang had learned in the Soviet Union, from Lenin himself, how to build such a party-state. Sun came up with a Chinese term, *yi dang zhi guo* (government by the party), that is authoritarian, even totalist in flavor. Here was an echo of the centralization, condescension, fusing of teachings (*jiao*) with power (*zheng*), and bureaucratic pretension that, during the dynasties, had spawned "father and mother of the people" (*min zhi fumu*) officials.

---

[48]Waldron, 1995, 8.
[49]Kirby, 2000, 227.

The bottom line was that government by the party meant government by *one* party, which excluded political pluralism, meaningful elections, or a free press.

Chiang made the situation clear by prohibiting all political parties other than the Nationalist Party and devising a national flag resembling his party's flag. This system demanded a Supreme Leader, who was part emperor, part Führer, part political tutor to the nation.[50] At Nationalist Party meetings, the first act was for the assembly to bow low three times before a portrait of Sun Yat-sen and hear his testament read aloud. Plans were drawn up (never to be fully implemented) for a Nanjing that would reflect the statism of Sun and Chiang. Drawings showed public buildings resembling Beijing's Temple of Heaven sitting atop Washington's Capitol. This was to be a patriotism-stimulating, high-tech, modernized Nanjing, "on a par with Paris and London."[51]

The Nanjing regime unified a substantial part of the country, reduced foreign control of coastal China, erected semimodern, semi-traditional government machinery, and set the plans and technological base (not much more) for modern industry. Chiang's regime was Janus-faced. It needed to be pro-West to get help against an expansionist Japan. But it also needed the crutch of certain Chinese traditions. For only the tip of the vast Chinese iceberg was modern.

The villages in body and soul were little changed from the Qing Dynasty. Only a tiny percentage of the Chinese people thought about politics in a liberal or democratic way. The number of students in secondary schools in Chiang's China (1,163,116) barely exceeded the number in the two American states of Illinois and New York (1,077,000), despite a population ratio of twenty to one between the two places.[52]

The Nanjing party-state was a membrane stretched tight and thin over a little-changed body sociopolitic. It was natural, therefore, for Chiang to reach for levers of governance available from China's previ-

---

[50]Kirby, 2000, 213, 215.
[51]Zwia Lipkin, "Struggle on the Margins: Nationalist Efforts to Turn 'Nanjing' into 'The Capital,' 1927–1937," talk at Fairbank Center, Harvard University, Nov. 30, 2001.
[52]Fairbank, 1983, 246.

ous experience. His regime saw itself as the guardian of a moral ortho-doxy. Antiforeignism appeared in some pronouncements. He began a New Life Movement that mixed Confucianism with fascism. In 1934 Confucianism again became the official cult of the Chinese state. Chi-ang was harking back to Yuan Shikai, who had in turn harked back to the Qing Dynasty. "The sky cannot have two suns," insisted Chiang Kai-shek to his aides, using a phrase from Confucius to affirm his supreme leadership over China and his imperial self-image.[53]

The Nationalist Party became more traditional than it had been under Sun. In his writings, Chiang said the Chinese past had been too sharply rejected. "During the last hundred years," he complained in *China's Destiny,* "the Chinese people . . . worshiped all foreign civiliza-tion and did not understand the innate spirit of the Chinese nation or the virtuous character of the people, both of which have their fine points."[54] Chiang's party-state succumbed to the factionalism that is prevalent in Chinese culture.

Chiang became a sharp-edged dictator. Soviet and Hitlerite influ-ence and Chiang's military instincts were blended with Confucian monarchical tradition. Certainly, at this time, Europe and the United States hardly set a shining example to China. The Nanjing regime coincided with fascist rule in Germany and Italy, Stalinism in Moscow, and capitalist depression in the United States, England, and many other places. No wonder "looking to the West" lost its glamour in the 1930s.

Chiang surrendered to the idea of a single, unified China, even though the reality before him differed. He declared: "If China today did not have the Guomindang, there would be no China."[55] Thus did this military politician with one foot in the Qing Dynasty conflate the idea of China both with the notion of a unitary state and with the rule of a certain party (his party) in a marriage with this state. Nanjing in 1936 controlled but a quarter of China's provinces,[56] yet Chiang was

---

[53]*Liji,* juan 7.
[54]Chiang, 1947, 230.
[55]Chiang,1947, 222.
[56]Ch'i, 1982, 23.

just as attached to the idea of "One China" as were past dynasties in a similar situation (and as Mao Zedong would be later).

In a general way, on paper, the Nanjing regime offered the modern political system many urban Chinese were seeking. But it derived little legitimacy from that constituency—Chiang Kai-shek had won power through the gun. The Nationalist party-state was unable to depart from Chinese authoritarian tradition because it had not come to power by the will of the people.

As Chiang Kai-shek ruled part of China from Nanjing, Mao Zedong was in the hills of Jiangxi Province, pursuing a different vision of China's future. Chiang the military politician was taking Sun's Nationalist Party to a neo-traditional right. In the villages, Mao was leading the Bolshevik-inspired Communist Party away from the path of urban uprising, toward a neo-traditional leftism of farmer rebellion. Chiang arrested Communists willy-nilly in Shanghai; one of them was Zhou Enlai, Mao's future premier in the PRC regime. In Mao's home province, Chiang's soldiers ransacked labor union and student move-ment offices to the shout "Long Live Chiang Kai-shek!" This was the ritual cry, *Wan sui, wan sui!*, literally "Ten Thousand Years, Ten Thou-sand Years!," with which people had greeted the Son of Heaven under the dynasties, and with which a future generation would greet "Chair-man Mao." Both Chiang and Mao, in their different ways, were pulling back from the ideals of May Fourth and the post-1911 republican goal of a democratic, federal China.

WE SHALL never know how long the Nationalist regime would have endured but for Japan's massive attack on China in 1937. Tokyo began by seizing Manchuria in 1931. Much of the world wrung its hands, but did little else. With northeast China as base, and a pact of 1936 with Hitler's Germany to nerve it, Japan used a clash with Chinese troops near Beijing in July 1937 as a pretext for attacking Beijing, Shanghai, and other cities. By 1940, when the Berlin–Rome–Tokyo axis was formed, Japan controlled the entire China coast. Chiang Kai-shek's government had to retreat, first to Wuhan and then to Chongqing in the southwest.

Eight years of war with Japan weakened the Chiang government and gave the Chinese Communist movement a chance to grow. By 1946, Mao's army numbered one million. Thanks to the Soviet Union, the Communists gained a foothold in Manchuria and were given Japanese arms left there. It was from the north that they were soon to overwhelm Chiang's defenses.

The Greater East Asian Co-prosperity Sphere was intended by Tokyo to blend Japan's superior power and experience of modernization with the lagging but promising societies of East Asia, especially China, and in particular with the untapped natural resources of China. This was an attempt, not reciprocated by the Chinese side, at one more China–foreign synergy. Seldom in East Asia had a synergy been attempted so heavily by the sword, and never did one bring about so much violence in so short a time; 15 to 20 million Chinese were killed as Japan marauded. Only in Manchuria did the synergy achieve a semblance of stability and produce progress. Japan's drive reshaped Asian history, but as a synergy it was a failure.

Chiang Kai-shek was the chief loser. The defeat of Japan by China and its allies (PRC textbooks gloss over America's role in the defeat of Japan) helped him not at all against Mao. From the euphoria of victory in World War Two there came—for Chiang Kai-shek—only the ashes of defeat by the Chinese Communists. Nationalist China was "lost," not by the United States, but by Japan. Tokyo had ultimately handed China's future to Mao.

No upward march of progress occurred from the revolution of 1911, through Chiang Kai-shek's national revolution of 1927, to Mao's revolution of 1949 and the Communist era it inaugurated. The nationalism that gripped China from the last years of the Qing Dynasty never delivered on the promise of popular sovereignty to replace the monarchical system.

Certainly there were connecting forward steps between the reforms of the late Qing, the storm of 1911–1912, the attempt to build political institutions in the 1920s and 1930s, and beyond. But a cyclical element was also at work. From the events of 1911–1912, through to the early twenty-first century, a back-and-forth movement occurred between authoritarianism and the aspiration to liberty, between Chinese nativism and foreign influence, and between the claims of the past and the lure of the future.

A key retreat took place after the second decade of the twentieth century. At the level of theory, the cause of the nation overwhelmed the cause of the individual; May Fourth's ambivalence on this point was resolved in an authoritarian direction. Typical was the disturbing remark of Guo Moruo, a leading writer and political activist, later one of Mao's house intellectuals, on his return from some years in Japan: "China was my sweetheart."[57]

In the political practice of the 1920s, the gun took over from political debate, first on the right, with the rise of the regional military leaders, then on the left, when the Communist Party turned itself into a farmers' army. In particular, the CCP's switch from the cities to the villages, and from cosmopolitan leadership to Mao's nativist leadership, however justified in strategic terms, was a step away from the hope of achieving a modern nation-state.

Of much of twentieth century China's post-1911 experience, it has been observed: "In general, the juggernaut of statism and nationalism overwhelmed the alternatives."[58] The tragedy of this dual victory from the 1920s did not go unprotested by Chinese. Zhang Junmei (Carsun Chang) in the 1920s criticized both the Nationalist Party and the Communist Party for not embracing democracy and the rule of law: "The basis of government must have as its principle the recognition of the personality and freedom of the individual," wrote Zhang in warning against communism and dictatorship in general. "If their [the Soviet's] political system clearly despises the personalities of others and takes away others' freedom, but [we], on the contrary, look to it as an ideal and do our utmost to promote it, this is nothing less than considering dictatorship the best plan, teaching people to worship heroes, and regarding the people as slaves."[59]

---

[57]Huang, 2000, 131.
[58]Brødsgaard and Strand, 1998, 5.
[59]Jeans, 1997, 67.

An "old China" did not end in 1911. Since 1900, the parade of cries announcing a "new China," followed by disillusion, reminds us that old and new, in culture and politics, are not holistic concepts. What China continued to do during the twentieth century was no less Chinese than what China did in the seventh century or the eighteenth century. Chinese still lived beside the same mountains and rivers, and made millions of personal decisions for or against "stability," "unity," and "change." Chinese elites still trod the same stage, and practiced some of the same smoke-and-mirrors political arts.

Esherick is surely correct to say the antiauthoritarian momentum of 1911 "reversed as it crashed upon the rock of Communist revolution."[60] True, the Communist revolution culminating in 1949 would involve the "masses" in a way that 1911–1912 did not. But it would also bring an intensification of the authoritarianism that 1912 had struck down (at the imperial center) and yet retained (locally). The Chinese term *zhengdang*, "leading party," used by the Guomindang, has a marked flavor of dynastic house, as in the terms "Ming court" or "Qing court." There would be no democracy and freedom as proposed by Carsun Chang, with his prescient warning about the "worship of heroes."

The turning point of 1911–1912 did establish one pattern that continued throughout the first half of the twentieth century, "a trend towards rule by a Westernizing urban elite." This trend Mao Zedong quickly reversed.[61] Yet, later still, Deng Xiaoping, Jiang Zemin, and Hu Jintao would in part reverse Mao's reversal. This story will take us through two further synergies in China's political history: one between Mao's Communist Party and Soviet Marxism (1920s–1970s), which produced poor results; and a somewhat more successful synergy (1980s–) between the post-Mao Communist Party and the foreign capitalist world. The late Qing's dilemma over reform's promise and its dangers would reproduce itself by the early twenty-first century. As the quip runs in Beijing today, there are two ways for the regime to die— one is to reform itself, the other is not to reform.

---

[60]Esherick, 1976, 256.

[61]Esherick, 1976, 259.

FIVE

RED EMPEROR

The Communist regime turned out not to be truly revolutionary; however, it was also still Chinese.

—Lyman Miller[1]

Why is it that morality is still difficult to make clear and social customs are not unified?

—Examination question, twelfth century[2]

Tocqueville's [*L'Ancien Régime et la Révolution*] pictures a long-persisting French state with a history that precedes the revolution and also survives it. May we, similarly, speak of a "Chinese state" that took shape during the late empire and survived the revolution of 1949?

—Philip Kuhn[3]

CHIANG KAI-SHEK looked Prussian, Mao Zedong looked Bohemian, as the two shook hands in Chongqing in August 1945, starting the last-ever negotiations between them. Chiang's jacket was pressed and dotted with decorations; Mao's was rumpled and unadorned. These two leaders of the twentieth-century Chinese party-state shared a strong will but little else. Chiang's family was commercial and cosmopolitan; Mao grew up on a farm. Chiang led a calm childhood, Mao a turbulent one. Chiang spent three months in the Soviet Union; Mao, as he took power in 1949, had never set foot outside China. Chiang read little; Mao's bed was half-covered with books. Chiang's mentor was Sun Yat-sen; Mao never had a political mentor.

[1]Miller, 2000, 40.
[2]Bol, 2001, 18.
[3]Kuhn, 2002, 92.

Chiang was the quintessential military politician; Mao was a semi-intellectual who became a military leader in spite of himself. Above all, Chiang never embraced socialism, while Mao took socialist remolding to an extreme.

The Communist army of rural youth wearing sneakers entered Beijing in 1948–1949, and some soldiers, new to city life, tried to light their cigarettes from light bulbs. From the Western Hills outside the city, Mao mused: "Will the tattered clothes change Beijing, or will the change run in the opposite direction?"[4] Both would turn out to be true. Yet a quarter century later, as Mao sank toward death from Lou Gehrig's disease, he was less struck by the new splendors of socialist remolding than by the biting jaws of the past.

Yuan Shikai had not been a real emperor, even after he placed himself on the Dragon Throne. Sun Yat-sen had not been the founding father of the nation (guofu), despite people calling him that. Chiang Kai-shek was not "the only sun in the sky," though he insisted "there could not be two suns." And Mao, at the height of the personality cult that swirled about him in the 1960s, was not the "Red Sun of our Hearts." All four Chinese leaders tried to re-create the role of Son of Heaven in an era when the beat of the music had changed, and the script did not match the gestures of the leading man.

Yuan, Sun, Chiang, and Mao, successive leaders of twentieth-century China, could not be emperors, but they could not quite forsake the imperial tradition either. The fundamental alternative to that tradition was not in place; these four declined to put it in place. There was no true politics from below to replace the politics from above that marked the dynasties. Still in 2003, with Hu Jintao at the helm of the CCP, sovereignty of the people has not been embraced.

Despite Mao's kinship with previous twentieth-century Chinese leaders, the state he bestrode proved sharply different from Sun's state and Chiang's state. Mao's state became far more intrusive than Chiang's (already authoritarian) state. Indeed Mao's state clamped itself upon Chinese society more tightly than virtually any regime in Chinese

[4]Junji Kinoshita, "Sekai wa chugoku kara dou mieruka," Sekai (Tokyo), Sept. 1963.

history. Yet, by his last years, Mao had also become more like a Chinese traditional ruler than his twentieth-century predecessors. "The CCP takeover," Fu Zhengyuan goes so far as to say, "was a counterrevolution against the first Chinese republican revolution of 1911."[5]

Mao's state, like Chiang's, was a party-state; one Party's privileged position and the state were almost indistinguishable. "Ultimately the Chinese civil war had offered no fundamental choice to the Chinese people," writes William Kirby of the struggle between Chiang and Mao from 1946 until 1949.[6] They were fed only renewed paternalism.

Yet Mao took the concept of the party-state into new territory. "The CCP takeover reversed the trend toward the development of an autonomous civil society [in the Nationalist era]," writes Fu, "and restored the traditional pattern of state–society relations in which society is almost totally subservient to the state."[7] Nongovernment forces had been unleashed by the 1911 revolution. But under Mao, there was no room for organizations or ideas outside the box of the centralized party-state.

A KEY TRAIT of the state in the Mao era was its *organizational reach*. China has more than two thousand counties, and by the early 1950s, CCP cells existed in every one of them. In the cities and towns, neighborhood committees enveloped each resident in a blanket of care and surveillance; benevolent paternalism was inseparable from busybody intrusiveness. At work, you were part of a "unit" (*danwei*) that also framed your total existence. The unit arranged for a place to live, kept a file on all aspects of your life (which followed you indefinitely), and decided whether or not you may leave that unit for another.

In the countryside, during the early years, the party-state's organizational reach was shorter. By the mid-1950s, however, most Chinese farmers were part of an "agricultural cooperative" that canceled the idea

---

[5]Fu, 1993, 2.
[6]Kirby, 2000, 229.
[7]Fu, 1993, 2–3.

of family farming. Decisions about planting and marketing were made by the party-state, as represented in every village by the machine-politics cadre.

The organizational thoroughness of the CCP soon had the world speaking of a "new China" or even a "new man." There was no new man, and China had not changed as much as the surface suggested, but Communist organizational skill was a fact. A resident of Shanghai could not have a visitor without the neighborhood committee knowing who it was and why he was there. A desire to read a newspaper? The only ones printed were licensed, staffed, and vetted by cadres of the party-state. If you had something to say about the situation of women in China, that would be done through the local unit of the Chinese Federation of Women; it could *not* be done, risk-free, outside that channel. Want a telephone number? No phone books were published; you obtained the number from the local party secretary or the neighborhood committee office; hence your call was not a private matter between you and the called person. You could not be a writer unless you were a member of the Writer's Union. You could not have contact of any kind with a foreigner or a foreign country without checking first with the cadre.

No dynasty ever attained this reach across Chinese society. Indeed, no government in the history of the world has wrapped so many people so tightly into a single organizational net as the party-state of Mao Zedong. In the Qing Dynasty there was the *baojia* system ("wrap up the households" system). A magistrate was supposed to organize households into groups of ten, one hundred, and one thousand; a placard on each house listed the occupants, and unlawful or suspicious activities were to be reported.[8] In the Chiang Kai-shek era there was the Blue Shirts, a secret, disciplined, consciousness-raising organization within the Nationalist army.[9] But Mao's urban neighborhood committees were a tighter, more privacy-denying bond than either the *baojia* or the Blue Shirts. They turned trusted grassroots folk into the

---

[8]Ch'u, 1962, 150–152.
[9]Eastman et al., 1991, 28–29.

eyes and ears of the party-state. Mao's state eliminated all loose ends. Beggars were no more to be found. In the process, Mao's state swelled to fill all available corners, an atomization of society occurred, and a lively people became cowed. In 1949, there were 720,000 state officials (cadres). By 1958 there were 7.9 million.[10]

Of central importance, *Mao's state had a doctrine.* Some of the doctrine we may be tempted to set aside, because it consisted merely of lies concocted to veil dictatorship. The more the Communists salted their speeches and publications with the terms "democracy," "people," and "constitution," the more one knew they were tightening the screws and thumbing their nose at law. In pre-modern world history there were Palace states such as Egypt (the default mode was to issue commands) and Forum states such as the Greek *polis* (the default mode was to persuade the populace).[11] The Communist states of the twentieth century were the first in history to be Palace states that spoke like Forum states, dictatorships that mouthed liberal words. This habit muddied the waters as to what the state's doctrine really was, but we can readily see, as the Chinese people at the time could see, the difference between the kernel and the husk.

Leaving aside the cynical aspect of Maoist doctrine, there was a formidable attempt by the party-state to fill the minds of the Chinese people with the iconoclastic ideas of socialism. *Serve the People. Fight Self. The Soviet Union's Today is China's Tomorrow. The Imperialists are Doomed. My Heart Belongs to Chairman Mao.* Scores of millions of Chinese tried—they *had* to try—to take these ponderous maxims aboard their personal ship. A far lesser number internalized the doctrine. "I am like a toddler," said a young socialist hero of the early 1960s, in a stunning echo of the Three Bonds of the Confucian-Legalist state, "and the Party is like my mother who helps me, leads me, and teaches me to walk. . . . My beloved Party, my loving mother, I am always your loyal son."[12] To their credit, most Chinese did not make fools of themselves in this fashion. The comic failure was as frequent as the earnest success.

---

[10]Wakeman, 1991, 87.
[11]Finer, 1997, 43.
[12]Sheridan, 1968, 53.

At a neighborhood meeting in Shanghai in the early 1950s, cadres required one illiterate elderly woman to praise the draft of the new PRC constitution. In Shanghai dialect, "constitution" and "magician's trick" sound similar. The lady thought she was being asked to say good words about a new magician's trick. As the cadres pressed her for a pledge of loyalty, she drew herself up and declared: "During my 73 years I can recall having seen only one magician's trick. The People's Government which is now about to perform a magic trick, therefore, has my support. I am determined to witness it."[13] Angry cadres kept the meeting going half the night, trying to inject political correctness into the elderly woman.

Still, the doctrines of socialism were omnipresent. Class categories were dragged into every realm of life and ideas; people learned to hate landlords and capitalists, and look up to workers and peasants. It was a daily gospel, expressed in a hundred ways, that the individual should be subordinate to collective purpose. In addition to socialist ideas, there was the Leninist organizational *use* of doctrine. The truth was whatever the CCP said was true, which made the party's authority absolute. Towering over the entire social engineering project was the "leader" and his "thought," both infallible, requiring unfailing loyalty and constant study.

A third key trait of Mao's state was its *sense of historical destiny*. The "people's democratic dictatorship" in Beijing was being outfitted as the vehicle of an eventual global worker-peasant political triumph. This historical confidence—not to say arrogance—made Mao's party-state obsessed with getting the labels right, even if they did not correspond to reality. "We have friends all over the world," said Mao's CCP, when, in the late 1960s, it had only Albania, North Korea, and Vietnam as friends. A similar mental technique existed at the dynastic court. For an emperor, cosmology required terminology to be correct, even if reality told another story. For Mao, Marxist teleology of history demanded the prettification.

---

[13]Loh, 1962, 122.

Mao's state called Chinese living outside China "Overseas Chinese," *huaqiao*, "sojourning Chinese." It was a misnomer, but much of the world gulped it down. The reality was that many of the 50 million Chinese outside China were Singaporeans, Americans, Hong Kongers, Australians, or whatever. They were of Chinese *descent*. Beijing referred to Chinese-Americans as *Meiguo huaqiao* (Overseas Chinese in the United States). Chinese-Americans should have been referred to, and mostly called themselves, *Meiguo huaren*, Chinese-Americans, comparable to African-American or Mexican-American. But in the make-believe world of the Mao state, all people of Chinese descent were part of Beijing's new socialist *jia* (household). The term "Overseas Chinese" suggested Chinese living away from the Motherland for the time being. Such a verbal adumbration served a political purpose for the Chinese state.

The party-state's appointment with history gave it the chutzpah to declare an innocent person "an enemy of the people," assert that "imperialism" was the source of the world's troubles, and vow that "China will never be a superpower." These statements could be believed (by the officials) because a sense of entitlement gripped the "people's democratic dictatorship." Virtue from birth was implied by the appellation "worker-peasant" state. It transcended empirical inquiry as to *who* was an enemy, *how* imperialism caused poverty in Africa, and *why* the Chinese empire was not an empire. "When a regime is *by definition* regarded as realizing rights and freedoms," J. L. Talmon wrote in an early work on the totalitarian party-state, "the citizen becomes deprived of any right to complain that he is being deprived of his rights and liberties."[14]

The state's sense of historical destiny explained why politics became theater. In a play, the villains can be made appalling, and the heroes spotless, because the plot will eventually justify these traits and reveal their consequences. So it was with the pantomimes that Mao's aides orchestrated during the Cultural Revolution. Military officers formed choirs to sing Mao Thought. When Mao swam in the Yangzi River to

---

[14]Talmon, 1952, 35 (emphasis added).

make his critics tremble, the official news agency declared: "The water of the river seemed to be smiling that day."

———————

LONG BEFORE Mao, Mongols, Manchus, and other foreigners established synergies with Chinese civilization. Reapplying an old pattern, Mao built a Chinese–foreign synergy with the Soviet Union and its socialist model. Every major new institution of the PRC in the years following 1949 was patterned on a corresponding Soviet institution. Said the *People's Daily* in a front-page editorial in 1953: "We must set going a tidal wave of learning from the Soviet Union on a nationwide scale, in order to build up our country. . . ."[15]

Mao received economic and technical aid, a security treaty backed by the Soviet atomic arsenal, membership in the socialist camp, which provided balance against a West now frosty toward China, and assistance with the development of Chinese atomic weapons. Within China, the synergy resulted in a bizarre marriage of Stalinism and Chinese traditional autocracy. A stone's throw from the old Forbidden City, where the emperors used to live and Mao now lived, there sprouted the Stalinist wedding-cake buildings of Mao's new government. Mao, who by the 1960s saw himself as an emperor,[16] was nonetheless called "Chairman," a bland term from the repertoire of international Communist organization. One of the wedding-cake monoliths was given a name, Great Hall of the People, that reflected the fakery of Stalinist word usage. It was the seat of an unelected government, not a place for the people.

In Mao's state, as in Stalin's, *top priority was control of the populace.* A cluster of people chatting at the street corner might turn into an antigovernment demonstration; nip it in the bud by sending people back to their homes! What is this landlord-son playwright getting at in his allegory? Ban his stuff and give the theater over to healthy plays! Why is a bearded Uighur in Turfan making a phone call to a foreign destination? Check him out!

———————

[15] *Renmin ribao*, Feb. 14, 1953.
[16] Li Zhisui, 1994, 480.

The obsession with control had its reasons. For decades prior to 1949, China experienced substantial disorder, and this *luan,* of which many Chinese have a horror, was both a genuine fear on the part of the CCP and a useful bogeyman to keep people from doing what the party forbad. The CCP, because it took power by the gun, was fearful that its "wife" (the populace) would be stolen from it, just as it stole this same woman from Chiang Kai-shek's Nationalist Party.

A more powerful rationale for control exists in China than in the United States. In America, federal, state, and local authorities exercise control in order to *avoid* unacceptable acts. Police are deployed to minimize crime. The National Guard may take preventive action in a tense situation to forestall a riot. Rules are promulgated about building safety to make sure structures do not collapse on people's heads. In China, the authorities long exercised control for these reasons but also in order to *attain* a social good. Under the dynasties, that social good was Big Family harmony up and down the realm. In the Mao era, it was a oneness of political outlook. Deviant people had to be taken in hand by the state ("remolded" or "struggled against"), not necessarily because they might do harm to others or to property, but simply because they deviated from the Way.

Under the dynasties, a criminal's *entire family* could be put to death, as well as the guilty one himself. In Mao's China, in a prison, if a crime was committed, it was not unusual to execute the offender, in the presence of his prison mates, within an hour of the offense; this was extremely effective in upholding the collective moral universe. As a former prisoner who witnessed one such execution said of the reasoning involved: "Those who do not behave as normal human beings should be punished, for the purification of society."[17]

MAO'S STATE set out to *direct the economy from top to bottom.* Resources were "allocated" from the top. Power counted more than money. The realm of the market, in which money ruled, was trivial

---

[17]Bao and Chelminski, 1976, 190.

compared with the political hierarchy, from which decisions on economic life cascaded. The Chinese *yuan* was not convertible with other currencies, so the Chinese *jia*, the household of China, was not plugged in by any rational economic mechanism to the world economy. In this isolated red Chinese family, production, housing, prices, wages, construction were all "planned" by the party-state.

Political direction of the economy held China back, but Mao was never able to face this truth. Heavy-handed control of economic life had punctuated Chinese history, often with poor results. There was a "tradition of nationalized production," Joseph Needham writes, referring to state monopolies in salt, canals, and iron that date back to the Han Dynasty.[18] Mao combined models of economic centralization from the dynastic era with the extra albatross of Leninist planning.

Since the collapse of the Soviet Union, it is widely recognized that the command economy cannot succeed in its goals, and that it strangles freedom in its attempts to plan what cannot be planned. Quite early, in the 1940s, the Austrian-born Friedrich von Hayek warned of the "synoptic illusion." There is no one point, he argued, where all the information bearing on an economy can be concentrated, observed, and effectively acted upon. Rather, the information is dispersed, changes constantly, and only comes into play in the bids and offers of market participants. Hayek, influenced by the scepticism of philosopher David Hume, stressed "the importance of our ignorance."[19] A "spontaneous order" forming from below brings the best economic results and maximum liberty for the individual.[20] Leninist five-year plans do the opposite. Mao seemed to know what Hayek meant. "Practically nothing comes to my ear in Beijing," he said to a group of finance officials in 1953.[21] To another meeting of local officials he declared, "Beijing is not a good place to acquire knowledge."[22]

If Mao experienced the "synoptic illusion" in the 1950s, he did not learn from it. The results of central planning attempts in China are now

[18]Chesneaux, 1968, 89.
[19]Hayek, 1967, 112, 39.
[20]Hayek, 1976, 162.
[21]Mao, *Selected Works*, vol. 5, 104.
[22]*Mao Zedong sixiang wansui*, 1969, 80.

well known. Mao's response to these hair-raising outcomes was extraordinary, if predictable. He could not accept the truth of the results, because he would not accept that socialism was flawed as a political idea. Economic policies could be made slightly less commandist, Mao conceded, under pressure from Liu Shaoqi, Deng Xiaoping, and Peng Dehuai, but the political line of the Great Leap Forward could be neither changed nor criticized.

Yet central planning in a Communist system *is a political policy.* Mao chose to hear only what he wanted to hear about the results of the Great Leap, and to blame "class enemies" for such of the disasters as could not be denied. In turn, this hunt for class enemies reduced the chance of truths being uttered and tightened the screws of political repression. Mao never renounced the centrally planned economy; he simply sought scapegoats for its failure.

Finally, Mao's state was notable for an *intimate link between domestic policy and foreign policy,* unmatched in the recent history of the major powers, including the Soviet Union. In 1958 Mao shelled the islands of Quemoy and Matsu, two outcrops between China and Taiwan, for no other reason than to signal to China, Moscow, and the rest of the world that he was embarked on a militant new domestic policy, the Great Leap Forward. The next year border skirmishes broke out between China and India. Said Khrushchev of Mao's boldness toward India: He "started the war out of some sick fantasy."[23] Khrushchev was not mistaken in failing to see a foreign policy logic to Mao's move against India. But, rather than a sick fantasy, the military move was another signal of Mao's new ambition to leap toward communism. Foreign policy was driven by a new twist in domestic policy. These actions go to the heart of one of our arguments about the Chinese state: Mao's control of his own people was of a piece, in doctrinal deceptions and Legalist modes alike, with his pretension to a world-arranging function in international relations.

MAO'S SOCIALIST AGENDA failed to produce the results he expected. "Serve the people" did not become the ethic of the land.

---

[23]Khrushchev, 1974, 300.

Communes came up against the human liking for privacy and respect for personal responsibility. "Class enemies" were not easy to remold. Particularly after Khrushchev's attack on Stalin, the goals of socialism became opaque, even for Mao. In 1960, shortly after the Great Leap Forward became a great lurch sideways, Edgar Snow, visiting Beijing, asked Mao what were his long-term plans for China. "I don't know," said Mao.

"You're being too cautious," the American journalist came back.

"It's not caution," Mao went on. "I just don't know; I don't have the experience."[24]

How Mao conducted China's affairs from the start often exhibited the imperial way. *What* he sought to accomplish was during the 1950s more distant from the imperial way. But from the late 1950s onward, the "what" took a back seat to the "how." As goals receded, methods and instincts became central. This made Mao more of an emperor, less of a socialist. He said of the Chinese Communist Party in a candid moment in 1966: "It would be monarchical if ours were the only Party allowed to exist." Was he looking in the mirror? Surely it was remarkable that Mao was aware of the parallel between his party of the proletariat and the Chinese monarchy. "The peasants are poor and blank," Mao also said, echoing the condescension of the dynastic court toward the villages of China.

During the later 1960s, at work units, people bowed three times before a blowup of Mao's moon face, asking for guidance with the day's work. Before going home, they bowed again before the portrait, reporting to the chairman what they had accomplished since morning. In newspapers and magazines, a quotation from Chairman Mao appeared at the top of the page, in bold large type, just as the emperor's words were written larger than an ordinary mortal's. The wisdom of Mao's thoughts made the blind see and the deaf hear, said the official media. On airplanes, the flight began with a hostess holding aloft a copy of *Quotations from Chairman Mao*, then reading a selected maxim to the passengers. In 1971, on a flight from Beijing to Xi'an, I recall a shrill

---

[24]JPRS, 52029 (talk of Jan. 30, 1962), 10.

voice delivering the quote, "Fear not hardship, fear not death," just before the engines started up.

A court of relatives and lackeys formed around Mao, often replacing the organs of the Communist Party. For a time his wife, Jiang Qing, became, together with Defense Minister Lin Biao, one of his two chief political associates, though Jiang, prior to 1969, held no senior post in the party. His daughter, Li Na, was thrust into the editorial chair at *Liberation Army Daily*, an office beyond her experience and capacity. His other daughter, Li Min, aged 27, ran the Science and Technology Commission (responsible for the development of nuclear weapons) at the defense ministry. As Mao's health sank, a nephew, Mao Yuanxin, became his effective chief of staff, and a girlfriend, Zhang Yufeng, controlled access to his quarters, finances, and papers.

Defense Minister Lin Biao, a super-leftist, also behaved in imperial fashion. During the Cultural Revolution, he instructed the police minister to search for a good-looking high school girl as a possible bride for his son Liguo. A similar search was ordered to find a suitable husband for Lin's daughter, Liheng. When Lin lost his post and his life in 1971, after clashing with Mao, the Tenth CCP Congress in 1973 expelled him from the Communist Party "once and for all." Expelling a corpse suggested that the party was, like the dynastic court, beyond history and part of the cosmos.

Under the Nanjing regime, foreigners lived and worked in China without difficulty. But the Mao era brought back the xenophobia of (some of) the dynasties. In a study of Qing Dynasty relations with the Dutch, John Wills writes that foreigners in China "presented a general danger of cultural contamination. Also, there was no place in the Chinese ritual order for residents of the empire who were subjects of another prince."[25] Much the same was true in China during the 1950s and 1960s, except for foreign diplomats and some Third World people. The party-state's security apparatus saw the nonofficial foreigner in China as a spy. Even if she was not a spy, she could not be expected to understand or fit into the *jia* (household) of socialist China.

---

[25]Wills, 1968, 253.

The son of head of state Liu Shaoqi, Yunruo, fell in love with a young Russian woman while studying in Moscow in the late 1950s. The parents would not permit marriage with a foreigner. "I'm a political leader," said Liu Shaoqi. "Once she enters my house, she has entered politics." When Yunruo continued to write letters to his girlfriend in Moscow, Liu instructed the ministry of aviation, supervising unit of the youth's college, to put beautiful secretaries and film stars into Yunruo's path.

One evening as the Liu family watched the movie *Five Golden Flowers,* Wang Guangmei, Liu's wife and Yunruo's stepmother, heard Yunruo murmur of the heroine, "She's beautiful, my, she's beautiful!" Next morning Wang was on a plane to Kunming, in southwest China, where the actress lived. The wife of the head of state told the young woman an important interview awaited her in Beijing. A few nights later, an awkward dinner party unfolded at the Liu residence, with the beauty from Kunming at the table. The president and his wife sought, in vain, to push Yunruo and the actress together in order to head off Yunruo's affair with the Russian. The young lovers continued their affair by letter. But during the Cultural Revolution, Yunruo, on the basis of his letter-writing to a Russian, was accused of being a "foreign spy." He spent eight years in prison. On his release in 1974, he was mentally ill. Three years later, still unmarried, his father dead and his step-mother in prison, he died of lung disease and sadness.[26]

MEETING WITH KHRUSHCHEV in Beijing in 1959, Mao tossed out a leading question: "How many conquerors have invaded China?" He supplied the answer. "Many. But the Chinese have assimilated all their conquerors." Why was Mao rehearsing past synergies between China and foreigners, in the presence of the Soviet leader? He did not leave the nonplused Khrushchev in doubt for long. "Think about it," the Chinese chairman resumed. "You have two hundred million people

---

[26]Interview with a Beijing source acquainted with Liu Yunruo; *Zhengming* (Hong Kong), Dec. 1979, 20ff.

and we have seven hundred million people."[27] A few years later, after Khrushchev fell from power, Mao said China would offer the ex-Soviet leader a room in a Chinese university to study Marxism, should he desire such "assimilation." Reconstructing history, Mao was pushing the CCP's imperial project.

The term for the Great Leap communes, *gongshe,* unlike most terms in the Communist lexicon, harked back to an old notion of primitive communism, and could be understood by any Chinese without reference to European Marxist thought. Mao rammed down Khrushchev's throat (he would not have dared do it with Stalin) the uniqueness of the Chinese language. "All the rest of the world uses the word 'electricity,'" he said to the Soviet chief in Beijing in 1959. "They've borrowed the word from English. But we Chinese have our own word for it."[28]

Mao the neo-emperor was ruling as if the Qing Dynasty had never fallen, Song Jiaoren had not won an election in 1913, Sun Yat-sen had not promulgated a democratic constitution or written *Three People's Principles,* the attempt to build a pre-democratic republic in Nanjing had not occurred. Indeed, as if his own proclamation of "new democracy" in the creative Yan'an period that followed the Long March were mere deception. It really was a counterrevolution against the 1911 revolution. Understandably, historian Alexander Woodside wrote of "disguised monarchism in contemporary China."[29]

Mao's gift to United Nations headquarters in New York, after Beijing took the China seat from Taipei in 1971, symbolized the PRC's attempt to buttress its legitimacy with Chinese tradition. The chosen gift was a giant tapestry of the Great Wall of China. When Beijing presented the 36-foot-wide tapestry to be hung in the North Lounge of the UN, its spokesman said the Great Wall depiction expressed "the new outlook and new style of the new China."[30] This was a remarkable comment on a 2,000-year-old icon. Yet perhaps the gift was fitting, for

[27]Khrushchev, 1974, 524.
[28]Khrushchev, 1974, 524.
[29]Woodside, 1991, 5.
[30]*New York Times,* Oct. 8, 1974.

the Great Wall is an emblem of both despotism and patriotism, and the two became inextricably entwined in Mao's China.[31]

As Mao became ill and weak, the battle for the succession grew bare-knuckled. In 1972, the two poles were Premier Zhou Enlai and Mao's wife, Jiang Qing. One day Zhou, concerned that Mao was resisting proper medical treatment for his lung and heart problems, went to talk with Mao. To maximize the appeal to Mao, Zhou went in the company of Jiang Qing. Mao's doctor was the fourth person in the room. Mao sat on a sofa, head back, eyes closed, breathing loudly. Jiang Qing disliked the doctor and felt his medicines were an attempt to "poison" Mao. Zhou thought Mao ought to follow the doctor's advice.

When Dr. Li, at Zhou's request, explained the treatment he favored for Mao's lungs and heart, Mao grumbled at all the pills required. Jiang Qing saw her opportunity. "Step out of the room," she said to Dr. Li, "You won't be playing your tricks around here anymore." Mao, ill yet imperious, called Dr. Li back from the doorway. He boomed that he would take no medicines at all, neither Dr. Li's nor the Chinese traditional herbs Jiang Qing was urging. Mao turned to Zhou. "My health is too poor," he said to the premier. "I don't think I can make it. Everything depends on you now. . . ." Zhou remonstrated that the chairman would feel well again before long. Mao went on addressing Zhou, as Jiang Qing watched in horror: "You take care of everything after my death. Let's say this is my will."

In fury Jiang Qing demanded, and got, an immediate meeting of the Politburo. At it she blazed at Zhou: "The chairman is in good health. Why are you forcing him to transfer power to you?"[32] But in Mao's China, as under most dynasties, smooth transfer of power was virtually impossible.

Following Zhou's death in January 1976, Deng, who had been brought back from the doghouse in 1973 by a Mao who needed him, became the great rival of Jiang Qing for the succession. Muddying the waters, Mao also quickly promoted a lesser figure, Hua Guofeng,

---

[31]Waldron, 1990, 226.
[32]Li Zhisui, 1994, 550, 556.

whom he felt he could trust. One night in April 1976, Mao got out of bed for a ten-minute talk with the prime minister of New Zealand. Before falling back into bed, he scratched out a message to Hua Guofeng: "With you in charge I'm at ease."[33] What did Mao mean? In charge of the next Politburo meeting? Of getting the New Zealand prime minister safely back to Wellington? Of China's future?

Over the following six months, the uncertainty led to plots, purges, military mobilization, arrests, and a total absence of any constitutional procedures. For millennia, forging and arguing over an emperor's "last will" had been recurrent. In Mao's China, echoes of the practice shaped the future of the Chinese people.

MAO TOOK TO dividing the history of the Chinese Communist Party (prior to his own control of it) into "five dynasties."[34] Professor Chen Duxiu and other 1920s and 1930s party leaders he repackaged as evil, failed emperors. Mao's own colleagues began to think of him as a neo-emperor. Mao was "brilliant," observed Zhang Wentian, a former ambassador to Moscow who had criticized the Great Leap Forward, but like the later Stalin, he was "very brutal in rectifying people." Hearing Zhang's remark, Peng Dehuai, who was purged as defense minister in 1959, remarked: "All through our history, the first emperor of every dynasty has been at once brilliant and brutal."[35]

Mao, who had hated Confucius since the age of eight, purged the famous philosopher from the mental space of the PRC. Yet the same Mao, in his use of Communist ideology, replicated the structural role of Confucianism in the Chinese polity. The Confucian underpinning of public policy had sometimes been in opposition to Legalism and at other times complemented Legalism. Mao's state displayed an update of the old ebb and flow between Confucianism (norms for the people's behavior) and Legalism (modes of control from the top).

---

[33] *Renmin ribao*, Dec. 17, 1976.
[34] *Mao Zedong sixiang wansui*, 1969, entry for June 16, 1964.
[35] *The Case of P'eng Teh-huai*, 1968, 36.

Under Mao, Confucianism, *functionally*, was succeeded by "Mao Zedong Thought." Like the ideas of Confucius and Mencius, Mao-thought was a Moral Way intended to guide conduct in society. Yet Maoists found, as Confucianists had found before them, that the Moral Way was not always upheld; many Chinese considered "serve the people" less attractive than "serve myself." At times, ideology was manipulated for power purposes. Traditionally, this took the form of Legalists taming and absorbing Confucianism to further their own law-and-order agenda. In the Mao era, too, there was both tension and symbiosis between values and *realpolitik*.

Mao ruled by a mixture of "neo-Legalism" and "neo-Confucianism." The neo-Legalism was Leninism grafted on to the state structure inherited from Chiang Kai-shek and Yuan Shikai. The post-1949 neo-Confucianism was Marxism as modified by the philosophical idealism of Mao's anarchist-influenced moral socialism. Mao blended, played off, and struggled with the incompatibilities of these two public philosophies.

Sometimes Mao put the Moral Way first. At the height of hostility between China and the United States, when *realpolitik* would have dictated mending fences with the Soviet Union, Mao did the opposite. In the mid-1960s, with war raging in Vietnam, Laos, and Cambodia, he escalated his moral denunciation of Moscow. At other times Mao unblushingly put *realpolitik* first. In July 1968, as the Cultural Revolution spiraled into factionalism and disorder, Mao pulled the plug on idealists of the left. "We want cultural struggle, not armed struggle,"[36] he said, in a retreat from previous instructions.

It was a familiar pattern in Chinese history; the iron and the silk had always belonged together. Only because Emperor Qin Shihuang built his state could the moral way of Confucianism endure as a semiofficial doctrine of the Chinese polity. In a longer perspective, only because there once had been a Qin Shihuang could there be a Chairman Mao.

---

[36] *Mao Zedong sixiang wansui*, 1969, entry for July 28, 1968.

As a moral socialist, Mao needed the repressive framework of neo-Legalism to build the PRC. Mao knew this. "Confucius, though famous," he wrote in a poem, "was really rubbish / The Qin order has survived from age to age."

WAS THERE DISSENT in Mao's China? There was, but it largely took the form of "petitioning the court," common in dynastic China. The Confucian critic typically did not confront the emperor with a fundamental difference on governing philosophy, but respectfully asked the emperor to make improvements at the fringes. Under Mao, those few intellectuals, religious figures, businesspeople, students, and others who dared to criticize fitted the same mold.

An April 1976 incident stemmed from sadness at the recent death of Zhou Enlai, anxiety that one result of Zhou dying before Mao was the resurgence of the left in Chinese politics, and disgust that Mao had become an emperor. Wreaths and poems to Zhou were placed on the Monument to the People's Heroes in the middle of Tiananmen Square. "The day of Qin Shihuang is done," ran one swipe at Mao. When police removed the wreaths and poems, there ensued a demonstration of 100,000 people that lasted fourteen hours. The regime declared it a "counterrevolutionary" incident. This "last great expression of popular resistance in the Maoist era," Frederick Teiwes pointed out of the 1976 demonstrations, "was in support of the experienced rulers of the state."[37]

In 221 B.C., Qin Shihuang established a new regime at today's Xi'an. In 1949, Mao Zedong established a new regime at Beijing. Both leaders brought unity after a period of division and turmoil. Both were levelers, standardizers, social engineers; they insisted on one language, currency, orthodoxy, and loyalty. Both began grandiose building projects. Both got rid of independent dukedoms, fiefdoms,

---

[37]Teiwes with Sun, 1999, 159.

"mountain tops." Both banished, or scared off, remnants of prior regimes to exile or the peripheries of China. Both looked down on merchants. Both clapped a hand over the mouths of cacophonous intellectuals.

Each dictator invented a new title for himself, to match his icono-clastic project. The ruler of 2,000 years ago called himself Qin Shi-huang. "Qin" was the name of his family. "Shi" meant "first-ever." "Huang" (with "Di" sometimes added) recalled ancient sovereigns, with a suggestion of the transcendent. Qin the First-Ever Emperor (of China). The ruler of the twentieth century was called "Chair-man," a bland term from the rule book of international communism. It was new; no leader of China had ever been *the Chairman* before. At the same time, the imperial wine inside the plain bottle could not long be denied; within two decades, grander appellations, with cos-mological echoes, were hung on Mao. "Red Sun of our Hearts" was one of them.

By then, Mao knew that he stood in the line of the emperors. "We must issue strict orders," he murmured in 1964, when Liu Shaoqi was riding high, but Mao was preparing a demarche. "There must be an Emperor Qin Shihuang. Who is Shihuang? It is [Liu Shaoqi]. I am his aide."[38] It was a treacherous remark; Mao was being ruthless while pre-tending to be humble. The post–Sino-Soviet-split Mao could have seen truth in a remark of his old adversary: "The Chinese Communist Party is not indigenous to China," wrote Chiang Kai-shek. "It is an outgrowth of Soviet Russia and the Communist empire."[39] Mao, in rejecting Moscow, was grafting Leninism on to dynastic Chinese autocracy. Friedman aptly calls the result "Tsarist-Qin-Leninism."[40]

Both Qin Shihuang and Mao Zedong, when death came, were lav-ishly entombed and harshly criticized. Their postdeath wills were forged and twisted. But the iron framework of their regimes, the one borrowing from the other over a gap of 2,000 years, endured.

---

[38]*Mao Zedong sixiang wansui*, 1969, entry for Dec. 20, 1964.
[39]Chiang, 1970, 11.
[40]Edward Friedman, communication to the author, July 29, 2002.

Mᴀᴏ'ꜱ ᴀɪᴍꜱ had been threefold. His *national* aim was to make China united, strong, and secure, as many a founding emperor before him had done. This he achieved in initial fashion in the 1950s.

His *social* aim was to turn China into the egalitarian, planned community that Marx and other socialists taught him was possible. Mao's admonition "Fight self" meant more than "Do not be selfish." The Chinese character *si* means "private" as much as "self." Mao was saying the individual could not dwell in a private realm apart from the socialist consensus. Real, local community was in truth an offense to Maoism. To permit pluralism would be to permit eight hundred million selfishnesses. "Fight self," at once a moral principle and a sociological imperative, meant "Stick with the team," and this team was the CCP, headed by neo-emperor Mao Zedong. The socialist remolding repeatedly failed, but Mao never abandoned the aim. Like a tennis player taking fifty extra serves after a double fault, in a vain effort for the world-class ace, he kept trying, grabbing another ball, varying the speed, putting a new spin on the endeavor.

Mao's *personal* aim was to transcend his own mortality by constantly revivifying the Chinese revolution and making it irreversible. This aim came to center stage in Mao's last decade, as the national aim was a finished achievement, and the social aim fell into eclipse.

A leading Chinese intellectual from the 1920s, Hu Shi, who later chose liberalism as Mao chose communism, on the eve of the CCP takeover in 1949, decided to go with Chiang Kai-shek, whom he had sharply criticized, to Taiwan. Explaining to a Nationalist Party official his reason for leaving his home in Beijing, Hu Shi fingered the difference between authoritarianism and totalitarianism: "The only reason why liberal elements like us still prefer to string along with you people is that under your regime *we at least enjoy the freedom of silence.*"[41] Under authoritarianism, it is said, many things are forbidden but the remaining things you may do; under totalitarianism, many things are forbidden and the remaining things you *must* do. Silence was not acceptable in Mao's state.

---

[41]Pepper, 1978, 227 (emphasis added).

History gave Mao his mandate, in Marx's schema of an upward march from feudalism, to capitalism, socialism, and eventually communism. Such a mandate was similar to the traditional Mandate of Heaven, since it was bestowed from above. No pact with the people could compare with the beckoning destiny of Heaven, enjoyed by an emperor, or the unfolding hidden goals of History, which promised a Marxist future. In the Cultural Revolution, Mao became a godlike supreme leader above his party-state, exceeding the aura of Yuan, Sun, and Chiang. He slipped, half wittingly and half pushed, into the emperor mode. As of the mid-1970s, the PRC seemed to be turning out not a solution to the political problems of pre-1911 China, but a fresh manifestation of them.

SIX

YOUR MOTHER IS STILL YOUR MOTHER

What the old China has left us with is a tradition of feudal autocracy, rather than a tradition of democracy and rule of law.

—*Deng Xiaoping, 1980*[1]

In our state, the [Communist] Party leads everything.

—*Zhang Youyu, senior legislator, 1981*[2]

From year to year, the story of [China's] twentieth century politics is chaotic and multidirectional. Viewed over a century, it is a story about the relentless march of the central state.

—*Philip Kuhn*[3]

DURING A 1998 VISIT to Hong Kong to mark the first anniversary of the end of British rule, President Jiang Zemin arrived at the New Harbor City Mall. He inspected the smiling southern Chinese faces and resplendent shops. Known to few, a renovation had preceded the president's 20-minute stop in midtown. A month earlier, the New Harbor City Mall was spruced up inside and out. Its music fountain was refurbished. New fittings were put on every door of its restrooms. Two weeks prior to the arrival of the president of China, four stores in the mall were

---

[1] Deng, 1983, 281.
[2] "Zhang Youyu tongzhi tan fazhi jianshe," *Zhongguo fazhi bao*, July 3, 1981.
[3] Kuhn, 2002, 132.

vacant. The Beijing regime was not too proletarian to reach for an imperial solution. Jiang's advance party leased the four stores for a three-week period. They supplied commodities to make the stores look prosperous. Reality was dismissed from view; a fresh vista was conjured up. On the big day, the emperor found his kingdom faultless. Sporting his dark Western suit and huge black eyeglasses, Jiang Zemin smiled so broadly his face seemed severed into top and bottom.

There are large discontinuities between the imperial state and the Communist party-state.[4] At the same time, many problems facing the party-state in the late twentieth century and early twenty-first century resemble those of dynastic China: center–periphery tension; periodic revenue shortfalls as defense and other costs rise; a tug between economic rationality and ideological purity; farmer unrest when the villages are squeezed hard for taxes; the need for symbols to focus the loyalty of a far-flung kingdom.

Such challenges were and are seldom subject to a final solution; rather, they persist or recur in variant forms. Hence a dual pattern exists in both imperial and PRC history. Fresh schemes are everywhere evident; yet a churning wheel of familiar remedies that leave a lot unresolved is also evident. Depending on the time frame of analysis, therefore, one finds *a continuity of cycles* beyond a *discontinuity of policies.*

From 1949, and then in a quite different form after 1978, the Communist dynasty adopted two varieties of a synergy well known from China's past. For Mao in the 1950s and 1960s, the Soviet Union was the partner. His successors, Deng Xiaoping, Jiang, and Hu Jintao practiced a synergy with Western and East Asian foreign capital. Such a switch of partners led some overeager analysts to say socialism had been replaced by capitalism.

One continuity between these two synergies of the PRC era was that China still sought the spark for its progress from outside China. It seemed like an abandonment of Moscow for Wall Street and right-wing ethnic Chinese businessmen in East Asia. Consider Shanghai. After 1949, "cosmopolitan Shanghai came to an end," writes Wang

[4]Miller, 2000, 41.

Gungwu. The city's people were to become bone-deep Chinese again. Yet they "were not asked to return to being Chinese in the Great Tradition, but to make their contribution to that curious mix of peasant simplicity and socialist experimentation" that was Mao's China. And when Maoism went out the window in 1978, and "an older Shanghai tried to be reborn,"[5] a "traditional" China did not come back. Rather, a synergy with foreign capital, amounting to an update of the Treaty Port system, took hold of Shanghai. In the Shanghai of 2003, there is both the Pudong skyscraper international financial quarter and, across the river, a newly constructed "China Town," in traditional architectural style; the dualism carries on the "imperialist era" dichotomy between the foreign concessions and the "Chinese" city.

A second continuity between the PRC before and after Mao's death in 1976 lay in the character of the Chinese state. There were major economic and social changes under Deng and Jiang, but a quarter century after Mao died, the Chinese state remained unelected, paternalistic, possessed of a doctrine (feeble as it was), obsessed with control, a project from above, and gripped by a sense of historical destiny. The sharp difference in spirit between the Mao years and the rule of his CCP successors came from a reshuffling of the old political dualism, "virtue" and "force."

"China entered the modern world not by abandoning her imperial tradition," Fairbank wrote of the Qing Dynasty, "but by adapting it to meet the problems of the mid-19th century."[6] Something similar became true of the PRC as it met twentieth-century problems. Through the adoption of two sharply different synergies, the mix of virtue (socialist ideals) and force (Leninist power) changed, but the neo-Legalist-Confucian state endured.

ASKED IF HIS NEW policies of the 1980s might bring peril to China, Deng shrugged and made a subtle crack at Mao: "I'm short and

---

[5]Wang Gungwu, 1999, 125.
[6]Fairbank, 1968, 257.

small, as you see. If the sky starts falling in, I can't be held responsible for holding it up, as taller, bigger men can be."[7] Five feet two inches high, a chain-smoker for sixty years, Deng had a bullet head sitting on wide shoulders with virtually no neck. As a presence, he could not compare with the imposing Mao.

Born into a rich landed family in the southwestern province of Sichuan in 1904, Deng went to France and the Soviet Union to study and agitate in the progressive fashion of the time. Back home from Moscow and Paris in 1926, he advanced in the CCP by doing concrete jobs and avoiding large conflicts in which others fell. He made the Long March in the mid-1930s, learning the power of the gun.

After the Communists won power in 1949, Deng became boss of his native southwest; by the mid-1950s he was secretary-general of the CCP. When Mao launched the utopian Great Leap Forward in 1958, Deng for the first time realized that his boss and mentor could be terribly wrong. He had to face the fact that more people, some 30 million, died in the famines of the Great Leap than in the war against Japan. But Deng kept quiet, and in the early 1960s helped pick up the pieces as Mao brooded on the sidelines.

Communist loyalty proved a powerful force. In the Cultural Revolution of the 1960s, Deng tried to appease Mao by joining in the denunciation of head of state Liu Shaoqi. But Deng himself was being marinated as the next goose for the red-hot oven; he soon was labeled "The Number Two Person in Power Taking the Capitalist Road." He was sent south in disgrace to work as a machine operator in a tractor-repair factory in Jiangxi Province.

After the death of Mao in 1976, Deng made a bid for power. His chief rival, Mao's widow Jiang Qing, was arrested a month after Mao's death and spent the rest of her life in custody. Half of Mao's Politburo were arrested as well. Deng as an anti-Mao had won. Jiang Qing as an extension of Mao had lost.

The Deng era was conjoined with the Jiang Zemin era. Deng took power in 1978 and ruled or reigned until his death in 1997. But due to

---

[7] Li Hongfeng, 1994, 291.

the Tiananmen crisis of 1989, when Deng unexpectedly toppled his latest heir apparent, Zhao Ziyang, Deng appointed Jiang Zemin head of the CCP. Jiang, an engineer by training, was plucked from his job as boss of Shanghai to be executive officer to neo-emperor Deng. By the mid-1990s, Jiang was essentially ruling the country in the shadow of Deng, who rasped an occasional judgment from the bridge table.

Jiang seemed an artifact to many Chinese, with his Grand Canyon grin, his habits of singing and combing his hair in public, and the difficulty in discerning what he actually believed. Yet he was the first leader of the PRC to be a university graduate and to speak some foreign languages. He had studied in the USSR and survived the ordeal.

Mao was teacher, ideologue, and warrior. Deng was organizer and warrior. Jiang was a technician with a career in machine building and electronics. Unlike both Mao and Deng, Jiang was never purged and knew little of the dog-eat-dog struggle, in the Communist Party and battling Japan and Chiang Kai-shek, that tempered Mao and Deng. "I climbed the stairs step by step," Jiang said truly of his apprenticeship in engineering and administration.[8]

THE DENG–JIANG era brought a number of major improvements to China, yet all had limits or side effects that revealed the anachronistic nature of the Chinese state and its need to clutch nationalism as a new legitimator. The post-Mao state *de-ideologized China.* Deng was not particularly devoted to Marxism as a youth, which made it easier for him to shake some of it off later. The references to Marx in his writings are lukewarm. "Marx and Engels lived and died in the last century," Deng said in one essay. "They were great, but we shouldn't expect them to come alive and help solve all our problems today."[9]

After 1978, Deng put less stress on class struggle than Mao had done; life and policy began to proceed with little influence from Marxism. When convenient, however, Deng sniped at "spiritual pollution"

[8]"Shanghai ren yanzhong de Jiang Zemin," *Guangjiaojing* (Hong Kong), July 1989, 13.
[9]Yang, 1998, 223.

from the West and raised the specter of "bourgeois liberalism" to knock down an opponent or rein in dissent. Such a maneuver found him purging two chosen successors, just as Mao had purged two chosen successors.

Three consequences for the nature of Beijing's rule flowed from Deng's downgrading of ideology. In historical-structural terms, neo-Confucianism was let go but neo-Legalism was retained. In contemporary parlance, Marxism was largely jettisoned but Leninism was retained. This gave a strong law-and-order flavor to the Deng era, providing a no-nonsense authoritarianism that, in the post-Mao CCP view, suited economic development. The "soft" power of Marxist doctrine subsided; the "hard" power of the police state continued. In six years from 1986, the number of legal professionals in China jumped from 21,546 to 48,094.[10] Yet, without the *rule* of law, the enhanced legalism was mostly used to facilitate commerce or as a repressive tool, replacing the mass political campaigns of the Mao epoch.

Second, the separation of faith in Marxism from Leninist power provided an opportunity, at times a necessity, for a revival of the "old" that Mao had struck down. On one level, the vacuum of values had to be filled with something, at least for those Chinese who felt themselves to be part of a civilization that lived by ideas. Officially, foreign doctrines—other than communism—could not be admitted into the vacuum. But Chinese ideas, if not antisocialist, and ideas far removed from politics, were candidates for the role.

"Modernization" was the stated thrust of the Deng–Jiang era, and it might have been expected that an international orientation would slight Chinese traditions. In some ways that indeed was true. China was partly integrated into the world economy, and the Chinese bureaucracy became more specialist and cosmopolitan than under Mao.

Nevertheless, a reaching back to the pre-1911 past was undeniable. Pro-Confucian sentiment strengthened in intellectual circles and in tens of millions of ordinary Chinese homes. Bookshops did brisk business in volumes on Qing Dynasty history, when China, as under

---

[10]*Zhongguo falü nianjian*, 1987, 892; and 1993, 955.

Deng–Jiang, was locked in a love–hate encounter with the West. When Deng traveled south to revivify reform in 1992, his trip was called "Southern Tour" (*Nanxun*), just as Emperor Kang Xi made "Eastern Tours" (*Dongxun*) to his native home of Manchuria.[11] Mao did not approve of farmers worshiping the Yellow Emperor, a mythical figure from the mists of pre-Shang Dynasty China (some say he reigned from 2697 to 2597 B.C.), but under Deng and Jiang it seemed to be encouraged. Mao referred to the Yao, Shun, and Yu rulers (who came after the Yellow Emperor) as mythical, but Jiang in particular made documenting pre–Shang Chinese history a high priority task of the party-state.[12] In 1993, Jiang wrote an inscription, "The Chinese Civilization has Distant Origins and has Run a Long Course," for a renovation of the grave of the Yellow Emperor, a blatant effort to grab an extra "1500 years [for] China's history."[13]

Deng and Jiang, hardly less than Mao, found in ancient Chinese autocracy and Chinese racial nationalism a prop for current repression. The ancient state as "the source of doctrine and moral values" was echoed in the Deng state's promotion of a "socialist spiritual civilization" in the 1980s. There was a "direct line of descent," Stuart Schram writes, from "the fact that the state in China was the sole font of authority, with no rival such as the church in the West," to "the concept of *yiyuanhua*—integrated leadership of the whole community by the [Communist] party-state."[14]

Heterodox uses of the past also proliferated. The breathing and exercise regimen of *qigong*, a 2,000-year-old tradition, won a large following among the health-conscious, the stressed, the elderly, and the apolitical. Farmers hassled by tax collectors or panicked by floodwaters clutched to their chests emblems of the Yellow Emperor, who, the farmers felt, offered solace and safety to a believing spirit. Joining two pasts together, the same farmers on occasion also clutched pictures of

---

[11]*Dachao xinqi*, 1992, 1; Elliott, 2000, 608.
[12]Friedman, 2000, 241; Li Xueqin, 2000, 1–2.
[13]Bøckman, 1998, 324; also Sautman, 2001, 105.
[14]Schram, 1985, xi.

Mao Zedong, with a similar hope in mind. Even the kowtow from a "feudal" past made a reappearance in some villages.[15]

Language reflected the trend to recover tradition. The Communist term "comrade" (*tongzhi*), a necessary prefix for most verbal exchanges under Mao, was heard less frequently in the Deng era and scarcely at all in the early years of the new century. The special Communist word for an official, *ganbu* (cadre), faded somewhat, and back came the traditional Chinese word, *guan*. Also in decline was another Communist term, *renmin*, meaning "people" in a politically correct Marxist sense. *Renmin* had been so ubiquitous in the PRC that the name of hundreds of organizations of the party-state began with it: People's Theater, People's Communes, *People's Daily*, People's University, and so on. Under Deng and Jiang, *renmin* was still used in a ritual fashion, but it lost resonance and was not applied to new institutions. Instead, the much older Chinese word *gongmin*, meaning "citizen" in a nonideological sense, was increasingly heard.

Unsurprisingly, in the crackdown on the Tiananmen democracy movement from June 4, 1989, *renmin* as the politically correct term for "the people" was thrown around like confetti at a wedding. The "People's Liberation Army," after all, was the force that "saved" the Chinese state from the "counterrevolutionary" protestors. However, some Chinese boldly rejected the term *renmin* in a grassroots protest against Deng and Jiang.

A few days after the massacre, as bus service struggled back in Beijing, I walked out of the Palace Hotel in Goldfish Lane and took a bus for the Western Hills. A yellow paper strip on the windscreen of the bus caught my attention. Handwritten on it in black ink were the four characters *wei min tong che*, "Run buses for the people." During these agonizing days, as vehicles crawled along streets littered with the debris of street fighting, I saw similar notices on many Beijing busses. Explosively, *renmin* was not the Chinese character used for "people"; *min*, a traditional, populist word, was used instead. In circumstances of stifling political orthodoxy, yet widespread anger at the Chinese government,

---

[15]Wilkinson, 2000, 107.

this was a stark substitution. *Min* carries none of *renmin*'s sense of "the people" as ideological scenery for a swaggering dictatorship. Bus drivers were reaching back to a pre-Communist past.

A THIRD CONSEQUENCE of Deng downgrading ideology was that nationalism entered the vacuum of values. By the era of Jiang, a surging sense of Chineseness was playing a double role in China. The party-state wielded it to perpetuate victimhood as a legitimating idea for the Chinese Revolution, after Marxist faith sagged. This manipulation of the imperialism-revolution myth threatened to trap the CCP in a surge of political fanaticism beyond its control. Still, Beijing pulled out the "national humiliation" stops in the wake of the NATO bombing of the Chinese embassy in Belgrade in May 1999, and after the collision of a Chinese and an American airplane near Hainan Island in April 2001. In both cases, the U.S. response was, "What happened? Let's get all the facts." The unspoken Beijing response was, "What ritualistic use, for nationalistic purposes, can be made of this incident?"

To any young Chinese who had read a textbook and done the compulsory school course "education in national shame," the NATO bombing, which killed three Chinese, seemed a logical new chapter in a lengthy saga of imperialist bullying. In China all textbooks are produced by the party-state. Those on modern history are a morality play of evil imperialists versus heroic Chinese revolutionaries. The bombing of the Chinese embassy in Belgrade was just the latest of thousands of cases, beginning with the Opium War, of aggressive foreigners trying to stop China's progress.

In 1994, the Jiang government began to select scores of "patriotic education bases" around the country.[16] These are museums or actual sites of past humiliation and heroism, much of it genuine, from struggles against Japanese, American, and other imperialists. Young Chinese are taken in groups to these places to heighten their sense of Chineseness. From guides, they hear about "Japanese devils" and "Hitlerite Ameri-

---

[16] *Wall Street Journal*, June 23, 1999.

cans." At such sites and museums, it is not uncommon to call Japanese and Americans "butchers." The city of Nanjing has six "patriotic education bases," including locations where Japanese soldiers killed Chinese civilians in 1937. Before graduation, each high school student must make three visits to each of the six shrines of memory.

The party-state also began to push nationalism in culture and history. A "valorized antiquity" was created, defying international archaeological consensus that early humanity emerged in Africa. Beijing claimed that Chinese civilization is 10,000 years old, China was the cradle of the human race, and surrounding Asian peoples are the cultural and biological descendants of Chinese.[17] In 1996, Jiang appointed a panel of 170 scholars to marshal evidence on the Xia Dynasty, a murky period in Chinese history prior to the Shang Dynasty (sixteenth to eleventh centuries B.C.), itself documented only from inscriptions on turtle shells and shoulder blades of cattle and other animals ("oracle bones"). Facts about the Xia being sparse in the absence of any contemporary written record, Chinese textbooks fill the vacuum with Marxist categories of "slave society" and "class struggle."[18]

When the Communist party-state seeks a report from a committee of intellectuals, it is made clear what conclusion the scholars must reach. Jiang wanted to boost Chinese national pride by establishing that the "Chinese nation" began as early as 3,000 years before Christ. The historians and archaeologists, as expected, came up with "proof" in a 2000 report under government auspices.[19] Said one leader of the project: "The party and the people are really proud of our work." Finally, the party-state could say that China's civilization was older than those stemming from today's Egypt, India, and Iraq. No foreign archaeologists were included in the 170 scholars who examined artifacts from Erlitou, just south of the Yellow River in Henan Province. The report is makeshift and fragmentary. It ignores evidence that calls in question its new clarity on the Xia Dynasty.[20]

---

[17]Sautman, 2001, 96, 97, 106, 108, 110.
[18]*Zhongguo lishi*, vol. 1, 20–22.
[19]Li Xueqin, 2000.
[20]Nivison, 2002, 1, 4, 6, 8; Shao, 2002, 2, 7.

International archaeological opinion is uncertain whether the arti-facts assembled are of the Shang or an earlier period. The report is for-malistic in focusing on mere chronology. It does not say what territory the purported Xia Dynasty encompassed.[21] Nor does it enlighten us much about the dynasty's emperors. It tells little of how the Shang and the Xia differed intrinsically from each other.[22] The triumphalism of the report's broad conclusion, about how ancient Chinese civilization is, was trumpeted to the world by the Chinese party-state. Perhaps the head of archaeology at the Academia Sinica in Taiwan summed up the project best: "It is a major political project, not just a major archaeo-logical project."[23] Historical myth became political weapon.

A further role for nationalism was not exactly planned by the party-state. By clinging to a public philosophy that was no longer believed in (Marxism), the party-state opened the door to unofficial substitutes. These included religion, cults, aesthetic theories, and nihilism. In addi-tion, especially as the Soviet Union disappeared and China became a lonely Leninist survivor, simple patriotism bubbled at the grassroots. After the passing of the ardent Mao years, Chinese of all strata, despite their suspicions of the CCP, felt an attraction to the Greatness of China as a substitute faith. For a comparison, consider the mental writhings of semimodernized Japan in the 1920s and 1930s. Japan felt alone, lacking an empire and a worthy role in international affairs. Even as it became more politically and socially Western, its mood turned anti-Western.

"You cannot be a Chinese patriot without being a socialist," cried Jiang, who did not want people to notice the link between authoritar-ianism and patriotism, much less to turn their eyes on democracy. "You cannot be a Chinese patriot without being a socialist" was a short step away from the traditional notion, "If you are not filial, you are not a real Chinese." By "socialist," Jiang meant obedient to the CCP. This was the throbbing heart of the Four Principles of Communist power-by-enti-

---

[21]On the poetic vagueness of Xia territory, see Zhang, 2000, 3.
[22]Li Xueqin, 2000, 83–85; author's interview with Prof. Li, Beijing, Oct. 19, 2001.
[23]Bruce Gilley, "Digging into the Future," *Far Eastern Economic Review*, July 20, 2000.

tlement. Under both Confucian and Jiang slogans, the people were being treated as children.

The imperative to carve out a post–Soviet Union future for a China still ruled by a Communist Party required more resources from Chinese tradition than expected. A comparison with Japan is again instructive. From the late nineteenth century, China threw out more of its past than did Japan. After the failures of communism, China under Deng and Jiang tried to correct the balance, for practical and emotional reasons. In particular, the fall of the USSR required Beijing to manufacture a new legitimation within China, to replace the legitimation stemming from the Bolshevik Revolution.

In retrospect, the late nineteenth-century convulsion in China was *both* about the drive to modernize *and* about resisting the West. The past was thrown out because this double drive seemed to require it. Logically, then, when the second task—pushing back the West—was finished, some tradition could be reclaimed. Embracing the modern, as Japan showed, never implied a total cancellation of the past. Many late nineteenth-century Chinese, of varying political views, thought Chinese culture and the Chinese state must stand or fall together.[24] Few Japanese ever took that view of Japanese culture and the Japanese state. Today, Chinese culture and the Chinese state must struggle back into synchronization.

———

DENG AND JIANG turned down the temperature of the official ideology, but they did not permit a plurality of ideologies. It was acceptable to be apolitical, but not to be independently political, or even to leave China and criticize the Chinese party-state from abroad. The citizens were to be trusted with their money, in the Deng–Jiang era, but not with their minds. "Do what you please," ran the saying, "as long as you please the Communist Party." Jiang had to take account of public opinion on some issues, but, as Fu Zhengyuan says, "the fact that the

———

[24]Bøckman (1998, 320) aptly says the modern term "political culture" fits well the sense of the society–state relationship in traditional China.

shepherd may take notice of the baying of his sheep does not make sheep participants in decision making."[25]

In the 1990s, people still honored two zones of expression, one for talking with family and friends, another for talking with anyone else. The latter was called "standard political talk" (*biaozhun shuyu*).[26] It was what one said to the boss, to foreigners, in a political study session, answering a public opinion poll, or exchanging views with anyone whose basic loyalty was to the party-state.

Dissent became stronger, more visible, and more frequent than it had been in Mao's China. Still, however, it mostly took the form of "petitioning the court," common in dynastic China. A writer, film-maker, or religious figure who questioned the basics of socialism was the rare exception. Mostly he or she would end up in a labor camp, silent passivity in a shuttered apartment, or in exile from China.

The method of stifling an independent voice in Jiang's China, or of belittling one who had fled from it, bore a close family resemblance to that in Mao's China. First step was to instruct an influential person to write an article saying that X, despite all appearances, was anti-socialist or anti-China. Next was to intimidate anyone connected with units or media outlets that might allow X to have his say. Probably a curtain of silence would then envelop X and the party-state's aim was achieved. This method is effective, because as Perry Link writes, Beijing uses "an essentially psychological control system that relies primarily on self-censorship." The party-state's pressure usually does not come as handcuffs or an arrest warrant. "It involves *fear* of such happenings."[27]

In 2000, when the Beijing Publishing Group decided to put out a translation of *Waiting*, a novel by the Chinese-American writer Ha Jin, the control system swung into operation. The attack dog was Liu Yiqing of Beijing University. The Beijing publisher had praised Ha Jin and his book and signed a contract with a New York house for its trans-

[25]Fu, 1993, 7.
[26]Li Qiang, 2000, 40–44.
[27]Link, 2002, 67.

lation. The Chinese text was half-done. But out of left field, primed for her task by officials of the party-state, came Ms. Liu.

The motive of her attack was less the content of the novel than irritation at the success in the United States and Europe of a Chinese who saw himself as a cosmopolitan (Ha Jin writes in English) rather than a Chinese nationalist. Liu said the writer was "cursing his own compatriots." He was a "tool used by the American media to vilify China." His novel "stressed the backwardness of China."

After her article, Chinese journalists were quietly told not to write anything about Ha Jin or his works. In New York, the author had won the National Book Award—not an everyday occurrence for a Chinese-born writer—but the PRC press ignored this and other honors. Said Ha Jin from his home in Atlanta: "My book is not about politics. It's about the human heart, about human flaws and the sinister nature of time." *Waiting* did finally appear in Chinese in Beijing in 2002, with two sentences cut to avoid political offense. "The novel went through a lot of difficulty with the Chinese authorities," said Ha Jin, "and gave me many heartbreaks, so I cannot feel any excitement over its publication in China at all."[28]

Jiang Wen, a well-known Beijing actor and film director, won the Grand Prize in Cannes in 2000 for his movie *Devils on the Doorstep*, set in the Japan–China war of the 1930s and 1940s. But the Chinese public could not see the film. Part of Jiang Wen's problem was similar to Ha Jin's: The foreign world saluted him as a Chinese artist, which intensified the Chinese party-state's view of him as an unreliable grumbler.

In Beijing, Jiang Wen met obfuscation. His film was not banned; nor was it approved. The Film Bureau, which must approve everything seen on China's screens, murmured that the film had "lots of problems." The bureau spokesman's only concrete statement was a claim to artistic global extraterritoriality. The film "was shown at a film festival abroad without prior approval, which is a clear violation." A Chinese, even in Cannes, was not outside the constraints of the socialist household (*jia*).

---

[28]*New York Times,* June 24, 2000; Ha Jin, e-mail to the author, Dec. 25, 2002.

Some film people in Beijing obtained a copy of the original report made on *Devils on the Doorstep* by the Film Censorship Committee of the State Administration of Radio, Film, and Television. It showed the paternalism of the Jiang party-state. "The Japanese military anthem is played many times throughout the film," complained the bureaucrats. "This signifies the strength of the Japanese military and severely hurts the feelings of the Chinese people." The father-and-mother officials felt there was not enough hatred shown in the Chinese characters' attitude to Japanese.

"It's all too much like a Hitchcock thriller," said Jiang Wen of his experiences with the party-state. "There's terror all around me, but I can't see what's going on."[29] The Chinese masses were permitted to see many Hollywood films, including scenes as racy as two Jiang Wen was criticized for in *Devils on the Doorstep*. But Hollywood directors, unlike Jiang Wen, are not assumed to be part of the socialist *jia*.

In 2000, Gao Xingjian, a Chinese-born citizen of France, won the Nobel Prize for Literature. He was the first author of Chinese descent to receive the honor. Beijing dismissed the choice as politically motivated. Gao's writing, said the Chinese party-state, is "very, very average." Gao had been harassed in China, and his work suppressed. In 1989 he moved to Paris.

How could Gao, an aesthetic, apolitical man, offend the Chinese party-state and draw such a sour response on winning the Nobel? Because he had no time for patriotism and was simply an individual. "Chinese people are too confined by their own culture," Gao told an interviewer in Sydney, where his major work, *Soul Mountain,* had been translated into English and published. "As far as I'm concerned, Chinese culture in general is meaningless."

In fact Gao is as Chinese as Jiang Zemin, but he does not see Chinese culture as holistic, and he refuses the patriotism–socialism link. "Too much emphasis on identity can become talk without real meaning and it can easily lead to nationalism," the slim, cerebral Gao said. "There is only one identity that is beyond doubt and that is that you are an individual."[30]

---

[29]*New York Times,* July 14, 2000.
[30]*The Australian's Review of Books* (Sydney), Dec. 2000.

Anathema to Gao is a single accepted doctrine, a single accepted view of history, a Great Systemic Whole. "There have been too many lies told over the past 100 years," observed this free spirit, "including the lies concealed within ideology." Gao was under no illusion that the decline of ideology since the Mao years, when he grew up, had brought freedom to China. In a cold rejection of the party-state as guardian of the household of Chinese people, he remarked in 2000: "China remains an authoritarian state, and I don't plan on returning while I'm alive. . . . I have my own personal China; I don't need to go there."[31] Ha Jin left China around the same time that Gao did. Jiang Wen may well have left China by the time this book is read.

What the party-state felt, but did not dare say, about the diverse artists—Ha Jin, Jiang Wen, and Gao Xingjian—was that they failed to behave like docile members of the Chinese socialist *jia*. Could socialism still have pull a quarter century after Mao's death? In truth it had little; ideology had declined. But, for the Leninist-Legalist party-state, the worn Marxist belief system still had the crucial function of maintaining authority. In tacit acknowledgment of the weakness of its belief system, the party-state, to stave off death, added the gaudy mask of nationalism. The bizarre result was a Communist-hijacked *jia* that was part socialist and part neo-imperial authoritarian. In Europe, the nation came to transcend the state. In China the nation still was defined by the state.

GENERALLY, vocal Chinese with a viewpoint contrary to the party-state respectfully asked the authorities for incremental adjustments to the system. This was true of most of the pro-democracy demonstrators in Tiananmen Square in 1989. Courageous as their actions were, the students showered praise on Hu Yaobang, a fallen Communist colleague of Deng's. They sought "a dialogue" with the Communist party-state. Few went beyond calling for "reform" to the Communist system.

------

[31] *New York Times Magazine,* Dec. 10, 2000.

After I wrote an eyewitness account of the 1989 Beijing crisis in *China in Our Time,* a Chinese student of that period, who later settled in Australia, sent me a letter that said: "What I don't understand is, during the peak of the students' demonstrations [in 1989], why didn't they wreak havoc on Mao's Mausoleum?" It is a good question. In 1989, a new society proved not yet strong enough to challenge an old state. Millions, better off under Deng than they had been under Mao, were "bought off" by economic considerations; they dared to be petitioners, but not to be opponents. As for attacking the Mao Mausoleum, the footprints of totalitarianism on a subject people can be heavy. Since Mao's death, there has never been an anti-Mao mood comparable to the anti-Stalin mood in the Soviet Union after 1953. In fact, for complex reasons, a pathetic need for Mao as a spiritual father can be found in some Chinese inured by the system to be upward gazers at the party-state.

The Tiananmen crackdown of June 4, 1989, was not the watershed that many, including me, thought it would be. It reaffirmed an existing truth (here I was not surprised). Its violent mode did not usher in a lengthy new era (here I was surprised). That is why Jiang did not make sharp departures from Deng, and why Jiang never criticized Deng in public as Deng did Mao. June 4 reaffirmed that the Beijing party-state will treat as the enemy any force that seems to threaten its monopoly over political power. Most people knew that beforehand, certainly most people in China. In the West, June 4 ended the illusion that Chinese communism had slipped away in the middle of the night.

In the Götterdämmerung of June 3–4, Deng performed an act rooted in a decision made forty days earlier. The demonstrators had mounted a "planned conspiracy," he told his colleagues on April 25. They would be shown "no leniency." The army's eventual shooting into crowds was a calculated act of state terror, to make the point, for 1989 and years to come, that Communist rule was a given that no one should question. That was, of course, an affirmation of a preexisting situation.

All of Deng's key decisions during the crisis were taken in violation of the CCP's own constitution. The dismissal of Zhao Ziyang, who had favored compromise with the students, and the appointment of new members of the Standing Committee of the Politburo went against Article 21 of the Party charter, which says these posts shall be filled by election of the Central Committee. The decision to impose martial law in Beijing, after Zhao's ouster, violated Article 67 of the PRC constitution, which says such a step must be made by the Standing Committee of the National People's Congress, the toothless parliament. When a member of this latter body, Hu Jiwei, former editor of *People's Daily*, got up a petition to convene a special meeting of the Standing Committee of the National People's Congress (which Hu was on), and the petition was signed by more than the requisite number of members, no meeting occurred. Instead, Hu was suspended from the CCP for two years and "recalled" from his post as a deputy to the Standing Committee of the National People's Congress.[32]

Before the crackdown of June 4, 1989, a student in Beijing, seeking to explain why he was not raising slogans calling for the overthrow of the Communist Party, said, "You may say that a mother acted wrongfully with good intentions, but you absolutely may not say that your mother is not your mother. Isn't this so?"[33] The day when the Chinese people refuse to accept dictators in the guise of parents had not yet come.

Several reasons existed for the ultimate deference. A certain fatalism in the Chinese spirit, after millennia of Us-and-Them governance and periodic humbling at the hand of nature, flecked the political culture. Fear of total disorder was strong, even among young people. A sense of Chineseness, even if it did not bring enthusiasm for the socialist *jia*, gave the benefit of the doubt to a "mother acting wrongfully." The CCP had been quite skillful in utilizing the Chinese past to maximize the advantage to itself of all these points. Finally, in the China of 1989, there did not appear to be an immediate *alternative* to Communist rule. Poland had Solidarity and the Catholic Church as alternative rallying foci; what did the Chinese have but their heavy-handed mother?

---

[32]Information from Prof. Chao Chien-min, Sun Yat-sen Graduate Institute, National Chengchi University, Taiwan.
[33]Han, 1990, 94.

Deng told his colleagues in a postmortem on the crisis: "This storm was bound to happen sooner or later. As determined by the international and domestic climate, it was ... independent of man's will."[34] This was still the imperial voice, invoking history (formerly, Heaven) as authority.

A SECOND BROADLY positive change in the reign of Deng, carried forward by Jiang, was a *higher priority to economic development*. The test of socialism, Deng said, was whether or not it produced economic progress. The mood became one of seeking efficiency and prosperity by almost any means. Many of Mao's collectivist economic policies were rolled back. In their place came a wave of commercialization, with a return to family farming in the villages, the sprouting of small-scale private enterprise in the cities, and expanded foreign trade. The results were excellent, first in the countryside, where the removal of collectivist shackles brought a fourfold increase in per capita income in a decade. China's exports rose from $20 billion in 1980 to $250 billion in 2000. There was much "catch up" to be done after the austerity of the Mao years; initially, economic growth came almost like water running down a hill.

The economic growth had momentous consequences. As the party-state encouraged people to be money-minded, there arose anxiety, inequality, crime, and corruption. But the new insecurity was inseparable from an exciting vista of opportunity for many Chinese. To be sure, statistics of economic growth in the Deng–Jiang era were exaggerated at times, as they were (dramatically) in the Mao era.[35] Nevertheless, the socioeconomic face of much of urban China is hardly recognizable in 2003 as compared with three decades earlier.

The control of the work unit weakened. Decisions about one's life could often be made without reference to the government. People

---

[34]*Beijing Review*, July 10–16, 1989.
[35]Cai, 2000, 787, 789, 796.

could buy and travel more, and enjoy more privacy. Mao focused on the land issue and saw socialism in terms of rural collectivism. By contrast, the Deng–Jiang reign focused on urban-based modernization. In this respect the post-Mao leaders were picking up from a post-1550s drive to urbanize and commercialize China, and, more recently, from the self-strengtheners of the 1860s and 1870s.

Thanks in large part to economic growth, by the late twentieth century China became stronger in relation to East Asia than it had been for two centuries. In Beijing, a desire and capacity grew to consolidate and even expand the empire as inherited from the Qing Dynasty. Key tasks were to knit Tibet, Xinjiang, and Inner Mongolia into China proper; to recover Taiwan; and to stake out a claim to disputed South China Sea isles, together with isles claimed by both China and Japan, as a basis for their future military capture.

It seems likely that Deng and Jiang were consciously picking up a theme, "Seek Wealth and Power," from the hard-pressed nineteenth-century Chinese self-strengtheners. An ignorant and complacent Chinese court spurned Lord Macartney's offer to talk and trade. Peter the Great led Russia to learn from the West, and the Meiji emperor did the same in Japan, but China under Qian Long was too proud. Some decades later, Zeng Guofan and other self-strengtheners attempted a partial correction of Qian Long's mistake. Deng and Jiang grabbed from the floor what Qian Long tossed off the table and the self-strengtheners knew should be pursued. On his Southern Tour of 1992, combating leftists who rode high in the wake of the Tiananmen tragedy, Deng remarked: "The Chinese, having more than once missed the opportunity to modernize, must not fail again."[36]

The West in the late twentieth century was even more eager to trade with China than it had been during the epoch of Macartney, and, later, in the years of the American Open Door Notes. But the China that the IMF and the World Bank came to inspect was hugely different from the China seen by Lord Macartney. Among the differences, Deng and Jiang knew more about the West than did Emperor Qian Long. Deng

---

[36]*Dachao xinqi*, 1992, 346.

admitted in private that China's doctrine (Marxism, in this case) had derailed China for several decades. And Deng and Jiang felt a fervor for economic development that recalled John Rockefeller, Henry Ford, and the English industrial revolution.

By the end of Jiang's hold on supreme power in 2002, as Hu Jintao became CCP boss at the 16th Party Congress, the "Rise of China" had taken on a quite new meaning. Under Mao, China as a revolutionary force gained the attention of her neighbors and the United States. By the early twenty-first century, the spotlight was on China using its economic clout and military capability to maximize its international influence.

ONE AREA WHERE Jiang did *not* put economics first was "reform" of the "state-owned enterprises." These industrial crown jewels of Stalinism, the "commanding heights," in Lenin's phrase, of the socialist economy, produce steel, machine tools, chemicals, weapons and ammunition, and such. The state factories are more than economic units; they are part of the socialist political establishment. This is in keeping with a Chinese tradition of economic paternalism. The very term for "economics," *jingji*, is an abbreviation of four characters, *jingji jimin*, which mean "to order the world and succor the people."[37]

From 1979, it had been comparatively easy to take initial steps of marketization. Small private firms and joint ventures between Chinese local government and foreign capital brought a real market to China. But the joint venture and private business sectors showed up the state factories as losers. When Deng came to power, the state factories produced 75% of China's industrial output. By 1995, seventeen years later, they produced a mere one-third. In the same period, most of these state factories lost increasing amounts of money. Only a minority could pay the interest on their debt.[38]

Deng and Jiang allowed these rusty industrial dinosaurs to bleed the party-state. The reason lay in the entwinement of three factors. Chi-

---

[37]Gernet, 1985, xxxi.
[38]Steinfeld, 1998, 12; Lardy, 1998, 38, 57, 76.

nese banks are virtually arms of the government. It became irresistible, given the political risks in privatizing large state factories, to instruct the banks to subsidize them. "Profit" and "loss" are almost meaningless terms in the state factories, since the connection to other arms of the government (tax bureau, economic ministries, banks) is so intimate.

The second factor was the party-state's fear of the social and ideological consequences of cutting the Gordian knot of the state factories. The Chinese Ministry of Labor and Social Security said in 2002 that urban unemployment would rise from 6.8 million in 2001 to 20 million by 2005.[39] The figure of 6.8 million for 2001 is almost certainly a huge understatement; the government seems to believe the real figure may approach 100 million.[40] What is stunning is Beijing's own prediction of a threefold increase in urban unemployment in a four-year period. To close or sell off to private hands most of the big state factories would bring a social crisis. Moreover, the PRC as a "workers state" would lose face if the industrial crown jewels of Stalinism were thrown out the window.

The third factor was that household savings gave the banks their money. The high savings rate of the Chinese people, who may be largely unaware of the hair-raising triangle of risk and folly in which they are unwitting participants, keeps the banks, if that is the term for them, in practical operation. Quite likely, the loyal Chinese savers are keeping the regime from collapsing.

By the late 1990s, a time bomb ticked under the three entwined factors. The banks were insolvent; bad loans were five times the banks' net worth. That could be borne in a socialist system, and in the crucial absence of a free press. The payments by the banks to the state factories—even payroll!—staved off social disorder. Part of the bank transfers to state factories came back to the government treasury as tax. Scratching for revenue, the party-state happily took what it could get.

But capital was not going to productive uses. The state factories were still being favored, against economic logic, in the interests of the sur-

---

[39] *Wall Street Journal*, June 21, 2002.
[40] Solinger, 2001, 183.

vival of the Communist party-state. Truly private firms were constrained to remain comparatively small. As of 2001, the largest private firm in all of China, the Hope Company in the southwest, was worth a mere $600 million (by comparison, India has private firms each worth $5–$7 billion). The state factories were not shrinking; in some respects they were actually growing, a cancer in the body of the nation.

It was all a house of cards, propped up by the smoke-and-mirrors of a paternalistic party-state that put its hope in the passivity of an ignorant populace, and its presumed preference for bread over political freedom. Everyone came to marvel at Mao's persistence in sticking to collectivist policies even when they produced lousy economic results. Fewer people noted that Jiang, with the state factories, was repeating this act of faith. Premier Zhu Rongji said at the Fifteenth Party Congress in 1997 that financial system problems and money-losing state factory problems would be solved within three years. The well-informed Nicholas Lardy found this "grounds for optimism."[41] Yet five years later there is little discernible progress.

As of 2003, the party-state still controls the economy far more than does any state in the Organization for Economic Cooperation and Development (OECD), and considerably more than any non-Communist state in East Asia. Power mostly wins any battle with money. The Chinese *yuan* is not a free-floating currency. *All* big industry is intimately linked with the banking–bureaucratic apparatus of the state. The party-state grows suspicious and avaricious when a private company flourishes. "So long as your business is below a certain size," said a successful businessman to John Derbyshire in 2000, "you're pretty much left alone. But when you get big enough to attract the attention of the authorities, they soon come knocking on your door with their hands out. *Like flies to meat they come!*"[42]

One of China's newest provinces, Hainan, born as a child of the reform era in 1988, was intended to be a model of "small government and big society" (*xiao zhengfu da shehui*). It set up only half the number

---

[41]Lardy, 2000, 148.
[42]*National Review*, Sept. 25, 2000.

of departments of other provinces. It omitted the prefecture level between province and city or county. Yet, a decade or so later, big government had reasserted itself step by step. The center at Beijing *required a counterpart* in Hainan for its eighty-odd ministries and commissions. Today, the state economy is the overwhelming sector in Hainan, even in agriculture. Only seven provinces have a higher number of bureaucrats, calculated as a percentage of total population, than the island meant to be a showcase of small government.[43] "The blueprint for a new state/society relationship," writes Feng Chongyi, "failed to materialize in Hainan."[44] The case suggests how government can be big and weak at the same time.

As the reform era began, there were 3.7 million bureaucrats in the governing structure of China, according to Kjeld Erik Brødsgaard, the leading student of China's administration, and by 2000 that number had increased to 9.72 million (leaving aside some 24 million party-state workers who are not civil servants as such). In step with rhetoric about downsizing the party-state, the actual administrative structures become ever more bloated.[45]

A THIRD CHANGE triggered by Deng was *steps toward constitutionalism.* Deng's way was to achieve a desired result without regard to image, theory, or elegance of rationale. This was in the Legalist tradition. He once described his political style: "I cross the river by touching my feet against the stones, this one and that one, to keep my balance and get to the other side." The "other side" of the river Deng had to reach was economic success; and for economic development, Deng knew, rules were a necessity.

After 1978, criminal and civil codes were introduced, and more predictability came to public policy and hence to private life. This did not mean individual rights existed or democracy was at the door. Deng had

---

[43]Brødsgaard, 2002, 380, 383.
[44]Feng, 2001, 25, 26, 33, 34.
[45]Brødsgaard, 2002, 365, 371.

little taste for political freedom. Words could still be crimes, as many a priest and democrat found out. At all times, the stability and unity of the socialist household outweighed any other consideration.

In 1986 Beijing enacted the General Principles of Civil Law, which bore the influence of Western, especially German law. Later came three specific laws on product liability, different in spirit from the General Principles: Product Quality Law, Unfair Competition Law, and Consumer Protection Law. There are two broad possible ways to deal with the problem of defective items doing damage to those who purchase them. One is to protect the right of the consumer to redress after buying a faulty product. The other is to deter manufacturers and retailers from allowing faulty products to reach the public.

The three Chinese laws on the subject are solely concerned with the latter. Beijing was concerned, as always, with the management of society as a whole, rather than with relations among individuals. "The principal function of Chinese product liability law," William Jones writes, "is to deal with the problem of product defects, only secondarily does it regulate the rights of individuals injured by defective products."[46] The practical method adopted by the party-state was to select an occasional egregious case—a space heater explodes and kills twin babies—and spotlight it. Rarely could the Chinese consumer rely on redress after buying a faulty product.

In the spring of 2001, an unemployed deaf-mute man with a grievance against his relatives was arrested for blowing up four apartment buildings, killing 108 people, including his relatives, in Shijiazhuang, the capital of Hebei Province, two hours south of Beijing. Of course he was executed. But a second person was also shot in the head, the usual mode of execution. Hao Fengqin ran a business selling explosives to local quarries. Forty-five years old, mother of two daughters, she said she had no idea the man to whom she sold ammonium nitrate was going to blow up buildings. He told her he ran a small quarry, of which there are many in the neighborhood.[47]

---

[46]Jones, 1999.
[47]*Renmin ribao,* March 17, 18, and 26, 2001.

Mrs. Hao, like other people in the local trade, lacked a licence to sell ammonium nitrate. Section 125 of China's Criminal law states that making, selling, storing, or transporting illegal explosives is punishable by 3 to 10 years in prison. From Hebei Province, Craig Smith wrote in the *New York Times:* "Typically, someone found guilty of making and selling unlicenced explosives would have been fined."[48]

Mrs. Hao got a bullet in the head, instead, for reasons that had little to do with justice among individual citizens. In Jiang's China, there were periodic, arbitrary crackdowns on crime based on the state's needs of the moment. Within these general waves, a basic technique was to single out someone *pour encourager les autres,* or, in the Chinese phrase, "to kill a chicken and thus scare the monkeys." Prior to the bombing in Shijiazhuang, China had seen a rash of such explosions. The tragedy occurred on March 16, and on March 18 *People's Daily* briefly reported the facts. A reward equal to ten years of salary for an urban worker was offered for finding the culprit. Beijing mounted China's biggest national manhunt in two decades and declared that the guilty ones would be nabbed within seven days. By March 25 a crime had become a political campaign. "This is a fight to bring terror to the soul," said *People's Daily* of the broad drive to deter such lawlessness. "This is a contest between righteousness and evil." As often with Chinese law, it is hard to be certain the right people were punished for the crime (the culprit, supposed to be a deaf-mute, was said by the official media to have spoken "in a mixed accent" when pursued, and to have cried on being apprehended, "Questions aren't necessary, I'm the man you want!")[49]

Compared with the consequences of the explosion that killed 108 people, and with the social context of a threat to the party-state's grip on the city of Shijiazhuang, Mrs. Hao's lack of evil intent was a minor consideration. After her execution, a sign in 6-foot-high characters went up in Hao's small town: "Crack Down Harshly on the Violent Crimes of Bombing, Arson, and Murder." An unexceptionable senti-

---

[48]*New York Times,* June 19, 2001.
[49]*Xinhua she,* March 24, 2001.

ment, yet the wave that yielded Hao the death penalty was reminiscent of the political campaigns in the Mao era. The goal differed greatly; the techniques much less so. Hao is dead not because her punishment was in proportion to the crime she committed, but because the interests of the party-state required her to serve a wider purpose.[50]

A SHARP LIMIT on the steps toward constitutionalism was the continued existence of a Supreme Leader. Of course, neither Deng nor Jiang attained or sought the godlike status that Mao possessed. That was due to personality differences, the backlash against Mao's arbitrariness, and the complex leadership demands of an era of economic development. But both post-Mao leaders, after a decade in office, took on neo-emperor traits. They disregarded party procedures (holding "enlarged" meetings) to get their own way. They put out "doctrines" and "theories" and "thought," whose banality was hidden by the loud implication that the Supreme Leader wielded truth with one hand and power with the other. Like Mao, they swam for the cameras.

The cult of the Supreme Leader can only exist as a two-way street. When the Hungarian philosopher Georg Lukacs heard of the denunciation of Stalin in Moscow in 1956, his first thought was not of personality but of the Communist Party's organization. "I pictured Stalin to myself as the apex of a pyramid," he said, "which widened gradually towards the base and was composed of many 'little Stalins': they, seen from above, were the objects and, seen from below, the creators and guardians of the 'cult of personality.' Without the regular and unchallenged functioning of this mechanism, the 'cult of personality' would have remained a subjective dream."[51] It was the same with Mao. From the top, a sense of entitlement, omnipotence, even immortality. From below, an institutional acceptance of this dictatorial pathology. In a lesser way, in the 1980s, the political culture entered a symbiosis with a cult of Deng.

[50]Cabestan, 1992, 471–472.
[51]Lukacs, 1963, 105.

And in a fresh fashion, the pattern recurred with Jiang. At the 14th CCP Congress in 1992, Jiang spoke of "two cores" in the history of the CCP. Mao had been the leader of the first core, Deng of the second. Five years passed, during which Jiang survived and few steps were taken to liberalize the political system. At the 15th Congress in 1997, Jiang discovered a new chapter to the CCP story. He presented himself as the leader of a "third core"! This was stark proof that economic reform was not going to be matched by political reform. A Supreme Leader still existed. Mao, Deng, Jiang: The children of Han would surely recognize their new father.

When the territory of Macao came back from Portuguese rule in 1999, two years after Hong Kong's reversion, the "family" metaphor was made palpable. A poem about Macao, set to music, was performed all over China by an eight-year-old: "I've been out of your bosom for too long a time, Mother!" it ran. "But they captured only my body. You are still the keeper of my soul, Mother! I want to return, Mother!"[52] Imperial language was used; the imperial way echoed on. "They" (the Portuguese) had captured part of the body of the children of Han, but the soul of the Han household was inviolable. The "Us-and-Them" syndrome was eternally valid, and politically useful.

Institutionally, both Deng and Jiang hit the brick wall of the succession issue, as most emperors did. We saw in Chapter 3 that the reality of imperial succession was frequently maneuver, plots, and disputed wills. All of these came into play as Mao sank and died. When Deng grew weak, the pattern was different. Fewer arrests occurred. The struggle over the succession generally stopped short of violence. Yet the political parallel remained. Two senior figures in Deng's party-state were purged (one put under house arrest) for growing too itchy at the prospect of succeeding Deng. At least two senior figures in Jiang's party-state had their careers cut short for a similar reason. At the 16th CCP Congress in November 2002, the exquisite difficulty of the unelected supreme leader syndrome was freshly on display. Jiang retired, but not entirely. Hu Jintao became CCP chief yet Jiang retained the top mili-

---

[52] *Wall Street Journal*, Dec. 15, 1999.

tary post at his own pleasure. The ruling Standing Committee of the Politburo was enlarged from seven to nine to permit the inclusion of a plurality of Jiang loyalists. It did not seem an easy prospect for Hu Jintao, lacking any mandate from the Chinese people, to emerge smoothly from Jiang's shadow and become a real new emperor.

In the post-Mao era, it was acknowledged that, even after 1949, "feudal despotism" had continued to plague China.[53] Though not acknowledged by official China, despotism still had not disappeared in the early years of the twenty-first century. Pilgrims flocked to the Jiang family home in Yangzhou, where a museum was being created to honor the third great leader of the PRC. "We never thought of [Jiang Zemin] as anything special," a local resident told a reporter. "It's hard to know who will grow up to be the next emperor."[54] Huge political change looms for China, but the back-door deal transferring power to Hu Jintao in 2002 was most unlikely to be its trigger. The entire 16th Congress seemed an exemplar of the anachronism of the Chinese party-state.

———————

DENG'S FINAL change was to *open China* to non-Chinese presence, capital, and ideas. More than Mao's readiness to accept technique from abroad, Deng's opening meant an end to the previously sacred principle of self-reliance. Deng and Jiang not only tilted to the West strategically, as the late Mao had done in full-blown fashion, but looked economically and even spiritually to the West. This historic step produced the latest synergy of the Chinese state. The Deng–Jiang regimes hitched their fortunes to a partnership with foreign capital and know-how. Consciously, Deng in particular tried to recreate the East–West blend that had brought success to Singapore and Hong Kong.

There were stark limits to Deng's opening to the non-Chinese world, and side effects judged unacceptable by the Chinese state. Police and security officials still viewed many foreigners as spies; flies and

———————

[53] *Zhongguo shi yanjiu*, no. 1, 1979, 13 (editorial commentary).
[54] *New York Times*, Nov. 9, 2002.

other pests were said to be buzzing through the open door. I learned this in Beijing in 1992, when I met up with a former leader of the Tiananmen democracy movement, Shen Tong.

By then a student at Boston University, Shen Tong was making his first trip back to China since the Tiananmen tragedy. He had traveled through a number of provinces unhindered for several weeks. But in Beijing, he was detained in the middle of the night at his mother's home. A warning phone call from the family reached me at the Jianguo Hotel just before the police cut phone lines at the house. Later that morning, Shen Tong was due to address an audience, including foreign journalists, in a reserved ballroom of the Jianguo Hotel. He clearly would not appear. I was the only person around, apart from the Chinese authorities, who knew he had been nabbed.

Around 9 A.M., as I began to explain to the assembled crowd why Shen Tong was not there, and handed out, in Chinese and English, a text of remarks he had prepared on democracy and China, hotel staff and plainclothes security men broke up the gathering. Pushing people away, they said the meeting was canceled, we were violating the law, literature may not be distributed, and the Jianguo Hotel was being threatened by chaos.

Plainclothes men hustled me upstairs and shuttered me in my room. Security officers of Beijing City arrived to grill me. Alerted by the foreign press, a diplomat from the U.S. embassy came to assist. With physical assistance from a Japanese cameraman, the diplomat was pulled into my room. But the police were firmly in charge. "You held an illegal press conference," said a security officer, as we sat on two unmade beds. "You distributed some documents."

I said it may have been unfortunate that I handed out materials on Chinese matters, but it occurred because of the even more unfortunate circumstance that Shen Tong was grabbed in the night and accorded no due process.

"You brought Western democratic ideas into China," said another security officer, above the noise outside the door of foreign journalists calling out to me. I said many Chinese had democratic ideas of their own. "What if Chinese went to America, the way you have come to China, and introduced materials hurtful to the American people?" The

U.S. diplomat snapped: "Chinese in the U.S. may say and write anything they wish."

After two hours a deal was struck. I would be released if I left the
Jianguo Hotel and went to the U.S. embassy for the rest of the morning. Still, around midnight, a swarm of public security agents arrived at
my hotel room. "You are being expelled from China." They took me to
a building near Beijing airport. Endlessly, the security police sought a
confession. I was unaware of my crimes and declined to confess.

As dawn arrived, my entourage explained they could not expel me
from China until I confessed. Finally, I agreed to sign a statement listing the activities I had engaged in, including taking some meals with
Shen Tong. I understood the police would then append a sentence that
said these were illegal, harmful to the Chinese people, "splittist," and so
on. This indeed was done in the English version of my "confession."

In the Chinese version, I was required to sign at the bottom of the
entire document, which I noticed, as I deciphered the hand-written Chinese characters, included the view that I had broken Chinese law. On the
tarmac of Beijing airport, a video was taken as I climbed the steps of a
ladder specially placed at one door of an aircraft bound for Hong Kong.
For the previous 24 hours, the opening of China to the West had seemed
to me rather limited. The security men had nothing in common with
urban Chinese whom foreign tourists meet. In goals and mentality, they
were father-mother officials of an unchanged Chinese party-state.

The Chinese state needed not only the video—to satisfy the boss—
but the "confession." In 2001, when the U.S.-based scholar Gao Zhan
was held in Beijing on spying charges, the party-state announced she
had "openly confessed her crimes."[55] This is a theme song when Beijing
deals with accused people, but what is its meaning? In China if you are
accused, you *have* to confess, for a fundamental reason. As there could
be no Catholic Church without confession, there could be no Chinese
Communist Party without confession. It affirms the infallibility of the
higher authority. It renews the sense of mission of the political priest-
hood to have the helplessness of the rank and file stated repeatedly.

[55] *New York Times,* March 23, 2001.

Each time a confession is made that contains untruth, as did the Chinese text of my own confession in 1992, the person concerned contributes to the mountain of lies on which the Chinese party-state is based.

When Shen Tong, after fourteen weeks, was released and dispatched back to Boston, the Chinese press said he had "asked for leniency" and "repented to some degree." At Boston airport, when I welcomed him home, he told me neither statement was true. The Qing Dynasty in 1727 forbad Chinese from living outside of China.[56] The PRC under Jiang compelled outspoken Chinese to live outside China.

IN THE AREA of information and publications, the Jiang state seemed to become a tougher state in the last years of the twentieth century and the start of the twenty-first. Newspapers and publishing houses were closed down every month for releasing politically incorrect viewpoints. Ethnic Chinese visitors to the PRC, some of them American citizens, were detained on false charges of spying. The first trials began of people accused of using subversive words on a website.

In 1996 *People's Daily* faced a sagging circulation that made its self-image as China's number one newspaper difficult to maintain. China had 1.2 billion people but only 800,000 copies of *People's Daily* were being sold. By comparison, in the United States, with 290 million people, the *Wall Street Journal* sells 1.8 million copies a day and *USA Today* sells 2.2 million. Worse, for Beijing, most of the 800,000 copies were not bought by actual people paying out of their own pockets, but by work units of the party-state.

The instincts of the CCP, which supervises *People's Daily*, did not lean toward solving the problem by permitting the paper to offer lively and objective stories. This would negate the didactic mission of the Communist Party. Instead, a directive went out to work units across the land, urging extra subscriptions to *People's Daily*. In ten days the circulation doubled to 1.6 million (according to government figures). The

---

[56]Elvin, 1973, 218.

father-and-mother officials felt better. Yet in the following months, the circulation began to sag again. The "solution" had been a piece of make-believe, unconnected with the appeal of *People's Daily*, or lack of it, to the Chinese people, serving only the self-image of the Chinese state.[57]

One could guess why few people buy *People's Daily* from its coverage of the teething problems of Hong Kong's new airport. A splendid facility, built on reclaimed land in Hong Kong harbor, the airport took seven years to build and cost more than US$20 billion. But its opening in July, 1998, was attended by mishaps hardly to be believed. Arrival and departure screens malfunctioned. Faulty conveyor belts sent luggage to unknown destinations within the bowels of the terminal. As flights were delayed, perishable cargo sat rotting by the runways. Extensive news coverage brought the nightmare to the whole world.

"Except to the people inside mainland China," commented Wang Ruoshui, a one-time deputy editor of *People's Daily*. "The people in China had no idea about what was occurring in Hong Kong. [On anything touching politics] the mainland media only brings them the good news."

After the airport opening, *People's Daily* wrote of its autopilot shuttle busses, world's best weather monitor, high-tech check-in counters, 24-hour runways—but not a mention of the chaos that had Hong Kong seething. "It is a long-standing problem," said Wang Ruoshui, who had been expelled from the CCP years before for speaking his mind, "that the Chinese media reports only the good news, never the bad. Even worse, Chinese officials dislike it when others report their bad news."[58]

All this occurred during Beijing's bid to enter the World Trade Organization and host the 2008 Olympic Games. But it was not surprising. The Communist party-state has a sense of its historical destiny to produce a world of harmony and light. Why publicize facts or figures that may call in question that destiny? On August 8, 2001, China Central TV (CCTV), the party-state television channel, announced

[57]Information from Liu Binyan; also, *China Focus* (Princeton), July 1, 1996.
[58]Wang Ruoshui, "China's Ban on 'Bad' News," *Los Angeles Times*, Nov. 29, 1998.

the party-state's "Seven Nos" for news coverage. Any publication could be shut down if it published reports that: "negate the guiding role of Marxism, Mao Zedong Thought, or Deng Xiaoping Theory; oppose the guiding principles [Four Absolutes], official line or policies of the Communist Party; reveal state secrets, damage national security or harm national interests; oppose official policies on minority nationalities and religion, or harm national unity and affect social stability; advocate murder, violence, obscenity, superstition or pseudo-science; spread rumors or false news, or interfere in the work of the party and government; violate party propaganda discipline or national publishing and advertizing regulations."[59] Try being a journalist in China! Dai Qing, a journalist who has spent time in prison for her views, said in late 2002: "In the Chinese media only the weather reports can be believed."[60]

An incident one evening in the fall of 1991 suggested that Jiang was less bold and more left-wing than his predecessor Deng. The 10 P.M. news on CCTV said an important editorial would follow the news and also be published in the next day's *People's Daily*. At 11 P.M., however, CCTV announced that the editorial, called "All for Reform and Openness," would be rebroadcast and alerted newspaper editors to heed the new, not the earlier version. At home, Deng had watched the first broadcast of the editorial and blown a fuse at the last part of one sentence: "In carrying out the party's policy of reform and openness, we should also persist in the Four Principles, and we should not forget to distinguish between Mr. Socialism and Mr. Capitalism." Deng phoned his secretary. A message went from Deng's office to the Politburo and then to the head of *People's Daily*, preparer of the editorial: "Delete the words 'and we should not forget to distinguish between Mr. Socialism and Mr. Capitalism,' then rebroadcast the whole thing!" "Why?" inquired the newspaper editor. "The general secretary [Jiang] didn't say there was anything wrong." The editor was rebuked: "Don't ask why. Just do it. This is from the top of the top." The editorial was rebroad-

[59]*China Rights Forum*, Fall 2001, 13.
[60]Dai Qing, talk at Fairbank Center, Harvard University, Nov. 21, 2002.

cast without the phrase drawing a line between socialism and capitalism that had offended Deng and published this way the next day.[61]

THE DENG–JIANG party-state was less ideological than Mao's state, just as the Song Dynasty, especially in foreign policy, was less ideological than the Tang Dynasty. The reasons for the difference in the two cases are similar. Deng and Jiang, like the Song emperors, had to tone down the doctrine because a lot of the actors on the political stage did not believe it. That the Song Dynasty eased up on Confucian cosmological doctrines in its policies toward the Liao, the Jin, and others did not mean the Chinese imperial polity was bankrupt and had to be replaced.[62] Likewise, the Chinese Communist state never broke down from 1949 to this day. It stopped saying American imperialists had one foot in the grave, war was inevitable, and the whole world loved Chinese communism, but its functions did not change fundamentally between the 1950s and the beginning of the twenty-first century.

In the Deng–Jiang era, as Marxism faded but Leninism remained, the party-state found a tool to shore up its sense of entitlement. The "four cardinal principles" (better rendered as "Four Absolutes," translating *yuanzi*, "principle," more contextually)[63] set in stone a marker between what it would tolerate and what it would not. The four are the socialist road, the proletarian dictatorship, the Communist Party's leadership, and Marxism-Leninism and Mao Zedong Thought.[64] In effect, the Four Absolutes, a summation of Leninism, are the unofficial constitution of the PRC.[65]

During the dynasties, emperors repeatedly turned aside from Confucian moral suasion to *realpolitik*. The first fifty years of the PRC saw a comparable shift from Maoism (functioning as neo-Confucianism) to Dengism (functioning as neo-Legalism). What was the content of

---

[61]Yang, 1998, 260–261.
[62]Xie, 1935, 81–82, passim.
[63]The translation of Mosher, 2000, 66.
[64]Yang, 1998, 207–208.
[65]Cabestan, 1992, 475.

Dengism (which Jiang also followed)? If Maoism was a version of Marxism, flavored with Mao's remolding vision, Dengism was a version of Leninism, blended with the nationalism and developmentalism of the nineteenth-century self-strengtheners.

In 1980, Liu Shaoqi, Mao's one-time closest colleague who was harried to death in the Cultural Revolution, was rehabilitated by the Deng regime. Purged in the 1960s as a "capitalist roader," he was in 1980 relabeled a "great Marxist revolutionary." The terms were meaningless, but the *use* of the terms was important.

Liu had always been an orthodox Communist organization person. When Mao, restless and disappointed in the early 1960s, tipped the balance between neo-Confucianism (Mao's moral socialism) and neo-Legalism (Leninist dictatorship) heavily toward the former, Liu was baffled. The Mao-Liu split became inevitable. Liu's career, and soon his life, was over.

When Liu was praised again by Beijing in 1980, many foreign commentators spoke of the "coming of capitalism" to China under Deng. That was not the point of Liu's posthumous return to honor. Rather, Deng was signaling a tipping of the balance away from neo-Confucianism (Maoism) and toward neo-Legalism (Leninist law and order).[66]

SEVERAL FORCES melded in the making of the PRC. One was a quest for economic modernization, common to many Third World countries in the later twentieth century. Mao gave it a utopian twist, which had to be corrected, but he shared the modernizing goal. A second force behind the PRC was belief in communism. Third was the autocratic state tradition of China. Just as the Qing Dynasty tried to adapt the imperial tradition to the challenge of the West and the task of modernization, so the PRC, in pursuit of its socialist modernization goal, built on both the traditional state and the pre-1949 party-state.

---

[66]Ross Terrill, "In China, 'Liuism' Is Back, But Not Capitalism," *New York Times,* Op-ed, May 16, 1980.

In the late twentieth century, two additional forces interacted with this tripod of influences. A nationalism that manipulated the Opium War project, but was in fact traceable to the China–Soviet Union split, the part-alarmed, part-calculated reaction to the fall of the Soviet Union, and a psycho-cultural resentment at the United States' sole superpower status. Second, China's substantial economic clout in Asia, which affected its thinking about both socialism and foreign policy.

The problem for PRC politics is that these five forces do not align smoothly. The economic modernizing drive is important to all Chinese, but it clashes with efforts to keep up Marxist appearances. The vision of a powerful and wealthy China playing a leading role in Asia, likewise, is welcome to Chinese people, and also in harmony with Chinese historical goals, but it puts at risk needed links with the West and residual claims to socialist morality.

Two worldviews have been shot down in short order within Chinese minds. The imperial mentality was attacked during and after the fall of the Qing Dynasty. A half century later, Maoist utopianism, sold to the Chinese as the "new" that replaced the imperial "old," was itself rejected. The solution had become another problem.

What, then, did the Chinese Communist revolution achieve? In Beijing's view, a "socialism with Chinese characteristics" has come into existence. Different from the socialism of the Soviet Union, it will endure. China is not on the way to capitalism; it is building a new genus of "market socialism." This Chinese formula for prosperity under authoritarianism will be Beijing's springboard to world leadership.

A second view is that the sole achievement of the Chinese revolution was to consolidate the unity of the Chinese realm. The Communist movement emerged in a situation of foreign encroachment on China and partial fragmentation of China. This crisis of national unity—but little else—was successfully addressed by 1949.

A third view of the PRC's scorecard could be called "Up the hill and down again." The years since 1949 fall into two parts, 1949–1976, and the post-Mao period. Mao tried to recast society and broach revolution to the world. Deng, Jiang, and Hu have essentially dismantled what Mao built in the first twenty-five years. So the revolution itself achieved no lasting change. Post-Mao China in many ways resumed a path trodden by Sun Yat-sen and Chiang Kai-shek.

A fourth view is a variation on the third. The Deng and Jiang period picked up from Li Hongzhang and other self-strengtheners of the nineteenth century. The Nanjing regime from 1928 forms a bridge between the two epochs. The warlord period and the Mao period were interruptions to a process of China evolving from monarchical empire to modern nation.

None of these four answers amounts to a realization of CCP revolutionary aims in 1949, much less the world-arranging aims of 1921, when the party was founded. We are forced to confront what did *not* change politically.

Mao is our best witness to the Communist system's evolution back toward Chinese autocratic tradition. "For the past four thousand years," he observed in 1923, when 30 years old, "Chinese politics has always opted for grand outlines of large-scale projects with big methods. The result has been a country outwardly strong but inwardly weak; solid at the top but hollow at the bottom."[67] But after Mao attained power he blamed all China's weaknesses on Western imperialism. At age 56, Mao declared: "The Chinese have always been a great, courageous and industrious nation; it is only in modern times that they have fallen behind. And that was due entirely to oppression and exploitation by foreign imperialism."[68] Mao changed his tune, the better to legitimate his autocratic party-state.

––––––––––––

THE AMBIGUITY of China's late twentieth-century domestic achievements lay in the ultimate impossibility of combining a market economy with a Leninist state. The revolution of 1949 brought to power a Communist Party that monopolized political power, and the post-1978 reforms opened part of the economy to market forces. But political paternalism and economic autonomy are not easy to mix. Fol-

––––––––––––

[67]Schram, 1992, 527.
[68]Mao, *Selected Works*, vol. 5, 16–17.

lowing one road in politics and a different one in economics does not make for a smooth ride or a settled destination. Reform-after-revolution suggested that something had gone wrong with the revolution. But this could not be openly admitted by the Communist Party.

The tension between economic rationality and the Tsarist–Qin–Stalinist crown jewels of the party-state came to a peak under Jiang Zemin, over the state factories, but it had existed ever since 1949. The arguments within the CCP over the Great Leap Forward displayed the tension.[69] Yet there was a difference between the economics–politics struggle in the Mao party-state and that in the Deng–Jiang party-state. In the 1950s and 1960s, the unique authority and strong personality of Mao often suppressed economic rationality. After the 1980s, the balance frequently tipped in favor of economic rationality.

Under Deng–Jiang, the privileged claims of the political crown jewels came under pressure from three directions. Missed economic opportunities of the Mao era could not be denied. Political gymnastics of the Mao era had exhausted the people; campaigns and "fights to the end" lost their capacity to seduce. Finally, the East Asian region as a whole took off economically after the Vietnam War; China, by comparison, looked like a laggard. No patriot could put up with that.

The balance sheet on the Deng–Jiang era synergy between the Chinese polity and foreign capital is not yet in. Are the United States, Japan, and other countries serving Chinese purposes without knowing it? Or is Communist China throwing out the baby of Chinese political paternalism with the bathwater of access to the world economy?

---

[69]MacFarquhar, 1997, 90.

SEVEN

BEIJING JUGGLES THE
LEGACY OF EMPIRE

The Globe, London, 1897:
China, in the natural order of things, cannot go on for long as an independent Empire, or even as a nation. In fact, it is not a nation; it is populated by peoples of different races, whose manners, customs, habits of thought and even language are quite different.

IN 1997, the most free-market and anti-Communist city in the world, the British colony of Hong Kong, half its families refugees from the PRC, went quietly under the wing of that same Marxist-Leninist state. After six years under Beijing's "people's dictatorship," Hong Kong was named "the world's freest economy" by the conservative Heritage Foundation and the pro-market *Wall Street Journal* in their *2004 Index of Economic Freedom.*

In truth, contradictions rear up from every fringe of the PRC. In the heavily Muslim province of Xinjiang, Communist officials enthuse about Central Asian oil flowing in pipelines through Xinjiang to China's east coast, yet a moment later warn of the danger of Xinjiang "splitting off" from the motherland. In Lhasa, more than a thousand miles south from the mosques of Xinjiang, the ruling officials continue a forty-year battle with the Buddhist Dalai Lama, now head of a government-in-exile in India, over whether Tibet belongs within Beijing's domain.

Historically, presently-defined China has alternated between unity and fragmentation, in roughly equal proportions. Within those swings, which generally were violent, a more limited, often peaceful alternation occurred between centralization in the imperial capital and devolution to the periphery. This limited ebb and flow has also occurred in the half century of the PRC. Historically, the centralization–devolution swings were sometimes a prelude to dynastic decline and fragmentation, but not always.

Take three cases of centralization and its cancellation, at intervals of a millennium. Wang Mang was a high official who grabbed the throne in the year 9. He ran a tight ship, brought in "new policies," and tolerated no deviations. He aggressively tackled the troublesome Xiongnu nomads, changed the names of counties and official posts, and sought to abolish the buying and selling of land.[1] Soon a disastrous Yellow River flood fueled the Red Eyebrow rebellion and helped undo Wang Mang's centralizing ambitions; he was murdered in his palace in the year 23. A thousand years later, Wang Anshi was the string-puller of a whirlwind period under Emperor Shen Zong of the Song, beginning in 1069, whose innovations included tax reform and central officials manipulating local trade as "entrepreneurial bureaucrats."[2] Believing in breaking down all barriers between the public and the private, Wang Anshi also established a Finance Planning Commission, and increased the size of the bureaucracy by nearly half.[3] Famine helped cut Wang Anshi's effective power to seven years. A further millennium on, Mao Zedong took China by the throat in the 1950s and 1960s; he was perhaps the most effective ideological and economic centralizer of them all. Mao updated what in Wang Anshi's day was called a quest, in the interests of reform, for "a single morality and a uniformity of customs" (*yi daode tong fengsu*).[4]

But Mao's death, and equally the fall of Wang Mang and Wang Anshi, was followed by devolution to the regions, enhanced scope for private interests, and a decline in central revenue as a proportion of total government revenue. The reputation of all three strongmen has fluctuated, as China oscillates between centralizing schemes and a retreat to localism.[5]

---

[1] Elvin, 1973, 31–32.
[2] Paul J. Smith, 1991, 111ff.
[3] Paul J. Smith, 1991, 114, 116; Bol, 1986.
[4] *Song huiyao*, xuanju 3.
[5] I owe the comparison of the Wang Mang, Wang Anshi, and Mao periods to Prof. Peter Bol of Harvard University.

The power and prestige of the center are subject to flux. Tight central control is followed by a loose rein. Harmony between capital and frontier during one decade can turn into revolt the next. A non-Han area may be sideswiped by national upheavals in domestic or foreign policy. Before and after the fall of the last dynasty in 1912, the flux was dizzying. A push for local self-government, the rise of regional military strongmen, and schemes for federalism all gave illustration to the age-old tension between a tight kingdom and a loose one. The opening line of the historical novel *Romance of the Three Kingdoms,* one of Mao's favorite books, comes to mind: "After a long separation, there is bound to be unity; after long unity, there is bound to be separation."[6]

Today, Beijing seeks to consolidate its far-flung imperial realm by juggling five variables: socioeconomic change, Communist doctrine, foreign relations, the evidence from history and archaeology, and the daily opportunities of governance in peripheral or non-Han areas. Just as Qing Dynasty policy in border areas was a "calculus of security, cost, and revenue potential,"[7] so too is the PRC's policy.

Few parts of China proper, or "inner PRC," possess separatist instincts. Guangdong displays some provincial chauvinism but of a politically toothless kind. The northern hinterland province of Shanxi, rich in political tradition but lagging economically, in the 1990s developed a provincial populism, but without separatist overtones. One might expect restiveness with Beijing's yoke in the southeastern coastal province of Fujian, which shares the culture and spoken tongue of Taiwan and lies a mere 100 miles away. Fujian speech is as different from Mandarin as Swedish is from English.[8] Yet one cannot detect serious signs of a "Greater Taiwan" or "Greater Fujian" movement, despite the fact that in modern history Taiwan was more nearly a "part of Fujian" (or "part of Japan") than "part of China."

Overall, the enhanced local sentiment and dissatisfaction with Beijing in Guangdong, Shanxi, Fujian, and other provinces of inner PRC

---

[6]Luo, 1970 (reprint), 1.

[7]Miller, 2000, 35, discussing John Shepherd's *Statecraft and Political Economy on the Taiwan Frontier, 1600–1800,* 1993, especially pp. 395–410.

[8]This is the well-informed opinion of Prof. James Watson of Harvard University.

does not involve, as it did in some provinces in the 1920s, an aspiration to independence. Today, devolution, by itself, is not a halfway house to fragmentation. Should some Han provinces (again) turn separatist, it would be less of their own volition than because Beijing fell into crisis over losing its grip on "outer PRC," the heavily non-Han periphery of China. Manchuria, now "northeast China," is a cross between a Han and non-Han territory. Historically, it was the homeland of the Manchu race, which overran China in 1644. But it later became Sinified, and today is hardly more independent-minded than Guangdong.

It is the ethnic issue that Beijing understandably sees as the chief peril to national unity. Discontent among the "minority peoples" of the west, southwest, and north has the potential to unravel the PRC. Here, as Edward Friedman writes, "The center experiences itself as overrun by the periphery."[9] In Xinjiang, Tibet, Inner Mongolia, and other non-Han areas, the old issue of empire is a current issue.

"Who is Chinese?" and "What is China?" are not settled questions, despite the socioeconomic success of the Deng and Jiang eras. Here is a woman in a village near Liangshan in southwestern Sichuan Province, a member of the Yi ethnic group, who cannot read Chinese, does not use chopsticks, and holds animist beliefs. But Beijing calls her a Chinese (*Zhonghua minzu*), not because she is Han, but because she is a citizen of the PRC. The Chinese government takes the same view of Tibetans, though most deny being Chinese in any sense. Here we see a concocted imperial project.

Is Chen Shuibian, the president of Taiwan, Chinese? Is Lee Kuan Yew, the former premier of Singapore, Chinese? In what sense is the New York architect I. M. Pei Chinese? Chinese identity can overlap with a second identity. A poll in Taiwan in 2000 found 42.5% of respondents saying "I am Taiwanese," 13.6% saying "I am Chinese," and 38.5% saying they were "both Taiwanese and Chinese."[10]

---

[9]Friedman, 1995, 331.
[10]*Taipei Review*, Dec. 2001, editorial.

What about the Chinese-American nurse, born in Vietnam and still a Vietnamese citizen, who lives near me in Boston? Or an elderly scholar in a suburb of San Francisco, who speaks only Chinese, eats Chinese food with chopsticks, and holds to the tenets of Confucianism? As a resident of the United States, he has an immigration green card, but he cannot read the English words written on it.

In these examples, we see the often clashing factors of language, culture, legality, and race that make "Who is Chinese?" a complex question. It is not unlike the question "Who is British?" when posed a century ago in far-flung English-speaking countries, such as Australia and Canada. "The notion of 'Chinese' can be political, ethnic, or cultural," writes Andrew Nathan.[11] Unlike the English-speaking world, the Chinese world does not even have a spoken language in common. As has been true for centuries, state and civilization are far from coterminus. Were Qin Shihuang to reappear today, he may be judged a Chinese citizen (*Zhonghua minzu*), but of minority nationality (*shaoshu minzu*).

JUST AS CHINA has found its most effective domestic policy path since 1949, a fresh issue, "What is China?" reappears. The economic dynamism of southeast China itself casts new light on the cohesion of China. Politics speaks of the unity of China, economics does not always do so. The PRC is a diverse empire. Even the definition of the Chinese motherland, today as often before, is contentious.

Large swathes of the PRC were not, historically, part of China. During the Qing Dynasty, China acquired extra land by imperial expansion, just as Britain acquired Hong Kong, and Japan acquired Taiwan, by imperial expansion. In the western half of the PRC, the beards, mosques, horseback economy, Tibetan version of Buddhism, minimal cultivation, yaks, and buttery tea do not seem at all Chinese. Not only is the western portion of the PRC alien to Chinese civilization, it evokes three other proud civilizations: Tibetan, Mongol, and Turkic.

---

[11]Hua, 2001, foreword, xi.

The PRC and the Qing empire bear comparison with Russia.[12] Like the Qing, the Tsarist empire was huge (one-sixth of the earth's landmass) yet subject to foreign invasion. Like the Chinese empire, the Russian empire was a combination of high ambition on the frontiers, and preindustrial, illiberal life at home. When Communist revolution struck, Romanov and Qing were repackaged as Marxist empires. In the Chinese case, as the PRC began, part of Mongolia had been lost to independent status (legally severed from China in 1946), thanks to Stalin, but otherwise the Qing empire was reborn as the new Chinese Communist empire.

Today, although Han people make up 92% of the PRC's population, 60% of the PRC's territory is occupied in considerable numbers by China's "55 minorities." A quarter of this segment is ethnically mostly Tibetan, a sixth is mostly Turkic, a tenth is mostly Mongol. The three largest PRC provinces, Xinjiang, Tibet, and Inner Mongolia, all represent non-Chinese civilizations. Mao put it bluntly: "We say China is a country vast in territory, rich in resources, and large in population; as a matter of fact, it is the Han nationality whose population is large and the minority nationalities whose territory is vast and whose resources are rich."[13] Beijing seeks to Sinify these ambiguous portions, diluting them with an influx of Han. Meanwhile, the non-Chinese inhabitants would mostly prefer independence from Chinese rule.

How much of the PRC *is* rim and how much is heartland? In southern streets and villages, Chinese may tell you that Thailand "really belongs to China." In the northeast, you may hear that Korea is but a variant on Chinese civilization, separate for the moment. The Republic of China on Taiwan until recently considered the Republic of Mongolia, which is an independent country with its capital in Ulan Bator, an integral part, together with Inner Mongolia (known by Beijing as the "Inner Mongolian Autonomous Region"), of the Chinese motherland.

---

[12]Crossley, 1997, 8.
[13]Mao, *Selected Works*, vol. 5, 295.

Often, over millennia, and repeatedly during the nineteenth and twentieth centuries, the Chinese polity changed the heartland–rim demarcation, or found it changed by others. In the Qing Dynasty, Beijing's empire reached its maximum extent (to be superseded in the Communist era, when some Qing losses were recouped). The Manchu court during the eighteenth century extended its rule to Mongolia, Xinjiang, and Tibet. It *doubled the size* of the Ming court's realm, which encompassed mainly Han people. Virtually all the Qing expansion was across land, into the nomadic north and west.

Astonishingly, the huge, unwieldy, multicultural Qing empire, after an interval, became the "nation" we know as the PRC. How did the Qing in essence bequeath its Gargantuan borders to the PRC? A key role was played by the Nationalist Party of Sun Yat-sen and Chiang Kai-shek. As William Kirby wrote of the Republican period, "The Qing fell but the empire remained."[14] The transition was completed by the leaders of the Soviet Union. Stalin, who in the 1940s essentially controlled northern Xinjiang, ruled as the East Turkistan Republic under Ahmedjan Kasimi, eased the way for Mao to take the whole of Xinjiang in 1949. Nikita Khrushchev in the 1950s took the Soviet Union out of Manchuria. Mao inherited an empire like manna from heaven.

Stalin's stamp on the shape of the PRC was made at the Yalta Conference in February 1945 and through the Sino-Soviet Friendship Treaty six months later.[15] At Yalta, unbeknownst to Chiang Kai-shek, the independence of Outer Mongolia was recognized, and Moscow's privileges in Manchuria, lost to Japan in 1904, were regained as a condition of the Soviet Union entering the war against Japan. After the conference, Stalin, negotiating with the Chinese government, cunningly addressed Chiang Kai-shek's four great concerns: the threat of Mao's Communists, and China's position in the three territories of Outer Mongolia, which was in limbo, Manchuria (which could well fall into Mao's hands through Soviet help), and northern Xinjiang

---

[14]Kirby, 1997, 437.
[15]David Wang, 1997, 83–84.

(where Turkic peoples had established an independent state). Stalin played the game of two for two. He promised the Chinese not to enclasp Xinjiang, and not to assist Mao in the civil war.[16] In return, Stalin got Chinese agreement to accept the independence of Outer Mongolia and Soviet privileges in Manchuria.[17]

This piece of world-arranging soon meant—given Mao's quick victory over Chiang Kai-shek—that the Qing empire, in its awesome complexity, became the PRC empire. "[T]he notion of China pertaining today," writes James Millward, "did not arise in 1912, or even in the late nineteenth century, but was invented in the course of a gradual accommodation by Han Chinese since the mid-Qing to the idea of a Greater China with the physical and ethnic contours of the Qing Empire."[18] Sun Yat-sen, Chiang Kai-shek, and Stalin were among the facilitators.

THE SELECTIVE REVERSAL of Mao's centralization in the late 1970s brought with it, as if the present were remaking the past, a changed view of the origins of the Chinese people and the nature of the Qing Dynasty. The post-Mao epoch of resistance to the all-encompassing demands of the central state saw a questioning by foreign scholars, and also some Chinese scholars in Sichuan and other places far from Beijing, of any clear-cut origin to the Chinese race in the Yellow River region, in favor of a theory of diverse cultural origins for "China." Tomb relics from Sichuan suggested that ancient southwestern events also shaped the Chinese people. Han identity may be a mosaic, the new research concluded.[19]

In addition, liberal Western Sinologists, newly apprised of the charm of diversity in Western society, discovered an exhilarating diversity in

---

[16]After Yalta and the Sino-Soviet treaty, Stalin gave no more encouragement to the Muslim independence movement in Xinjiang. Chiang Kai-shek, for his part, sent a pro-Soviet official to take care of Xinjiang.

[17]Jiang, 1989, 54, 55.

[18]Millward, 1998, 19.

[19]Wang Guanghao, 1988, 3–4, 45–46, 461–463; Wilkinson, 2000, 344, 345.

reexamining the records of the Qing Dynasty. The Qing was no longer viewed as fitting into the Chinese system like a hand into a glove, or as being a wall-to-wall autocracy. Using fresh Manchu-language sources, revisionists put less stress than the Fairbank generation on China's assimilation of the Manchus. Sessions of the ruling Grand Council, it is now claimed, were routinely conducted in the Manchu language as late as the reign of Emperor Qian Long.[20] In Xinjiang during the eighteenth century, the Qing "rarely placed Han Chinese . . . in positions of authority over Inner Asians."[21] Much the same was true of Qing rule in Tibet, Mongolia, and Manchuria.

The Manchus, successful in expanding the realm of China, were culturally less successful in resisting the seduction of Han and Confucian ways. As Henry IV of France converted to Catholicism in 1598 the better to rule the country, so Manchu leaders aspired to be Confucian sages. They showed flexibility, however, in deploying non-Chinese mechanisms to deal with Mongols, Tibetans, and others in special cultural or geographic circumstances.[22] Lyman Miller concludes that the Qing "was a multiethnic empire utilizing a diversity of governing institutions and routines."[23] It was pluralist, not politically, but racially. Some say the Qing was an empire *rather* than a dynasty. Manchu rule, writes Evelyn Rawski, was "a creative adaptation to problems of rulership that was not simply a repetition of the dynastic cycle."[24] Revealingly, the 1719 scroll version of Emperor Kang Xi's atlas marks place names within China proper in Chinese characters, but, in a seeming admission of colonialism, marks the names of other parts of the Qing realm in Manchu.[25]

To reinterpret the Qing top to bottom in echo of today's "diversity" and "decentralization" would be unwise. Actually, the new views are an amendment to, not a replacement for, the Fairbankian view. Millward

---

[20]Rawski, 1998, 829.
[21]Millward, 1998, 234.
[22]Li Shiyu, 2000, 22–23.
[23]Miller, 2000, 25.
[24]Rawski, 1998, 302.
[25]Hostetler, 2001, 33, 75.

insists that the Qing employed a tributary system only for foreigners, and says Fairbank misunderstood this point. It is true that "tributary system" overstates the coherence of the Qing's modes of handling people at lower rungs of the ladder of its hierarchical worldview,[26] but it remains true that the Chinese polity did not make a clear distinction between international relations and control of its own subjects. Millward says that during the Qing "the question of who and what comprises 'Chinese' and 'China' is problematic." It is also problematic in the west of the PRC today.

The empire attained during the Qing should be understood, not in terms of race, but as a certain type of state. It was a state whose basic framework the Manchus took from Chinese tradition. They employed it "to achieve a long-lasting political merger of Inner Asia and East Asia."[27] This state possessed an Us-and-Them outlook on Chinese imperial subjects and Turkic (and other non-Han) imperial subjects alike. The "Chinese world order" theory is "misleading," complains Millward. Less so, if it is thought of as a Chinese *political* order, which is a reasonable interpretation given the murky line between domestic and foreign affairs. The Chinese state has a middle kingdom mentality due to its inherent nature. This does not mean Beijing's foreign policy replicates that of the Tang or Song dynasties, but that the PRC's worldview is rooted in its method of rule.

Despite an exaggerated rejection of the Fairbank view, the fresh understanding of what the Qing did greatly illumines today's China-rooted imperial project. To depict the Qing realm, Millward replaces Fairbank's "concentric rings" with a series of ethnic blocs. This parallels my "building blocks" depiction of the Communist Chinese empire in Chapter 1. At the center of the Qing enterprise lay not Chineseness—many Han scholars opposed the Qing's expansion into the western regions—but an ingenious form of state power.

What the Qing reengineered was basically the Chinese state in its Legalist tradition. The reach of this state was not, as it is not for Bei-

---

[26]Hostetler, 2001, 43.
[27]Rawski, 1998, 300.

jing today, coterminous with Chinese civilization. Being Muslim did not prevent Tungans fighting with the Qing against Kokandis. Being Chinese did not prevent a Han official marrying a Uighur woman.[28] And, in our time, being Tibetan has not stopped Ngabo Ngawang Jigme Shape from faithful service to the Chinese Communist Party for many decades starting with the "Seventeen Points Agreement" in 1951.[29]

The Qing were not especially racist; certainly they were less so than some Chinese dynasties. They wanted control and prosperity, not racial triumph. They began with the Ming idea of the western Muslims as "dogs," and ended up calling them "imperial subjects." In this respect today's new Chinese empire is similar. As during the Qing, security and money are as important to the governance of Xinjiang as ethnicity. The central issue, in understanding both Qing and Communist empires, is not culture or race. It is a vision, and modes, of central control.

The Chinese state was and is obsessed with unity. This predilection is as old as the Warring States and as current as Beijing's repression of Xinjiang Muslims post-9/11. "If there is unity of opinion, then one can govern well," says the *Lu shi chunqiu* of the third century B.C.; "if there are divergences, then there will be disorder. Oneness fosters safety; difference brings danger."[30] Emperor Qian Long had a vision of Muslim and Han held together politically in a Great Unity (*da tong*). "Once the names are unified," he said, "there is nothing that is not universal."[31]

But who does the unifying, and on what basis is it done? The pluralism of Qing rule may be compared with the two-way process in operation today between Hong Kong and Beijing's polity, and between Taiwan and that polity. One territory is in Beijing's polity (Hong Kong), one is outside (Taiwan), but both are engaged with the PRC center, sending and receiving influence. The "name is unified" by the emperor, however; whether currently inside or not, they are both, in the CCP view, building blocks of Great China.

---

[28]Millward, 1998, 171.
[29]Shakya, 2000, 198, 300.
[30]Chen Qiyou, 1984 (reprint), 1124.
[31]Millward, 1998, 199.

APART FROM CHINA, the world's other multiethnic empires have all gone. Austria-Hungary and the Soviet Union were among the last to expire. Yet the PRC has put the world on notice that it expects to acquire *more* territory than it presently holds. Taiwan will be acquired next, other territories will follow. The rationale is a political theology called "One China." It is a fiction created to deny the reality of China's diversity and the anachronism of the PRC's mode of governance. There is just One China, runs the mantra. "Since ancient times," Tibet and Xinjiang have been part of it. Taiwan, despite appearances, *cannot possibly be* a sovereign entity. Variations of the mantra cover Mongolia and Manchuria.

In historical materials and current secret reports, further areas fall helpless before One China, including portions of Russia's Siberia and scores of islands east and south of the PRC. Said Mao in 1964, "About a hundred years ago, the area to the east of Lake Baikal became Russian territory, and since then Vladivostok, Khabarovsk, Kamchatka, and other areas have been Soviet territory. We have not yet presented our account for this list."[32] If China becomes a superpower, the account will be presented. By 1973, Mao seemed to have augmented the territory he feels was stolen by Moscow. "In history," he complained to Kissinger, "the Soviet Union has carved out one and a half million square kilometers from China."[33] During the 1970s and 1980s, the same Communist Party that rules in Beijing today claimed as Chinese large parts of the territory of today's Kazakstan and Tajikistan.

A fixed cry in Beijing's international rhetoric, One China is the bone of contention between China and countries that wish to deal with Taiwan. But One China casts a net beyond Taiwan. It is the signature maxim of the new Chinese empire. To be a true member of the Chinese *jia* (household), anywhere in the world, you must believe in One China, applied to Tibet no less than to Taiwan. Any foreign government that does not annually recite the catechism of One China is "interfering in the internal affairs of the Chinese people." This is the imperial voice.

---

[32]Doolin, 1965, 44.
[33]Burr, 1998, 187.

In fact, One China is unsupported by history or culture. Repeatedly, Mao himself broke the rule of One China. "From now on, there are two totally different states in the territory of China," he said when his separate "Soviet Republic" was proclaimed in 1931, as Chiang Kai-shek ran the Chinese government, called the Republic of China, from Nanjing. "One is the so-called ROC, which is a tool of imperialism. . . . The other is the Chinese Soviet Republic, the state of the broad masses of exploited and oppressed workers, peasants, soldiers and toilers." Two Chinas, anyone? Mao did not stop at two; "it would be better," he wrote in 1920, "to divide China into twenty-seven countries."[34]

Mao, expressing a factual situation plus an ideological preference, was replicating many a scenario in Chinese history. More than one claimant to be the government of China often existed on the territory of China, each with its values and constituency. People in Taiwan, Hong Kong, Inner Mongolia, and elsewhere say this can also be true of the contemporary era, but the Chinese government gets "angry" at the suggestion. One China helps Beijing exaggerate the longevity of Chinese identity, the degree of cohesiveness of Chinese civilization, and the legitimacy of the PRC regime.

Beijing's fears on these scores make it touchy about any probing of One China. In 1998 the *Washington Post* published an article by me that called in question the validity of One China. Interesting was a response published in the leading Beijing daily *Guangming ribao*. Rejecting my statement that One China is an ideal rather than a reality, Li Rong (a pseudonym) thundered: "This is indeed an absurd and ridiculous view aimed at confounding black and white and calling a stag a horse." In questioning One China in the *Washington Post*, I was "an ant trying to topple a giant tree." Yet this futile ant was "part of a plot to split China," and a "saboteur of U.S.–China relations."[35] Both points could not be true. Could an ant split China? The angry confu-

---

[34]Short, 1999, 287; Schram, 1992, 545; also Yan, 1992, 19.

[35]Ross Terrill, "Chairman Mao's Sacred Cow: One China Doesn't Make Sense Anymore," *Washington Post*, Outlook, Sept. 22, 1996; Li Rong, "Luosi Teliya de rimeng," *Guangming ribao*, Oct. 29, 1996.

sion of the author of "The Daydreams of Ross Terrill" suggested my article had struck a nerve.

The idea of China is like the idea of the British Empire. Both China and the British Empire, as physical entities, grew and shrank over time. Before, during, and after the jewel of India was ruled by Britain, the *idea* of the British Empire existed. Taiwan, Tibet, Vietnam, Korea, and other "parts of China" have gone back and forth from rule by Beijing. Sometimes there was "China proper" (*Zhongguo benbu*), ruled by the emperor and his bureaucracy, and "Outer China" (*fanshu*), mostly non-Chinese areas that had a loose relation to the Chinese court. Meanwhile the *idea* of China endured.

A glance at Puerto Rico highlights China's unique stance. Puerto Rican society differs from the rest of U.S. society to a degree comparable to the difference between five or six areas that Beijing considers part of China, and the rest of China. Puerto Rico is currently part of the United States, under the special arrangements of commonwealth status. Most Puerto Ricans like the present setup; but some would like independence from the United States, and others would like full statehood within the United States. Why is there little tension surrounding this matter, whether in Puerto Rico, Florida, or Washington? Because it is accepted by everyone involved that any change in Puerto Rico's status would occur by the ballot box. As a project from below, any change in Puerto Rico's situation is a manageable issue. No one in Washington describes as "splittists" those Puerto Ricans who favor independence.

Within and adjacent to the PRC, there *is* great tension over situations comparable to Puerto Rico's, because Beijing does not see sovereignty (when China is involved) as having anything to do with the will of the people involved. Here is the pretension of Beijing's concept of One China. The realm of China is composed, not of sovereign people, but of the building blocks of an imperial edifice. Beijing says the entire Chinese people support the PRC concept of One China. In fact, this is unknown. The people of the PRC have not been consulted on the matter. In Taiwan, where the population *has* been consulted, voters have chosen two successive leaders who did *not* agree with the PRC concept of One China. Meanwhile, Beijing whines about "U.S. imperialism," shines a light of approval on any Puerto Ricans who support independence, and claims they soon become targets of U.S intelligence services and often "political prisoners."[36] Zhou Enlai also called Hawaii a "vassal" of the United States. The Americans, he said in 1957, try to "make Taiwan like that vassal land Hawaii."[37]

Beijing's formulation of One China seems threatened from inside China and beyond. History's lesson is that the parameters of China have regularly changed. Beijing's present view of One China is arbitrary. Three twentieth-century Chinese leaders, Sun Yat-sen, Chiang Kai-shek, and Mao Zedong, all drew the map of China differently. Each one during his career changed his mind over whether one or other territory was part of China. Why is Taiwan "in" the PRC's One China (Mao once said it was probably bound for independence) and northern Mongolia "out" (Chiang wanted it in)? There are answers to these questions, but they do not lie in a Heaven-given concept of One China.

———

CHINA ESPOUSES a questionable unity that sweeps ethnic differences under the carpet, for the glory of a state constructed from above. This building blocks approach to ruling a diverse society dominates Chinese political thinking. Increasingly, as Marxist ideology recedes, it is a vision of a Han-race-led empire. The minority peoples are caricatured, exoticized, applauded for their culture even as they are kept at arm's length in decision-making. "Under communism," quips Anthony Daniels, "all minorities dance." China, like the Soviet Union before it, hides its nonrespect for the individual by enshrining "diversity" in its formal arrangements.[38]

An alternative to a "unity of building blocks" is unity won from the allegiance of free individuals. Certainly, this is the only concept of the state that American political science (these days) takes seriously. As Eric Nordlinger writes, "only by making individuals central to the def-

[36]*Renmin ribao*, Feb. 28, 2000, and Nov. 16, 2000.
[37]Zhou, 1971, 327.
[38]John O'Sullivan, "As the World Turns," *National Review*, Jan. 28, 2002.

inition [of the state] can Hegelian implications (substantive and meta-physical) be avoided when referring to the state's preferences."[39] The situation of a "hyphenated" citizen illustrates the difference between a unity of building blocks, where, in the spirit of Hegel, history is des-tiny, and a unity centered on the individual. China does not acknowl-edge the existence of individuals such as "Korean-Chinese," "Ameri-can-Chinese," or "Tibetan-Chinese." Beijing speaks only of "national minorities," ethnic blocs, whose members are Chinese persons (*Zhong-guo minzu*). The Chinese media regularly speaks of "Tibet compatriots" (*Xizang tongbao*), or "*Zangbao*" for short, which does not seem com-patible with calling Tibetans a "nationality" (*tongbao* literally means "born of the same parents").[40]

In addition, the Chinese party-state reaches beyond China to call people of Chinese descent "Overseas Chinese." They are seldom called "Chinese-Australians" or "Chinese-Singaporeans," just "Overseas Chi-nese," as if they really belong to Beijing. Reporting on Chinese-Kore-ans in Seoul celebrating the return of Hong Kong to China in 1997, *People's Daily* spoke of them as "Overseas Chinese in Korea" (*Hanguo huaqiao*).[41]

Late in 2001, I found myself in the delightful new museum in Wuhan that houses the contents of the tomb of Marquis Yi, a states-man of the Warring States era. Among the treasures are a set of sixty-four bronze bells. Together, they form an orchestra. Struck by a rod, each bell is capable of different sounds depending on where it is struck. Said an official of the Hubei Provincial Museum with pride: "Yo-Yo Ma, the Overseas Chinese cellist, played a replica of the bells at a con-cert in Hong Kong. It was wonderful."

"I love the bells," I said to the guide, "and I am glad Yo-Yo Ma, whom I know, made fine music from them. But Ma is *not an Overseas Chinese* [*hua qiao*], he is a Chinese-American [*meiguo huaren*]." An

---

[39]Nordlinger, 1981, 9.

[40]*Renmin ribao*, Feb. 19, 2002; June 15, 2001; June 5, 2001; May 26, 2001; Aug. 11, 1995; and Aug. 11, 2001.

[41]*Renmin ribao*, July 5, 1997.

uncomprehending silence followed, underscoring the powers of indoctrination of the Chinese party-state. Power, of course, can turn illusion into dogma.

One may contrast Taiwan's usage. "Renowned violinist Lin Cho-liang visited Taipei in December to give performances," wrote a state-owned weekly in January 2002. "Born in Taiwan, the American musician thrilled audiences and helped bring 2001 to a close with a bang."[42] When Yo-Yo Ma himself visited Taiwan in 2002, the Taipei press referred to him as "the Chinese-American cellist."[43]

Mao, when talking privately, acknowledged China's cultural narrowness. "The Chinese are very alien-excluding," he remarked to Kissinger in 1973. "For instance, in your country you can let in so many nationalities, yet in China how many foreigners do you see?" Prime Minister Zhou Enlai, who was sitting nearby, said "Very few." Mao went on: "You have about 600,000 Chinese in the United States. We probably don't even have 60 Americans here."[44] Proportionately, not much has changed since.

African students in China have experienced undeniable racism at the hands of Chinese students and Chinese authorities over many decades. Soon after Zhao Ziyang, then head of the CCP, said in 1988 that racial discrimination was common "everywhere in the world except China," horrendous campus riots broke out in Nanjing between African and Chinese. A certain number of Chinese students unabashedly declared blacks backward, ignorant, ugly, uncultured, and drunken. "When I look at their black faces," said one Chinese of Africans, "I feel uncomfortable. When I see them with our women, my heart boils."[45]

The problem goes beyond cultural narrowness to the logic of authoritarian empire. Emmanuel Hevi, the author of *An African Student in China,* found the denial of individualism in the political system a more

---

[42] *Taipei Journal,* Jan. 11, 2002.
[43] *Taipei Journal,* March 15, 2002.
[44] Burr, 1998, 95.
[45] Sautman, 1994, 420, 425, 435; Hevi, 1963, 163, 173–174.

fundamental offense than Chinese people's racial attitudes.[46] In CCP eyes, an individual can hardly make a choice that affects his citizenship status. The Chinese state makes the choices. "Chinese-American" or "American-Chinese" suggests individuality. "Korean minority people" and "Tibetan minority people" are components of an imperium. "[M]en can have validity," wrote Hans Buchheim of fascist and Communist systems, "only as building blocks or structural elements, raw material, 'human materiel'; totalitarian rule cannot as a matter of principle acknowledge the citizen's personal autonomy, on which political liberty is based."[47]

"As with every region on the Chinese rim," wrote Steven Sage of China's big southwestern province, "Sichuan's history is part of world history."[48] Still more so is the history of Hong Kong, Korea, Mongolia, Vietnam, Manchuria, Taiwan, East Turkistan, and other areas intermittently ruled by China. Yet this truth comes up against Beijing's view that any territory touched by China has entered the family of China, and its history has become Chinese history. Europeans typically do not take this view. By 1810, Napoleon's France ruled central Italy, most of the Low Countries, the Illyrian Provinces, and all areas on the left bank of the Rhine. Also essentially controlled by France were Spain, Switzerland, the Grand Duchy of Warsaw, and other non-French territories. Yet France today does not dispute the "loss" of all these places.

During a 1996 lecture in Hong Kong on the ancient Vietnam Dong-son bronze drums, a Chinese member of the audience remarked that since "Vietnam belonged to China during the Han Dynasty," the

----

[46]Hevi, 1963, 12, 183, 187.
[47]Buchheim, 1968, 14. It is true that in recent years Beijing has begun to speak of *meiguo huaren hua qiao*, which seems to acknowledge the two categories of Chinese who were born in the United States and those who were not (*Renmin ribao*, July 24, 2001, and Feb. 13, 2001).
[48]Sage, 1992, 7.

drums are really Chinese, not Vietnamese.[49] When the Chinese Academy of Social Science published a translation of the *Cambridge History of China* in 1992, it baldly substituted a different map of Ming China from the one in the original English-language edition. Instead of the Ming reaching westward only to Yunnan, Sichuan, and Gansu, Beijing's version had the Ming extending to the Pamir Mountains and north beyond Lake Baikal! This is more than a lie; it reveals the past and present world-arranging pretension of the Chinese imperial state.[50]

The contemporary Beijing geographer Tan Qixiang draws historical maps that suggest the lines between China and Southeast Asian countries have been for 2,200 years roughly what they are today. The territory of many border peoples who were separate from China simply becomes a province of China. This is imperial imagination, not empirical research. Tan's map from Qin times puts Yunnan and Guangxi inside China, but they did not become Chinese until during the Ming. That of the Eastern Han Dynasty gives China northern Burma and northern Vietnam.[51] The shrinking of China under the Ming is concealed by lumping the maps of the Yuan and Ming Dynasties together. No account is given of the Chinese polity's expansion, for instance during the Qing, or of the military expeditions that were involved. The implication is that the realm of China, given by Heaven, simply realized itself as the centuries marched by.

Peter Perdue's remark is apt: "Maps control people, not just land." They are "valuable instruments of power."[52] In 2002, the Shanghai Museum map of Minority Peoples included the Nan Sha, Xi Sha, and Dong Sha islands, southeast of China, most of which are in no sense Chinese territory. The main textbook for Chinese middle schools includes Taiwan (under the name Liu Qiu) in its map of Sui and Tang

---

[49]Wade, 2000, 28.
[50]Mou, 1992, front matter, Map 1, and 249.
[51]Tan, 1996, 15–16, 19–20.
[52]Perdue, 1998, 265, 272.

Dynasty China.[53] Until forced to accept the reality of Western and Japanese power, Chinese mapmakers depicted the world not as it actually was but "in terms of how they wanted it to be."[54] Some wishful thinking continues today.

––––––––––

CONSIDER THE CASE of Parhae, a state from the years 698 through 926, located partly in the northeast of today's PRC (Manchuria), and partly in Russia and northern Korea. The people of Parhae (in Chinese, *Bohai*, the same characters as the nearby Gulf of Bohai) were a mixture of Korean and Malgal (in Chinese, *Mohe*), a people who are today one of the fifty-six official nationalities in the PRC.

Whose history is Parhae's? Archaeology regularly changes our view of the past. Yet archaeology is quite often carried out as a national enterprise, even a nationalistic one. In particular, a party-state that wields doctrine as well as power cannot easily accept fluctuations in historical understanding based on relics. The result in the case of China is that historical understanding is at the mercy of current international relations. "That history be sacrificed to power," writes Philip Kuhn, "has seemed inescapable to Chinese of the modern age."[55]

Korean archaeologists, north and south, say Parhae's origins lie with the Koguryo (a polity rooted in the Korean peninsula).[56] Archaeologists from Russia and China mostly see Parhae as a Malgal nation. "At the end of the 7th century," runs a typical statement in the press of Jiang Zemin's China, "the Malgal people of our country's northeast established the Kingdom of Parhae."[57] Of course, archaeological research may be able to settle differences over Parhae's origins. But China will not allow Korean or other foreign archaeologists access to the Parhae

––––––––––

[53] *Zhongguo lishi*, vol. 2, 1; although the characters *Liu qiu* are the same as those later used for the Ryukyu Islands, in the Sui-Yuan period they were used for Taiwan (Wilkinson, 2000, 137).
[54] Richard J. Smith, 1996 ("Mapping . . ."), 96.
[55] Kuhn, 2002, 1.
[56] Byington, 2000, 2.
[57] *Heilongjiang ribao*, Oct. 27, 2001.

historical sites located within the PRC.[58] A Korean history professor, Song Ki-ho, a student of Parhae, was ejected from PRC museums and sites during the 1990s for seeking to examine Parhae relics. "One museum granted me entrance," he recalls, "but employees followed me wherever I went, prohibited note-taking, and eventually told me to leave in the middle of my tour."[59]

The political kernel of Beijing's closed door to archaeological enquiry is that the Korean "minority" living in the northeast of China (Manchuria), according to Professor Song, "consider Korea their mother country."[60] Beijing declines to call PRC citizens of Korean descent "Korean-Chinese." It refuses to allow them to socialize at functions hosted by Korean dignitaries visiting China.

Song Ki-ho complains of Beijing's exclusionary nationalism: "[A]ll that took place within the bounds of what is now Chinese territory is used to bolster the official narrative of Chinese history today. This perspective tends to assimilate the history of minorities [and] to provide the ideological basis for the claim of a single Chinese race." Taking this view, Beijing cannot see archaeology merely as a scholarly pursuit. Viewing Parhae as part of Korean and Russian history would be tantamount, for the Chinese party-state, to splitting off the former Parhae from the motherland of China, now the PRC.

During the nationalistic post-Mao years, Beijing took its imperial approach to the Manchurian past a step further. It began to claim Koguryo history as part of Chinese history![61] In fact the Koguryo kingdom (37 B.C.–A.D. 668), which arose in the Manchurian area and later moved its capital to Pyongyang, is one of the Three Kingdoms that belong to the history of Korea.[62] In an angry exchange that led to the premature closing of a Chinese–Korean conference on Koguryo in 1993, a North Korean archaeologist inquired: "Does history change just

---

[58]Byington, 2000, 6–7, 9, 10.
[59]Song, 1998–1999, 59.
[60]Song, 1998–1999, 59.
[61]Zhang and Wei, 1998, 18–28.
[62]Byington, 2000, 14–16.

because territory has changed hands?" The imperial mind thinks it does. Twisting history to buttress current empire is irresistible to Beijing.

But is territoriality forever? As Song Ki-ho wrote, "If I receive a piece of land, does its history then become mine? If I lose that land, then do I lose that history?"[63] Surely the history of Parhae, which blended Koguryo and Malgal people, has a place in both Korean and Chinese history? For now, a collision occurs between "Chinese political agenda and South Korean historical belief."[64]

To their credit, some PRC historians take a subtler view of the matter. "Koguryo was part of Chinese history," writes Zhang Bibo, "but then [when its capital moved to Pyongyang] of Korean history. It is a case of 'One history, Two uses.'"[65] But in the twenty-first century, the Chinese party-state was hardening its view on Parhae and Koguryo. In 2000, Professor Song, visiting Heilongjiang Provincial Museum, was not allowed to take notes in the Parhae section. In 2001, taking a photo of a stone lantern at a temple at the Parhae capital site, he was fined US$250 for his transgression. "Under the CCP," he says of Beijing's view of its peripheral areas, "China will never embrace objective history."[66]

THE QING DYNASTY saw Manchuria as its home place. When the Manchus became Sinified, where did that leave the status of Manchuria? As with many frontier areas of China, destiny lay in the flux of international power. Russia was stopped from making Manchuria its protectorate only by Japan's military defeat of China (1894–1895) and of Russia (1904–1905). During the twentieth century, as Russia and Japan pressed in on a weakened China, and the Manchu Dynasty disappeared, most people in Manchuria did not see their homeland as part of any other nation, but as a place with its own identity, seeking sovereignty.[67]

[63]Song, 1998–1999, 60, 61.
[64]Byington, 2000, 19.
[65]Zhang, 2000, 7–8.
[66]Song Ki-ho, e-mail to the author, Aug. 9, 2002.
[67]Elliott, 2000, 607, 619, 639, 640.

Japan's military takeover in 1931 prejudiced the case for Manchuria's separate existence. Yet, says Prasenjit Duara, if Japan's state of Manchukuo was "imperialist in intent, it was nationalist in form."[68] Paradoxically, the period of Japanese rule gave Manchuria as strong a sense of identity as it ever had. Even the Chinese Communist Party during the 1930s used the Chinese term for Manchuria, *manzhou*, as a toponym, acknowledging its uncertain relationship to China. Said an American diplomatic dispatch from China in July 1949: "The Chinese Communists have recognized the special status of Manchuria and have kept it under a different type of government regime from that prevailing in China proper."[69]

Chiang Kai-shek was prepared to let Manchuria go to Japan, according to Chinese Communist textbooks, as a bargaining chip in his battle with Mao's Communists. The warlord Zhang Zuolin wanted to make an independent fiefdom of Manchuria, but the Japanese military beat him to it. Logic, justice, will of the people—none of these decided Manchuria's fate. The PRC takes care to wipe out any memory of Manchuria as a toponym. To Beijing, Manchuria is a building block in the new Chinese empire. Koreans, Manchus, anyone who lives in the three northeastern provinces is, by definition, "Chinese." In Manchuria as elsewhere, "Chinese" has come to mean anyone under the control of the new Chinese empire.

Sun Yat-sen opened the door to this imperial assimilation with his formulation, "the five races united in the Chinese nation" (*Zhonghua minzu*). These races were Han (as the leader), Tibetan, Manchu, Mongol, and Turkic. Sun coined another, disturbing, fascism-tinged phrase, "A Great Nationalist State" (*Daminzu zhuyi de guo*), that foreshadowed the PRC's imperial project.[70] State and a vanguard race were fused.

Duara remarks in a mischievous paraphrase of Lenin, "Anti-imperialism is the highest stage of nationalism." China learned the nation-state system from the West and the Soviet Union, in the late nineteenth and twentieth centuries, and made it the framework for a new

---

[68]Talk at Fairbank Center, Harvard University, May 14, 2001.
[69]David Wang, 1999, 416.
[70]Brødsgaard and Strand, 1998, 19–20.

Chinese empire. In the period following World War One, until the end of the twentieth century, an ideology of the nation-state became triumphant. "To join the Club, you had to become a nation," says Duara.

Garbed in the costume of a nation, the PRC seemed to be *against* imperialism. The soothing language of "autonomy," "minority nationalities," "proletarian unity," and "we will never seek hegemony" hid the magician's trick. Shouting anti-imperialism, China hid its own imperial acts. China managed to have its steady integration of Manchuria, Tibet, Xinjiang, and Inner Mongolia judged unobjectionable by much of the international community. Today, identical terms from the Qing Dynasty—"employ culture and doctrine" to "control" the peripheral peoples of the realm, and bring them to "know the laws" (*zhi guo fa*)— are considered by PRC historians suitable for dealing with Beijing's "minority nationalities."[71]

Of course, in the twenty-first century we have entered a new phase: The nation-state itself is under pressure. The sovereignty of small countries is nibbled at by various international forces. Globalization, once more, has acquired momentum. Among the major countries, only China grinds away at the identity of small nations by incorporating them into an empire, in the name of an anti-imperialist, revolutionary nation-state. "In reality," says Duara truly, "contrary to the ideology of the matter, nationalism and imperialism are very closely related."[72]

The lesson of the past is that the play of external forces, more than sense of identity within, is the key to the fate of a territory that has gone in and out of the Chinese empire. This occurred when Britain bested the Qing Dynasty and grabbed Hong Kong in 1842, and, in reverse direction, when Britain's relative decline led to a weakened will in London to hold on to Hong Kong in the 1980s. It did so when Tibet delivered a military defeat to the Tang Dynasty in 745, and, in reverse, when India and Britain caved in and allowed Beijing to claim Tibet after 1949. It did so when Chiang Kai-shek's weakness allowed the establishment of an East Turkistan state in northern Xinjiang in 1944,

---

[71]Li Shiyu, 2000, 22, 29.
[72]Talk at Harvard University, May 14, 2001.

and, turning the tables, when Stalin's maneuvers allowed Mao to incorporate all of Xinjiang into the PRC a few years later. It did so when Mao, who had told Edgar Snow that Mongolia would "automatically" be part of a shining new socialist China, found Stalin had a different plan, leading Mao, by 1952, to lamely speak of China's "border" with the "People's Republic of Mongolia."[73] Further jolts in the international balance of power surely lie ahead, and will no doubt affect China's ambiguous territories.

---

[73]Snow, 1961, 110; Takeuchi, vol. 7, 98. See also Hoshino, 2000, 112, on the role of the CCP–KMT civil war in determining Mongolia's future.

EIGHT

MARITIME EMPIRE

> [T]he big China that has existed for four thousand years has no foundation. Even if we say there is a China, it is only China in form, not in reality, because it has no foundation. . . . The foundation of a big country is its small localities. . . . It is the individual citizens who comprise the foundation of the citizenry as a whole.
>
> —*Mao Zedong, 1920*[1]

"The problem of Taiwan has to be resolved," says Beijing, and diplomats of dozens of nations echo the call. What problem, one may ask, and what solution exists to the problem as defined by the Chinese dictatorship? Does Taiwan not flourish? It is a stable democracy with the third highest per capita GDP in Asia. It ranks eleventh among the world's trading nations, despite being only forty-sixth in population. With 22 million people, it buys as much from the United States in an average year as does the PRC with 1.2 billion people. With 2% of the PRC's population, Taiwan's GDP in 2001 was nearly one-third of the PRC's GDP.[2]

Moreover, relations between Taiwan and the PRC have been a success story of peaceful coexistence since 1950. While Beijing has fought with many of its neighbors, no war has occurred between the PRC and Taiwan. "The problem of Taiwan" is Beijing's dissatisfaction with the status quo. Beijing insists on saving Taiwan from itself. Writes Nicholas Kristof in *China Wakes:* "Sheryl and I are never so optimistic about the future of mainland China as when we stroll the bustling streets of

---

[1]Schram, 1992, 546.
[2]*Far Eastern Economic Review*, Oct. 4, 2001.

Taipei."[3] The premise of this remark is explosive: Taiwan foreshadows the mainland's future. But Beijing says the PRC foreshadows Taiwan's future.

Of the ambiguous territories I broached in Chapter 7, Taiwan is a major case of a country separate from the PRC, but staunchly claimed by Beijing. The island's situation starkly focuses the imperial issue. The themes of Chapter 7 come together like a tangle of thread bunched at the eye of a needle: historical claims, imperial entitlement, democracy versus autocracy, One China, high consciousness of enemies, a "building blocks" polity versus the citizenship of individuals, and the influence of balance of power on boundaries.

SOMETIMES, as the youthful Mao Zedong avowed, the issue of belonging to China, or not belonging, hinges on popular will and social justice. Three decades prior to the founding of the PRC, Mao wrestled with his loyalty to Hunan Province on the one hand and his patriotic feeling for China on the other. Twenty-six-year-old Mao said of the unity of China: "I would give my support if there were a thorough and general revolution in China, but this is not possible." Instead, he concluded: "We cannot start with the whole, but must start with the parts."[4] Mao's ultimate goal was a revitalized China. But his key concern in 1920 was what kind of governance China should have.

The unity of China viewed as an ideal, or as an unstoppable historical locomotive, does not take away the importance of popular will and social justice. The context for the push by the CCP to include Taiwan in the newly established PRC in 1949–1950 partook of a moral dimension. Taiwan in the 1940s stood in uncertain relation to a China throwing off Japanese invasion and resolving a civil war, not least because it became a province of the Chinese empire only in 1884, and for most of the intervening years had been ruled by Tokyo. This uncertainty was eclipsed, however, by the fact that the losing party in the civil war, the

[3]Kristof and Wudunn, 1994, 347.
[4]Schram, 1992, 547.

Nationalist Party of Chiang Kai-shek, fled from southwest China to maintain a continued existence as the ROC on Taiwan.

Given Chiang's presence in Taipei, Beijing possessed support and momentum as it planned to include Taiwan in mopping up the last phases of its dynastic conquest. This was strongly suggested by the absence of any stand by the United States against the CCP's continued advance to the island of Taiwan. Washington considered the fate of the Chiang government in Taipei in the context of the final stage of the civil war that began in 1946.

The 1949–1950 context of the Taiwan issue changed dramatically when North Korea attacked South Korea. From the spring of 1950 Mao was sympathetically aware of Kim Il-sung's plans to bring his revolution to the south. "We should help Little Kim," he said to Stalin in Moscow.[5] A North Korean army was still operating with the Chinese People's Liberation Army. Kim asked for it back to aid his unification of Korea; Mao agreed. Stalin, masterful and selfish, had been pressuring Mao to be tougher with the United States since 1948, but Moscow did not want direct involvement in a Korean war. "For you [Chinese] it is possible to help the Korean people," Stalin said to Zhou Enlai as Chinese troops prepared to go into Korea, "but for us it is impossible because . . . we are not ready for the Third World War."[6]

Contemplating intervention, Mao juggled support for Kim's aggressive aims, concern for his own relations with Stalin, and an ideological conviction that consolidation of China's revolution required a revolutionary foreign policy. He did not seek a fight with the United States. In going along with Kim's plan to take Seoul, he assumed Washington would not intervene. At least he told Stalin so, hoping Stalin would also believe Washington would not intervene as Mao moved to take Taiwan. In a string of regrettable statements, President Truman and Secretary of State Dean Acheson had given Mao, Stalin, and Kim every reason to think the United States would keep its distance.[7]

---

[5]Goncharov, Lewis, and Xue, 1993, 130.
[6]Shi Zhe, 1991, 496.
[7]Chen Jian, 1994, 89, 102, 156–157, 213–215.

But the United States did intervene. Quickly, Kim Il-sung was thrown on the defensive. Both America's Korea and Taiwan policies were turned on their head by Kim's attack on South Korea. General Douglas MacArthur cemented the Korea–Taiwan connection by flying from Tokyo to Taipei to see Chiang as the Korean crisis unfolded. In a word, Taiwan's relation to the mainland changed when Beijing's reunification project gained a context broader than completion of the Chinese civil war.

After the CCP decided to intervene in Korea, Mao sent a telegram to the head of the New China News Agency, ordering him to back off from any public statement that Taiwan would be taken within a given period of time. "Please note that from now on," he wrote, "we will only speak about our intention of attacking Taiwan and Tibet, but say nothing of the timing of the attack."[8] This recently available telegram is one of the most striking proofs in diplomatic history of the power of deterrence. Mao recognized that the context of the Taiwan issue had been transformed. He, no less than MacArthur, now accepted the reality of a broad international struggle between socialist and capitalist forces. It was called the Cold War.

Taiwan's mid-twentieth-century saga repeats a pattern familiar in Chinese history. Comparable ingredients often affected the emperor's relation to Tibet, Hong Kong, Xinjiang, Mongolia, eastern Siberia, Taiwan, and other peripheral areas. Ming leaders did not think or behave as if Taiwan were part of China. Of the Qing Dynasty, John Wills writes: "The Court and Fukien officials were willing to allow the Dutch to reoccupy Taiwan, which had never been part of the Chinese empire and would be very hard to govern."[9] A millennia ago, the eastern coastal state of Wu Yueh used a non-Chinese state, the Khitans, against the Song Dynasty.[10] In our time, Taiwan, since the Korean War, has used the United States, especially, and also Japan—as the state of Wu Yueh used the Khitans—to pluck a practical freedom from a theoretically unpromising situation.

---

[8]Mao, *Jianguo yilai Mao Zedong wengao*, cable of Sept. 29, 1950.
[9]Wills, 1968, 233.
[10]Rossabi, 1983, 7.

The One China concept only got its rhetorical hands around Taiwan's neck in recent times. The Taiwan Communist Party, founded in secret in Shanghai in 1928, and affiliated with the Japan Communist Party, began its life with Taiwan independence as a plank of its "Political Program." This occurred under the influence of Lenin's strong support, backed by Mao and the Japan Communist Party, for the self-determination of peoples. Three years later, the Taiwan Communist Party (TCP) underwent a split and the reorganized party became a branch of the Chinese Communist Party. The new leaders of the TCP were all Taiwanese who held membership in the CCP as well as the TCP. After 1931 the goal of independence for Taiwan remained in its platform! A cluster of three principles was embraced: "Taiwan people" or "Taiwan nationality" (*Taiwan minzu*); "Taiwan revolution" (*Taiwan geming*); and "Taiwan independence" (*Taiwan duli*).[11]

The TCP's embrace of independence for Taiwan, backed by the Chinese Communists, was by no means merely tactical or a "first phase" to be followed by unification with China. The Political Program supported Taiwan independence with a lengthy analysis of the historical development of the Taiwan nationality, including during the period when the Qing Dynasty was the formal ruler of Taiwan. The "Chinese revolution" was discussed in the program as being quite separate from Taiwan's struggle to found a "Taiwan Republic." Chen Fangming concludes from a study of the relevant documents: "In the Chinese Communist Party's platform, resolutions, and policies [all the way from 1928 to 1943], there was never any divergence from the position that the Taiwan nationality [*minzu*] must be independent." Mao's party repeatedly called Taiwan one of the "weak and small nations" (*ruan-xiao minzu*).[12]

Beyond the deliberations of the Taiwan Communist Party, the CCP in its own councils and documents recognized Taiwan's "nationality" or "nation-hood." At the Sixth CCP Congress in 1928, the Taiwanese were spoken of as separate from the Han, as a separate race (*zhongzu*)

[11]Chen Fangming, 1998, 233–234.
[12]Chen Fangming, 1998, 219, 222, 237.

or "stock" (*zongzu*).[13] Mao's CCP put Korea and Annam (Vietnam) and Taiwan together as nationalities headed for an independent existence. In one of Mao's most important speeches of the 1930s, he five times used the phrase the "nationalities of Korea, Taiwan etc."

Here is Zhou Enlai in 1941: "We should sympathize with independence-liberation movements [*duli jiefang yundong*] of other nation-states [*minzu guojia*]. We will . . . assist the anti-Japanese movements of Korea or Taiwan, or anti-German, anti-Italian movements."[14] As for Chiang Kai-shek, his Nanjing government, the ROC, had a consulate in Taipei in the 1930s, implying Taiwan's separateness. Only after 1943, when Roosevelt, Churchill, and Chiang Kai-shek at Cairo decided that Japan, once defeated, must yield Taiwan to China, did the CCP talk of Taiwan as destined to be part of the "motherland" (China).

———————

BEYOND THE COLD WAR, a third context for the PRC's reunification agenda appeared in the 1990s. The Taiwan issue took on a dimension that transcends the bilateral ties between the PRC and various nations, even the United States, let alone "mopping up" after the 1949 revolution. As a result of bold decisions in the later 1980s by Chiang Kai-shek's son, Chiang Ching-kuo, who succeeded his father in 1975, Taiwan turned into a democracy.

People opposed to the Nationalist Party (Guomindang, or KMT) came out of prison and ran for office. Diversity of opinion appeared in the formerly monolithic press. A party-state eased its way to political pluralism. Former dissidents, exiles, and political prisoners, including a lawyer named Chen Shuibian, became prominent in a new opposition party, the Democratic Progressive Party (DPP). By 1996, after Chiang Ching-kuo's death, Taiwan conducted the first-ever direct presidential election with full adult franchise in the history of Chinese civilization. At the next presidential election, in 2000, Chen Shuibian became president of Taiwan. His DPP, not long before a bunch of semi-under-

———————

[13]Hsiao and Sullivan, 1979, 447.
[14]Hsiao and Sullivan, 1979, 448, 451, 453, 451, 454.

ground amateurs, had ended the long years of dominance by the Nationalist Party.

Taiwan had become a nation. To be sure, factors other than the coming of democracy played a role in the island's new status. A steady maturation of Taiwan's dealings with countries in the region as if it were a sovereign state took place in the years after Taipei stopped talking about "retaking the Mainland." The robust Taiwan economy proved substantially invulnerable to the Asian Financial Crisis of 1997–1998.

Meanwhile, concern grew on the part of the Association of Southeast Asian Nations (ASEAN) and Japan with Beijing's trigger-happy obduracy over the much-disputed Spratly Islands. "There is but one sovereign state in the South China Sea," runs a typical article from Beijing, "namely China. China possesses entire and complete [*wanzheng, chongfen*] jurisdiction in the southern seas region."[15] And there was the simple factor of the passage of time. The PRC argues reasonably that the ROC regime, now on Taiwan, was succeeded historically by the PRC regime in 1949. But, for the next half century, Beijing failed to take Taiwan. Here kicks in the argument of "territorial persistence."[16] Wrote Ho Ping-ti of the Qing Dynasty's dealings with surrounding powers: "The true status of any of China's peripheral areas depended on China's ability to exert effective control."[17] By the 1980s, Taiwan's "status" had changed as a result of Beijing's failure to exert effective control over it. The consequence of such long delay was compounded by the springing up of democratic institutions, through which the Taiwan electorate evolved its own point of view on the receding ROC–PRC historical struggle.

In December 1991, early in Taiwan's democratic era, after a stay on the island during the first all-Taiwan National Assembly election campaign, I wrote: "The Nationalists aren't really pushing reunification and the Progressives [DPP] aren't really pushing independence. As in other democracies, each party promotes its ideal only to the degree necessary

---

[15]Li Guoqiang, 2000, 81.
[16]Lovelace, 2000, 58.
[17]Ho, 1967, 190.

to persuade the electorate that it cares most for the true welfare of the people. . . . It is highly unlikely that Taiwan will either 'declare its independence' or unite with the mainland. The great majority of the Taiwan citizenry doesn't favor either extreme course."[18] Twelve more years of the democratic process have made the point ever more clear.

The result is an undermining of the reunification agenda of the PRC. But the Beijing party-state is blind to how democratic processes create sovereignty. It misunderstands the relation of elections to sovereignty so badly that it can say: "Sovereignty over Taiwan belongs to all the Chinese people and not to some of the people in Taiwan."[19]

In truth, where democracy sprouts, as recently in Taiwan and to a degree in Hong Kong, the rug is pulled out from under Beijing's concept of legitimacy. A string of elections in Taiwan has crystallized the sovereignty of the territory and solidified its identity as an island nation unto itself. "I must say quite simply," said President Lee Teng-hui in his office, in my hearing, on July 28, 1999, "I'm the president of a country. I must stand up for the national interest of this country."

One China, on the other hand, was spawned from the self-image of a Leninist-imperial state, an anomaly in today's world. One China is redolent of an era when the Chinese court undertook to arrange the surrounding world according to its principles. It does not fit an era when the source of change, and the roots of foreign relations, are chiefly in the internal evolution of societies.

Beijing cannot construe "interference in domestic politics" other than in imperial terms. When the Dalai Lama goes to Prague, or Washington, or Sydney, and a foreign government talks to him, that is "interference in the domestic politics of the PRC." But the principle looks different when Chen Shuibian, president of the Taiwan government since 2000, visits the United States. In 2000, when Chen stopped in Los Angeles en route to South America, Beijing demanded that President Chen not meet with any U.S. officials, including members of Congress. In their sense of imperial entitlement, the Chinese Commu-

---

[18]Ross Terrill, *Newsday,* Dec. 10, 1991.
[19]*White Paper on the One-China Principle and the Taiwan Issue* (Beijing), Feb. 2000; excerpted in *New York Times,* Feb. 21, 2000.

nists failed to see this stance as "interference in the domestic affairs of the United States."

In December 2001, President Chen gave a first-ever broadcast by an ROC president in Taiwan to a Mainland audience. Chen said his dream was to see "the leaders of the two sides shake hands." He also referred to his Fujian Province ancestry: "I hope I will have an opportunity to search for my roots one day."[20] Six months later, I asked President Chen how he would relate these two remarks should he meet Jiang Zemin. "There is no conflict between the two remarks," he replied. As he spoke, the president took from his wallet a document. "This is a copy of my birth paper," he said. "Two days before my inauguration as president, a Taiwan TV station presented it to me. Until I can investigate [in Fujian] for myself, I keep this copy in my wallet." By juxtaposing the two themes of his ancestry and his role as an elected leader, Chen Shuibian, in his radio broadcast and subsequent remarks, seemed to be shooting down the PRC's notion of One China. He is of Chinese descent, yes. But he is also the elected leader of a democracy that is not part of the PRC. "As a person of Chinese descent," he said at our meeting, "and as president of the ROC, I have to discuss with President Jiang Zemin the issues of peace and progress across the Taiwan Strait."[21]

––––––––––

THIRTY YEARS AGO I was co-speaker at a forum at Caltech in Pasadena with Peng Mingmin, law professor, Taiwan independence leader, and a pioneer of the movement that brought Chen Shuibian to power in 2000. It was an exciting period, just after President Nixon held his summit with Mao; U.S.–China relations were the success story of the decade. In the audience were middle-class Chinese-Americans highly relieved that "Communist China" was no longer the enemy. From the safe distance of California, they felt One China was a reasonable concept for Nixon to acknowledge.

––––––––––

[20] *Taipei Update,* Nov. 28, 2001.
[21] Meeting with President Chen Shuibian, as part of the 31st Sino-American Conference on Contemporary China, Presidential Palace, Taipei, June 4, 2002.

Professor Peng, who had spent time in a Chiang Kai-shek prison for his Taiwan nativist views, challenged these Chinese-Americans. "You have an image of China in your mind," he said with some passion to one questioner, "which corresponds not at all to the concrete realities of Taiwan and China. It's easy for you to call for One China," continued Peng, whom Beijing regarded as a "splittist," "but which China, and by what concrete steps will we get this [United China] of your imagination?"

To another ethnically Chinese member of the audience, Peng riposted: "Are you any less a traitor for becoming an American citizen than I am for wanting a Taiwan separate from China?" In 1972, Peng Mingmin's view was unusual in Taiwan. Today it is a majority view. This change has transformed Taiwan as an issue between Beijing and Washington.

The premise of the famous Shanghai Communiqué, signed by Nixon and Zhou Enlai in 1972, was that Chinese on both sides of the Taiwan Strait upheld One China. Mao and Chiang Kai-shek were still, in theory, fighting over the Chinese throne. That premise was no longer true by the 1990s. A third to a half of Taiwan disagreed with it. These 8–11 million people oppose reunification with the Communist regime in Beijing. The change does not affect the outlook of an imperial state, but it does sway democratic states, including Taiwan, Japan, and the United States. The three communiqués signed by Washington and Beijing in 1972, 1979, and 1982, insofar as they deal with Taiwan, have been undermined. The Taiwan they referred to was a dictatorship. Now Taiwan is a democracy. The wishes of its people have become known.

The private American policy on Taiwan in 1971–1972 differed from the public one. To the American people, the Nixon administration said in 1971 that Taiwan "is an unsettled question subject to future international resolution." This was reasonable, and not incompatible with the historic Beijing–Washington reconciliation. But in private Nixon and Kissinger denied that U.S. policy in three ways. They told Zhou Enlai that Washington accepted that Taiwan was part of China, would not support Taiwan independence, and would recognize the PRC diplomatically (by implication using the Beijing formula on One China), in

Nixon's second term.[22] Democracy in Taiwan over the past decades has left these hair-raising undertakings in the trash can.

The American leaders had been seduced by the Chinese imperial style. Awed by Mao and Zhou, the Nixon team accepted that Beijing "would never give in on principle." Actually, the Chinese state, past and present, frequently caves in to foreigners. I recall in 1964, 1971, and 1973 seeing billboards, hills, and rocks in the PRC inscribed with the characters "We Shall Certainly Liberate Taiwan" (*Women yiding yao jiefang Taiwan*). At that time, Beijing said it would never normalize relations with the United States unless all arms sales to Taiwan ceased. Later, Beijing gave up talk of "liberating" Taiwan, and established diplomatic relations with the United States while Washington continued to sell arms to Taiwan.

For all the huff and puff, it seems the public State Department position of 1971 remains a factually correct description of reality in 2003: For U.S. policy, Taiwan "is an unsettled question subject to future international resolution." Within that formula, Beijing can "unify," if it is able. Within that formula, Taiwan can continue its independent existence, if it is able. Within that formula, the United States and Japan can together, if they wish, keep the new Chinese empire from grabbing Taiwan.

Much of the "problem" of Taiwan is of the PRC's own making. It is surprising to read Robert Ross say Taiwan "is a vital interest" of China's and yet "does not entail the vital interest" of the United States.[23] Ross considers China "a conservative power." Yet we read in Beijing's defense white paper this description of the international scene: "There is a serious disequilibrium in the relative strength of countries. No fundamental change has been made in the old, unfair and irrational international political and economic order."[24] The same white paper warns about unresolved "questions left over by history." It complains about an international scene marked by "the strong bully-

[22]Mann, 1999, 33, 46, 61.
[23]Ross, 1999, 113.
[24]*China's National Defense,* 1998, 2, 3, 4, 20.

ing the weak" and "certain powers" that "impose their own will on others." A conservative outlook?

In truth, the entire balance of power in East Asia would change if Taiwan went out of existence as a separate entity. Japan's confidence in its security relationship with the United States would be reduced; the Philippines, Vietnam, and others would reconsider their view of China; parts of East Asia would look to India as a balancer for China. Yet the Chinese people have no need to absorb Taiwan. In no way is Taiwan a threat to the Mainland. Meanwhile Taiwan and the Mainland benefit each other economically. Trade between them reached US$32 billion in 2001.[25] A Taiwan that was indefinitely separate from China but non-hostile to it, as Finland was to the Soviet Union, or as Panama is to the United States, could be in Beijing's interests. Such a Taiwan, perhaps entering into a security agreement with the Mainland, would be less of a threat to China, and to the balance of power in East Asia, than a smoldering, armed-to-the-teeth, foreign-backed Taiwan.

But, over the years, we have seen that it suits the Chinese Communist state to keep the Taiwan Strait tense. It fires missiles into "splash zones" close to the northern and southern edges of Taiwan. It speaks of the Taiwan leaders in barnyard language. It gives Mainland people no details of Taiwan's elections. It amasses huge military forces in Fujian Province opposite Taiwan.

In Taiwan, the issue of relations with the Mainland has become embedded in democratic politics. In the Mainland, however, the relationship with Taiwan is a "state matter" that has nothing to do with the will of the people. It is the centerpiece of the CCP's concocted imperial project. The exiled writer Liu Binyan remarked of the Beijing leaders in the mid-1990s: "These men in their seventies and eighties are warriors. The lives, loves, happiness of hundreds of thousands of people mean nothing to them."[26] This is the point missed by Robert Ross. Absorbing Taiwan may be a "vital interest" of the Chinese Communist state, but not of Chinese society, of the Chinese *minzu* (people).

---

[25] *Taipei Journal*, editorial, April 5, 2002.
[26] Liu Binyan, conversation with the author, 1993.

Writes Louis Henkin: "In relations between nations, the progress of civilization may be seen as a movement from force to diplomacy, from diplomacy to law."[27] The receding prospects for the PRC to take Taiwan may be a case study in Henkin's point. In 1949–1950, force was the name of the game in both Beijing's reunification project and the thwarting of it following the outbreak of the Korean War. In the years embraced by the "three communiqués" of Washington and Beijing (1972–1982), the name of the game was diplomacy. In the 1990s and 2000s, since the collapse of European communism and the coming of democracy to Taiwan, law in its broadest sense has become an indispensable part of relations across the Taiwan Strait.

———————

AT THE TRANSFER of Hong Kong from British to Chinese rule in July 1997, Jiang Zemin spoke of the territory's achievements as due to "Hong Kong compatriots" and the "hinterland." No hint that British institutions played any role. Indeed, Jiang seemed to deny that Hong Kong had a history. He spoke of "six million Hong Kong compatriots who have now returned to the embrace of the motherland," as if those people had once been ruled by China. Yet when the story of British Hong Kong began, the territory was a fishing town of five thousand people. Jiang referred to the period under British rule as "one century of vicissitudes." If Hong Kong's history was simply "the humiliating state of Hong Kong under occupation," how did the territory, by the date of the handover, attain a per capita GDP ten times that of the PRC?

When Beijing reclaimed it, Hong Kong was Asia's third most prosperous society (after Japan, and very close to Singapore). As the clock struck midnight on July 1, 1997, and Hong Kong became China's, the GDP of the PRC rose 20%. Simply in the decade prior to the British departure, Hong Kong's per capita GDP more than tripled. East–West synergy had produced its finest daughter. "In Hong Kong," said a Japanese filmmaker, "East and West may not have been in love, but they were having sex."

———————

[27]Liu, 1999, 21.

The 1997 event, for Jiang, was simply a feather in the Chinese party-state's cap, a day of glory for the motherland. It was a triumph of identity politics, with race counting more than values, national glory more than individual freedom, payback above historical fact. The Chinese Communist state was expanding; Western law was in retreat.

A motif of Beijing's celebrations was the Great Wall. This was fitting. For the Great Wall symbolizes both despotism and patriotism, and the two are inextricably entwined in China. Waldron has shown the Great Wall's limited use as a barrier, but its potency as a symbol. Remove the myth of the Great Wall, and the Chinese–Barbarian gap would have been less clear-cut, as the Ming Dynasty knew. Today, remove the myth of One China, and the claim of Beijing to its empire becomes problematic, as Hu Jintao knows.

Hong Kong has little that is rooted, much that is transient. Foreign businessmen sign a contract and depart. Twelve million tourists a year come and go within a few days. The British arrived from afar to rule Hong Kong and in 1997 they departed.

The populace itself comes and goes. Hong Kong's population grew fast in the mid-twentieth century, essentially because people fled the PRC. In the later 1940s, the colony's population was 1.6 million, the same as before World War Two. With the Communist Revolution of 1949, numbers jumped. In 1952 Hong Kong had 2.25 million; in 1960, 3 million; and by 1980, 5 million. In the years leading up to Beijing's takeover in 1997, hundreds of thousands of professionals left Hong Kong for the United States, Canada, Australia, and other places. Today there are as many people (6.2 million) in Hong Kong as there are Tibetans in the PRC.

In 1944, Stalin urged Mao to grab Hong Kong while the revolution had momentum. But Mao had a subtler plan. Let Britain build it up. Keep it as a listening post on the world, and make money from it. Under the dynasties, Khitans and other Barbarians supplied the Chinese court with horses in return for tea and silk; in the second half of the twentieth century, Hong Kong supplied Beijing with hard currency in return for Guangdong chickens, vegetables, and water. Hong Kong's market, know-how, and capital was a major reason why Guangdong outstripped northern China in the first reform years, and why Shen-zhen, a special economic zone between Hong Kong and Guangdong, surged ahead even of Guangdong in the 1990s.

Unlike Tibet, Xinjiang, and Inner Mongolia, three other ambiguous territories broached in Chapter 7, all of which have regularly been the scene of violence, Hong Kong has been peaceful since the end of the Japanese occupation in the 1940s. From the 1960s, London did not expect to hold Hong Kong much longer, and from the 1980s it lacked the will to do so.

Hong Kong knew shaky moments in the Mao era. During the hunger brought on by the Great Leap Forward in 1959–1960, crowds protested in Guangdong, demanding to cross the border to British Hong Kong. Some cried out that they wished to celebrate Queen Eliz-abeth's birthday in the Crown Colony! During the Cultural Revolution of the late 1960s, the British governor of Hong Kong would not have been surprised to receive a phone call from Beijing saying the Chinese Communist army was on its way to take the colony.

But Hong Kong, a successful synergy between Chinese industrious-ness and British institutions, hung on. Turning its face away from pol-itics, the colony kept reinventing itself economically with acrobatic skill. It changed from "barren rock" (Lord Palmerston's phrase when Britain took it in 1842) to fishing township, place of refuge, modest trade entrepôt, revolving door for the Chinese revolution, cheap man-ufacturing base, financial hub, bastion of re-export trade, and mecca for shoppers and tourists. All the while it made much out of little, lacking resources and a secure outlook, responding as best it could to a world it never made.

In the end it was Britain that broached with Beijing arrangements for adjusting Hong Kong's situation, as the expiry date on the lease of part of the territory approached in the 1980s.

During the 1990s, when the atmosphere between China and both Hong Kong and Britain was poisoned by the after-stench of the Tiananmen tragedy of 1989, Beijing feared two things. Hong Kong might seek to "contaminate" the Mainland in the direction of liberty and democracy. "Well water may not intrude into river water" (*jingshui bu fan heshui*), the Communists warned, in characterizing Hong Kong's modest role in relation to the vast land to its north. Unfortunately, they seemed to think "interference" by Hong Kong in China's affairs began the moment a person in Hong Kong opened her mouth to express a belief in liberty and democracy.

China, with more justification, also was upset when Britain, at the eleventh hour, brought in liberalizations designed to protect the territory from the eventual chill winds of Beijing rule. Zhou Nan, the chief Beijing official in Hong Kong, complained to me in 1990 that Britain was "playing tricks," by talking of the need to "internationalize" Hong Kong in preparation for its future, and of its concern for "popular will" in Hong Kong. It was true that London, with the appointment of Chris Patten as governor of Hong Kong in 1993, struck a new note, pushing democracy and grand projects like a US$20 billion airport. The reason was British nervousness at how Hong Kong and the world would stomach the arrival of Chinese rule in 1997, given the shadow Tiananmen had cast on the early 1990s.

"China is terrified of elections," the Hong Kong democratic leader Martin Lee said to me at that time. "The Beijing leaders are more afraid of us [in Hong Kong] than we are of them." I expressed some doubt that pushing for democracy in Hong Kong during the 1990s could lead to anything but disappointment after a nondemocratic Beijing took over Hong Kong in 1997. "Democracy in Hong Kong can be like a paper door in a Japanese restaurant," Lee responded. "You can walk through it; no one can stop you if you really want to. But if you respect the people on the other side of the door, you will knock and ask permission before you go through. The same with Hong Kong and China."

Piquant to recall that the one British governor of Hong Kong—prior to Chris Patten—who wanted to move the colony toward democracy, Alexander Grantham, finally desisted in 1952 in part because of worries that Chinese politics could infiltrate an elected Hong Kong legislature!

The 1990s saw a drama of words and laws, behind which lay a looming change of imperial grip. Never before had a nation (in this case

Britain) handed over to another preexisting nation (in this case China) not just a strip of land, but an entire flourishing society, which knew years in advance the exact date of its transfer. By contrast, in Tibet, Xinjiang, and Mongolia, the struggle for control was often unprogrammed and violent.

For decades some countries worried that China might try to take another wayward piece of the Qing maritime empire, Taiwan, but it turned out that Hong Kong, long unprovocative toward Beijing and concerned only with business, "went back" first to Mainland rule. Hong Kong, which had thrived under British law, was sentenced to a new future by British law. Taiwan, which had long lived by the sword, was enjoying independence thanks to the sword.

Is Hong Kong today in a "tributary" (*chao gong*) situation vis-à-vis Beijing? Historically, directly ruled territories paid tax to the Chinese dynastic court; independent territories sent tributary missions. Hong Kong, still a golden goose for the Mainland economy, or at least for the pockets of some of its officials, seems in between. Beijing treats the territory's chief executive (CE) as a provincial official. Jiang viewed the handover ceremony as being about China more than about Hong Kong. When a prickly issue, such as how to handle the protesting *Falungong*, comes up, Beijing feels Hong Kong's policy toward the idiosyncratic Buddhists must serve, not necessarily Hong Kong's interests, but the security and stability of the central state.

In Beijing in October 2000, just prior to a meeting with Tung Chee-hwa, CE of Hong Kong, Jiang met with a roomful of Hong Kong media. The journalists knew that Jiang had backed Tung for a second term in his post, which replaces the British governorship, far in advance of the "election" process for the CE within Hong Kong. Prior to China's takeover of Hong Kong in 1997, Jiang had said the CE of Hong Kong will be "elected by the Hong Kong people."

A reporter from Hong Kong's Cable TV station asked Jiang if it was "an imperial order" from Beijing that Tung ought to be reappointed. Jiang rose from his chair. "You pressmen need to learn more. You know much about the West. I tell you—I've seen a lot. Which part of the West have I not been to?" This was not an answer to Cable TV's question, but it did display Jiang's mixture of arrogance and insecurity. "I am not a journalist," said the dictator, jabbing his finger toward the Hong Kong visitors, "but I must tell you the truth about life." He threw in a threat: "If your reports are not accurate enough, you will have to be held responsible."

Communist engineer Jiang said he gave no imperial order and the Hong Kong media, "good for nothing" in his view, "should not criticize me."[28] He overlooked that for the president of China to back Tung for a second term was to make it impossible for any other candidate to become CE. It was unhappily close to the "project from above" approach followed in Tibet, Xinjiang, and Inner Mongolia.

During his tirade Jiang said: "Hong Kong belongs to the Government of the People's Republic of China!" Beyond contradicting the notion of the CE being "elected," Jiang had been rattled by the (all too pertinent) use of the word "imperial." He had condescended to the Hong Kongers, behaving as a jumpy autocrat, an emperor addressing lesser folk from the fringes.

———

"Use the Western Regions to rule the Western Regions," ran a dictum of the Qing Dynasty, and today Beijing applies a southern version of it to Hong Kong. In "using Hong Kong people to run Hong Kong," Communist Beijing displays its least unsuccessful technique of rule over a peripheral area so far. Initially, in 1997, the new CE kept on twenty-two of the twenty-five cabinet secretaries, the civil service heads of the Hong Kong government's departments, from the British regime. So far, despite apparent pressure on the CE to blunt civil service independence, Beijing has generally supervised Hong Kong with the "loose rein" that wise emperors chose for distant regions. Tung Chee-hwa has regrettably reduced the role of the English language in schools and increased the role of government in the Hong Kong economy, but it is not clear he did so under Beijing pressure. One hears folk

———

[28] *South China Morning Post*, Oct. 28, 2000.

in Guangdong, Xinjiang, and other provinces say they would like Hong Kong's "one country, two systems" status for themselves.

Different ways exist to handle heterogeneity within a single political form, even for authoritarian Beijing, and it would be agreeable to think of Hong Kong as a pattern to be followed in Tibet, Xinjiang, and Inner Mongolia. In Hong Kong, Beijing has gone outside the box in showing how a Leninist state can handle a peripheral area. But few truths can be learned about the new Chinese empire from the Hong Kong case. The barren rock turned modern city-state, unlike all other peripheral areas with "autonomous" status, was far ahead of the rest of the PRC in standard of living when it entered the Communist *jia*. And Hong Kong is more than 90% Han, unlike most of the other ambiguous territories.

So far, for Beijing, Hong Kong has been an easy morsel to digest, with its prosperity and legacy of effective political, legal, and educational institutions. Moreover, Beijing will continue to walk on eggshells in dealing with Hong Kong because it wants to impress Taiwan with the good points of "autonomy." Digest the duck, then reach for the side of beef. In truth, so far, Hong Kong may have Taiwan to thank for its relative independence from the grasping Beijing party-state.

One respect in which Hong Kong differs from other "autonomous" territories now within the PRC is that influence between it and Beijing is two-way. In Tibet, Xinjiang, and Inner Mongolia, the question is whether Beijing can hold on to a heterogeneous fringe as it modernizes. In Hong Kong, the question is whether Beijing can digest a modernized city-state without upsetting its own health. Hong Kong offers capital and skills, but it also poses a problem not posed by Tibet, Xinjiang, and Inner Mongolia. Beijing fears winds of liberalization from the direction of Hong Kong. In this respect a shadow falls on Hong Kong. If it proceeds further toward democracy, peril may arise as Beijing sees the "well" polluting the "river." Too good to be a model, Hong Kong may be good enough to be a danger.

A synergy between Chinese civilization and foreign forces, Hong Kong is a test of the new Chinese empire's ability to withstand the influence of globalization. In the past, influences on the Chinese court included Buddhism, the Mongols, the Manchus, the Soviet way; now comes the international economy of high tech and open flow of information. Hong Kong's way of life is seen by some influential people in Beijing as heterodox to Chinese Communist values. This is quite different from the cultural and racial issue in Tibet, Xinjiang, and Inner Mongolia. Hong Kong does not threaten the Chinese way, as the non-Han areas may appear to do. But its experience with capitalism and the cosmopolitan international economy threatens Chinese Communist autocracy.

It is unlikely that the Hong Kong tail will wag the PRC dog. In the 1980s and 1990s, the lines of influence ran this way: The adjacent special economic zone of Shenzhen learned from Hong Kong, Guangdong learned from Shenzhen, and the north and west of China learned from Guangdong. But Hong Kong's magic as the lofty peak of the Chinese realm derived from its being outside the PRC. Wealth and power were separate in British Hong Kong. Now the territory is within the Chinese *jia* and wealth and power are merging. Freedom cannot but shrink. In 2002 the squeezing out of top journalists already began.

In his quest for the meaning of Chineseness, historian Wang Gungwu finds that Hong Kong Chinese, prosperous, modern, and free, "can claim to have developed their own version of a new Chineseness. . . . The question is, will they be rewarded for that contribution? Or will they have to pay a price for having gone their own way?" In the end Wang Gungwu, who has lived in Malaysia, Australia, Hong Kong, and Singapore, concludes that, maybe, "the Chineseness of China will always be considered the only authentic kind, and those outside must choose to return or forever confront their dilemmas of place and practice."[29] If so, this would confirm the Beijing state as arbiter of the soul of every Chinese person.

Under what circumstances could the present stability and prosperity in Hong Kong continue for a long time? A formidable list of conditions must all pertain: ongoing economic growth in the PRC; calm in Tibet, Xinjiang, and Inner Mongolia; Japan–China relations remaining

---

[29]Wang Gungwu, 1999, 127, 129.

cordial; no crisis in the Taiwan Strait that requires neighbors to choose between Beijing and Taipei; no reversal of the devolution from Beijing that gives Guangdong room to breathe and prosper. Most important, China must give up its "fifty-year deadline" for thrusting the medicine of socialism down Hong Kong's throat.

A PARADOX about China early in the twenty-first century is that it is more secure than for centuries, yet its mood is agitated, strident, and fearful. It talks of "splittists," locks people up for uttering words that question the unity of the Chinese empire, and even says "anti-China forces" put the nation's survival in doubt. It is true that China lives in an unenviable environment, with land borders of 22,000 kilometers, a coastline of 18,000 kilometers, and twenty close neighbors, fourteen contiguous and six separated by slim stretches of sea. But China's jumpiness is ultimately due to the Chinese party-state's fear of democracy and national disunity, and its understanding of the relation between the two.

To Beijing, the decline and fall of the Soviet Union showed that political liberalization endangers national unity. To a degree, the reform movement during the last decades of the Qing Dynasty sends the same message to the CCP. Gorbachev did not intend *perestroika* to lead to the dissolution of the Soviet Union. Kang Youwei did not mean the Hundred Days of reform in 1898 to undermine the Qing. Yet both political liberalizations had unintended and drastic consequences for national unity.

A second connection between political liberalization and the CCP's view of the unity of the realm has been demonstrated within China each time a post-Mao leader got to the brink of political reform. When Hu Yaobang in 1986 encouraged open-ended political reforms, Deng decided these would threaten the CCP's grip on its realm. Three years later, during the Tiananmen crisis, Zhao Ziyang, whom Deng had chosen to replace the "weak" Hu, indulged the pro-democracy students enough to convince Deng he was "splitting" the CCP and the country. Deng dismissed both political liberalizers.

In 1987, Communist Party chief Zhao Ziyang, pressed by Hong Kong journalists about China's plans for Hong Kong, said with agitation: "What is it that scares you so much?" Zhao had signed the Joint Declaration with Margaret Thatcher in 1984 that laid plans for the 1997 transfer, promised a "high degree of autonomy" for Hong Kong, and an unchanged socioeconomic system for "fifty years." But Zhao, two years after his remark to the Hong Kong journalists, was purged by Deng Xiaoping for "splitting the party" in the wake of the crushing of the student democracy movement in 1989. Perhaps Zhao in his disgraced state understood better than at the 1987 press conference why the prospect of Communist Party rule scared many Hong Kongers.

Taiwan and Hong Kong offer a third connection—in Beijing's perception—between political liberalization and the unity of the realm. Large numbers of people in both Taiwan and Hong Kong would approve of being part of China if the Chinese polity were democratic. Likewise, but in reverse, the CCP sees the issue of unity as inseparable from that of its authoritarian political system. In the 1990s, for the first time in history, democracy made a major, successful appearance within Chinese civilization. For the authoritarians in Beijing, this stirring of freedom in China's maritime empire was even more appalling than the coming of democracy to East Europe and Russia.

Taiwan and Hong Kong are not neighbors with a Chinese background, in the CCP's eyes, but the southeastern maritime fringe of the PRC. They are embracing ideas of freedom and democracy that are alien to the Chinese socialist *jia*. Water from the "well" threatens to pollute the "river." It was no surprise, indeed it was impeccably logical, that Beijing called Lee Teng-hui's commitment to electoral politics in Taiwan "separatism." In result, if not in direct intent, it was exactly that.

Ethnic Chinese democrats in Taiwan, Hong Kong, and other places evoke didactic tirades from Beijing. Lee Teng-hui and Chen Shuibian in Taiwan, Martin Lee in Hong Kong, the pro-democracy veteran Wei Jingsheng in exile in New York, all are a pain in the stomach for the Communist party-state. Their offense is their existence as Chinese. Politically, they are outside the Chinese household's orthodoxy. The CCP knows that a substantial degree of individuation exists in Taiwan and Hong Kong, and it fears the growth of the same phenomenon in the cities of the PRC.

Well may Beijing be afraid. The Chinese party-state does not represent Chinese society, but takes its mandate from a Marxist-concocted "history," the contemporary manifestation of "heaven." This is the irreducible problem of legitimation of a government that has never been elected. On the one hand, Taiwan has a government based on the sovereignty of the people. "Our decision-making mechanism here operates from the bottom up," said President Chen Shuibian, "and the public has much say in this process."[30] On the other hand, the Beijing government's legitimacy is the bedraggled Four Absolutes of a failed Marxism.

It is likely that any future U.S. administration, and most of the American people, will continue to favor a democracy-plus-deterrence approach to Taiwan policy. The starting point is that any "reunification" of Taiwan with China depends on the will of the people involved. As an expansionist project for the glory of the Chinese state, it is not attractive. The burden of proof will be on those who would allow Taiwan to go out of existence to show why this would be preferable to the current situation. Only one context exists for a reunification not contrary to the interests of the United States and China's neighbors: if sovereignty of the people pertained in the Mainland as it does in Taiwan.

The unfolding drama of democratization within and beyond Chinese civilization will continue to have a bracing and unpredictable effect on international affairs. A multilateralization of the Taiwan issue within the Asia–Pacific community will also occur. Taiwan is not only an American concern. The survival and success of the Taiwan democracy is important for the peace and prosperity of East Asia as a whole. The challenge for Washington is to coax a coalition of Asia–Pacific countries to jointly take a stance, in the name of true stability in East Asia, against any involuntary change in the situation of Taiwan.

---

[30]Video remarks to Council on Foreign Relations, New York, Oct. 16, 2000, cited in *Taipei Update*, Nov. 3, 2000.

If we forget the balance of power and practice naive engagement, Beijing will take advantage of our innocence to combine mercantilism with expanded international influence. If we follow a policy of clear-eyed engagement, maintaining an equilibrium in East Asia, centered on the alliances with Japan, Korea, Australia, and others, two processes will occur. Increasing economic interdependence will continue to put pressure on China's autocratic political system. And Beijing will hesitate to expand its maritime empire because the United States stands in the path.

NINE

STEPPE EMPIRE

In building the Great Wall, China sought to keep its own people in. Wrote Lattimore: "From early times the Chinese, when they penetrated too deeply into the steppe environment, were likely to break away from the main body of the nation." But, in the south, "the Chinese never broke away from China but added to it new territories, whose peoples they recruited and converted gradually into Chinese." Thus was Guangdong Sinified during the Tang Dynasty, Fujian and Jiangxi during the Song Dynasty, and Guangxi, Yunnan, and Guizhou "pacified" during the Ming. The south became "an open frontier of indefinite depth," Lattimore went on, while the north was (and is) a frontier "artificially closed but never quite successfully closed."[1]

"Chinese Turkistan," as today's western province of Xinjiang was called by foreigners during the Qing Dynasty and the first half of the twentieth century, formed the western end of the steppe, with Manchuria at the eastern end. In between was Mongolia, epicenter of the alien way of life of the inland China–periphery. The key to the steppe was "the control of animals by men."[2] Cattle, sheep, horses: from each sprang a variant form of nomadic life. Animals were the "Detroit" and the "Boeing" of the steppe's economic history.[3] Tibet, overlooking

---

[1]Lattimore, 1962, 23.
[2]Lattimore, 1962, 23.
[3]Edward Friedman, communication to the author, July 29, 2002.

China from the southwest, was a late-blooming part of the frontier with special traits lent by geography and religion.

Thanks to the roll of the dice of power politics, and the divide-and-rule policies of Stalin and Mao, Tibet, Xinjiang, and Inner Mongolia have been repackaged as provinces of China, the three largest in the PRC. This is recent and perverse. An illustration of the illogic is that more than 4 million of the 6 million Tibetans in the PRC do not live in "Tibet," as Beijing has drawn the boundaries between the "Tibet Autonomous Region" and other Chinese provinces. Stalin taught his Chinese pupils well.

Like the Russians, but unlike the British and French, the Chinese did not carve out their empire "overseas." Russians and Chinese acquired territory along their own frontiers. They practiced what Michael Khodarkovsky calls "organic colonialism," a colonialism shaped largely by a defensive need to "secure and stabilize" the empire's borderlands.[4] The result, writes Alexander Chubarov of the Russian case, was that "metropolis and empire became territorially indistinguishable."[5]

The Orthodox Christian faith (in the Russian case) and the Confucian Way (in the Chinese case) were the norm in metropolis and frontier alike. Imperial Britain never allowed Ceylon or Hong Kong to impinge on Britain's self-image; nor was the French sense of self changed by the acquisition of Senegal or Tahiti. But Chinese and Russian consciousness was deeply affected by the presence of diverse peoples on various sides. "The empire *was* their mother country," says Chubarov of the Russians.[6] So it was with China.

The Chinese empire was never quite *seen* as an empire by Beijing. Because it was not "overseas," it could (and can) be seen as the buffer zone of China, just as Siberia and Manchuria were intended to be Russia's buffer zone. In such circumstances, there is a frontier but few rational boundaries. Of the Altai region of Xinjiang today, Millward

[4]Khodarkovsky, 2002, 229.
[5]Chubarov, 1999, 206, 201, 205.
[6]Chubarov, 1999, 206.

says, "a jeep carrying Chinese officials drives round, they may see you [a traveler] and ask for your papers, or they may miss you, and you don't know what country you are in."[7]

WHAT IS TODAY CALLED Central Asia, with its largely Turkic civilization, has been China's front door for most of the last 2,500 years. Turfan, an oasis city now in western China, was "the Shanghai of the overland approach [from the Near East] to China."[8] North of India, south of Russia, and east of Persia, Central Asia gave China trouble, yet also formed a bridge to the Middle East and Europe. By contrast, the Pacific Ocean flank was of little strategic import to the Chinese dynasties until the eleventh hour of British arrival and the rise of the United States.

The United States has long yawned at the Muslim world of Central Asia. The PRC has long felt the West poorly appreciates Beijing's security worries on its inward flank. Uzbekistan, Kazakstan, Tajikistan, Turkmenistan, and Kyrgyzstan, all left involuntarily to their own devices by the collapse of the Soviet Union, have felt distant from the neon lights of world politics and neglected by Washington.

The terrorist attacks of September 11, 2001, canceled all this. Thereafter, Washington grew active in shaping the next phase in Central Asia and South Asia. Tashkent, Samarkand, Peshawar, and other ancient Muslim cities, once the world's crossroads, returned to the stage for an encore. And Beijing saw an opportunity to win sympathy for its undemocratic but arguably successful "building blocks" approach to unity and security in Xinjiang and other frontier zones. Stunningly, it cooperated to a degree with Bush's war on terrorism.

In 2001–2002, so gravely did Beijing take its imperial role, that it compromised on substantial points in return for a hoped-for buttressing of its empire. The U.S. military swarmed over Afghanistan, halfway house between South Asia and Central Asia, which borders the PRC.

---

[7] Panel at Association for Asian Studies annual meeting, Washington, D.C., April 2002.
[8] Lattimore, 1962, 179.

Japan, in response to the same crisis, asserted a wider role for Japanese troops around the globe. Russia, which in the preceding years had stood with China as supervising gatekeeper of Central Asia, greased the path for American military operations launched from Uzbekistan and Tajikistan.

This looked like a Beijing nightmare come true: NATO on the border of Xinjiang. U.S. encirclement of a vulnerable PRC flank. Japan spreading its military wings once more. Afghanistan a client of the "hegemonists." Moscow and Washington in each other's arms. But a pearl of great price attracted Jiang Zemin. It concerned the pivot of Eurasia, China's "Xinjiang Uighur Autonomous Region."

XINJIANG TAKES UP one-sixth of the PRC map. It borders eight nations, and is larger than all of Britain, France, Spain, and Italy. In this land rich in oil, tin, mercury, copper, iron, uranium, and lead, four cultural worlds abut: Han, Mongol, Turkic, and Tibetan. One example of the entanglement is Lamaist Buddhism in Tibet and Mongolia, to either side of Xinjiang; the "Dalai" in Dalai Lama is a Mongol word, and the 4th Dalai Lama was a Mongol.

Starting in the fourteenth century, after the fall of the Mongol (Yuan) Dynasty, Islam made huge strides in Xinjiang. Although Buddhism and other faiths remained, by the seventeenth century the area was thoroughly Islamicized.[9] Like Christianity and Judaism, Islam "sprang from a culture that attempted to coordinate the two societies of pastoralism and the oasis and to create a community of outlook in town and tent and field, between trader and peasant and herdsman."[10] That was China's problem with it. Islam became rooted in the desert-plus-oases of Xinjiang because it offered a social sinew that Confucianism could not match.

Most of the Turkic people in Xinjiang are Uighur. Now numbering nine million, the Uighurs became prominent in the region in the sev-

---

[9]James Millward, communication to the author, Oct. 11, 2002.
[10]Lattimore, 1962, 80–81.

enth century. In 744 they took Mongolia. Later they retreated to their present habitat, leading a partly nomadic life, but practicing some agriculture. A people of notable musical and literary flair, they are nonfanatical Muslims of the Sunni persuasion.

People in Beijing and Shanghai routinely remark, and Chinese children learn in school, that Xinjiang has been China's since the Han. The truth is different. For a thousand years from the eighth century, China-based polities exercised some influence, but no control over the Xinjiang area as a whole. It was the Qing Dynasty that staked out "East Turkistan" for China, and Stalin who secured it for Mao's China. In the Muslim view, the Chinese are interlopers. To name the area Xinjiang, "New Border," as the Qing did, was an insult to Uighurs long resident in the Tarim Basin and Turfan area. Of course, the Qing's choice of "New Border" also showed Xinjiang had *not* been China's since the Han Dynasty.

People in eastern China have little idea how colonial is the atmosphere in Xinjiang (and Tibet). Mao called the Soviet Union's presence in Xinjiang in the 1930s "colonialism." Was it so different from the PRC grip? Selective memory stores up danger, just like the fictions of dynasties that declared Barbarians "obedient" when they were hostile (discussed in Chapter 3).

The modern history of Xinjiang and its environs recalls Julian Huxley's remark: "A 'nation' is a society united by a common error as to its origin and a common aversion to its neighbors." In the nineteenth century, Russia and Britain each tried to influence politics in Xinjiang. In the early twentieth century, Turkey backed pan-Turkism in the area. Most dramatically, in the 1940s the Soviet Union encouraged Muslims in the Ili region of northwestern Xinjiang to declare independence from (Chiang Kai-shek's) China.

Across the border, Stalin mixed and matched "republics" in Central Asia, by the 1920s part of the Soviet Union, like a child with a cutout book. He evidently believed that to multiply Turkic identities, including Kazak, Kirghiz, and Uighur, then shuffle them to ensure irrational borders, would forestall pan-Turkism. A Xinjiang warlord of the 1930s, and later Mao as well, learned "minority policy" from Stalin, and rearranged the non-Han peoples in western China to minimize separatism.

As Xinjiang in the nineteenth century was "the most rebellious territory in the Qing empire,"[11] so today, resistance to Beijing's policies in Xinjiang, mainly by Uighurs, is constant. The East Turkistan People's Party, a pro-independence group based outside China, claims to have 60,000 members and 178 underground branches inside Xinjiang.[12]

Doak Barnett wrote that Xinjiang "was, historically, more associated with Central Asia than with China."[13] This is China's Xinjiang problem. During the 1990s, the Taliban regime in Kabul trained a number of militant Muslims from Xinjiang, whose aim is to eject China from Xinjiang and restore the independent state of East Turkistan, which existed as recently as 1945. "The situation in Xinjiang is the main element in China's Afghanistan policy," a Chinese Central Asia specialist said in October 2001.[14] Beijing's efforts with carrot and stick to dissuade the Taliban from meddling in Xinjiang had not solved all problems. By the time 9/11 arrived, the PRC had good reason to wish the Taliban into the trash can of history. That is why Jiang Zemin spoke up for Bush's drive against terrorism.

———————————

IN XINJIANG, we see apartheid with Chinese characteristics. Towns and streets all have Chinese names, unreadable for most Uighurs. The Han wear the uniforms. All college textbooks are in Chinese. Han regulations strangle the life of the mosques; the Muslim doctrine, "pure and true," is often a cry in the wilderness. Han officials pay Chinese females money if they marry a Uighur—not an everyday occurrence—thus contributing to the melting away of Uighur identity. No one from Xinjiang is permitted to study in Iran or Pakistan. "The Uighur people have suffered for years under Chinese discrimination and oppression," said Abdulhekim, executive chairman of the East Turkistan Center in

———————————

[11]Fletcher, 1978, 90.
[12]*Taipei Times*, Oct. 11, 1999.
[13]Barnett, 1993, 343.
[14]*Far Eastern Economic Review*, Oct. 4, 2001.

Istanbul. "The ethnic hatred is like water boiled to 100 degrees and could explode at any moment."[15]

Hundreds of "splittists" are arrested in a typical month. A sizeable batch of these militant Muslims is executed every few months.[16] For their sympathy for the Muslim cause in Xinjiang, Beijing periodically protests to Turkey, Uzbekistan, Saudi Arabia, and Kazakstan. But most neighboring countries are afraid to give assistance to Xinjiang rebels. "Uighurs and the local population in Xinjiang want the Turkic-speaking states to help them," said the Uzbekistan president in a candid moment in 1998. "If we support this aim, our relations with the great China might be destroyed tomorrow."[17]

On a trip to Xinjiang in 1997, I found a political atmosphere like eastern China during the Mao years. The radio and newspapers spoke of Mao Zedong Thought, "class struggle," and the danger of enemies undermining the PRC. The CCP's fear of national disunity reaches maximum intensity in Xinjiang. While in Turfan, in the central part of the province, I turned on the official TV News (there is no other) and heard an editorial in Chinese: "Every friend of ours in religious circles should recognize that only the Chinese Communist Party represents the interests of the people of all ethnic groups." This is the imperial voice, abstract, dogmatic, divorced from reality.

In 2001, Beijing detected its antiterrorist, pro-imperial opportunity in a crack in the logic of the U.S.-led war. President Bush and most Americans saw themselves striking against broad forces of unfreedom. Beijing saw the war against terrorism as a defense of the unity of China. In addition to the common interest in opposing Islam-influenced terrorism, Beijing benefited from a certain opportunism in America's eclectic choice of partners in the antiterrorist coalition. Nondemocratic leaders were embraced by Washington, among them Pakistan's military dictator—and Jiang Zemin.

Jiang joined the antiterrorism coalition because he saw a chance to strengthen his control over Xinjiang and further his ambitions to take

---

[15] *Taipei Times,* Oct. 11, 1999.
[16] *Kaifeng* (Hong Kong), July 1996, 39–40.
[17] Becquelin, 2000, 71.

Taiwan. In Kashgar, Yining, and other Xinjiang cities, where Muslims, as a gesture of dissent, set their watches two hours earlier than Chinese imperial time laid down by Beijing, hearts sank as Jiang joined the antiterrorist drive in 2001, declaring that the world might finally grasp China's "splittist" problem in Xinjiang.

Xinjiang and Taiwan! Separated by two thousand miles, like book-ends on either side of China proper, of which both are wary. Chalk and cheese in way of life, economic structure, and standard of living. One attuned to Mecca and the call of the minaret, the other to the capital-ist zones of the Pacific. But the Communist Party in Beijing sees itself as the rightful ruler of both.

The two bookends adopt opposite strategies toward Beijing. Taiwan advances separatism without overtly questioning Chinese imperial unity. Uighur militants seek separation, some using violent methods, while objecting to Chinese imperial unity, but so far without success. Abdulhekim of the East Turkistan Center in Istanbul has signaled that trouble in the Taiwan Strait would be accompanied by uprising in Xin-jiang. "If China attacks Taiwan at four o'clock in the morning," he said, "we will have an uprising at three o'clock."[18]

As of this writing, we do not know how enduring the new post-9/11 political reality will be. The PRC is by no means in the terrorist camp. But neither is it in the liberal and democratic camp, the chief target of Al Qaeda. For the CCP, the place of Xinjiang, Tibet, and Taiwan as building blocks within the PRC has nothing to do with the wishes of the people in those "provinces"; it is not a project from below but an imperative from above. Time will tell whether Beijing, where the untested Hu Jintao has taken over the top CCP post from Jiang Zemin, really can use Bush's antiterrorist war to solidify the new Chi-nese empire.

WHY (LONG PRIOR TO 9/11) has the PRC had more troops in Xinjiang—one million—than before the Soviet Union collapsed? It

---

[18] *Taipei Times*, Oct. 11, 1999.

cannot be because of an enhanced foreign threat in the 1990s. India–China ties were less tense in the 1990s than for decades. The five new republics of Central Asia pose fewer problems to China than the Soviet Union did. No, it is the task of *securing empire* that explains the militarization of Xinjiang, as well as Tibet, Inner Mongolia, and other places. The Qing Dynasty built a similar framework of colonial control, with similar anxiety and expense.

A Qing official declared, "The center gives up people to benefit the west, and the west gives up wealth to benefit the center."[19] This is the logic of Jiang Zemin's 2000 campaign to "develop the west." In the 1830s, scholar-official Wei Yuan proposed flooding Xinjiang with Chinese people. "To call in Chinese people and turn this rich loam into China proper," he wrote, "would greatly ease the exercise of our authority and greatly increase our profit." This policy has been aptly called "defense by assimilation,"[20] and it is Beijing's policy today. The twenty-first century "profit" will come, if at all, mainly from oil. Xinjiang's economic strategy is "one black, one white," meaning oil plus cotton.

This "defense by assimilation" policy has boosted the Han population of Xinjiang from 5% in 1940 to 40% today. The Uighurs, in their own country, are now but one of the fifty-six nationalities of the large family of China. Many feel swamped. Runs an irreverent Uighur quip, "If they [the Han] all stood on the Great Wall and pissed down, we Uighurs would be washed away."

"[A]s the numbers of [Chinese] soldiers and people increase over time," wrote a Qing Dynasty official of Xinjiang in 1827, "the Muslim's strength will gradually weaken, and naturally they will no longer entertain ulterior aspirations."[21] A Beijing historian, writing about Qing Dynasty policies of controlling non-Han peoples by "revivifying culture and doctrine" (*xing wenjiao*) and "making the [indigenous ones] know the national law" (*shi renmin zhi guofa*), adds, "these were efficacious measures, and they also have a role today."[22] For the CCP as for the

---

[19]Millward, 1998, 241.
[20]Millward, 1998, 244.
[21]Millward, 1998, 227.
[22]Li Shiyu, 2000, 28, 29.

Qing, economic development is intended to serve a strategic purpose. That does not mean the economic development is unwelcome. Xinjiang has gone ahead, if less swiftly than coastal China. Beijing claims that life expectancy rose from 33 years in the early 1950s to 63 years by 1998.[23]

During Qing rule over Xinjiang, exchange of gifts between the territory and Beijing began a continuum at the other end of which lay warfare. In between came commerce, internal immigration, religious rules, map-drawing, and bargaining over official appointments. A similar continuum of modes of control exists today. For instance, Beijing has been generous (until recently) in granting concessions to Uighurs on birth control. It has been tough in closing mosques where "splittist" talk takes place. During the Qing, there arose a continuum of modes of resistance to Beijing's control, from deception to rebellion. The expense of subjugating non-Chinese peoples, occasional distractions from the maritime flank, and bouts of Beijing apathy about non-Chinese areas all countered the imperial aspiration to hold any territory once stamped as belonging to the emperor. Similar strains put a question mark over Beijing's grip on Xinjiang in 2003.

Unlike Tibet (and most of the potentially defecting Russian regions), which has "nowhere to go," Xinjiang has millions of people with racial, religious, or personal connections in nearby Tajikistan, Kyrgyzstan, Kazakstan, and Uzbekistan. The CCP is ill-placed to handle this issue, because it practices an Us-and-Them condescension both with its non-Han peoples and with the Central Asian republics.

Even little Kyrgyzstan, the smallest of the former Soviet portions that border China, sometimes allows its irritation with Beijing's imperial voice to show. During 1997 China protested to the Kyrgyz foreign ministry about the newspaper *Res Publica*'s reporting of Uighur riots in Xinjiang. Beijing spoke of "impudent interference in China's internal affairs," and claimed the paper, published in the Kyrgyz capital of

---

[23]Becquelin, 2000, 67–68.

Bishkek, had "seriously offended the feelings of the Chinese people." This is the normal response of the new Chinese empire to any objective reporting of its internal realm.

But, surprisingly, *Res Publica*, like the occasional Barbarian in dynastic times who shot back at the Chinese court, replied with backbone. The newspaper said it "reserves the right to publish materials without sharing the author's opinion and also publishes opinions (sic) expressing opposing opinions." Impishly, *Res Publica* said it was willing to publish an article from the Chinese embassy in Bishkek, describing conditions in Xinjiang, so long as it "does not insult the feelings of the peoples living in Kyrgyzstan."[24]

So far, CCP rule over Xinjiang is the second longest in Chinese imperial history, exceeded only by the century of Qing control that ended with the rebellions of the 1860s. Sustained independence has proved difficult for Xinjiang. In the 1940s, when the Soviet Union encouraged a separate state, Stalin had mixed motives and he soon pulled the rug out from underneath the struggling regime. He manipulated the Turkic leaders in Xinjiang in order to get the Chiang Kaishek government to accept the terms of Yalta.[25] As the power balance tipped toward Mao, the CCP, Stalin, and the leadership of the "Three Districts Revolution" in Xinjiang juggled ideological categories to fit a new reality.[26] Beijing drew a veil over the ethnic elements, including anti-Han feeling, involved in the Three Districts regime.[27] It conveniently said that regime was aimed against the "Guomindang reactionaries and the imperialists." In a word, the cause of East Turkistan independence became an international football.

Beijing's repression deepens Uighur resentment of the Chinese, yet it also erodes sympathy for the separatists. "We just want to make money and live in peace," a young Uighur businessman in Kashgar said in December 2001. "The separatists have brought pressure on every-

---

[24]Burles, 1999, 56–57.
[25]Benson, 1990, 136–147; David Wang, 1999, 18.
[26]Xu Yuqi, 1998, 1, 259, 260–261, 264.
[27]David Wang, 1999, 12–13.

one."[28] Modernization, however, can be a two-edged sword. As Xinjiang becomes more prosperous and more important to China, the options of the Uighurs may grow. The Deng era in some ways spurred ethnic identity, and brought indirect religious revival. An Islamic college in Xi'an began to offer courses in "Muslim entrepreneurialism." A Muslim who prospered could finally make the trip to Mecca. Money can bring mobility, self-esteem, group pride, and a sense of an open door westward.

Any "pure and true" claim is a challenge to Marxist dogma; that was Mao's problem with the Muslims. But "pure and true" assertiveness in an atmosphere of "to get rich is glorious" (Deng's words) can be a challenge to Beijing's notion of unity and stability. Historically, in Xinjiang there were two roads to success, military and bureaucratic. With the growth of the market in the Deng and Jiang eras, new roads of private enterprise and foreign connections have opened. This provides Uighur, as well as Han, with opportunity.

AS TIBET FORMED, with Buddhism as the oxygen of its state, Tibetan society was shaped by topography: far away and hard to penetrate. Tibet specialized in sheep-breeding and cultivated barley, buckwheat, and other crops that do well at high altitudes. Mountains rendered the Buddhist redoubt unattuned to large-scale political organization or expansion. At the same time, Tibet, far more populous than Xinjiang, Mongolia (horseland), or Manchuria (favorable to cattle), was not always isolated and sometimes encroached on China. In the eighth century, during the Tang Dynasty, a strong Tibet pushed into western China (it also came in contact with the Arab empire based in Baghdad). During the Tang, China and Tibet signed eight bilateral treaties.

The Song Dynasty of the tenth and eleventh centuries left Tibet alone, but in the thirteenth century the Yuan (Mongol) pulled it into

---

[28]*New York Times*, Dec. 16, 2001.

line as a vassal. The Ming Dynasty from the fourteenth century accepted tributary missions from Lhasa but did not rule Tibet directly. The final dynasty, the Qing, sent military expeditions into Tibet and sought to rule it as a province.[29] By the 1940s, following almost a century of essential independence as the Qing and the republic dealt with more pressing problems, Tibet had few cards to play; when India and Britain caved in, Beijing was able to claim Tibet after 1949.

Beijing reads its current imperial control of Tibet into two millennia of Chinese history. Talking of Yuan, Ming, and Qing times, it calls the Tibet government "local." That is untrue, but it fits present reality. "China's Tibet" and "Our Tibet" are common phrases in Beijing today. "Tibet is China's Tibet, not the United States's Tibet," says *People's Daily*, as if speaking of a colonial possession.[30] Behind the proprietorial tone is more than a legal claim. Han paternalism and Marxist self-entitlement also flavor the Chinese stance. The legal issue is subsumed within the presumption of primacy that the doctrine of One China bestows on the Communist party-state.

During the Qing, as today, some Chinese argued that the western frontier was not really Chinese. Then, as now, the argument cut two ways. One possible conclusion is that Tibet, Xinjiang, and the rest do not belong in Beijing's realm. A second is that they can be *made Chinese by strong measures*; then they will belong with China. The latter is the point of view of today's CCP. However, "being made Chinese" is not acceptable in Lhasa, still less in the Tibetan countryside.

A gaggle of confusions results. Nation-state principles are mooted, but they seldom apply. A religion–politics divide is in evidence, but it is not understood the same way by the two sides (plus the international actors involved). Class analysis is broached, but sometimes the denunciation of "feudalism" sounds like Han (*hua*) criticism of Barbarians (*yi*). Boundaries are invoked, yet an imperial boundary is seldom a line.

Ultimately, a gap of way of life yawns. "When I drove from Chengdu to Lanzhou," said the Tibet specialist Robert Thurman, "I changed my

---

[29]Courant, 1912, chap. VII.
[30]*Renmin ribao*, May 31, 2001.

view of the proper boundaries of China. I saw that Chinese settlement worked at the lower levels of the mountains, but not at the higher levels. This experience turned my cultural sympathy for Tibet into a political sympathy."[31] Geography, in a word, is on the side of the separateness of Tibet.

But, unlike Mongolia and Xinjiang, which also traditionally objected to Chinese domination, Tibet has "nowhere to go." It cannot look across the PRC border and see a missing part of Tibetan civilization. The elevated Buddhist kingdom is simply and innocently itself. The Lhasa king in the seventh century, to achieve balance, took one wife from China and one from Nepal. Still today, Tibet stands between China and India, a misfit in Inner Asian politics.

TODAY, as during the Qing Dynasty, struggles over the selection of a new Lama, the holy figure of Tibetan Buddhism, the most important non-Han Buddhist strain in the Chinese empire, pit Beijing against Tibetan public opinion. Neither the Dalai Lama nor the Panchen Lama typically leave written instructions on which boy should be groomed as his successor. For Tibetans, including the two million-odd that remain in Beijing's "Tibet Autonomous Region," the Dalai Lama and Panchen Lama are both religious and temporal leaders. For Beijing, they are but religious figures.

The Qing preferred to send a golden urn to Lhasa, have the boy candidates' names written on slips of paper, then pick the new Dalai Lama or Panchen Lama by having the Chinese *Amban* (administrator of Tibet) dip a pair of ivory chopsticks into the urn and draw out one slip of paper. The Tibetans preferred to put before the boys a selection of relics from the previous incarnation's life, mixed in with extraneous relics, and see if one boy spotted the authentic items. Often, Lhasa, duplicitously, would tell the Tibetan people the traditional mode had been followed, while telling the Qing court the golden urn had been used.

---

[31]Robert Thurman, talk at Fairbank Center, Harvard University, Nov. 2000.

In the PRC period, everything became tenser because of Beijing's contempt for religion and fear that Buddhism would be used as an "anti-China" force. After the tenth Panchen Lama died (perhaps poisoned) in 1989, while Hu Jintao ran Tibetan affairs for the CCP, the Tibetan Buddhist leaders appointed a senior figure, Chadrel Rinpoche, close to the Dalai Lama, to search for the right boy. Beijing, in turn, appointed a pliant Lhasa figure to head a search procedure.

The Dalai Lama's representatives visited the Yumboli and Lhamo Latso sacred lakes to watch for signs of who the next Panchen Lama may be. But Beijing wished to use the Golden Urn, essentially a lottery process that they could manipulate, and keep the choice out of the hands of the Dalai Lama. The Tibet Buddhist establishment, centered on the Tashilhunpo Monastery, tried to arrange for the Dalai Lama, from India, to choose the eleventh Panchen Lama.

In May 1995, a boy, Gedhun Choekyi Nyima, from a remote Tibet village, was chosen by the Dalai Lama and the Buddhist leadership in Tibet, after search parties, prayer, and divinations. From India, the Dalai Lama announced the choice. Beijing rejected the Dalai Lama's selection. The Beijing press said the six-year-old was a nasty person who "once drowned a dog" and whose parents were "notorious for speculation." Some monks in Lhasa were told that anyone in possession of a photo of the boy would be executed. Six months later, in a rigged meeting held in Beijing, under the direct supervision of Jiang Zemin, the CCP chose its own boy, Gyaltsen Norbu.[32] This six-year-old, whose parents are both Communists, declared his loyalty to the Communist Party of China.

Chadrel Rinpoche, who had conducted the search on behalf of the Dalai Lama, was accused by Beijing of "splittism." Cultural Revolution-style, the Dalai Lama's chosen boy and Chadrel were subject to criticism meetings all over "China's Tibet." Beijing declared in a chilling sentence: "Any legitimate religion invariably makes patriotism the primary requirement for believers."[33]

---

[32] Hilton, 1999, 283, 264, 277.
[33] Hilton, 1999, 286.

Beijing's boy met and was photographed with Jiang, who told him to "uphold the leadership of the Party, have a deep love for the nation, for the people, and for socialism." Then the six-year-old was shut away in a villa near Beijing. By early 1996, the Dalai Lama's boy had mysteriously disappeared from his village. Later, Beijing said they had put this boy "under the protection of the government at the request of his parents." During 1996, not surprisingly, there were violent confrontations at Tibetan monasteries between monks and Chinese authorities. Propaganda was spewed out to attack the Dalai Lama, not only as a flawed temporal leader, but as a miserable religious leader. In 1997 it was revealed that Chadrel Rinpoche had been tried for "leaking state secrets" and "splitting the country" and sentenced to six years in prison.[34]

Almost certainly, Beijing will "remold" both the chosen boys to fit CCP purposes. Eventually they expect to do the same with whoever emerges, from divination and prayer, or from a Golden Urn, as the new reincarnation of the current Dalai Lama. For Beijing thinks the Dalai Lama, not Tibet itself, is the problem, and that after he goes Tibet will cooperate with "the central government."

———

AFTER PRESIDENT BUSH met the Dalai Lama in Washington in May 2001, Beijing said the Dalai Lama was "traveling further and further down the separatist road." Since the Tibetan Buddhist leader has been walking the same protect-Tibet road for half a century, one may wonder just where the road leads. The "problem of Tibet" has not been solved. Why is this? The basic reason is that one man's empire is another man's family.

Han paternalism rubs, and probably long will rub, Tibetans the wrong way. Chinese guards stop a Tibetan and, even if the guards know Tibetan, require the interrogatee to answer questions in his broken Chinese. High schools in Tibet teach Chinese as the first language. Here is an exam question for a "patriotic education" course in a Tibetan

———

[34]Hilton, 1999, 291, 299.

middle school: "Do you consider that the Dalai Lama is a religious leader or a political leader?"[35]

The mere appearance of the Tibetan flag above the Jokhang Temple in Lhasa in February 1989 led to repression and revolt, leaving scores dead and hundreds injured. Beijing officials supervise Tibetan Buddhism, which is akin to a monkey conducting an orchestra. No one likes foreigners to rule them in their own land. And Han people dislike the Tibetans they live among in Tibet, because pervasive Tibetan resentment at Chinese overlordship chips away at the Han sense of entitlement.

The Marxist vision of progress, now modified at times to mean economic development, is a mixed influence. Leaving aside the condescension, it is likely that Chinese Communist control has modernized Tibet more than an independent Tibet government would have done. Unfortunately for all concerned, bounty from the hand of a traditional bully is not necessarily welcome—as Japan found out when it modernized its Korean colony.

Incidents displaying the age-old problems occur month by month. The captions at the splendid "Tibet Relics Exhibition" in the Forbidden City in 2001 were in Chinese and English, but not Tibetan. One caption said Tibet officially became part of China in 1247! China rebuked the European Parliament in October 2001 for allowing the Dalai Lama a platform "to unscrupulously discuss his plot to split China." The EU should "stop doing things which hurt the feelings of the Chinese people," Beijing declared, like a teacher addressing a class.[36] In Lhasa, the Beijing party-state, with no excess of tact, is building a monument opposite the Potala Palace to commemorate Tibet's "liberation" by the People's Liberation Army in 1950.

Widespread world sympathy for the subjection of Tibet does not translate into governmental support for the Tibetan government-in-exile. No government in the world recognizes Tibet as a country (but, then, no government recognized the Ukraine in 1990; by 2002, 117 governments had embassies in Kiev). When Jiang Zemin visited Lon-

[35]"Education for Minorities," *China Rights Forum*, Summer 2001, 12.
[36]*China Daily*, Oct. 29, 2001.

don in 1999, the Blair government arrested people who tried to march in the streets in favor of Tibet independence. Yet when the Japanese emperor visited London in 1998, Blair permitted large demonstrations against him. In Europe and many other parts of the world, no middle ground exists between grassroots emotional support for Tibet and a sense of helplessness in official circles. The world has enough "failed states," it is said with a sigh in the chancelleries. Do we want to bring one more into existence?

Yet Beijing's tight control of Tibet risks an explosion damaging to China, Tibet, and some other countries. It is possible to envisage indefinite stability in Hong Kong, under Beijing's sovereignty, but not in Tibet. Yet major progress on Tibet is unlikely without overall change to the Chinese party-state.

A new irritation for Beijing from the late twentieth century is international public opinion on human rights. The Dalai Lama taps it in proposing a referendum in Tibet. "If the majority of the people in Tibet are really happy and willing to live under Chinese rule," he wrote, "it would be foolish and unreasonable on the part of 100,000 Tibetans in exile to stubbornly act contrary to their wishes." This point can be a knife in Beijing's back. "So far," the Dalai Lama says, "it is only the Chinese publicity organs and their recognized spokesmen in the West who claim the Tibetans in Tibet are happy."[37]

Beijing lacks a good answer to this point. When the Dalai Lama in his talk at the European Parliament in 2001 again suggested a referendum, "to determine people's wishes on their relation with China," the Chinese government said: "Since Tibet is an inseparable part of China, there is no need to conduct a 'referendum' on Tibet's future."[38] Beijing confronts the global wave of freedom and democracy with an assertion of imperial entitlement.

Still, it is easier to put up with world criticism for repression in Tibet than, as with Taiwan, to find a way to militarily invade a territory that is well-armed and backed by the United States. Unlike Hong Kong

[37] *World View*, Jan./Feb. 1980, 39.
[38] *China Daily*, Oct. 29, 2001.

and Taiwan, Tibet is not a source of "polluting influence" within the PRC. Beijing will only allow Tibet a separate existence, or a semiseparate one such as Hong Kong's, if it sees gain in doing so. Today it does not; tomorrow may be different.

Historically viewed, China is now strong in relation to Tibet. Yet, as China proper changes faster than Inner Asia, the choices in Tibet policy are not easy. Repressing Tibet solidifies Tibetan identity, the chief obstacle to turning Tibetans into "Chinese people" (*Zhongguo minzu*). Yet liberalizing Tibet policy allows Tibetans to use new freedoms to rebel against Beijing.

The Dalai Lama in 2003 was asking little more than the substantial autonomy Beijing offered decades ago (in the "Seventeen Points" of 1951); he does not ask full independence for Tibet. Perhaps this means that Beijing is gaining the advantage in its effort to turn Tibet irrevocably into a "local government" of the PRC. Said the Dalai Lama while visiting Taiwan in 2001: "The views of the mainland Chinese leaders should change along with the world."[39] Is that his only hope?

———————

FOUR SCENARIOS SUGGEST themselves for future relations between Center and Periphery, of which we have considered some maritime and steppe examples.

One scenario sees Beijing hold on to its entire realm, mostly inherited from Qing China, by democratizing and federalizing. If Deng sought to save Leninism with consumerism, a future leader of China will save the unity of the realm by liberalization. Certain federations have come into existence to preserve a national unity that would otherwise have been impossible. This was the case with India in 1947 and Spain in 1974. A federation by definition is based on law, and ethnic groups and cultural minorities therefore have rights. Under Scenario One, a federal system proves appropriate for the new society and economy produced by the Deng and Jiang eras. The countryside, never

———————

[39] *Lianhe bao* (Taipei), April 6, 2001.

really incorporated into the state structure since the end of the dynasties, finally wins a stable fiscal and policy role within a federal structure.

As a liberal multiethnic federation comes into existence on Chinese soil for the first time, Taiwan is encouraged to accept associated status as one of the regions of the federal democracy of China. Said a Taiwan scholar in praise of such a vision: "[The] regions of China are quite different. . . . Power must be devolved towards the periphery, and the people of each region must be allowed autonomy, so that all these people can see their dignity respected. . . . China must become like Europe."[40] Although Scenario One sees China flourish, it is by no means unfavorable to America's interests.

Edward Friedman writes that a "federalist or confederalist notion of Chineseness could better serve future Chinese greatness than would purist, centrist racism."[41] Unfortunately, a Leninist party-state, jittery and defensive, does not think in such terms. Mao in 1937 gave lip service to the federal vision. "The Mohammedan and Tibetan peoples," he pledged, "will form autonomous republics attached to the Chinese federation."[42] But Communist Party rule could not and cannot accommodate such a vision.

Scenario Two offers a gradual homogenization of the races, languages, dialects, social policies, and cultures of the PRC. This knitting together facilitates a continued authoritarian, unitary-state rule within the present borders. Such an evolution brings continual tensions, but no climactic crises over some decades. The result gives updated expression to a vision already imposed on the Chinese past by Communist Chinese official scribes: Han-led multicultural harmony, as the minorities wake up to find themselves fundamentally Chinese.

Beijing, runs this scenario, will go on diluting Tibetan, Mongol, Uighur, and other minority areas with Han internal migration, spur enough economic development to keep the minorities passive, and prove, over time, that the Qing Dynasty reinvention of China has taken grip. The non-Chinese peoples on China's fringes, already called retro-

---

[40]Tu, 1998, 60.

[41]Friedman, 2000, 242.

[42]Schram, 1985, 82; see also Takeuchi, vol. 9, 220.

spectively "national minorities," will indeed smoothly transmogrify into "Chinese citizens." Implicit is the idea that the Han are more advanced and will, as surely as night follows day, assimilate surrounding peoples.

So China under Hu Jintao, if he truly becomes established as red emperor, will achieve what Lattimore hoped for. "It will be possible [after the defeat of Japan]," the Inner Asian specialist wrote, "to link together and integrate farmland, steppe, and forest by the use of industrial techniques, which were lacking in China's past, and thus to eliminate for the first time in Asiatic history the old processes by which different environments have generated different economies, which in turn have nourished mutually hostile societies."[43] This is the integrationist vision that the CCP, under Scenario Two, will pull off.

Under Scenario Two, the PRC carries forward both the universalism and the imperialism of the Chinese dynastic polity. Of course, Beijing avoids the term "Barbarians" in favor of "minority peoples." Actually, the Qing Dynasty already made a similar shift of gears. *Way of life* was the decisive difference between Chinese and others for the Qing. Way of life, the CCP believes, is changeable, and Beijing will prove able to change it in Xinjiang, Tibet, Mongolia, and the rest. All this is just possible, but unlikely.

Scenario Three is a consensual return to "Ming China." China loosens up politically, and in circumstances of liberalization, parts of Outer China become separate states, by amicable arrangement with Beijing.

Ming Dynasty officials did not see profit or justification in ruling those areas beyond China proper that the Qing later acquired. The Ming Dynasty, as a result, ruled a China far smaller than the Qing, or than Beijing rules today. Influential people in the PRC, under Scenario Three, come to feel that the China of the Ming is the essential China, more nearly coterminous with Chinese customs and language than the Qing or the PRC as presently defined. They fear growing international resistance to Beijing's effort to keep the Qing boundaries.

Large states become that way in diverse ways, some by conquest, others by the nonviolent extension of free settlement. Similarly, large

---

[43]Lattimore, 1962, 149.

states become smaller in different ways. The shrinkage can happen as a result of war (as in the birth of Bangladesh in 1971) or by mutual agreement of the parties involved (as in the emergence of Slovakia and the Czech Republic in 1993). Under Scenario Three, the PRC loosens to the point of becoming a plurality of one large and several small states. There is little violence, as both Beijing and the outlying cities involved—Lhasa, Hong Kong, Kashgar, Taipei, and Huhehot—are softened by the winds of freedom.

In such a vision, the new states are not hostile to Beijing. As time passes they become associated with the Beijing government, now called the Democratic Federation of China, in a league of sovereign countries acknowledging their overlapping civilizational roots. This optimistic picture is favorable to America's interests, and Washington and some other capitals encourage it. Like Scenario Two, it is possible but unlikely.

Under Scenario Four, there occurs a multiple crisis. In the west, an uprising occurs in Xinjiang or Tibet, and Beijing is close to losing control. Simultaneously, a challenge arises on the southeast coast. Beijing has chosen to meddle in a messy Taiwan political situation, hoping this will be a step toward "reunification." But Guangdong and Fujian join Hong Kong in dragging their feet over Beijing's political drive into Taiwan, on the ground that Taiwan is a Golden Goose for southern China's economic development that is best left alone. In Beijing, intraparty dispute flares over these issues. The massive unemployment following several years of membership in the World Trade Organization feeds fresh ingredients into the intraparty dispute, diluting the government's competence in handling problems in the west and the southeast.

China's history offers cases of such a coincidence of events. It is one reason why China has had so many periods of disunity and even fragmentation. As recently as 1915, after Yuan Shikai made himself emperor, the leaders of Yunnan, Guizhou, and Guangxi provinces disowned the center and declared independence. The last phase of the Soviet Union showed what a time bomb the link between empire and autocracy can be. When Gorbachev loosened the screws of authoritarianism, the artificial construction of a mighty empire came apart. Boldness against Moscow's yoke in one place (Poland) fed boldness in other places (Latvia, Lithuania). International and domestic crises overnight became a seamless web. The seismic movements fueled intraparty quarreling in Moscow. Economic modernization proved no guarantee against rebelliousness (Czechoslovakia).

A violent "return to the Ming" boundaries is arguably a tragic vision. Nonetheless, the tightness of Beijing's rule over its empire points to involuntary breakup. Scenario Four is likely if Beijing continues to reject steps toward political pluralism, a future economic downturn is severe, and the balance of power should tip against China in East Asia and Central Asia at the same time. In some ways, modernization makes the governance of the new Chinese empire not less, but more difficult. For each religious or linguistic wrinkle smoothed out from the imperial rug, there appears a fresh wrinkle of socioeconomic interest-differentiation. Moreover, the difference in economic environment between China proper and the minority areas does not go away quickly. Wet fields are not high steppes.

Additionally, environmentalists see nonpolitical roots to the possible fragmentation of China. These include resource scarcity in parts of the country, environmental degradation (water, air) of such severity as to cause uprising, and consequent internal refugee flows. The environmentalists fear a "Chinese Chernobyl," involving biological weapons or nuclear power, its appearance initially kept from notice by the absence of a free press.

An economically growing China, remaining authoritarian, and still imperial in reach, must encounter hostility in some of the realms it abuts. "The renaissance of the China Spirit," runs a typical current nationalist sentiment from Beijing, "will be like the ringing of the morning bell of the Pacific Age. All glory belongs to Great China. The future lies with the modernized China Spirit—in the name of the new century!"[44] The phrase Greater Japan is still a curse in much of East Asia. Some Chinese figures and many Western Sinologists speak lightly of Greater China, yet for many surrounding peoples, Viet-

---

[44]Zhao, 1992, 252.

namese, Mongols, Kazaks, Koreans, and Uzbeks among them, it is hardly less problematic than was Greater Japan in the 1930s and 1940s.

By 2002, the United States and Russia were much more active players in Central Asia than before. Other countries, including the European Union, paid fresh attention to the point of view of Uzbekistan, Kazakstan, and other western neighbors of China. The more the rest of the world focuses on Central Asia, the less tenable becomes the picture that Beijing paints of Xinjiang. All this may eventually loosen up, not tighten, Xinjiang's situation.

In seeing Scenario Four as quite likely, I acknowledge that Beijing would have to be clumsy and perhaps unlucky, internationally and domestically, to lose portions of the PRC as a result of a multipronged crisis. But the fundamental point is that the Chinese state in its anachronistic condition probably will not be able to deal successfully with multiple setbacks.

China's exposed situation, the forces playing upon it, its extraordinary size and diversity, the freakish way in which the last dynasty of an ancient political order bequeathed its boundaries to a Communist state, and the very success of post-Mao economic and social development, all may put the new Chinese empire in a peril that CCP leadership is ill-equipped to handle. Beijing's unfailing instinct to put the maintenance of Communist autocratic power at the center of its calculations will eventually be its undoing.

FOREIGN POLICY

Imperial Goals and Modes

. . . foreign policy is the extension of China's domestic policies.
— *Foreign Minister Qian Qichen, 1990*[1]

Negotiating in the Chinese capital gives the Chinese the opportunity to manage the ambience so as to maximize the sense of gratitude, dependence, awe, and helplessness they evoke in their guests.
— *Ambassador Richard Solomon*[2]

ONE DAY IN 1972, Prime Minister Lee Kuan Yew, sitting at his orderly desk in the Istana Complex in Singapore, talked with a visitor about China, his ancestral homeland. In Beijing, Mao still reigned.

"It is certain that China will extend its power into Southeast Asia," Lee said.

"Are you concerned about Chinese missiles, Mr. Prime Minister?"

"Not at all—why would they hit Singapore?"

"Well, why would Beijing subvert Singapore?" I asked.

Replied Lee Kuan Yew, who previously battled Communists in Singapore politics, "It's part of their ideology. They can never give it up. They want a string of fraternal Communist states around their borders."

---

[1] *Beijing Review,* Jan. 15–21, 1990.
[2] Mann, 1999, 52.

In those days, Lee refused to establish diplomatic relations with the PRC. He felt Singapore, populated mainly by Chinese people, needed more time to develop its separate identity as "not Chinese." Until it did (helped by the English language) and a sense of loyalty to Singapore had taken root, he felt a Beijing embassy could subvert his city-state.

The Singapore leader got history half right. Three decades later, Beijing has few ideological aspirations in Southeast Asia. Yet the Chinese party-state retains an imperial sense; it seeks a string of compliant states around its borders. Skillfully, China has changed gears from ideological to economic and military methods. Its aim, unchanged from the Mao era and much earlier in Chinese history, is to make Beijing the centerpiece of Asia. Strikingly, the Chinese state's view of its centrality to a wide Eurasian zone has endured for more than 2,000 years.

In 1996, former Japanese prime minister Morihiro Hosokawa said in a speech in Washington: "There is a need for Japan to pay sufficient attention to the latent desires of the Chinese state and the instability this introduces to the whole Asia–Pacific region."[3] The remark was a throwback to Lee Kuan Yew's wariness of a quarter-century earlier. In between, the 1980s saw a relaxed view of the PRC in most of Asia. Hosokawa's speech reflected a fresh apprehension about China during the 1990s, in Tokyo, Delhi, Hanoi, Jakarta, and other Asian capitals. Beijing multiplied military spending, voiced claims to multiple territories beyond its own borders, and breathed dissatisfaction with the world.

What does China want of its neighbors and the world community? Part of discerning the future is recalling the past. This does not mean that "history is merely rephrasing itself," as the Norwegian historian Harald Bøckman points out, "but rather that it is used in a transactional manner in order to make sense of the strains of modernization."[4] China as it changes is still China, with age-old challenges of governance, some due to geography, and unique traits of culture. The transi-

---

[3]Morihiro Hosokawa, "Rebuilding the US–Japan Security Structure," Washington, D.C., March 12, 1996.
[4]Bøckman, 1998, 311.

tion "from a Qing Dynasty empire to a Chinese nation-state," as Millward themes the century following 1911, is not yet complete.[5]

During the later twentieth century, while Americans alternatively viewed China as mirror, demon, or economic animal, depending on the pressure or impulse of the moment, the Chinese party-state took a long-range view of the United States. In America, the myriad components of China policy fill the air like so many snowflakes. In China, the key components of policy toward the United States are never mentioned in public.

For the ears of the world, Beijing says it seeks "peace and development," favors "multipolarity," and will "never seek hegemony." It purrs that all countries in the world are equal and the UN is the hope for peace and justice in the world. Yet such pabulum is not a foreign policy. Rather, a foreign policy is "an integrated structure of assumptions, objectives, and means."[6] In practice, Beijing has quite different goals: use international relations to shore up the party-state at home; build up wealth and power in a mercantilist fashion; be seen as an equal of America; have the United States and the world believe they need China more than it needs them; supplant the United States as the leading force in Asia.

It follows from the last three of these aims that China expects a showdown with America (unless Americans accept illusion as truth, and lie down and roll over), that it plans for the strongest military it can afford, and that it treats cooperative international institutions as decoration (behind which power is what counts). Beijing pursues these aims with persistence, a sense of history, and indirect methods. Its stance toward America continues, whether consciously or not, some traditions of the Chinese Legalist state.

Privately, Deng Xiaoping set forth a foreign policy strategy in the difficult year of 1990 that reflected tested techniques of the Chinese state. The Tiananmen tragedy of June 1989 had mauled China's image. The United States, Europe, and Japan had slapped sanctions on the

[5]Millward, 1998, xvi.
[6]Tsou, 1963, preface, ix.

PRC; foreign leaders stayed away from Beijing. "Watch and observe calmly" (*Leng jing guancha*) ran Deng's first maxim. "Secure our own position" (*Wen zhu zhenjiao*) came next. There followed four methods: "Behave with confidence and patience" (*Chen zhuo yingdui*), "Hide our capacities and bide our time" (*Taoguang yanghui*), "Be good at keeping a low profile" (*Shan yu shou zhuo*), and "Never play the leader" (*Jue bu dang tou*).[7] These six stratagems from Chinese state tradition were extremely apt for the year after Tiananmen. Deliberately deceptive, they separated the immediate from the long term. Nothing further removed from the razzle-dazzle of 1990s American diplomacy could be imagined.

COMING TO POWER in 1949, the CCP was fundamentally wary of an "imperialist-dominated" world. Chiang Kai-shek had signed international agreements, bilateral and multilateral, that implied China was one nation among others. Under Mao, steps toward the international order were reversed. Only in the 1970s during the last years of his life, when the synergy between the Chinese party-state and the Soviet Union crumbled, did Mao continue the Nanjing regime's entry into the nation-state system.

To be sure, the United States did not throw down a welcome mat for the PRC. If relations among the CCP, the Soviet Union, and the United States during the late 1940s had turned out differently, and the United States and the PRC had established diplomatic relations in 1949, the PRC might have evolved to a socialism comparable to Yugoslavia's, and Mao from the start might, like Tito, have adopted a middle position between Moscow and Washington. I doubt this scenario, but, given it, Mao's "proletarian internationalism" would have been diluted two decades earlier than happened.

Initially, Mao's objection to the existing international system was Marxist. The setup was "bourgeois." In line with his view of domestic

---

[7]*Renmin ribao*, Dec. 24, 1996; July 13, 2000; Jan. 3, 2001; *Mingbao* (Hong Kong), June 23, 1998.

policy and foreign policy as a seamless web, the Communist dictator saw "proletarian internationalism" as an approaching replacement for the bourgeois international order. Mao said the West was on a quick trip toward collapse. He said the more countries with atomic weapons the better for peace. Later, Mao's objection to the international system turned cultural and emotional. Insufficient respect was being shown to China's brilliant past and the manifold sufferings of the Chinese people at the hands of foreigners. The resulting "Go it alone" outlook was a manifestation of Marxism-plus-tradition.

The first phase of PRC foreign policy saw adherence to the "socialist camp," a Marxist view of the world scene, and a tight link between foreign and domestic policy. Mao's state did not sit at the UN, spurned disarmament talks, and largely limited its diplomacy to the socialist bloc and other "anti-imperialist" forces such as Sukarno's Indonesia. One-time foreign minister Wu Xiuquan said the UN was full of "truth-distorting proposals," called it "a dirty international stock exchange in the grip of a few powers," and said the Chinese delegation, while participating in UN debates on the Korean War, often had to "leave the conference room in anger."[8] All this was a far cry from Chiang Kai-shek's cooperative participation in ideologically diverse international meetings and agreements.

The PRC's initial foreign policy was military-minded. Within a year of seizing power, Mao sent 300,000 troops into Korea. Soon after reunifying China in 221 B.C., Emperor Qin Shihuang sent a 500,000-strong army to attack Vietnam. Military assertiveness often marked the start of a dynasty. Mao's reasons for intervening in Korea in 1950 partook of Qin Shihuang's reasons for going into Vietnam.[9] Protect the recent achievement of unification, and flex the muscles of a new polity in a wider sphere.

The early consolidation of the Tang Dynasty also resembles Mao's first decade in foreign policy. A dualism of (neo) Confucianism and (neo) Legalism was evident during the 1950s. The Tang knew relations

[8]Wu, 1991, 273, 274.
[9]Chen Jian, 1994, 213–216.

with the Turki were unequal; Mao saw the same with the United States. So Mao, like the first Tang emperor, practiced caution toward a superior force, yet without changing the doctrine ("the United States is declining"), the ritualistic denunciation of class foes, or China's sense of moral superiority. What Emperor Tai Zong said when the Tang expanded—we did not aggress, they just submitted—is what Mao said in grabbing Tibet, and what Mao's "younger brother," Kim Il-sung, said in invading southern Korea.[10]

Phase One of PRC foreign policy saw vigor, as in Korea and bombardments in the Taiwan Strait, but within the parameters of Moscow's leadership. In the 1950s, Beijing had no important tie with any capitalist nation. A smiling face was directed toward India, Indonesia, and others of the Bandung group (named after its summit in the Indonesian city in 1954) of Nonaligned, in the name of a shared anti-imperialism. "Peace" was the number two catchword. Many demons in the psyche of the Chinese party-state were, for the moment, kept out of sight.

———————

THE SECOND PHASE of PRC foreign policy, from the late 1950s to the late 1960s, brought a militant policy that might be called United Front from Below. Within the logic of United Front from Below, the enemy is only part of the point. Almost as important is struggle within the ranks of the coalition forged against the enemy. For China in the 1960s, the "soft" left of nonalignment was destined to be pushed aside by the "hard" left of Maoism. Security against the current foe mattered less than world revolution. Frustrated and impatient, Mao ached to relive the glory of the wars against Japan and Chiang Kai-shek. He was also trying to replicate an imperial stratagem.

The decade was marked by a souring on the socialist camp, arguments with Moscow, and a sharper delineation of Chinese communism's social way. Mao displayed a militant rural romanticism, which echoed the 2,000-year-old scholar-official elite's nod to agriculture and belief in the moral superiority of rural life. At home, he attempted to

———————

[10]Perelomov and Martynov, 1983, 83, 141–142, 144, 148; Goncharov, Lewis, and Xue, 1993, 130.

"leap to communism" by dragooning farmers into communal life. Abroad, he spurred the "countryside of the world" (soon called the Third World) to surround the cities of the world (imperialism). "Anti-imperialism" was still the heart of the cause, but "Liberation" became number two catchword. Jaded, status quo Moscow, said Mao, could not possibly lead the national liberation struggles of the world's rural dispossessed. Only China could do that.

Such an analysis wiped the smile off the face of the Bandung Non-aligned countries. Beijing was kicked out of Jakarta for seeking to overthrow the Indonesian government. It fought with the previously well-disposed India of Nehru in 1959. By the Cultural Revolution of the mid-1960s, ethnic Chinese loyal to the "Red Sun of Our Hearts" (Mao) were using spears and bombs against the authorities in friendly Burma and Cambodia.

During Phase Two, the awkwardness of the Middle Kingdom in the modern world was jarring. Mao's state defied everyone and everything at once. Not passively and serenely, as many emperors withstood Barbarians; rather, frenetically and angrily. The Chinese *jia* (household) fronted the world; in a projection identification of the *jia*'s unease with the non-Chinese world, Mao denounced the world's unease with China. Like alcohol in the belly of a church-going burgher, the Cultural Revolution brought out dark truths from a Chinese psyche not yet adjusted to a post-1911 world.

The 1960s brought the nearest approximation in PRC history to an eclipse of neo-Legalism by neo-Confucianism. China's national interests seemed overwhelmed by Beijing's belief in doctrine. Yet, even during the Cultural Revolution, Mao disappointed the purists by cracking the Legalist whip. When Red Guards captured Foreign Minister Chen Yi, Mao put his foot down. Chen Yi "has lost twenty-seven pounds," he said. "I can't show him to foreign visitors in this condition." Even amidst the tears and shouts of the Red Guard summer of 1966, Qin Shihuang was not absent. "I will definitely protect Chen Yi," Mao said, expressing the dualism of his neo-Legalism and neo-Confucianism, "but first let the Red Guards put the heat on him."[11]

---

[11]Gurtov, 1969, 92.

As 1949 USHERED IN the socialist camp, and 1959 signaled a United Front from Below, 1969 began what might be called a United Front from Above. Two problems had arisen during the militant 1960s. Disorder at home got out of hand. Abroad, members of the United Front from Below did not appreciate being manipulated by Beijing. Nehru was called an anti-imperialist in 1956, but a stinking bourgeois by 1960.

In a United Front from Above, which became Phase Three of PRC foreign policy, the coalition's enemy is the sole target. The agenda does not include struggle within the ranks of the united front. Stalin had given Mao a successful example of United Front from Above in his World War Two alliance with the United States and Britain against the Berlin–Rome–Tokyo axis. Moscow and Washington did not subvert each other, or even criticize each other's society, for the duration of the antifascist struggle. Geopolitical location in the international system, not class analysis, is the alpha and omega of this variety of united front.

From 1969, when the Soviet Union and China fought a border war in northeast Asia, Moscow was the target of Mao's United Front from Above. Beijing embraced any country that was staunchly anti-Soviet. Included were Pakistan, post-Allende Chile, the Shah's Iran, and other right-wing, militarist, antirevolutionary regimes. Beijing lost interest in meddling in the domestic affairs of insufficiently leftist nations. The world was put on notice that Beijing was just as good at *realpolitik* (neo-Legalism) as at ideology (neo-Confucianism).

Mao milked a traditional Legalist doctrine, "Make friends with ones afar and attack ones nearby" (*yuanjiao jingong*). He returned to feelings he had expressed in a youthful poem: "In the northern mountains hate-filled enemies abound."[12] In both the 1950s and 1960s, in different ways, Mao had aligned domestic policy and foreign policy. But in the 1970s he separated them, allying with the West and other anti-Soviet forces strategically, while sticking with the socialist road at home. Nixon abroad, purges at home.

In the tradition of nimble switches between Confucianism and Legalism, Mao departed from his doctrine without canceling a role for

---

[12]Schram, 1992, 64.

doctrine. When Moscow replaced Washington as the enemy, Mao said the Soviet Union had become "social imperialist." Thus could he cling to the theory of imperialism. "The Americans are bastards," he said to the Yugoslav ambassador, showing he could be practical, "but they are honest bastards. The Russians are also liars."[13] Soon, "hegemony" became (for a time) an intellectually more convenient word to use than "imperialism." But Mao still thought he had history in his pocket.

THE FOURTH PHASE of PRC foreign policy, launched as the post-Mao leadership settled into the cockpit in 1979, is marked by independence, economism, and nationalism. With Deng, foreign policy and domestic policy again marched in step. In the 1980s and 1990s, a major goal of both was the wealth and power of the nation, leading, in due course, to a dominant place for China in world affairs.

Deng took the claims to Marxist moral exceptionalism ("class struggle" against "imperialism") out of China's foreign policy and yanked it toward national aggrandizement, a traditional aim. By Jiang's time, China boasted an "independent foreign policy of peace." The PRC by the 1990s, while not valued in the West as much as before Tiananmen Square and the collapse of the Soviet Union, was more influential in Asia than before. And it secured the incorporation of Hong Kong into the PRC in 1997.

If Deng sounded like a warrior, fighting Vietnam, threatening Taiwan, calling the Tiananmen students "the enemy," and adopting a unilateral position on disputed islands in the South China Sea, he indeed came into politics through war. The border war between China and Vietnam in 1979 revealed his readiness to reach for the gun when faced with conflicting forces. He showed the same tendency for military solutions at Tiananmen in 1989.

The spirit of Deng's remarks on attacking Vietnam in 1979 was close to that of Tang emperor Gao Zu's words on attacking the trou-

---

[13]Yugoslav diplomat (colleague of the ambassador concerned) to the author, Beijing, July 1971.

blesome Turki early in the seventh century: "Earlier, since All Under Heaven had not yet been fully pacified, I displayed generosity toward the northern Barbarians, so as there [to secure] peace on our frontiers. [But] now, since they have breached the accord, I have decided to destroy them, and will pamper them no longer."[14] The common premise was that China possessed a world-arranging role for its periphery. In assaulting Vietnam, Deng said he was "punishing" a misbehaving Hanoi.

Deng's mind, formed in the anticolonial era, amidst civil and international violence, was not equipped for the Economic Age of the 1990s, when nations were increasingly interdependent and human rights concerns became prominent. Jiang Zemin was blander, and he deployed the cards of economism and nationalism with some success and no disaster. The eternal blend of neo-Confucianism and neo-Legalism shifted further toward the latter.

By the Jiang era, "reactive, developmental nationalism," in James Gregor's phrase, had succeeded revolutionary Marxism as the operational force of Chinese foreign policy, still mounted by a Leninist (neo-Legalist) party-state. Revealing were the fresh instructions given (in secret) to officials dealing with foreigners and the outside world. They were told to cancel their "boasting and verbiage" about the "so-called world revolution." It was laid down that they should "stop stuffing socialism! communism! and other revolutionary stuff down [foreigners'] throats." As Chinese tradition emerged from under the weight of imported Marxist ideology, junior officials were required to produce "foreign propaganda with Chinese characteristics."[15]

Thirty-five years ago, Benjamin Schwartz said "the external situation that made it plausible for the Chinese to regard their state as unique has . . . disappeared beyond recall."[16] The phrase "beyond recall" went too far. Maybe the Chinese no longer think of their state as unique (I doubt it), but they do think it may again become Number

---

[14]Perelomov and Martynov, 1983, 140.
[15]Brady, 2000, 950.
[16]Schwartz, 1968, 284–285.

One. That is a giant step toward recovering uniqueness. Beijing would not be alone in seeing special claims ride on the back of rising power. The U.S. claim to "exceptionalism" was inseparable from its rapid and early success.

Schwartz said the revolutionaries of the Sun Yat-sen era "were quite willing to exchange the Chinese universal world order for a strong Chinese nation." In fact, that was the essential project of the Chinese polity from the time of Qin Shihuang. Schwartz said the PRC government appeals to international law when it suits. So did the Qing Dynasty in the 1840s. The dialectic of universal theory and national interest is an old song.

As early as Qin Shihuang, there existed a Chinese foreign policy doctrine using both Legalism and Confucianism. After maximizing domestic power, the emperor looked abroad, to ward off foes and procure good horses for antinomad wars.[17] Into this framework it is possible to fit much of the PRC's mercantilism, insistence on independence, bureaucratic caution, and obsession with the unity and security of China's territory.

"We cannot draw direct conclusions about contemporary China from any analysis of her imperial strategy," writes Peter Perdue, "unless we believe either that leaders of the People's Republic actually rely on Ming and earlier texts for their strategic planning, or that an unconscious set of assumptions has been transmitted to them unchanged over many centuries."[18] There is a third possibility: Beijing repeats aspects of China's past because it faces comparable challenges to those faced by various dynasties and because the Chinese state remains an Us-and-Them authoritarian polity.

Defining traits of Chinese foreign policy include: Difficulty in practicing give and take with other nations; open compromise occurs but it comes hard. Small interest in international solutions to problems; a preference for warding them off. Capability of caving in—the other side of the coin from high arrogance—when stonewalling proves coun-

---

[17]Tikhvinsky and Perelomov, 1981, 185.
[18]Perdue, 2000, 260.

terproductive. Wariness of "enemies," against which the Chinese *jia,* as a vast household, must do battle. All of these traits stem from the hierarchical, Us-and-Them nature of the Chinese dynastic state.

All mark PRC foreign policy, as, in sequence, Beijing is unable to settle World War Two issues with Japan, refuses a multilateral approach to South China Sea island disputes, flip-flops on issues related to Taiwan in its policy toward the United States, and expresses paranoia over NATO's Kosovo operation in 1999.

The old-new Chinese foreign policy has little role for allies. We saw that "international relations" was a dubious concept to apply to the Chinese dynastic court's view of its dealings with surrounding peoples. "Because of China's own size, bureaucratic unity, and defensive military strength," writes Wills, "she seldom needed foreign alliances to defend herself." A "solitary eminence"[19] marked China's situation. It is similar today.

With no country, unless it be North Korea (what a prize!), has Beijing had a continuous friendship between 1949 and the present. Attempts at alliances during the 1950s and 1960s ended bitterly. The closest partners—Vietnam, the Soviet Union, Albania—became the most excoriated foes. The United States, ever since the late Qing Dynasty, has been close to China only when a common enemy loomed. The partnership in each case was difficult; only the enemy kept it (somewhat) in shape. Deng fumbled for a quasi alliance with the United States in the Carter period, but it did not materialize.

The tenacious legacy of China's discomfort with allies is suggested by the split between Moscow and Beijing and its outcome. The more China diverged from the Soviet model, the fewer allies China had, a reversion to past practice. In the end, Beijing ditched a dozen allies by rejecting the socialist camp. In 1963, the PRC listed the number one contradiction in the world as "between the socialist and imperialist camps." By 1969 it changed that to "between the oppressed nations on the one hand and imperialism and social imperialism on the other." (Social imperialism meant Moscow and company.) With none of the

---

[19]Wills, 1968, 254.

"oppressed nations" did Beijing, post-Soviet split, proceed to form an alliance.

Why the tendency not to seek or hold allies? Historically, we find four reasons. Hierarchy as a way of thinking about political reality. The Chinese polity's sense of being propelled to a predestined future. A certain lack of interest in other cultures and societies except as they served China's needs. Recurrent ambiguity as to the territorial definition of China. All four points have weighed heavily during the PRC years—as in Beijing's condescension toward Vietnam, insistence that socialism is a "higher stage" than capitalism, ethnocentrism in approaching Africa, and refusal to give details of its "historic" claims to the Spratly Islands.

In the mid-1960s, Schwartz could not see as clearly as we may see today that China can be both nationalistic and, when strength permits, a great international center (in its own eyes). In the 1990s, even as Marxist faith sagged, Beijing began to call its post-Soviet system "socialism with Chinese characteristics." Here was a hint of an updated "Chinese perception of world order." The overseas front is but an extension of the home front.

The anti-imperialism of the days of international communism has been transmuted from a global ideology into an expression of China's own nationalism. The primary agenda has become domestic: preservation of the CCP's power and building up the nation's economy. As we saw in Chapter 7, "Chinese world order" may better be called "Chinese political order."

The aim of securing China's "wealth and power," an update of a late nineteenth-century aspiration, has large future foreign policy implications. As early as the Twelfth Party Congress in 1982, the CCP altered its priorities to put modernization ahead of antihegemonism. Of course, only a modernized China will be able to grasp the baton of chief hegemon from the (presumed) weakening hand of America. For the moment, China still has a Third World economy married to a Superpower ego. The four priorities of Beijing's foreign policy, in descending order, are: control of the regime's own people; economic development; managing security issues around China's borders; unfolding plans for China's rise to replace the United States as the dominant power in Asia.

GOALS ARE ONE THING, capacity to achieve them is another. For dynastic China, fluctuating capacity was a major variable in the oscillation between hauteur and compromise, between high Confucian vision and low Legalist dogfight. In the PRC period, China regained unity and made strides toward modernization. But judged by Beijing's own standard—aspiration to be the equal of the leading powers—capacity still lags behind goals.

Except for intoxicating moments during the Cultural Revolution, Beijing has been aware of the gap between dreams and capacity. Mao, discussing nuclear weapons with French culture minister Andre Malraux, said, "Six bombs will do."[20] He knew China could not afford a large arsenal. The utopianism of the Great Leap Forward ("We shall teach the sun and moon to change places," "Overtake England in Fifteen Years!") was an attempt to bridge the gap between aspiration and capacity. Of course, the self-delusion of utopianism can kill people, as it did in the Great Leap.

Juxtaposing ritual and the gun, as the emperors did, the PRC leaders try to turn weakness into strength, and use doctrine to picture that weakness as strength. As a result of such skills, China often boxes above its weight. "Come and be Sinicized" (*lai hua*)—the redemptive power of coming to Beijing—is a technique of turning weakness into strength. The foreigner comes to China "raw" (unaware of the Middle Kingdom's greatness); he leaves "cooked" (with full respect for China).[21] The result serves China's national interest.

In 1971, a pair of poems about Nixon and Kissinger, written by a man in Xi'an, circulated informally across China. Calling China a "demons-demasking-mirror" that laid bare the nature of the pathetic foreigner, the verses were an interesting update of *lai hua*. "Blazing fires of revolution burn the world over," one poem began. "Boiling oil is poured on the Pentagon." It offered a solution: "A visit to China is the only way out / For a brief respite from blazing flames that singe the eyebrows."[22]

---

[20]Nixon, 1978, vol. 2, 24.
[21]Bøckman, 1998, 315; there was a term for the raw Barbarian, *shengfan,* and another for the cooked Barbarian, *shufan.*
[22]Translation based on that of Dr. Cornelis Schepel of the University of Leiden, adjusted after consultation with Dr. Ch'en Li-li.

The second poem also portrayed China's beneficence as the answer to America's problems large and small:

For next year's national presidential elections
Two promises made have not at all been redeemed
The key to capture votes is a visit to China . . .

Of Nixon, the poet said, "He will not hesitate to use grease paint and to peddle his sex-appeal."

In the face of Nixon's many dilemmas, "Kissinger's trip to Beijing brought a joyful message." Of Nixon's presidential journey, the man in Xi'an wrote: "With painted face-mask, disguised as a beauty, he comes to negotiate / But the demons-demasking-mirror in the city of Beijing is truly inexorable."

In the end, China shows up the pathos of the visitor: "There is no way out but to go to church, and in profound worship / Pray to high heaven and beseech God: 'Protect me through this difficult passage.'"

Interesting in all this doggerel is the imagery of theater, the language of religion, and the sharp spiritual divide between China and foreigners.

In the first years of the Communist dynasty, as in the early years of the Ming Dynasty, the court sought tribute and respect from wherever. The Ming faced a poor situation in the north and west, so it focused on "countries of the South Seas." Mao faced a poor situation in the northeast and in contemplating the Western powers, so he threw down the carpet for tribute from distant parts of the Third World.

Said a Ming emperor in 1372, as quoted earlier: "Countries of the western ocean are rightly called distant regions. They come [to us] across the seas, and it is difficult for them to calculate the year and month [of arrival]. Regardless of their numbers, we can treat them [on the principle of] 'those who come modestly are sent off generously.'"[23] The Ming hauteur and largesse were equalled by Mao's welcome to Asian and African figures in the 1950s and 1960s.

"Having ascended [the mountain] I perform sacrifices," a Tang emperor said, defining a happy state of affairs, "a hundred Barbarian

---

[23]Perelomov and Martynov, 1983, 184.

clans bring gifts, ten thousand states visit the court, the court and the provinces rejoice, China and the Barbarians are exultant."[24] The tributary (*chao gong*) system expressed dynastic China's sense of centrality and cultural superiority. Non-Chinese, which at first meant nomads of the north, would come to the Chinese court and be touched by its civilization. A secondary aim was trade.

From the border, Chinese officials took charge of a foreign mission. They paid the bills, escorted the visitors to the capital, and coached the foreigners in proper behavior for a session with the emperor. The visitors prostrated themselves to the floor in a kowtow before the Son of Heaven. Gifts were exchanged and admired. It was made clear the foreigners must leave when the ensuing commercial business was done. The whole process showed the overarching power and sense of responsibility of the Chinese state, and the limited scope for *un*-official activity.

In 1971 a group of Australians made a mission to Beijing and found themselves part of a comparable process. The occasion was a bid by Gough Whitlam, leader of the opposition Labor Party, to talk with the Chinese leadership. One person from among the Barbarian tribe, myself, was chosen by Beijing as a "vanguard officer," as Premier Zhou Enlai referred to me when I met him as the visit unfolded. After the departure of the Barbarian chief, Whitlam, the "vanguard officer," myself, was kept on for some weeks, as reward and resource.

I arrived in Guangzhou from Boston and planned to spend some days in the southern city, but the foreign ministry insisted I come at once to Beijing for "discussions." Officials tried to establish that I had been "invited" to China and that I was a "guest." These terms were inaccurate, but they were important to Beijing because they implied obligations. Two millennia ago, the Han Dynasty scholar-official Ban Gu distinguished between paying tribute and coming to China as a guest. Sometimes he manipulated the difference to preserve face and make the emperor happy.

It was progress of a sort, then, that the Australians were "guests" and not tributaries. In truth, Whitlam could not be a tributary as he was not

---

[24] *Tang da zhaoling ji*, 14.

in office. Certainly it was better to be "guest" than "foreign friend." The term friend, in Beijing's mouth, was (and still is) used as a suction pump to draw all objective juices from a visitor. Yet, even "guest" and "invitation" were a dictatorship's technique to mask the lack of freedom of movement between China and the outside world.

The Australians were escorted from commune to Children's Palace, some side trips were paid for by the Chinese party-state, suggestions were made about etiquette, and the accompanying Australian journalists were guided in how to portray China and its "invitation" to the Australian political opposition. Banquets were used as a weapon to charm, soften, or awe the visitors. During the delicious meals, as dishes were awaited, the host had the chance to propose toasts to edify or rebuke the Barbarians. "Hospitality is political," secret Chinese Communist documents state accurately.[25]

When the Institute for International Affairs gave a banquet for Whitlam, the distinguished intellectual Zhang Xiruo spoke, a glass of *maotai* in his hand, about relations between China and Australia. Despite "vast oceans that separate us," said the Columbia University Ph.D. from the 1920s, there is a "tradition of rich contacts." He illustrated the tradition by listing sportsmen, writers, scientists, and others. All were Australian visitors to China. He gave no example of a notable Chinese visiting Australia.

"The Barbarians covet Chinese products," claimed an official Ming Dynasty history, "and make enormous profits by trade and the roads are packed with them."[26] One day in the summer of 1971, over dinner in Xi'an, foreign ministry official Zhou Nan said to me: "Everyone wants to come to China! Our ministries can't keep up with the applications from businessmen, journalists, politicians." Both statements were exaggerations. Both exhibited the self-importance of the Chinese state. The late 1990s version was Beijing's canard that the United States needed China more than China needed the United States. "If a 'trade war' occurs between the U.S. and China," inquired the official Chinese media in 1998, "is it possible that the U.S. economic growth that has gone on for

[25]Brady, 2000, 955.
[26]Cited in Perelomov and Martynov, 1983, 184.

more than 80 months will not be seriously affected?"[27] But the United States sells *only 3% of its exports* to China!

Compare China–Australia ties in the 1970s and China–Holland ties in the Qing Dynasty.[28] Each relationship, three centuries apart, revealed a similar blend of interests and ritual in Chinese foreign policy. The ritual served to maximize influence, to narrow the gap between Beijing's capacity and its goals.

Encountering the Dutch East India Company in the later seventeenth century, the Qing was dealing with a distant land of which it knew little. Beijing thought Java and Holland were one place. Likewise, in 1971, the Chinese bureaucrats we met were hazy about the distinction between Australia and New Zealand. The Qing needed the Dutch in struggles over Taiwan, where Ming Dynasty remnants led by Zheng Chenggong (Hoxinga), hostile to the Qing, had retreated. It used the Dutch desire for trade as a bargaining chip in this goal. In 1971, Beijing was trying to pry Australia from diplomatic relations with Taiwan to relations with Beijing. Purchases of wheat were dangled before the Australians as a reward. Exquisite ritual was practiced by the Chinese court in both cases, to impress the visitors with Chinese civilization and suggest the wisdom, patience, and resources of Chinese diplomacy.

In 1667, a Dutch embassy brought as gifts four dwarf horses from Persia and four dwarf oxen from Bengal. The emperor agreed to view the eight beasts, but declined to accept them. In 1971, one evening after dinner, Whitlam was told by his Chinese hosts to stay in his hotel. This created suspense, during which the Australian side fumbled to ready its questions and gifts, in case an imperial meeting was at hand. Came a near-midnight summons to a session with Prime Minister Zhou Enlai.

Two years later, after Whitlam's trip to China had helped make him prime minister, a similar drama was created for his visit to see Mao in his Ming Dynasty quarters by the Forbidden City. First making a

---

[27] *Xinhua she,* June 19, 1998.
[28] Wills, 1968, 228–246.

nervous wreck of the Australians by the uncertainty of the plans, the Chinese officials suddenly delivered Whitlam to the presence of Mao, who threw out imperial perspectives for the enlightenment of the Antipodeans.

The Dutch did not fret like the British (who came to Beijing later) over the requirement to fit into Chinese ritual. Likewise, the Australians were more informal with the Chinese than were Americans. Wills found that bad translation often helped reduce the Dutch–Chinese values gap, and Dutch requests sometimes disappeared in the Beijing–local political gap. These bittersweet mishaps occurred also in Australia–China dealings.

By 1690, China and Holland lost interest in each other. Zheng Chenggong's menace to the Qing on Taiwan ended. The Dutch no longer sought revenge against Zheng and cooled on Chinese silk and gold. Likewise, Chinese and Australian mutual excitement eased. After the Nixon–Mao opening of 1972, Whitlam's Australia was far less important to Beijing than was Nixon's United States, and Australia reaped few bonanzas from China trade in the 1970s and 1980s. China's deployment of ritual to maximize interests turned to other arenas.

"Visits were considered a reflection of the internal state of the middle kingdom," write two Russian scholars of a number of Chinese dynasties, "of its greater or less success in world arranging." Foreigners came to China, in the Chinese view, because virtue existed at the emperor's court. Early in the history of the Chinese polity, we find in a Shang Dynasty hymn, "None has yet dared to come without tribute."[29] Such ancient tradition was cited by later dynasties as they used and extended it.

The Tang ruler, Zong Zhi, in a welcoming verse to a mission from Dunhuang (today part of the PRC), said of the visitors: "You offer territories to the emperor / And have come far across the deserts to assure us of your loyalty." The same verse looked back on a mission from an ancient, showing an amusing awareness of the gap between ritual and

---

[29]Perelomov and Martynov, 1983, 114, 112.

reality. "So, today, we smile to recall that in ancient times / The Liu tribe came to show its submission by offering the court / A large dog named Ngao / History has noted this useless tribute as a spectacular gift."[30] During the Qing, Emperor Gao Zong wrote a verse that also made ancient parallels:

> *Heavenly Qing also accepts tributes,*
> *The ten thousand lands are in harmony.*
> *The patterns of writing, the tracks of carts,*
> *Who could remain out of them?*
> *[Among those whose] soles are square and whose heads are round*
> *None have failed to arrive . . .*
> *. . . The Shang court accepts the ritual jade,*
> *A hundred times [Heaven] has sent its blessings.*[31]

Mao deployed such literary symbols of world-arranging in the 1950s and early 1960s. Beijing looked in the mirror of Asia and Africa and parts of Latin America to confirm the glory of China. "It was like going to the court of Louis XIV," the first Indonesian ambassador to the PRC said of his visit to Mao to present credentials. "I felt I shouldn't ask Mao any questions. He was like a god. I think he believed in [the Heavenly Middle Kingdom]." The ambassador's boss, Sukarno, complained that he eight times invited Mao to visit Indonesia, with no sign of an acceptance.[32]

As for the "failure to arrive" of a Barbarian, we note that Jiang Qing, Mao's wife, on meeting President Nixon at a theater performance in 1972, inquired archly, "Why did you not come to China before now?"[33] Fortunately for Nixon, on stage, a drama of a heroic girl's struggle against landlords, one of Madame Mao's "model theater pieces," suddenly produced shouting and clatter, obviating a reply that would have required Nixon to broach the McCarthy era and the Vietnam War.

---

[30]Chen Tsu-Lung, 1966, 32–34.
[31]Perelomov and Martynov, 1983, 114.
[32]Mononutu, interview with the author, Jakarta, Dec. 1, 1979.
[33]Nixon, 1978, vol. 2, 39.

The classical canon observes that the appeal of China's virtue had a flip side. "When the power [*de,* virtue] of the Tang Dynasty declined," says the history of the Song dynasty, "the surrounding tribes stopped coming."[34] This is what happened to Deng and Jiang for several years after the Tiananmen tragedy of 1989.

In 1998, British prime minister Tony Blair visited Beijing and declared, "I want Britain to be China's number one friend in Europe." With this statement Blair locked himself into an old imperial device. His aim was the same as that of missions from Lhasa under the Ming Dynasty: Praise the emperor and then seek favors. Few favors for the British were on offer from Jiang Zemin. Blair spoke in grand terms of British investment in China, present and future. Yet, as Jonathan Mirsky reported, "No contracts were signed and no one mentioned that Britain invests much less in China than it does in tiny Belgium."[35]

Beijing supplied the imperial device of "friendship," which it had conjoined with friendship as a Soviet Communist technique, and Beijing benefitted from its deployment. After Blair declared his desire to be a Friend, the Chinese government announced that he was indeed a Friend. Blair was told he was such a good friend, "you can say anything you want to us." The only outcome of being declared a friend—inappropriate in the sphere of international relations—is an obligation to deliver what friends deliver. The rest was, as Mirsky said, Beijing Opera.

In this Chinese theatrical form, the outcome is known, the heroes are extremely heroic, and the villains are downright nasty. What counts is costumes, makeup, and precision of speech and movement. The imperial libretto moved from scene to scene. Blair handed over to Jiang a list of twenty Chinese political prisoners. The official spokesman later said the Chinese side had no memory of such a list.

Calling each other a Friend was an end in itself for China, and Blair might as well have packed his bags and left at that point. But he stayed on for the bells and whistles. The final badge of co-option came when Blair was allowed to write an article on the front page of *People's Daily.*

---

[34] *Song shi,* juan 485.
[35] *International Herald Tribune,* Oct. 12, 1998.

The Beijing Opera permitted Beijing to pretend that the world was in conformity with the Chinese way.

It had all been seen before under the Qing Dynasty. "The Chinese view of their empire as the sole center of civilization," wrote Wills, "[was] largely confirmed by experience and seldom challenged by foreign visitors to China."[36] In 1793, Macartney declined to perform a full kowtow before Emperor Qian Long. Some said the poor results of his mission were a consequence. This was not the case. The Dutch sent a mission to Beijing soon after Macartney, did the full kowtow, yet got nothing more than the British did from the court of Qian Long.

Blair's fellow Briton, Chris Patten, the former governor of Hong Kong, could have warned him the visit would be theater; you leave the auditorium and find the street outside unchanged. Patten discerned the two levels of Chinese diplomacy: theater (neo-Confucianism) and interests (neo-Legalism).

For a month, Governor Patten would face a barrage of insults from Beijing. Suddenly the attacks would stop; the party-state wanted something concrete, which it would not get by vituperation. Patten observed the well-oiled mechanism of The Threat ("You will have to bear all the consequences"). In fact, the threats to Governor Patten generally fizzled. They were theatrics. "There does not really seem to be any relationship between political good conduct in China's eyes and trade performance," Patten concluded.[37] Hong Kong under his rule did not suffer concrete (as distinct from verbal) "punishments" from Beijing at all.

"There are some officials who equate diplomacy with being nice to foreigners," Patten wrote after leaving the Hong Kong governorship.[38] But the Chinese, skillfully deploying their two levels of diplomacy, quickly see through foreign flattery. A Hong Kong businessman began a session with Prime Minister Li Peng by telling him he was "the greatest leader of the Chinese Communist Party since Mao." Li Peng inter-

---

[36]Wills, 1968, 254.
[37]Patten, 1999, 239.
[38]Patten, 1999, 92.

rupted to snap that he was not in fact leader of the CCP.[39] The flattery, amusing in retrospect, seldom makes the Chinese think more highly of the foreigner. Some British critics of Patten said his refusal to "shoe shine" (as south Chinese call flattery), and his bold steps toward democracy for Hong Kong, would together destroy British exports to China. This did not happen. Neo-Legalism was alive and well.

In 1998, the Dalai Lama visited Prague and the president of the Czech Republic, Vaclav Havel, spent much of the two-day trip at the Tibetan leader's side. The Beijing propaganda machine almost blew a gasket. Trade would suffer. Cultural exchanges could not but be devastated. The Chinese people's feelings were being crushed. A year later, I asked the Czech ambassador in Washington if the Dalai Lama's visit brought repercussions to Czech–PRC relations. "Absolutely none," he replied. With the Dalai Lama's departure from Prague, the curtain came down on the Beijing Opera. Everyone had played their roles. The grease paint was washed off, the costumes went back into the closet.

THE IMPERIAL LIBRETTO of "friends" and "anti-China forces" covers not only foreign nations, but also foreign individuals. Beijing saw Jimmy Carter as the best thing since the invention of chopsticks, because he set up full diplomatic relations with the PRC. Chris Patten was called "the Whore of the East," because he gave Hong Kong a bit of democracy before turning it over to China.[40] These were exaggerated, too-personal characterizations.

In a small way I have played both "hero" and "villain" roles in an imperial libretto. In 1971, I was singled out to get a much-desired visa, because I had helped Beijing (indirectly, in the course of helping the Australian opposition leader Whitlam). Having been given a visa and the hint of some interviews to come, I was expected to cooperate with Beijing as a "vanguard officer" in its plans for Whitlam's visit. I was

[39]Patten, 1999, 74.
[40]Patten, 1999, 57.

called by the official news agency "a good friend of the Chinese people." Later, I was given an award by Sichuan Province.

But the "hero" label lacks intrinsic meaning. Carter and Patten could switch roles in an instant if the script required it. What counts is the function being served for the interests of the Chinese party-state. Both Western leftists and rightists could and can be darlings of Beijing, depending on the issue at stake. After the Tiananmen Square tragedy, the same Australian-American person who had been a Friend, myself, became an anti-China force. In 1992, the official media that once praised me called me a "splittist" and the secret police said I had "hurt the feelings of the Chinese people" (a recurring lament of the party-state that seems to express both insecurity and arrogance).

In Beijing's classic divide-and-rule strategy, heroes and villains are cast for each historical phase. In the 1970s, when talk of "recognition of the PRC" was in the air, I was in the positive column. In the 1990s, when the question of democracy within Chinese civilization came up, I was moved to the negative column. Beijing's priorities had changed.

Anne-Marie Brady has shown that "foreign friend" and "foreign spy" are Siamese twins. The entire "Handling the Outside" (*waishi*) system, she writes, exists "to manage a balance between the two extremes [hating foreigners, fawning on foreigners] among the Chinese population, manipulating pro- or anti-foreign sentiment in accordance with the political needs of the time."[41] An underlying maxim for handling foreigners, "Distinguish between inside and outside" (*neiwai youbie*), is found in secret Chinese documents today. As the era of the apparently modern-minded Hu Jintao was proclaimed, at the upscale resort of Beidaihe, east of Beijing, the beach was still divided into a section for Chinese and one for foreigners.

It is difficult to imagine any other major nation laying down these rules Beijing promulgated as recently as 1993: "It is forbidden to engage in immoral behavior with foreigners, and it is forbidden to collude with foreigners to engage in illicit reselling of state products. Unless the permission of *waishi* offices has been given, it is forbidden

---

[41]Brady, 2000, 962.

to visit foreign embassies, consulates, apartments and other foreigners' residential quarters. It is forbidden to disseminate to foreigners expressions of discontent, or reactionary views that attack our Party or socialist system."[42]

China's psychocultural love–hate of the West may continue until the Chinese Communist party-state is replaced by a less world-arranging Chinese government. Pending that day, the dualism of "foreigners as the Other in contrast to the Chinese Self," functional for the new Chinese empire, is nevertheless an obstacle to China's much-vaunted "integration into the world community," and to Chinese and non-Chinese persons relating as equals in the PRC.

———————

THE SAGGING OF MARXIST faith in Beijing does not seem to have eliminated the Chinese imperial view of the world. Did Marxism stipulate that America was "imperialist"? Very well, the Marxists-in-transition in Beijing hardly miss a step in declaring America "hegemonist." Not, in fact, a very big difference. China now shouts its antihegemonism just as the China of Mao shouted its anti-imperialism; the tune is identical even as the lyric is adjusted. The song really means that a muscle-flexing China *itself wants to be the hegemon.* It aims to eclipse America in Asia and ensure that nothing is done there against China's wishes. Equipped with its own unstated version of the Monroe Doctrine, Beijing wants to be in Asia what Washington is in Latin America. That the goal is far distant does not reduce its sweetness.

At one level, as we have seen, the foreign policy goals of Beijing are the mother's milk of "peace and development." This is real enough, as far as it goes; China wants to be unmolested and knows a large agenda of economic development lies ahead. Yet, at another level, Beijing also seeks redress for the past. The details of this revanchism are secret, kept in reserve until the CCP can back up words with actions. But is this second goal programmatic or merely symbolic?

———————

[42]Brady, 2000, 958.

The question arises because myths about the past are wrapped up with the legitimacy of the Communist party-state. The roots of China's dealings with the outside world have always lain in vigilance toward the home front. The same considerations were translated from managing the Chinese people to dealing with the wider sphere: order, hierarchy, ritual, the unity of all things, correct doctrine. Perhaps the myths serve domestic stability, more than they flag tomorrow's foreign policy?

Some will say the legacy of the past may not necessarily make for a vigorous and positive foreign policy agenda. Under the dynasties, it could be said, three factors often made for *absence* of foreign policy ambition: insouciance, pragmatism, and a feeling that nothing beyond the Chinese realm mattered much. Sometimes in the PRC period, these same factors have produced a foreign policy consisting of little more than bureaucratic management and colorful words.

What did Beijing seek from Cambodia in 1966–1967 as Red Guards loyal to Mao rampaged in Phnom Penh? How did Beijing drift into conflict with the Soviet Union at the Ussuri River in Manchuria in 1969? What exactly was China's aim in frothing at the mouth over the American EP3 plane incident near Hainan Island in 2001? To ask these questions is almost to answer them: There seemed in all three cases to be no clear policy. Yet these spastic gestures are by no means the summation of Chinese foreign policy.

Are the ambiguities of the Chinese state due to latent desires (and dilemmas) that should worry China's neighbors? Are they merely an imperial style of behavior, ultimately as toothless as France's clinging to its *mission civilisatrice?* Are they essentially a drama of domestic policy, a strutting nationalism to legitimate an ideologically struggling Communist dynasty?

The truth is the current Chinese state weighs all three considerations. Revanchism, traditionalism of style to maximize influence, and a quest for fresh legitimacy; the three together make up the real PRC foreign policy. The Chinese state, a project from above and guardian of a doctrine, translates its condescension toward its own people into a sense of entitlement in world affairs.

ELEVEN

FOREIGN POLICY

Half-Empire and Half-Modern Nation

> . . . whereas India, after independence, came to good terms with her former rulers, the British, China interpreted the turn of history in 1949 as a glorious shift from a century of dishonorable inferiority to a brilliant age of ascendancy over her former invaders.
>
> —*Chusei Suzuki*[1]

Each time a flap occurs between Beijing and Washington over Taiwan or Tibet, the State Department and White House assure Beijing that our "One-China" policy is unchanged. Clinton's State Department did it in the aftermath of Taiwan president Lee Teng-hui's low-key visit to the United States in 1995. Clinton officials did it each time the president popped into a room (usually the vice president's) and spoke briefly with the Dalai Lama, encounters that Beijing protested. President Bush and his foreign policy team in 2002 and 2003 did much the same.

Why should the world's top power repeatedly recite, at Beijing's insistence, support for One China? We did not endorse the territorial integrity of the Soviet Union. On the contrary, we declined to accept the incorporation of Latvia, Lithuania, and Estonia into Moscow's realm. The Soviet leaders lived with that. Why in the case of China, a

---

[1]Suzuki, 1968, 189.

comparable Communist empire, do we endorse its questionable view of its own boundaries?

Countries friendly to Indonesia do not speak of One Indonesia, when questions arise about the rights of the turbulent provinces of Aceh and West Irian. No global tears are shed for Mongolia as a "divided country," yet it is one; should there be a doctrine of One Mongolia, to match One China? But China is special. China must be treated like a Ming vase, in Chris Patten's phrase. All this benefits the new Chinese empire. Beijing can pretend to be an aggrieved former semicolony, rather than the only multinational empire to survive into the twenty-first century.

After the Nixon–Mao opening of 1972, Washington unwittingly conspired with Beijing's view of itself as a special country. This was usually done for good reasons, but the effect was to sweep under the rug the problem of the Dynastic-Leninist state. At times, the awe in which the Washington leaders held the Beijing court led to variant private and public policies.

Zbigniew Brzezinski, national security advisor to President Carter, impressed with Deng's plan to attack Vietnam, echoed Kissinger's admiration for the crisp methods of the Chinese dictatorship: "I secretly wished that Deng's appreciation of the uses of power would also rub off on some of the key U.S. decision makers." During the ensuing China–Vietnam conflict, Brzezinski met daily with the Chinese ambassador to the United States, giving him helpful information on the war. This may or may not have been in American national interests. Certainly it was a success for Beijing's diplomatic skill to induce Washington to back it in "punishing" Vietnam.

Even as China attacked Vietnam in 1979, U.S. Treasury Secretary Michael Blumenthal went to Beijing to work out details for China to get Most Favored Nation trade status. When Blumenthal mildly criticized the Chinese invasion of Vietnam, Brzezinski cabled him, "Shut up and stick to trade issues."[2] Careful of the Ming vase!

---

[2] All U.S. officials' words from Mann, 1999, 71, 99, 107, 108.

During Deng's visit to Washington in January–February 1979, he told Carter that if China got Most Favored Nation status, U.S. trade with the PRC would become ten times its trade with Taiwan. It was a ridiculous pledge/prediction, but Carter evidently believed it. In fact, after two decades of MFN status for China, U.S. trade with the PRC was very far from being "ten times" its trade with Taiwan. In 1999, U.S. exports to the PRC were *less* than its exports to Taiwan.

The story of American China policy from 1972 is one of reasonable success for a number of years. But, in retrospect, with Watergate and the replacement of Nixon by Ford, the best years of that policy were over. Most of the benefit for U.S. interests of U.S.–China detente had been reaped. The later picture, from Carter to Clinton, was mixed. Beijing has quite often bested, outlasted, or deceived Washington.

For this there are diverse reasons. Our democratic system precludes the long-term outlook of the Beijing dictatorship's America policy. The loss of executive power to Congress, during the 1990s especially, allows enhanced influence for lobbies, and a resulting fragmentation of foreign policy vision. Most important is the inability of some on the American side to see through Beijing's imperial behavior.

Ritual to confuse, impress, and put off balance the opposing side is one mode. The repertoire includes scripted banquets, linguistic mystifications, and the mileage obtained from ambiguity. Many a time, from Nixon to Clinton, American diplomats have lost a battle to the techniques of this repertoire. A *posture of infinite patience* is a second mode. It is displayed in Taiwan policy, and in earlier years it was used to gain moral force in policy toward Britain on the Hong Kong issue. This posture conveys the impression of unshakeable principle, leads Americans in particular to admire China's cultural depth, and obscures Beijing's incapacity or unwillingness to match words with actions. These two modes are as old as the Han Dynasty.

A third mode springs from modern history. An *aggrieved stance* gives China a presumed upper moral hand. This legerdemain is able to locate China in the world's have-not "South," exploited and obstructed by the filthy-rich "North." The premise of all public discourse is that the West is declining, and that the Third World will flourish the moment Western imperialism crashes. Enough hangover exists from the Marxist sense of entitlement to portray China's rise as held back only by anti-China machinations. The Third World gleams with virtues, while the capitalist world is a cesspool of racism, poverty, and violence (is that why so many Chinese want to leave the PRC and go there?). China (apparently alone among all powers that have risen toward being Number One) will never seek hegemony. In fact, China matches itself against the great powers and disdains the Third World. In the main Chinese textbook for history teaching in middle schools, of the fifty-two chapters on non-Chinese history, only eight or nine are on the Third World.[3]

In all this behavior, we see a Chinese state that is anachronistic, a special case in foreign policy as it is in domestic policy. This is not a state that will allow economic development, by its own logic, to shape the future. Not a state into whose policies public opinion has any institutionalized input. Nor is it a state that expresses some intrinsic, never-changing Chinese essence. This is a Communist state trying to survive by leaning on those aspects of an autocratic tradition that suit its purposes. For this self-appointed state, Leninist, imperial, and paternalistic, neither economics nor culture is destiny. Its own political will, unaccountable to no one, is the compass that detects a future.

───────────

IN 1895, two proud Asian political leaders sat across a table in the Japanese seaport of Shimonoseki. Li Hongzhang spoke for the Qing Dynasty, Ito Hirobumi for the government of Meiji-era Japan. A war had given Japan victory over the Qing government of China; negotiations began on the Treaty of Shimonoseki. Japan, open to the West, was rising. China, battling the West, was tottering. Count Ito, in the box seat, criticized China as aloof, deceitful, and uncooperative toward the "family of nations."

───────────

[3] *Shijie lishi*, 1993; in vol. 1, 29 chapters are on world history from the beginnings, and 5 or 6 could be said to be on the Third World; in vol. 2, of 23 chapters on modern world history, 3 are on the Third World.

At one session Ito inquired: "Why does not China observe the rules of all other nations?" Li Hongzhang, a self-strengthener and a major figure at the Qing court, replied that it was "a very difficult matter in our country for the Servant [i.e. Li] to propose a change to the Sovereign [i.e. the emperor]." Ito observed that "the Imperial Wisdom" must surely "recognize the necessity for such a reform." Said Li: "Every change will certainly take time."

Li Hongzhang had a proposal of his own: "It is quite time the yellow-race should prepare against the white." But Ito did not see merit in an anti-West phalanx by China and Japan. "I think it would be wise," he riposted to Li, "to make your young men well acquainted with things European." But China looked down on Japan and would not take advice from it. As S. C. M. Paine wrote of the Chinese stance, "Japanese success at a time of mounting internal difficulties in China, instead of being seen as a way out of China's turmoil, became another 'loss of face' for the Chinese."[4]

A century and more later, China is still trying to pry Japan away from the West, still torn between disdaining Japan and learning from its best points, still imitating the West yet rejecting the West, and still sensitive to "face."

Japan's achievements after World War Two did not take away Chinese condescension toward a cultural younger brother. When Beijing and Tokyo reconciled in 1972, Mao dealt with Prime Minister Tanaka as if he were a vassal. Zhou Enlai brought Tanaka through an anteroom to Mao's armchair. "Did you finish your quarrel yet?" Mao inquired. "Quarrels are good for you," he declared grandly, without waiting for a response from the Japanese leader.

"We've had amiable talks," said Tanaka, sweeping under the rug the difficult issue of whether the (second) Japan–China War had caused "disaster" (the word proposed by Beijing) or merely "trouble" (Japan's term). When Tanaka tried to apologize directly to Mao for Japan's 1930s invasion of China, Mao resisted and said the "help" of that inva-

---

[4]Paine, 1996, 345–346 (including Li and Ito quotes).

sion made possible his Communist victory in 1949![5] Mao was positioning himself on a philosophical plane, above the policy level. He was the emperor, dealing with the Japanese visitor ritually, preserving the image of Japan, despite its advancement, as a manageable offshoot of Chinese civilization. Mao had updated for current purposes a Chinese cultural nationalism of largesse and condescension.

In the quarter-century since the Mao–Tanaka conversation, Tokyo has continuously and unsuccessfully tried to settle past and symbolic issues and focus on a current agenda. For the Chinese party-state, however, Japan symbolizes the World War Two past, and looms as a worry for the future, but is not easily accepted as a present reality.

On a 1998 trip to Japan, Jiang Zemin made a score of speeches about what he called "questions of history," centering on Japan's attack on China in the 1930s and its later role in keeping Taiwan out of Beijing's grasp. He spent time with "friendship organizations," urging them to "counter militarism," as if, in 1998, the big military buildup in East Asia was coming not from Beijing but from Tokyo. He complained that Japanese textbooks were nationalistic. Jiang did not say whether the CCP has ever "faced up to the history" of the ruinous Great Leap Forward that led to 30 million deaths.

Jiang's Japan policy was a piece of theater that moralized Japan's aggressive past. Beijing knows how to "move on" when it suits—hence its lack of historical memory of the Great Leap Forward—but, with Japan, the Chinese Communists find dwelling on the past irresistible. It permits the imperial style to be utilized, buttresses the legitimacy of Communist rule ("without the CCP, China would not have defeated Japan"), and milks Japanese guilt for practical concessions.

Jiang must have realized that the 1998 trip to Japan was short on fruits, but the imperial posture was not given up. In the spring of 2001, the new Japanese prime minister, Junichiro Koizumi, said he intended to visit a Shinto shrine that honors Japan's war dead on August 15, anniversary of the official end of World War Two. In July at an ASEAN meeting in Hanoi, the Chinese foreign minister, Tang Jia-

---

[5] *Tokyo Shimbun*, Sept. 27, 1972.

xuan, protested to his Japanese counterpart about Koizumi's planned visit to the Yasukuni Shrine. After that meeting, Tang met Japanese reporters and cried "Stop this!" to indicate Beijing's view on the shrine visit. "The words were spoken in Japanese," reported the *New York Times,* "in an imperative voice usually reserved for children."[6]

The result of Tang's outburst was similar to the result of Jiang's harping in 1998: Japan dug in its heels. Koizumi went to the Yasukuni Shrine as planned (though on August 13, a token two days away from the World War Two anniversary). After Jiang's 1998 speeches on World War Two in Japan, the Japanese chief cabinet secretary, Hiromu Nonaka, said in frustration, "Isn't this a finished problem?"[7] But Japan's past transgressions will never be a finished problem while the imperial state exists in Beijing. "Just how long do we have to repeat the apology?" asked the Tokyo daily *Sankei.*[8] Until the Chinese state ceases to legitimate itself by means of receiving such apologies; until empire becomes modern nation.

Beijing criticizes Japan for textbooks that "sanitize" Japan history, yet PRC textbooks also sanitize Chinese history. The main text for middle school history in China devotes nine chapters to Japan's aggression against China in the nineteenth and twentieth centuries, but does not mention China's invasion of Japan in the Yuan Dynasty. Vietnam comes off even worse than Japan in *Zhongguo lishi* (Chinese History), the multivolume work, which, like all textbooks in China, is a party-state book. Nothing is said of the Han Dynasty's conquest of Vietnam or of China's 1,000-year colonization of Vietnam! The only discussion of Vietnam in the four volumes that deal with Chinese history concerns the France–China war of 1885. Vietnam was the "place," as it were, where China and France encountered each other. France "invaded Vietnam, using it as a springboard to invade China."[9] Likewise, Chinese invasion and colonial rule of Korea are simply omitted.[10]

---

[6] *New York Times,* July 26, 2001.
[7] *South China Morning Post,* Nov. 28, 1998.
[8] *South China Morning Post,* Nov. 28, 1998.
[9] *Zhongguo lishi,* vol. 3, 64.
[10] *Zhongguo lishi,* vols. 1, 2, 3, 4; lesson 11 of vol. 3 deals with the 1885 war.

The recent political history of China is just as selective. The text-book does not mention the Great Leap Forward famine. It gives the impression the CCP was the reason for the success of Chiang Kai-shek's Northern Expedition of 1927 that unified much of China. Also that the CCP was in charge of the Chinese nation in the 1937–1945 war against Japan.[11]

Actually, the criticism by Beijing of Japan's textbooks is not about history, but about the present and the future, just as Chinese textbooks are didactic tracts designed not only to inform but also to inculcate nationalism. "It is true that the controversy is about history," writes Han Xiaorong in a trenchant discussion of the Chinese–Japanese text-books dispute, "but it is about the pieces of history that are still closely linked to current controversial issues."[12] The PRC, like past Chinese regimes, uses history as a means of control and a weapon in struggle with non-Chinese. The technique is more dangerous in China than in Japan because in Japan, unlike in China, there are both government-sponsored textbooks and independent ones. In April 2001, the Chinese government sponsored a group of soldiers who had fought against Japan to gather in Harbin and fire a blast at a Japanese textbook. "I cannot understand what on earth the Japanese government wants its young people to become in the future," said one veteran, "with this textbook distorting history."[13] In China's textbooks the distortion is worse, but not a dog barks against it.

———

THE SONG DYNASTY, in a multivolume work called *Cefu yuangui* (Outstanding Models from the Storehouse of the Past), gave voice to two enduring themes of Chinese foreign policy as it related historical precedent to its own border problems in the tenth and eleventh centuries. The themes of the key editorial prefaces in *Cefu yuangui* were: concealing weakness with the appearance of strength, and juxtaposing ideals and *realpolitik*. Though the Khitan ruler, in the north, who led

———

[11]*Zhongguo lishi*, vol. 4, lesson 22; vol. 3, lesson 27; vol. 4, lesson 1; vol. 4, lesson 10.
[12]Han, 2002, 11.
[13]*Xinhua she*, April 6, 2001.

the Liao Dynasty, was an equal of the Song emperor, Song documents call him an "Outer Minister" (*wai chen*) of the Chinese court.[14] To make the limits on Chinese power more bearable, the Song, in its book designed to make history serve the present, reviewed and affirmed a foreign policy tradition going back to the Xia Dynasty that (purportedly) began in the twenty-first century B.C.[15]

The Song historians could hardly deny that the Han Dynasty had not been strong enough to repulse the Xiongnu nomads. Their solution was to gloss over three post-Han centuries, prior to the rise of the Sui Dynasty, in five lines of the compilation. The Tang period was revised by the Song writers to bring Chinese power and Chinese virtue as close together as possible.

The first and longest preface in *Cefu yuangui*, "General Preface on Outer Ministers," has Tang emperor Tai Zong, in reviewing the past, frankly drawing a distinction between a Han Dynasty that had to compromise with non-Chinese, and a Tang Dynasty that did not need to. "Formerly during the Han," he wrote in 642, in response to advice not to break a promise over a marriage pact, "the Xiongnu were strong and China was weak; therefore the daughters were richly adorned and married to the *Shan-yu*. Now, China is strong and the Northern Ti are weak, and a thousand soldiers can defeat their several tens of thousands." A marriage pact could be broken at will in periods of Chinese strength.

The Song book, covering a period when Tibet was the equal of China, had to admit that the same Emperor Tai Zong entered into a marriage pact between China and Tibet that he had to honor. Similarly with a marriage pact between another Tang emperor and a Uighur leader. Still, the *Cefu yuangui* decided to tell a useful lie, to disguise Legalism as Confucianism, and say the Uighurs, from the time of the marriage pact on, "paid tribute [to China] without cease."[16]

The Song Dynasty itself, in a treaty with the Khitan of 1005, just eight years before the "General Preface on Outer Ministers" appeared,

---

[14]*Cefu yuangui,* book 19, juan 956, 11237.
[15]*Cefu yuangui,* book 19, juan 956, 11237, 11238; Wang Gungwu, 1983, 56.
[16]*Cefu yuangui,* book 19, juan 956, 11240.

had to treat its partner as an equal. Gifts of silk and silver were handled so as to be viewed either as tribute from the Khitan to China, or as *tribute from China to the Khitan*. The Song had to swallow Korea paying tribute, not to China but to the Liao (Khitan) Dynasty. Also, in the south, some kingdoms paid tribute to Vietnam rather than China. In this precarious situation, the Song—here was the point of the painstaking historical review—drew reassurance from knowing that the ancients had been realistic without ceasing to be virtuous Chinese.

The *Cefu yuangui*, which in total runs to twenty volumes, created workable precedent out of a blend of Confucianism and Legalism. It clung to Chinese superiority even as it embraced modes employed when China was in fact inferior. Mugged by reality, the Song had to accept that doctrine and reality could diverge. "After 1005," writes Wang Gungwu in a brilliant analysis of the compilation, "as they contemplated the continuities of Chinese history, Song officials began to see that there had been a respectable tradition of dealing with reality separately so that there was no need to change the rhetoric. When all you could do was hold the line, there was obviously no Chinese world order. But even for a lesser empire, perhaps especially for one so perceived, the rhetoric of tribute was immensely comforting and reassuring."[17]

These intellectual and political processes have been adapted for use in the PRC, not out of scholasticism, but because the two operational themes identified earlier continue: alternation of strength and weakness, and mixed application of ideals and *realpolitik*.

An immense amount has changed in foreign policy from the Song Dynasty until today, including the following: Beijing now deals with every corner of the globe, belongs to 451 international governmental organizations and 2,986 international nongovernmental organizations,[18] possesses in Marxism-Leninism an ideology more genuinely universal than Confucian all-under-heaven doctrine, accepts continuous intercourse with foreigners in Beijing, has the military capacity to wreak havoc on nations far across the seas (including the West Coast

[17]Wang Gungwu, 1983, 62.
[18]Union of International Associations, *Yearbook of International Organizations*, 38th ed., 2001/2002, vol. 5, 42.

of the United States, as it has chosen to boast), and has joined UN peacekeeping operations in Cambodia, East Timor, Mozambique, Iraq–Kuwait, Western Sahara, Liberia, and Sierra Leone.[19]

Nevertheless, we cannot simply draw a line between the dynasties and the PRC. A great deal also changed between the third century B.C. and Qin Shihuang's era. The chaos after the fall of the Han in the third century was a far cry from the Tang at its height in the eighth century. The Song Dynasty before and after its military defeat at the hands of the Jin in the north in 1126–1127 was a different beast. Economically, China enjoyed a medieval leap forward—Elvin calls it an "economic revolution"[20]—but it was followed by a slump until the sixteenth century. The activist-state economic policies of the early Song were not found in the Ming.[21] Between the Qing Dynasty in full extension in the eighteenth century and the retreating Qing of post-1860, there was a sharp change.[22] These fluctuations, in scale and general nature, may be compared to changes within the span of the PRC between the Mao era and the Jiang era. We see, in ancient, medieval, and contemporary China, oscillation between tight control and disorder. Between holding the line and pushing for maximum goals. Between pursuit of prosperity and pursuit of national glory. Between moral suasion and the sword. Between attention to the outside world and neglect of it. The important thing is to grasp the laws behind the changes.

For thousands of years, the two themes mentioned above have been evident in these repeated changes. Sometimes China is strong, sometimes it is weak; a link between the two conditions lay, and lies, in the Chinese polity's efforts to maximize its influence by hiding the difference and repackaging weakness as strength. Benjamin Schwartz saw the variables involved in rising and falling. One was "contingent external factors." We may illustrate this variable. The Xiongnu nomads were a challenging menace to the Han; the Soviet Union was a menace to Mao. The Khitan were an obstacle for the Song; the United States was

---

[19]*China's National Defense,* 1998, 23.
[20]Elvin, 1973, 215.
[21]Paul J. Smith, 1991, 318; Elvin, 1973, 205.
[22]Perdue, 2000, 266; Hostetler, 2001, 26.

for Jiang Zemin. And so on. Schwartz's other variable was "the strength of inner cosmological foundations." The Han Dynasty enjoyed prestige among some surrounding peoples; after the Han fell, a divided China enjoyed less. Mao's communism had a global appeal to the far left in the 1950s and 1960s; by 2003 the communism of Jiang and Hu Jintao had virtually no ideological appeal.

A second theme that is constant for thousands of years of repeated change is the Chinese polity's ambidextrous use of morally laced language and naked *realpolitik*. The dualism (not unknown, in a different form, in American diplomatic history) is as old as the difference between Confucius and Han Fei; as current as the difference between Premier Zhu Rongji telling Americans that China is "a reliable friend" of the United States,[23] and a secret army report saying, "it will prove impossible to fundamentally improve Sino-U.S. relations."[24] The Chinese Communist duet of the ideal and the real stems from a long and largely successful tradition.

The Song Dynasty was often frustrated at its inability to impose a Chinese world order, just is Beijing is frustrated at the gap in wealth and power between China and the West. For the Song, coping with the frustration involved falling back on "inner cosmological foundations." Today, the equivalent ideational crutch is Chineseness-plus-Marxism, with the balance tipping increasingly toward the former. The strength–weakness factor, for the Song and other dynasties, was connected with the idealism–realism factor. Fluctuating capacity was a major variable in the oscillation between hauteur and compromise, between high Confucian vision and low Legalist dogfight. The connected dualisms are both in evidence during the PRC decades.

A comparison of President Reagan's and President Clinton's relations with China is revealing of the Beijing party-state. Surprisingly, U.S.–China ties were smoother under Reagan than under Clinton. This was not because Reagan was better disposed toward the values of Chinese communism than was Clinton! Rather it was because, with his mil-

---

[23] *Wall Street Journal,* April 6, 1999.
[24] Munro, 1994, 358.

itary buildup and other signs of strength, Reagan was perceived in Beijing as a leader who would not readily back down. The Chinese state, which for two thousand years has known when and how to retreat, compromised with Reagan. With Clinton, who wavered and pecked intermittently at China policy, Beijing simply pushed for more and more.

JIANG ZEMIN'S visit to the United States in October–November 1997 was worthwhile for U.S.–China relations, yet it also displayed the Chinese party-state's self-glorifying techniques. The Chinese press and film coverage of the trip depicted a historic triumph. Jiang "conquered the hearts of Americans." He was shown strumming a guitar for adoring Americans, banging his hands together at the New York Stock Exchange, speaking in English to a Harvard audience, and appearing to answer each question at a Washington press conference. The Chinese press later said Jiang "possesses a wide knowledge of things ancient and modern, speaks fluent English, plays the guitar, sings Beijing opera and is good at swimming and dancing." He is "extraordinarily quick-witted and charismatic." He is "amiable and worthy of respect."[25] This is the picture the Chinese people received of Jiang and his impact on America.

The processes involved in the Chinese state pursuing its purposes abroad were revealed in Jiang's visit to Harvard. In Memorial Hall, Jiang spoke of China being united for millennia, a shaky assertion. Limning China's historical exchanges with other nations, he never mentioned the import of Marxism-Leninism! I heard no one at Harvard in the ensuing days remark on the omission. Some may have felt it was a sign of Jiang's post-Communist liberal cosmopolitanism that he left out Marxism. The truth is Jiang at Harvard, as during the entire U.S. trip, essentially hid his foreign policy agenda.

During his Harvard appearance, Jiang was affable and spoke some English. Some Harvard people clutched at such straws to declare his visit a triumph. To make thin pickings a little fatter, a few read into a

---

[25]All cited in *New York Times*, June 16, 1998.

boilerplate answer an admission of error over Tiananmen Square; actually it was not. Two days before, in Washington, with Clinton at his side, Jiang had stated that the Chinese government "long ago" arrived at a "correct judgment" of the Tiananmen incident. Everything said by Beijing on the June 4, 1989, event in the six years since Jiang's appearance at Harvard buttresses the point that Jiang was not conceding error.

Unfortunately, Harvard did not permit an open session of questions to Jiang. A committee filtered out submitted questions beforehand. At the speech, the chairperson read out chosen questions that had no bite and did not differ from those Jiang had already been asked in Washington and New York. Still, an apology was made to Jiang for the "toughness" of the questions he was asked! After the two "selected" questions, a third from the floor was announced. The chairperson said, "President Jiang Zemin would like to hear from an American." Up stood American citizen Lee Tun-Hou, Professor of Virology at the Harvard School of Public Health. "I do not recognize you, please sit down," said the chairperson, evidently overlooking that an American may be of Chinese origin.[26]

One question the screening committee received that was not put to Jiang was: "You say Taiwan should be part of China and the USA has long prevented the reunion of Taiwan with the Mainland. Looking back, was it a good thing or a bad thing that Taiwan, by being separated from the PRC, missed out on the Great Leap Forward and the Cultural Revolution?" On a Boston radio program a few days before, I had suggested this as a stimulating question. A member of the screening committee told me as I walked into Memorial Hall that this question had been received by his group. A radio listener had evidently submitted it. But the committee may have thought this question would upset the Chinese dictator. Expressing a perennial American illusion, the chairperson told a reporter that by showing Jiang "how we conduct open public discussion in a peaceful democratic way without creating disorder, it will be meaningful for public debate in China."[27]

---

[26]Lee Tun-Hou, e-mail to the author, Feb. 19, 2002.
[27]*Boston Globe*, Oct. 31, 1997.

There is no public debate on political issues or foreign policy in China, there was virtually none at Harvard on that day in Memorial Hall (posters, no threat to security, were forbidden), and all that was "meaningful" for the people within China—all they were shown—was Jiang speaking before a backdrop of the emblem "Veritas" of a great American university. The crimson and white banner "Veritas" was one of two images the Chinese party-state most wanted from the trip. The other, which it maneuvered to conjure into the record, was of Jiang standing before the Liberty Bell in Philadelphia. "American negotiators preparing for the visit," wrote the *New York Times*, perhaps not wishing to pinpoint Clinton officials' failure to understand the centrality of ritual for the Chinese state, "have said they were perplexed by the way their Chinese counterparts seemed extremely particular about the details of protocol and symbol."[28]

Outside Memorial Hall, one pleasant feature of the scene was pro- and anti-Beijing ethnic Chinese debating with each other. But in general the day was a missed opportunity on Harvard's part. Inside the hall, a prettified ritual. Outside, chanting demonstrators. Each fed on the other. To have engaged Jiang Zemin in dialogue within Memorial Hall would have created a middle ground. It was startling to hear Harvard president Neil Rudenstine welcome Jiang in the name of freedom of speech, and then sit through a meeting for which the ground rules had been proposed by the authoritarian Chinese party-state, and accepted by Harvard. Back in Beijing, the Communist media did not focus on Harvard's attachment to free speech. Instead, it thundered that people in the United States should "give up their cold war mentality." From Washington to Cambridge, the Chinese party-state had enjoyed an excellent week. Jiang was treated as a Ming vase.

PRESIDENT CLINTON, accompanied by 500 support staff and 200 reporters, in a total entourage of 1,200 people, returned Jiang's visit to the United States with a trip to China in June 1998 that sent Beijing

---

[28]*New York Times*, Oct. 28, 1997.

into high heaven. The official Chinese news agency wrote on the eve of Clinton's arrival, "Some anti-China elements and politicians in the U.S., with all sorts of excuses, have been vociferously attacking the White House policy of engagement with China, and they have also tried to obstruct Clinton's trip to China."[29] Beijing backed Clinton to the hilt politically. In return, Clinton leaned heavily toward the Beijing view of Taiwan and U.S.–China relations. And he gave a ringing endorsement, at the end of the trip, to the top Communist dictatorship.

In Beijing, standing beside the leader of a government that has never expressed any remorse on behalf of the Communist Party for the Great Leap Forward and the Cultural Revolution, Clinton said Americans must "acknowledge the painful moments in our own history when fundamental human rights were denied." Positioning himself just where the Chinese state wished, he continued: "we must say that we know we still have to continue to work to advance the dignity and freedom and equality of our own people." Beijing played the American president like a violin. If *lai hua* ("Come and be Sinified") had not been invented two thousand years before, it would have had to be crafted for the 1998 summit.

The die was cast before Clinton left Washington. Hoped-for agreements on trade, human rights, and the environment did not materialize, so the White House declared the *trip itself* to be the message. "The single most important outcome," said the administration's trade representative, "would be to introduce China to the United States." That was what the Chinese side wanted. But "introduce China to the United States" was an odd phrase for the U.S. side to use in 1998. The phrase really meant, "discredit the 'anti-Beijing regime' sentiments of some Americans," which the CCP strove to achieve and Clinton happily assisted them to achieve.

"He's not going to meet with people who are in jail or under house arrest," said a senior administration official. "This is not a road show to play to the galleries back home." Actually, it was. But the road show, whose strings were being pulled by the Chinese party-state, "played" to

---

[29]*Xinhua she,* June 19, 1998.

combat the "anti-China forces" back home. For weeks prior to Clinton's trip, as prior to Jiang's trip to the United States, Chinese authorities questioned and intimidated Chinese, some in America and many in China, whom they feared may strike a discordant note during the summit. Chen Bangzheng, a molecular biologist who works for the Food and Drug Administration, visited his mother in China prior to Clinton's trip. Security police nabbed him for questioning about dissenting Chinese in the United States. "It was clear to me," he said, "that they didn't want anything to happen to interrupt any honeymoon between Jiang Zemin and Mr. Clinton."[30]

On the eve of Clinton's departure from Washington, Beijing, by telephone, canceled visas—recently issued—to three reporters from Radio Free Asia who were to cover the president's China trip. The head of Radio Free Asia, which is a publicly funded network set up by Congress in 1994, asked the White House to allow the three reporters to travel on the plane chartered by the government to carry media on the trip. The White House said no, hiding behind "international aviation requirements, which state that you have to have a valid visa to board the aircraft."[31] This overlooked that the three reporters had valid Chinese visas stamped in their passports. In a similar situation in 1991, the British prime minister simply told Beijing that a journalist China wanted to exclude was coming on the British plane; at Beijing airport, China gave him his visa.[32] But Washington let Beijing keep the three Radio Free Asia reporters from covering his trip. It quaked before the Ming vase.

The Chinese party-state even outclassed the White House in handling news of Clinton's best moments within China. The *People's Daily*, reporting the joint press conference between Clinton and Jiang, omitted Clinton's excellent words on freedom, Tibet, and the Tiananmen tragedy of 1989. The day after Clinton went to church and spoke well to a congregation of 2,000, *People's Daily* did not mention that event. Nor, the next day, did *People's Daily* offer the barest word of Clinton's

---

[30] *New York Times,* June 9, 1998.
[31] *New York Times,* June 24, 1998.
[32] *International Herald Tribune,* June 25, 1998.

free-wheeling speech at Beijing University the previous day.[33] But did Beijing not keep its promise to televise the press conference and the university talk? It did, but as Jonathan Kolatch reported, without prior announcement to the Chinese public. On the Saturday and Monday mornings concerned, few Chinese were in their homes and few watched.[34]

Clinton officials, giving transcripts of Clinton's remarks on all three occasions to the U.S. press for dispatch around the world, and basking in the American public's appreciation of the film they saw of Clinton on the three occasions, did not seem to realize that, thanks to the policies of *People's Daily* and Jiang's office, the Chinese public, the presumed object of many of his remarks, missed them. In these ways, the Chinese Communist party-state turned weakness into a kind of strength.

Jim Hoagland of the *Washington Post*, not given to excess, wrote an unwitting tribute to Chinese theatrical skill: "His [Clinton's] China trip is being scripted around a set of fictions. Clinton joins the Chinese in manipulating himself for their purposes, which he mistakes as identical to his own."[35]

"What I would like to see," Clinton told a press conference in Hong Kong after leaving China, "is the present government, headed by this president and this premier, who are clearly committed to reform, ride the wave of change and take China fully into the 21st century."[36] The Chinese people had no say in the selection of this Chinese government that so pleased Clinton. Clinton found in Jiang a Chinese Gorbachev. Had he looked closer he would have seen a Chinese Brezhnev.

Meanwhile Jiang pursued his unexpressed goals, and a *New York Times* editorial after the visit must have helped convince him that he attained one of them: "[Jiang] used his appearances with Mr. Clinton to present himself as a statesman who could meet on equal terms with the leader of the world's richest and most powerful country."[37] That is

---

[33]*Renmin ribao,* June 24, 25, 1998.
[34]*Washington Post,* July 28, 1998.
[35]*Washington Post,* June 21, 1998.
[36]*New York Times,* July 4, 1998.
[37]*New York Times,* July 4, 1998.

turning weakness into strength, a fundamental aim of the Chinese party-state.

Interviewed by *Newsweek* in connection with Clinton's visit to China, Jiang ended with a remark he obviously planned to get in. "I'd like to conclude," he said, "by quoting a famous poet from the Song Dynasty. . . . 'Despite the efforts of the mountains, the river will keep flowing eastward.'"[38] This was nothing less than an update of Mao's Cultural Revolution maxim, "The east wind will prevail over the west wind."

David Sanger of the *New York Times* seemed to understand Beijing's manipulation of Clinton, yet he never criticized it. "They wanted the imagery of Air Force One flying right past Japan," he said cheerily of Clinton's capitulation to Beijing's demand that Clinton not stop in Japan en route to the Middle Kingdom.[39] Just after Clinton returned home, Premier Zhu Rongji, in a secret speech, expressed satisfaction that Clinton "made no stopover in Japan on his way to China . . . with the result that Japan has lost face."[40]

"World public opinion" highly rated the Jiang–Clinton summit, said *People's Daily.* The Chinese official press basked in any comment from outside China that Clinton and Jiang had met on equal terms, that Beijing's direct telecast of Clinton's words showed Jiang's "confidence," that the two leaders together had made Asia "more stable" and the "world more peaceful."[41]

The two summits between Clinton and Jiang bore out Waldron's remark that "China can act special in its relations with us only when we treat it as special."[42] The occasions displayed a successful manipulation, by means of ritual, an aggrieved stance, and a posture of patience, of the most powerful country in the history of the world by a Communist dictatorship grabbing at the lifebelt of any slim hope to renew its legitimacy.

---

[38] *Washington Post,* June 21, 1998.
[39] *New York Times,* June 21, 24, 1998.
[40] *Jingbao* (Hong Kong), Aug. 1, 1998.
[41] *Renmin ribao,* June 29, 1998.
[42] Waldron, *New Republic,* May 17, 1999, 44.

Wrote a pair of Russian scholars of the foreign outlook of Chinese dynasties from Tang to Ming: "[T]he clear cut ideological principles, coupled with the well-orchestrated ritual, and with the stake the [foreigners] had in maintaining commercial relations with China, enabled the imperial officials to create the illusion of a dependence far and away greater than the true political influence of the celestial empire."[43] Every word of this could be said of Washington's wishful thinking about China during the 1990s.

The only difference was that in the 1990s the commercial bonanza was more imagined than real. Clinton's commerce secretary called China "the pot at the end of the rainbow."[44] But, while the Clinton administration saw China becoming capitalist and democratic, Beijing saw itself becoming a mercantilist state, every muscle strained toward being a superpower to eclipse the United States. In the process, during the 1990s, China's trade surplus with America rose from $6 billion to $83 billion.[45]

THE COMING TO OFFICE of George W. Bush did not ring down the curtain on the smoke-and-mirrors performance of the Chinese state in U.S.–China relations. Consider the sequence of events surrounding Secretary of State Colin Powell's July 2001 trip to Beijing. On the eve of Powell's arrival, two imprisoned scholars with U.S. connections were convicted of spying and immediately deported. This gesture, easy to repeat when circumstances require it, had no impact on the fate of thousands of other political prisoners. In Beijing, Powell's TV interview was eviscerated to omit his criticisms of the PRC human

---

[43]Perelomov and Martynov, 1983, 128.
[44]*New Republic,* March 10, 1997, 15.
[45]The astonishing rise in China's trade surplus with the United States during the 1990s, according to U.S. Census figures, is as follows (rounded to the nearest billion): 1990, $6 billion; 1991, $12b; 1992, $18b; 1993, $22b; 1994, $29b; 1995, $33b; 1996, $39b; 1997, $49b; 1998, $56b; 1999, $68b; 2000, $83b; 2001, $77b. Beijing has a different way of measuring the trade figures, but on its own calculation, China's surplus with the United States rose *more than 45%* in the first six months of 2002 as compared with the equivalent period in 2001 (Beijing General Administration of Customs).

rights record, in breach of an agreement with the U.S. Embassy that Powell's remarks would be relayed in full. In terms of political effect, this withholding of information from the Chinese public was more consequential (for Beijing's benefit) than the selective release of a few political prisoners (for American benefit). Both the deception and the grand gesture, redolent of the traditional Chinese party-state, were devices to pluck strength from weakness.

Beijing's schizophrenic performance of good-cop bad-cop during Powell's visit won plaudits in the American media. Wrote the *Wall Street Journal* after Powell returned from China: "Just three months after the nasty U.S.–China face-off over a downed American spy plane, the advocates for engagement with Beijing have won."[46] Why such a conclusion? Victory, in truth, went to the crafty Chinese party-state. Within China, the chilling effect of the original arrests was ongoing; yet Beijing reaped benefit from its "largesse" in releasing two persons. Powell himself seemed a victim of the tricks. On September 9, two months after his trip to China, I asked him about the condition of U.S.–China relations. "I had an excellent trip to Beijing," the secretary of state said. "Very encouraging indeed."

One current school of thought, which may include Powell or some of his State Department aides, worries that President Bush may "make Beijing angry" or "displease China." If we understand the nature of the Communist party-state, this is an unnecessary fear. There is no way the United States can please Beijing. The craving for respect could not be fulfilled by a thousand American concessions. Sometimes, to be sure, Beijing is justified in being upset. But often the PRC's anger is beyond analysis or disregard. A near-theology exists that China's feelings, above those of all other nations, must never be hurt. The Barbarians were required to accept that in the Han Dynasty; Americans are asked to do so in the twenty-first century.

Beyond feelings, China's anti-Americanism is a cold political calculation. With Marxism no longer the root of China's social and eco-

---

[46]Neil King in *Wall Street Journal,* July 26, 2001.

nomic policies, how can Beijing justify the Communist Party's continued guaranteed monopoly on political office? By asserting that without
the Communist Party, the Chinese nation would face destruction at the
hands of "imperialists" and "hegemonists" who seek to quash its rise.
Thus does the evil of the United States become essential to the
refreshed legitimation of the Communist party-state.

It would deflate some of this mythology if foreign nations steadily
treated China as an ordinary country—not as an evil empire; nor as a
magic kingdom for which heaven or history has made special rules. If
they asserted that a relationship with Beijing is a two-way street whose
success depends on both parties. Beijing has managed to convince the
world that a poor relationship with Beijing is always and forever the
fault of the non-Chinese side. Yet good relations with China, Chris
Patten observes, are not a "commodity that can be offered or withheld
by Beijing," but a result of "the aggregate of business—agreements and
disagreements—that each of us does bilaterally with China."[47]

As of early 2004, some people feel U.S.–China relations have a rosy
glow of health because of 9/11. Washington and Beijing stand together
against terrorism. Let us be clear-eyed: Terrorism is a method, and
democracy also is a method. The pair are opposite poles. The antithe-
sis is that the terrorist is not accountable to any human constituency,
whereas the leader in a democracy faces the voters. Al Qaeda, as a terrorist organization, operates analogously to a nondemocratic government, that is, a dictatorship. As dictatorships go, the PRC is quite
rational. Still, it is a dictatorship; Hu Jintao, the CCP chief, has never
faced the voting choice of the Chinese people, any more than has Al
Qaeda's head Osama bin Laden ever faced voters. Al Qaeda will kill
anyone; the PRC executes to punish particular behavior. But there is no
accountability in either case. The Chinese state is at once a foe of the
anarchy of wanton terrorism and a semiterrorist outfit itself. Here is the
strangeness of Beijing as a partner in Bush's antiterrorist drive.

Leftist elements around the world, devastated at the existence of a
single superpower that is not their first choice, speak of a U.S.

---

[47]Patten, 1999, 258.

imperium. No one can deny the reach and influence of the United States beyond its borders. But this "hegemony," as Beijing calls it, is mostly the result of the free choice of individuals. The forces that promote "American hegemony" are immigration to America from the entire world, open information, technological prowess, and a free market. The difference between the U.S. state, shaped and fueled from below, and the Chinese state, a construct from above, is far from incidental in a war between terrorism and free societies.

———————

Is China still recovering from past weakness, in the CCP's view, or has it begun a positive agenda for a larger place in the world? The question brings us back to the Chinese state's hang-up with the West that Count Ito noticed in Li Hongzhang in 1895. One hundred years after Count Ito and Li Hongzhang met in Shimoneseki, Beijing in 1995 called Chris Patten "the snake, the liar . . . the man condemned for a thousand antiquities." In 1998, it criticized Patten's memoir *East and West* with the words: "China deserves respect and equal treatment rather than venomous slander and hostility in the world arena." These two quotations about the Briton who was governor of Hong Kong from 1992 to 1997 encapsulate the contradiction of Chinese foreign policy. China lectures the world in imperial didactic tones, yet wants "respect" as a modern nation alongside other great powers.

In 1995, at an Asia Society conference in Houston, a Chinese scholar from Beijing University said Chinese foreign policy was basically a reaction to the power of the United States. Is there psychological unfinished business about the West festering deep in Chinese society, or is the CCP manipulating feelings about the West for political purposes (the United States needed as enemy)?

In December 2001, another Chinese scholar of international relations from the same university complained to a Harvard seminar that the United States keeps trying "to change China." Yet a moment later, he said "America must change," a statement he repeated half a dozen times. He also said, "only the American people can bring about the change," implying that the sole superpower was too formidable to be much influenced by Beijing. The bottom line seems to be both unawareness of the CCP's constructed imperial project, and hankering for a sign that America respects China.

If the second point is indeed the case, this is startling, given China's greatness as a civilization. Recall, however, that during the twentieth century China stood for little and made very modest contributions to the world. "For two hundred years we [Chinese] haven't produced a great thinker," lamented the Chinese writer Liu Binyan.[48] Whereas during the Qing Dynasty, Chinese styles in porcelain, furniture, textiles, and wallpaper intrigued the West,[49] little of twentieth-century Chinese culture (beyond talented people, cuisine, and some film) has graced the outside world. Worse, today, there is an awareness, as Lowell Dittmer and Samuel Kim write, "that China has been inferior to the Western powers in the very domain of normative politics and the very principles of proper behavior which Confucianism has held to be the hallmark of China's civilizational greatness."[50] The old Chinese empire, like all empires, was created by force, yet its distinction and durability mostly lay in culture and social morality. China has lost the old virtue, but failed to learn a new virtue. Thus is it half-empire and half-modern nation.

The hankering for respect may surprise us for a second reason: The Chinese party-state does little to earn our respect. Throughout the 1990s and into the new century, the Chinese government opposed the United States on most international issues. On many it attacked us. On some—including Kosovo in 1999 and the Hainan Island plane incident of 2001—it excoriated us as "Hitlerite" and more. Beijing regularly deceives and lies to Washington (and some other governments).

The Chinese government bristles with historical grievances. It takes the view that in the eighteenth and nineteenth centuries, when China was weaker than Russia and the West, any treaty signed by China was "unequal" and therefore invalid. Actually, Beijing did well to stop the

---

[48]Buruma, 2001, 23.

[49]Crossley, 1997, 8.

[50]Dittmer and Kim, 1993, 281.

Russian empire from expanding farther than it did into Qing territory. The Treaty of Nerchinsk in 1689 was not obviously unequal.

Why was India's response to a sustained colonial past more moderate than China's response to a brief semicolonial past? India, like China, knew frequent attacks from the north. But India, unlike China, did not repeatedly seek to extend its own civilization into the north. There was less sense in India of entitlement to prevail culturally than there was in China. Hence, as Chusei Suzuki says, the two Asian powers reacted differently to the achievement of independence. China was hell-bent on revanchism; India was relaxed toward the Western colonial powers. "If imperialism leads to eventual revolt," wrote Northcote Parkinson, as if in prediction of the PRC's future, "the revolt leads as inevitably to the new imperialism."[51]

The CCP's perpetuation of the imperialist myth, in an epoch when imperialism has ceased to be the key fact about the world, exacerbates the gulf between China and parts of the non-Chinese world. The Chinese people are led up the garden path of excessive hostility to supposed "anti-China forces." Beijing cannot look at contemporary Japan without seeing (or pretending to see) a replay of the long-past militaristic Japan of the 1930s and 1940s.

At the same time, the imperialist myth is a springboard to China's future ambitions. The Pretentious, Aggrieved, and Fearful State will segue into the Vengeful State. The Chinese leaders regard China's ownership of the oil-rich and strategically located South China Sea islands known as the Spratleys as essentially nonnegotiable, "from ancient times part of China's territory,"[52] even though five of China's neighbors lay claim to all or part of the island chain.[53] They condescend to 60 million non-PRC Chinese in Asia and around the Pacific Rim, whom they regard as a displaced part of the Chinese household. One day they want to see Beijing acknowledged as the head of this "Overseas Chinese" and "compatriot" family.

---

[51]Parkinson, 1963, xviii.
[52]*Zhongguo lishi*, vol. 3, 7.
[53]Li Guoqiang, 2000, 80, 81.

The CCP's pretentious, aggrieved, and fearful worldview has been internalized by part of China's populace, which will complicate China's passage from empire to modern nation. In the wake of the NATO bombing of the Chinese embassy in Belgrade in 1999, and again when Chinese and American aircraft collided near Hainan Island in 2001, the party-state's anti-Western nationalism received considerable (if unmeasurable) support in urban China. Starved of information from one side of the issue, many Chinese people naturally became indignant on behalf of their party-state.

After fifty years of Communist rule, spearheaded by three red emperors, many Chinese people still heed dictators in the guise of parents, still regard the West as anti-China, still look upon Asia as China's backyard. The religion of the Chinese, in the absence of a pervasive transcendental religion, and in the presence of a party-state controlling virtually all information channels except the Internet, and propping itself up by bribes to the nation, may be said to be China itself.

AUTOCRACY'S LAST LEGS?

National goals are set, yet the literati are not obedient. The rules are clear, yet policies have not been entirely successful. Why is this?

—Examination question in the Song Dynasty, 1106[1]

Although we Chinese get upset when Japanese scoff that China is not really a nation, we should calm down and reflect. Have we laid the organizational foundations for a modern nation or not? In the society of a modern nation, there are elections so that people can participate in politics, freedom of publication to assure accurate news, and various kinds of associations that draw together the feelings of different segments of the people . . .

—author He Luzhi, 1929[2]

This is Shanghai, a big city on Chinese soil. How dare you call us Communist China. Communist China has become history. Such a term no longer exists.

—Tang Jiaxuan, PRC foreign minister, upbraiding a Taiwan reporter at the 2001 APEC meeting in Shanghai[3]

RECENT REVIVAL OF ESTEEM for Sun Yat-sen and Chiang Kai-shek, inside China and beyond, follows a dawning realization that the CCP half century has been a cycle, in some respects a step forward for the Chinese people, in others not. The half century prior to Mao's victory in 1949 was not one of failure and mess, later remedied by a problem-solving half century of CCP rule. On the contrary, the last years of the Qing Dynasty, the period of regionalism that soon fol-

---

[1] Bol, 2001, 19.
[2] He, 1948 (1929), 12.
[3] *South China Morning Post,* Oct. 19, 2001.

lowed the fall of the Qing, and the Republican era all saw steps away from autocracy and a totalist mentality. Shelly Yomano suggests that the warlord period, although flawed, carried the hope of reunification *without* autocracy and totalism.[4] Certainly, after 1949, autocracy and totalist thinking came back stronger than ever.

To see the 150 years following the Opium War of 1839–1842 as imperialism-plus-revolution makes the PRC seem a culmination of the post-1840 story. A "new China" arrived at last. This view of history obscures a good deal. It *is* a historical shift that China's power has grown, with zigs and zags, during the PRC period. China is probably better off internationally than for two centuries. It has become an economic player in East Asia of greater weight than since Emperor Qian Long's heyday. But China's increased power in the later twentieth century is not explained by the morality play of imperialism-plus-revolution.

"Imperialism" and "revolution" are not clear-cut terms, and both are used polemically. Chinese dynasties practiced imperialism—metropolitan manipulation of peripheral peoples—no less than modern China experienced imperialism from Europe. A number of Chinese dynasties killed more non-Chinese people on China's borders than Europeans killed Chinese people in the two Opium Wars.[5] The Ming Dynasty's expedition to Yunnan in 1381 was no more nor less than an imperial grab to incorporate that southwestern area, then controlled by local kings and "barbarians," as a province under Ming rule.[6] Official PRC maps say delicately that the Ming "extended itself" to Yunnan.[7]

Today, a focus on imperialism and revolution misses most of the key issues facing China. Some are intrinsic to governance in a rapidly changing huge society, some are due to the pathologies of the Chinese state. The following challenges stand out.

An aging population.   Demographically, China is quickly heading for a phase that will strain government revenue and social cohesion. In 2001,

---

[4]Yomano, 1987, 26.
[5]Paine, 1996, 8.
[6]Ma, 1987, chap. 6; see also Hostetler, 2001, 102, 105, 114–115, 132, on the Qing Dynasty's blunt colonialism in Guizhou and Yunnan.
[7]Tan, 1996, Mingshi qitu, 1, shuo, following 61–62.

some 10% of the population was 65 or over. By 2030, a hefty 25% of the population is expected to be in that elderly group.[8] Pensions, health care, and other services will soar in cost. An only child in Shanghai today, whose parents are also from one-child families, all products of the party-state's deliberate policy, will tomorrow have six dependents on his hands, two parents and four grandparents. All the while, expectations of a better life grow. Wisely, the post-Mao leadership has slowed population growth, but the economic and social implications for twenty to thirty years ahead of an old population of some 300 million are hair-raising.

Military relations with civilian power.   One of Jiang Zemin's political achievements was to buy off the military with heavy spending on arms and military wages, and thus gain peace with the generals. Such a strategy may not survive recession or major political struggle.

Widespread health care problems.   Much of rural China is an arena of social Darwinian struggle when it comes to competent treatment for illness or injury. AIDS is not being confronted squarely, storing up future problems, and any new pandemic would find China a juicy target. The World Health Organization ranks China's health system one of the worst in the world, coming in number 144th among all WHO members. Most sick farmers needing hospitalization are not admitted because they cannot pay.[9] SARS in 2003 was only a foretaste of more health shocks to come.

A cultural predisposition to political escapism.   Apathy toward public life, a long-standing Chinese trait,[10] was initially encouraged by the post-Mao regime, and it has been reciprocated by a populace disgusted with ideology and eager to prosper. This political numbness can give implicit welcome to soft authoritarianism ("let others take care of public affairs, while I pursue family, business, art") and produce stability. But true stability arrives indirectly, when safety valves exist to drain away potential threats to stability. The Brezhnev period in the Soviet

[8]Wong, 2001, 84.
[9]Pei, 2002, 104.
[10]Pye, 1968, 13, 129–131, 247.

Union, when Moscow's leadership was thick with engineers, as the Beijing leadership is today (the nine top figures are all engineers),[11] was a time when Brezhnev, like Jiang for the past twelve years, prevented turbulence at the top of the Communist Party. "Stability," indeed, marked the eleventh hour of the Soviet Union's existence. The political escapism that temporarily serves stability can also be a ticking time bomb; a neglect of citizenship allows pathologies to grow unchecked within the polity. This contributes to the danger of fascism, rather than democracy, replacing Communist rule.

The problems of legitimacy and succession in the absence of elections. Even in theory, the sovereignty of the people does not exist in China. It is history (frozen into the Four Absolutes) that is presumed to give the CCP its mandate to monopolize political power. In modern conditions, this makes for tension, struggle, and ultimate instability. A growing economic gulf between jumping coast and lagging hinterland adds to the implausibility of the claims of the Chinese party-state to be based on "workers and peasants."

The importance of science and technology for China's future progress, and an atmosphere of free enquiry that will nurture them. Three decades ago Elvin wrote: "The technological creativity of the Chinese people has deep historical roots, and slumbered for a while mostly for practical considerations. As it slowly reawakens, we may expect it to astonish us."[12] It will one day, but not under Communist repression.

The absence of an authentic banking system.   Major banks are insolvent, loans are made on noncommercial grounds, 30% of bank loans are "bad," and an ill-informed public pours household savings into the sagging government banks. The rotten industrial-financial core adds to the revenue paucity at the center. A secret struggle goes on between Beijing and key provinces over revenue, and Beijing may not be winning it.[13]

---

[11]Li and White, 1998, 231; the nine top Chinese leaders form the Standing Committee of the Politburo.
[12]Elvin, 1973, 319.
[13]Friedman, 1995, 336; Pei, 2002, 105–106.

Dangers to the environment. Half of China's rivers are putrid, cultivable land shrinks, and investment in agriculture is insufficient. With nine of the world's ten most polluted cities, the PRC's urban air stunts children's futures.[14] China's mines have the world's worst safety record and nuclear weapons are dispersed in more than half a dozen provinces and subject to capricious use if certain provinces disobey Beijing. These issues are often unaddressed, because there is no free press and the state's operation has all the transparency of a brick wall. In Judith Shapiro's words, "political repression, utopian urgency, dogmatic formalism, and state-sponsored relocations" all distort society's relationship with nature.[15]

None of these social, economic, cultural, and ecological issues is illumined by the Communist party-state's mantra of "revolution" beating back "imperialism," or "China's rise" being quashed by American "hegemonists." Most of the problems are rendered more difficult by the nature of the Chinese party-state and its obsession with control and uniformity of thought.

It seems irresistible to conclude that political ideas will publicly revive before long in China. Franco's Spain, Suharto's Indonesia, Salazar's Portugal, Chiang Kai-shek's Taiwan—all these regimes suppressed political ideas; yet, when each regime fell, political debate revived. And Chinese civilization for 2,500 years has lived by ideas. Today, beneath the surface, and on the Internet, an astonishing variety of political theories, 90% of them incompatible with the CCP's worldview, are whispered and weighed.

But *what* political ideas will spring out from the long-shut closet of Chinese political debate? A revival of Europe-derived socialism is the least likely. Less unlikely is rural leftism based on traditional Chinese ideas of community. Full-throttle pro-West liberalism, lurking in China ever since the May Fourth Movement of 1919, and present in the Tiananmen movement of 1989, is possible, but not likely. Otherworldly philosophies cannot be ruled out. Secular, rational China, after all, produced the heaven-struck and apocalyptic Taiping Rebellion.[16]

---

[14]Pei, 2002, 105.
[15]Shapiro, 2001, 195.
[16]On the frequent exaggeration of China's secularity, see Wilkinson, 2000, 571, 659, 667.

When *Falungong* leader Li Hongzhi declared, "We live in a despicable age," he may have implied an impulse to replace the CCP status quo with *Falungong*'s supernatural alternative.

THE TWO CHINESE CHARACTERS for "revolution" mean "withdrawal of the mandate." When the French and American Revolutions occurred, the Chinese applied this term, *geming,* to both foreign upheavals. When the Qing Dynasty fell in 1911–1912, "withdrawal of the mandate" was also what happened, as described in Chinese. Thirty-eight years later, Chiang Kai-shek, in turn, lost the mandate to build a post-Qing republic using Sun Yat-sen's ideas. Mao Zedong "took away" Chiang's legitimacy in 1948–1949.[17] In the years ahead, some form of "withdrawal of the mandate" will occur once more. Chinese socialism as defined by the Four Absolutes is in its final phase.

In October 2001, in Chongqing, a local schoolteacher who drove me around the city stressed people's desire to have a comfortable life. We saw billboards advertising apartments with swimming pools, gardens, and modern kitchens. "People here don't want any more Cultural Revolutions or wars," said the teacher with a shrug. "We like these [material] things. We're keeping our fingers crossed. Jiang Zemin keeps it smooth for the moment. In the future, who knows what's going to happen." Of course, I do not know how and when Communist rule will end in China, any more than does the Chongqing schoolteacher. Nor, probably, could the current head of the CCP, Hu Jintao, give the scenario and date.

In the Soviet Union and East Europe during 1989–1991, two forces interacted. A failure by the party-state to deliver a modern way of life to the people. And reduced acceptance by the people of the regime's supporting myths. In China, belief in the supporting myths has already eroded considerably. But the party-state has facilitated an improving standard of life for a substantial part of the population.

------

[17]Rozman, 1981, 52.

In daring to predict the end of Communist rule, one must acknowledge the strengths of the Chinese Communist regime after half a century in power. It shrugged off the disaster of Tiananmen in 1989 and within three years recovered its poise and policy line. Less than a decade after Tiananmen, it became confident and effective in foreign policy.[18] Why has the regime not yet gone down the drain like the Soviet Union?

Lessons have been learned from Moscow's collapse. Living with contradictions is less difficult for the Chinese mentality than for the Slavic. Chinese have long been capable of being "Daoist in private and Confucian in public." In addition, a Chinese who entered public service also became "in some measure Legalist."[19] Foreign and non-PRC Chinese influence on post-Mao China has moderated the Chinese Leninist state. A useful marriage has been effected between Leninism and Chinese autocratic tradition. The PRC is secure internationally. Most of the Chinese millions don't lack for a shirt on the back or gadgets in the home. The party-state is aware of its political predicament and unlikely to commit suicide in an obvious way. Pride in China could help the nation ease away from (Europe-derived) communism without losing face.

One must also note Beijing's vulnerabilities. Communism has outlived its world historical role. Economic growth and crude nationalism are insufficient supports for long-term continuance of a regime. No cultural tissue connects government and people. A hovering army of unemployed grows. The party-state's condescension to the Chinese people is unlikely to be accepted indefinitely. The same nationalism that comforts could also hurl China into fascism.

Three traits of the Chinese state ill-fit the changed society and economy. First, the Beijing party-state is a project from above. It sees

---

[18]Compare the change in Jiang Zemin's summation of his U.S. policy from 1992 to 1997. In 1992 he proposed, "Increase trust, reduce troubles, develop cooperation, and avoid confrontation" (*Zengjia xinren, jianshao mafan, fazhan hezuo, bugao duikang*). In 1997 he put forward the more assertive "Increase understanding, expand consensus, develop cooperation, and together create the future" (*Zengjia liaojie, kuoda gongshi, fazhan hezuo, gongchuang weilai*). (*Mingbao* [Hong Kong], June 23, 1998.)

[19]Hucker, 1975, 69.

its legitimacy as coming from a mandate of history, just as the dynastic mandate came from heaven. Virtually everything political in China is state-driven; little gains entry from below.

In the spring of 2001, the International Olympic Committee came to Beijing to inspect the city as a candidate for the 2008 Games. In preparation, the government spray-painted roadside grass in bright green. Beggars, cripples, and "floating people" from the countryside were hustled away. Factories that belched black smoke—a not incidental part of the Beijing scene—were ordered to stop operations. Here was Beijing's determined pursuit of raison d'état. The high interests of the state eclipse the low priority of citizen rights.

The implied message in the nightly news from the party-state CCTV is that only the CCP stands between the Chinese people and the horrors that hit the Soviet Union and East Europe in the late twentieth century. Chaos looms for those unlucky enough to lack strong Communist leadership. "Unity and stability" bless those overseen by the father and mother officials of Beijing's bureaucracy. But this project is never put to the Chinese people for approval.

A second vulnerable trait of the Chinese state is its fusion of doctrine and power. Whether rejecting the concept of a Korean-Chinese or a Tibetan-Chinese, styling Taiwan Vice President Annette Lu "the scum of the Chinese race," finding it impossible to sustain an alliance with any major foreign country, perceiving *Falungong* as a threat to the CCP—in all cases the premise is that a single moral universe and discourse exists, its epicenter the Chinese party-state.

When truth and power issue from a single fount, society lacks room for free expression. Corruption goes through the roof as there is no one to blow the whistle. The party-state does not even allow *the past* to be dispassionately analyzed. In 2001 at a street stall in the city of Suzhou, I came upon a white porcelain plate that depicted Mao and Lin Biao together. "Isn't Lin a bad man?" I inquired of the stall proprietor, a beaming middle-aged lady, mindful that the former defense minister had "tried to kill" Mao and was now a nonperson. "*Buhao shuo,*" she said—"Not good to talk about that." I said, "I'm surprised you have these two guys together on your plates." The lady shrugged. "Well, it's history; you know, it's history!" Actually, Lin is not part of PRC political history. That is why he is found on souvenir plates for tourists visiting Suzhou, but rarely in official accounts of recent CCP history.[20]

A third fault line of the Chinese party-state is its inability to value the individual. Wrote Harry Wu, a dissident who is a Catholic believer, after burying a friend who died in the labor camp where both men were confined: "Human life has no value here, I thought bitterly. It has no more importance than a cigarette ash flicked in the wind. But if a person's life has no value, then the society that shapes that life has no value either."[21] Chinese economic achievements notwithstanding, there is a moral bitterness about such a society, and ultimately a limited horizon.

The problem of the undervalued individual in Chinese communism is deep. Mao as a youth wanted strong individuals for the purpose of saving the Chinese nation. The May Fourth Movement also failed to embrace individualism as an end (self-fulfillment). Chinese communism only intensified the strain in Chinese tradition that saw the individual purely in functional terms. Today, the CCP's well-known fear of foreign influence ("spiritual pollution"), of which the Internet is the cutting edge, is ultimately a fear that widespread individuation in China would undermine the present regime.

Can China *evolve* from its autocratic state, or must the polity *crash*, as the imperial system crashed in 1911–1912? A common view among Western Sinologists is that if Beijing drives over the cliff gradually no one will notice. I believe the Chinese populace and the rest of the world really will notice when the CCP loses its monopoly of political power. No regime in Chinese history has ever given up power without bloodshed.[22] I do not believe the CCP party-state will be the first.

A crash looms because the Leninist core of the regime is unchanged from Mao's construction of it in Yan'an six decades ago. Michel Oksenberg, the leading China political scientist of his generation, in his final

---

[20]When Lin lost his posts and his life in 1971, even phrases associated with him were weeded out of dictionaries (Wilkinson, 2000, 89).
[21]Wu and Wakeman, 1994, 129.
[22]Wakeman, 1991, 102, n159.

article in 2001, said of the Chinese political system: "at its core it is still a Soviet-Leninist state."[23] Guo Sujian distinguishes "hard core" features of totalitarianism from "operative features." The "hard core" is philosophic absolutism, inevitable goals, official ideology, and single-party dictatorship. Each trait is evident in post-Mao China. Guo's "operative features" changed sharply under Deng–Jiang. A "protective belt" was adjusted in order to preserve the core.[24]

Much of the economy is still micromanaged by the party-state. There is only one acceptable worldview for the Chinese people. Not a single major social organization can exist with impunity other than under the supervision of the Communist Party. No fundamental foreign policy debate occurs in the Chinese media. The history textbook for middle schools aims to "make pupils ardently love China, the Chinese Communist Party, and the enterprise of socialism, and lead them to uphold the Four Absolutes [of the Leninist state]." The textbook says, "Only by using the concepts of Marxism will correct conclusions be reached." In particular, only analysis by "historical materialism" will result in a "correct view point."[25] Why was "spiritual pollution" from the West a threat to the party-state in the 1980s, and *Falungong* a threat in the 1990s and beyond? Because the CCP is deadly serious about its claim to be the sole source of truth for the Chinese nation.

Guo Sujian cautions us to be wary of concluding that a totalitarian system can change smoothly into another system. "Totalitarians are by nature utopians," he writes, "whose ultimate goals and other claims are actually unachievable and therefore contain the limits of their realization."[26] Falling short, then, does not necessarily mean the CCP's totalitarian drive dies. Instead, we see the thrashing around over "political reform" that occurred in the Deng era. An agenda of political institutional reform appears, as the regime fleetingly faces up to the futility of the socialist goal; then it disappears, as Beijing retreats to the faith. Sometimes the reversal is swift indeed. On December 7, 1984, *People's*

---

[23]Oksenberg, 2001, 25.
[24]Guo, 2000, 203.
[25]*Zhongguo lishi*, vol. 1, shuoming, 3.
[26]Guo, 2000, 203.

Daily said Marxism-Leninism could not solve the current problems of China. The next day the newspaper corrected its statement: "Marxism-Leninism cannot solve *all* the current problems of China," it freshly laid down. "It is of the totalitarian essence that the goal is never reached,"[27] writes Buchheim. To cope with the goal's fading credibility, Jiang, hardly less than Mao and Deng, regularly re-dressed the goal in a new costume. As Hu Jintao takes the CCP mantle from Jiang, economic success only widens the gap between the socialist goal and the rationale for pursuing it.

A second reason why a crash looms is the legacy of Legalist autocracy. In the history of Leninism, the longer and stronger the past authoritarian tradition, the more tenacious the twentieth-century Communist rule. Poland and Czechoslovakia slipped more nimbly out of the Leninist straitjacket than did Russia. China may have an even harder time than Russia.

Chinese culture is no more "imperial" than most other cultures. Many ancient civilizations, in various ways, knew autocracy and encroached on other peoples. China's autocracy is a problem not because it is "Chinese," but because it is autocratic. The issue is that a tradition of governance, and a matching mentality, have been appropriated by a Communist Party in an era otherwise done with autocratic empire.[28] We have not seen the end of the Chinese imperial state, but simply its modernization.

A crash may seem unlikely to a reader familiar with Shanghai, Beijing, and Guangzhou. But regimes do not always fall because of stagnation; witness the stable failure of the governments in Burma and Laos. Often regimes fall because of high ambition undercut by reality. It is not because the Chinese political system is the bottom of the barrel that it will fall, but because it is riven with contradictions between old and new, politics and economics, Chinese particularism and the tug of universalism.

What does it mean to "reform" communism? For the CCP, it means holding on to Leninism after abandoning much of Marxism. Foreign

---

[27]Buchheim, 1968, 38.
[28]Yan, 1987, 87.

Minister Tang in Shanghai in 2001 objected that "Communist China" is a term that "no longer exists." It never did exist as a legal term, but as a political fact it has not ceased to exist. The Marxist flesh may be gone; the Leninist bones remain. Rising officials in their thirties and forties in the CCP and the State Council are not socialist believers; they are often pragmatists. But, functionally, they are also Leninists. Their meal ticket stems from the Four Absolutes. Leninism, indeed, even in Lenin's day was never as much about socialism as it was about power.

At the 15th Congress of the CCP in 1997, Jiang verbally solved the great contradiction of today's China by stating that "reform is a revolution." But Jiang also stated that the goal of this second revolution is not open-ended. This can only mean that reform is intended, not to negate the revolution, but to perfect it. It is a fallacy to think further reform is all that is needed to cancel communism in China. "You can skin an onion leaf by leaf," R. H. Tawney wrote in a different context, "but you cannot subdue a tiger paw by paw."

Did Jiang believe in his bones that the Communist system is doomed? Maybe he did not. "I cross the river," Deng said, "by touching my feet on the stones beneath the water." Crucial in this apparently planless maneuver is whether or not the walker believes a bank exists on the other side of the river. In East Europe, "reform" was in essence a pulling of the plug on socialism. The walker knew he was leaving behind the "land" of communism and would not rediscover it beyond the waters of reform. But it is also possible that crossing the river by feeling for the stones is the mode of an authoritarian trying to salvage totalist goals. This is certainly the view of Li Peng, who was powerful near the top of Chinese politics for a decade and a half until the 16th CCP Congress in 2002.

Huang Yasheng, a specialist on Chinese economic development, said in 2000: "It matters greatly whether the Chinese government believes in capitalism, or whether it just wants to play around on the fringes of capitalism." I believe Beijing merely seeks to use capitalism for an authoritarian purpose. Truly private firms are constrained in manifold ways and cannot grow into very large firms. Private firms fear expropriation, for the party-state "eyes" the best and most profitable private companies. A dismal choice faces many private businessmen, Huang finds. Make no profit at all, or make a profit by engaging in illegal practices, and get assailed and maybe destroyed by the government. A looming showdown is suggested by the fact that most private firms keep three sets of books. One for the bank, one for the tax bureau, and a real one for themselves.[29]

The future of any political system, especially a dictatorship, including the Soviet Union in the 1980s and China in the first decade of the twenty-first century, is not to be predicted only on the basis of personality, anecdotes from the grassroots, speeches by leading figures, and official statistics. It is equally important to grasp the theory of a dictatorship's situation, or a democracy's situation. The cacophony of an American election campaign might suggest instability to an observer from afar. Heeding the theory of democracy, however, the observer would draw an opposite conclusion. We fight our grassroots campaign *before* the change of administrations. Beijing changes its government (in secret) *then* conducts a top-down campaign.

Of course, it is valid to ask why a given dictatorship is able to last for a sustained period. It is also important to utilize theory to locate the system's fault lines. Beijing is trying to do something impossible— combine a market economy and Communist paternalism—and the resulting strains will not go away. It is a mistake to speak of economic reform and political reform as two separate agendas. "In China, economics is never simply economics," writes Zhu Xueqin in the preface to a courageous book by economist He Qinglian, "but composed of a definite political content. Our planned economy is the product of a certain political system. The moment the planned economy interacts with the real world, each cell of it drips with politics." To chatter about reform, Zhu says, yet ignore the political content of economic structures, "is once more to weave a set of emperor's clothes."[30]

---

[29]Huang Yasheng, talk at Fairbank Center, Harvard University, April 2000.
[30]He, 1997, 9.

With good reason did Adam Smith in *The Wealth of Nations* call the market economy "a system of natural liberty." Likewise, the Leninist state is a system of natural repression. No amount of detail can obscure Beijing's current impasse. As society and state interact, the balance between them shifts over time. In the Tiananmen crisis of 1989, the state–society relationship was on a knife-edge. Tanks against students, it tipped in favor of the state. Next time, in different circumstances, it will tip toward society and the economy and a new politics will be born.

WE MAY IDENTIFY a number of factors prominent in the fall of dynasties that bear on Beijing's future.

Diminishing leadership quality. Often, a dynasty's early emperors were masterful, while later ones were feeble, low in motivation, or simply puppets.[31] This factor is probably not a threat to the PRC. Hu Jintao may be a pale shadow of Mao, but China does not need a Mao. Current problems do not invite Mao-style solutions. CCP rule will not end because of weak leadership, but because Communist leadership becomes irrelevant to China's needs.

Corruption. Use of office for profit put an end to reigns and doomed dynasties. Ho Ping-ti summed up the link between corruption and assaults on late Qing rule: "It was the widespread peculation from the Qian Long era [reigned 1736–1794] onwards," he wrote, "that transformed the benevolent despotism of Kang Xi [reigned 1662–1722] and Yong Zheng [reigned 1722–1736] into a malevolent despotism that had so much to do with the outbreak of the White Lotus and subsequent rebellions."[32]

Corruption is a grave threat to the PRC. Any Communist regime that loosens up is ripe for corruption. Power and money intersect without benefit of the rule of law to supervise the encounter.[33] For the same reason, the presence of foreign money adds to the temptation. "To get

---

[31]Dunstan, 1996, 98.
[32]Ho, 1967, 195.
[33]Cabestan, 1992, 470–471, 473, 476.

rich is glorious," said Deng. But the Communist Party continues to call the shots. The result is a lottery of money-seeking at the grassroots and full pockets for the bureaucrats who move the goalposts around. Corruption distorts the distribution of resources, impedes the expansion of China's domestic market, and increases inequality.[34] One percent of China's population owns 40% of China's wealth, much of it built up through corrupt acts. The 1980s economic activity was largely driven by the industriousness of a newly unleashed people. The 1990s economic activity owed more to political power and connections. Not stopping corruption will destroy the country, the saying runs; stopping it will destroy the Communist Party.

That spectacular cases of corruption occur in the lagging northeast is an illustration of the logic of Communist-style corruption. In the "rust belt," where the command economy reigns supreme, power exceeds the money available; hence officeholders scramble for spoils. When the game was finally up in 1999 for the crooked mayor of Shenyang (formerly known as Mukden), urban bastion of the northeast, US$6 million worth of gold bars were found in his house.[35] His salary as mayor had been $3,500 a year.

Succession struggle. Many reigns became obsessed with the choice of a new emperor. The basic reason was the absence of firm rules about the succession. It has been similar, so far, in the PRC period. In 1976, the struggle over filling Mao's position did not bring down the dynasty, but it did replace Mao's reign with a sharply different reign. In recent years, succession struggle has eased in Beijing. Still, there are no rules for the choice of a new boss of the CCP that cannot be ruptured by political maneuver. In 2002 Jiang Zemin, echoing previous Chinese rulers, had second thoughts about following a prior undertaking to leave all his posts and hand full power to Hu Jintao. At the 16th CCP Congress, Jiang relinquished the party general secretaryship to Hu, but retained the top military post and filled the ruling core of the Politburo with his supporters. A modern solution to the suc-

---

[34]Wu Junhua, talk at Fairbank Center, Harvard University, Dec. 11, 2001.
[35]*Washington Post,* March 6, 2002.

cession issue, election from below by the entire membership of the party, was not broached.

Farmers' uprising. Extra taxes and arbitrarily levied fees were the immediate grievance in rebellions against the dynasties. Apocalyptic politics often accompanied the farmer uprisings. Lucian Bianco shows that the twentieth century exhibited the same tax-related triggers for rebellion. Thomas Bernstein finds a similar dynamic in villages today; tax is 20–30% of farmers' income, he concludes, and it is "open-ended, unpredictable, and regressive."[36] Parts of rural China are becoming lawless, violent frontiers. A Beijing official told Bernstein in a candid moment, "We can't support village elections, because if we did, and they proliferated, farmer political parties would appear, and we urban Chinese would be swamped." The overwhelming strength of religion today is in rural areas, where alienation from the CCP–foreign capital synergy is greatest (and where three-quarters of Christian church members are female, among whom a sense of the apocalyptic tends to flourish).

Farmers' discontent, caused by high taxes and expressed in apocalyptic politics, is a danger to CCP rule. It will only shake the regime, however, if links are made between rural grievances, which often win the sympathy of local officials, and urban unemployment. World Trade Organization pressures could bring these into existence. Apocalyptic ideas are ready and waiting, including bizarre forms of Buddhism and Christianity. "When regimes weaken," the pro-democracy exile Wei Jingsheng said, linking history with the present, "popular religious movements and superstitions become significant. There are a hundred sects like *Falungong,* which means that people long for faith in some ideology, a new source of guidance. The government recognizes the danger and is anxious for ways to control their growth."[37]

Military defeat. Early in a dynasty, military victories were numerous. Later, vigor lacked, the cost of campaigns led to excessive tax on farm-

---

[36]Lucian Bianco, Thomas Bernstein, Papers at the panel "Taxation and Resistance in Twentieth-Century China," Association for Asian Studies annual meeting, Washington, D.C., April 2002.
[37]Wei to Safire, *New York Times,* June 3, 1999.

ers, and wars were lost. The Han Dynasty lost battles to the Xiongnu, the Song met defeat at the hands of the Jin, the Qing were beaten by Britain in the Opium War three-quarters way through the dynasty.

Military defeat does not loom for the PRC. The "first reign," Mao's, brought costly war with South Korea, India, and the Soviet Union, as well as skirmishes in the Taiwan Strait. China suffered no clear-cut defeat in any of these. At the start of the "second reign," Deng's, China attacked Vietnam without much success. In the Jiang period, there was no war but a high level of military spending.

The PRC faces no internal armed challenge. Foreign powers do not impinge on China's sovereignty, so far, which allows Beijing to utilize foreign capital and know-how without seeming to lose control of its own affairs. A danger is that the mood of nationalism could lead to an unwise war. This could be devastating if Hu Jintao's China, like the Qing, found itself stretched by wars on two flanks. Beijing may fight for political reasons with Taiwan, in Central Asia, or with Japan over disputed islands.

Legalist policies did not satisfy the Chinese people's moral sense. A vacuum of values appeared, causing unease, and Confucian morality was reasserted. This was the pattern in the eventual replacement of the Qin by the Han, and the change from the late Yuan to the Ming. During the PRC decades, the Mao era pushed neo-Confucianism. The Deng era swung to neo-Legalism. After the Tiananmen Square repression, worn-out ideology could do little to rescue legitimacy. By the end of the Jiang period, a hunger for new meaning was a cloud over the CCP regime. A phrase—"crisis of belief"(*xinxing weiji*)—arose to describe the mood.

Demographic change. Flux of population explains much in Chinese history and will help explain the eventual fate of the CCP. Quick population growth, adding to pressure on land use, was one of two fundamental reasons, together with pressure of the West and Japan, for the Qing's demise. China had some 200 million people in 1580, and 410 million by 1850. The Taiping Rebellion, a blend of recycled Christianity and farmer revolt, drew huge support from a displaced populace.

In a flash of realism, Mao remarked to an audience in 1958: "Our population of 600 million will one day in the future have to line up when we go into the street. . . . The streets will be jammed with people. How will we distribute newspapers? How will we go to the movies? How will we go to the park? All these will become problems." In the forty-four years since Mao spoke, another 600 million Chinese have arrived. The problems Mao foreshadowed have also arrived. Some are Mao's fault. The biographer of Ma Yinchu, a leading economist who clashed with Mao over population policy in the 1950s, writes: "In broad figures, had Ma's [birth control ideas] been accepted and continued to be implemented [rather than Mao's the-more-people-the-better ideas] the population of China in 1986 [when the biography was published] would have been 250 million less than it was."[38]

Unimaginable to Mao, upward of a hundred million "floating people" are now living elsewhere than where the regime wishes them to live. For the moment questing and restless, rather than rebellious, these ex-farmers are a time bomb beneath the CCP's "stability and unity."

Isolation of the court. An emperor was misled about food supply in a province experiencing drought. A child found himself on the throne, oblivious to his kingdom, manipulated by power-seekers who cared little for the image of the Chinese polity in China's villages. Conspiracy and revolt erupted without warning, proving that the center was out of touch with some provinces. The Empress Dowager in August 1900, as the Qing Dynasty tottered, fled from Beijing in fear, losing respect from ordinary Chinese who knew of her panic.

In physical ways, Beijing's dictatorship today would make "the first totalitarian" Qin Shihuang envious. The center can do things it never dreamed of being able to do in ancient and medieval times. Better transportation, electronic communications, and statistics with a passing resemblance to reality have made the modern Chinese state a sharp instrument of rule. Nevertheless, the CCP, intellectually and spiritually, is out of touch with most Chinese people. Moreover, although the party-state is usually well informed about local conditions, local officials sometimes "cooperate" with Beijing by padding their reports to

---

[38]Yang, 1986, 157.

the center.[39] At the level of popular culture, including religion, the Communist Party might as well be on another planet from the villages. People feel the chief ingredients of recent progress have been foreign money, products, and techniques. The CCP's contribution has been to refrain from harm, rather than to do good. Once, the motive for joining the CCP was idealistic; today it is careerist.

The CCP, sensing its isolation from the nation's actual preoccupations, offers Jiang Zemin's theory, "The Three Represents." It is a "new development of Marxist theory on party construction." In 2000, a Mao-like political campaign pushed Jiang's doctrine. Of the eight factors that historically threatened the Chinese polity, the "Three Represents" showed particular worry over corruption, succession struggle, and vacuum of values.

The Communist Party, said its unelected leader, must be representative of "the most advanced productive forces, the most advanced culture, and of the people's interests." In the military, the party cell in each unit held sessions to apply Jiang's "scientific theory" to "arming the thoughts of officers and soldiers" and "winning wars." Mischievous Chinese whispered, "Hasn't the glorious Party always been representative of the best things in China?"

Clearly, the three represents had nothing to do with Marxism. Class analysis was absent from them. But the doctrine had everything to do with a party slipping out of kilter with a changed socioeconomic situation. Jiang's CCP was trying to catch up with society, to move from being exclusionary (capitalists are beyond the pale) to being inclusionary (the CCP can successfully supervise anyone and anything).

In Europe, the idea of representation arose in the Middle Ages. At first a "representative" was a presumed mirror for those he was to represent; he "stood for" them. Later, the idea of representation took on a flavor of accountability, influenced by elections held in the Cistercian, Dominican, and other Christian orders. Such accountability became a root of democracy in Europe. The middle link was the growth of parliament. With parliaments, the idea of representation became a twin of the idea of sovereignty of the people.

---

[39]Cai, 2000, 787, 789, 796.

The earlier, nonaccountable or "mirror" notion of representation was entirely compatible with the paternalism of the Chinese Son of Heaven, both traditional and Red versions. A father or mother can plausibly "represent" their children. CCP cadres feel they "represent" the people.

Jiang's "three represents," reaffirmed by Hu Jintao at the 16th CCP Congress as "important thinking," proclaimed the CCP a mirror to the high points and key interests of Chinese society. But the party does not represent anyone in the sense of being accountable to them. Jiang was simply telling the CCP to *think of itself* as hyperadvanced! Here was a mixture of Lenin's theory of a revolutionary "vanguard" and the Confucian scholar-official's sense of entitlement. The "three represents" was like the "ritual and music" used a thousand years ago to ensure the common people knew what was good for them.[40]

The problem is you cannot have "representation," or "unity" or enduring "stability," when you have no politics. "Politics is the result of the planning and wishes of many," wrote Buchheim in his classic study of authoritarianism, "totalitarian rule actualizes a single all-encompassing plan."[41] Without freedom of expression and association, there can be no political life. In China there is "*bureaucratie politique,*" but there is no politics.[42] "Representation" in some mystical way beyond being chosen in an election is a fraud.

What role can remain for the CCP by the time Hu Jintao, 60 years old at the time of writing, is an old man? If the rule of law comes, that leaves party directives in the dust. If private property and the market grow, what price "allocation" by the party-state?[43] Where in the world has a Leninist party retained its power after the economy ceased to be state-directed?

―――――――

FINER SUGGESTS IN HIS history of world government that a tripod of belief-system, social stratification, and political institutions is the key to a system's stability. All three have to be congruent for the

―――――――

[40]Bol, 2001, 13.
[41]Buchheim, 1968, 41.
[42]Cabestan, 1992, 479.
[43]Waldron, 1999, 104.

polity to endure. "Where the claim of the ruler to authority is out of kilter with the prevalent belief-systems of the society," Finer writes, "he must either 'change his plea' . . . or else de-legitimize himself and fall." Confucianism was a belief-system congruent with the hierarchical social organization of dynastic China, and with the emperor-at-the-top political institutions that developed.

But, in China today, Finer's "social stratification" has broken ranks with both the belief-system and the political arrangements. Individual autonomy has grown in the cities. The impulse to self-fulfillment, in economic and cultural life, is a Pandora's box that threatens Beijing's paternalistic rule.

A popular sentiment in a survey of youth, "Do what you yourself want to do," departs from the Communist view (and some traditional views) of the individual as a cog in a collective moral apparatus. As does a second theme, "My choice may not be everyone's, but I believe it is right for me." And, "If at first I fail, I won't give up—some day I'll succeed."[44] In one afternoon on the streets of Shanghai in 2002, I twice saw the slogan "It's not impossible!" (*Bushi buke nengde*), in advertisements for education and purchase of real estate. Such a sense of individuality and rejection of fatalism may be the seedbed of democracy. In the medium to long run, Chinese totalism cannot survive the winds of modernization.

Using the Internet, the skillful individual, in Beijing or 2,000 miles away, 8 years old or 80, wearing a suit or underwear, can communicate more anonymously with far more people, both speaking and listening, than ever before in history. He can browse in the Bible, in English or Chinese, for example, without anyone knowing that he is reading religious material. He can, if he is assiduous, gain a second and third point of view on the Chinese party-state's views and acts. Distance evaporates; even exile loses its sterility; the chat room could become a practice ground for democracy.

On the other hand, it would be wrong to see Internet use as a direct step to democracy. Many Chinese will go online to play games, seek educational opportunity, make money, or look at naked bodies. More-

---

[44] *Zhongguo qingnian*, no. 9, 1992, 12–13; also Yu, 1999.

over, the Beijing party-state has made a decision to use the Internet in a massive way for *its* purposes, including publicizing its policies. And by the end of 2002, the government had imprisoned thirty-three people for "subverting state power" by expressing wrong political thoughts on the Internet. The Internet both strengthens the state and empowers the individual. So far, this new struggle occurs on the margin of China's state–society tension, since only a tiny percentage of Chinese (mostly young urban males) use the Internet in a substantial way. Tomorrow, should an elite disagreement interact with the expression of grievance and opinion from below, popular Internet use could become a political factor. One day, stopping "subversive" use of the Internet may come to be as futile as the radio jamming of the Cold War era looks in retrospect. Chinese Communist totalism could suddenly lose its point in the face of the Internet's instantaneous mobilization of information.

In rural China, too, there is a disconnect between belief-system and political system. Under the dynasties, popular religion linked each village to the emperor via cosmology. Holidays were laden with historical memory. By contrast, the new holidays in the PRC (May Day, Army Day, National Day) "have little cultural meaning and elicit no special behavior except that arranged by local cadres. The contrast with the lunar New Year and other traditional festivals," Myron Cohen writes, "could not be greater."[45]

In the China of 2003, religion means only state-approved religion. All else, including local popular religion, with its gods of the underworld, heaven, and earth, not to speak of Buddhist-flavored *Falungong,* is "superstition," to be fought. "Because political relationships in modern China have no shared cultural framework," adds Cohen, "they are largely expressed in the form of naked commands." The power of the state is not facilitated by natural cultural links. Instead, there is a forced culture of "compliance, of slogans, posters, and mobilizations conveying messages and commands rather than meaning." Witness Jiang Zemin's "three represents."

---

[45]Cohen, 1991, 128.

From below, the impulse to recover a believed public philosophy occasionally flickers, as in the "latent demand for salvation" of *Falungong* in the late 1990s[46] or the case of "Emperor Li" of Hunan Province in 1992. As a youth, Li tended cattle, picked pockets, and peddled pots and knives. Later, in a socialist work team, he became a leader by promising bounty and filling the vacuum of values with an enticing idea. He proved his superior powers by healing diseases and conjuring up watches and tape recorders from Hong Kong. Certainly Li was a swindler. But when he *claimed to be emperor*, many farmers accepted him.

Li was showered with gifts and money. He persuaded believers in his emperorship to go with him to sacred Mount Omei in Sichuan Province to study magical arts. To show their sincerity, some farmers gave the emperor their own daughters as his concubines. Money, miracles, and sex spun a web of enchantment.

Ann Anagnost writes in her exhumation of Li's saga that the "mythic or historical images" of the "Hunan emperor" expressed "present-day political sentiments unacknowledged in the official order."[47] This rural would-be hero "managed to tie the mythic past to the very material present." He rallied people anxious at marketization and forlorn at a cultureless party-state. Despite his unsavory aspects, Li achieved a fleeting belief-system link between leader and people that the Communist Party has lost.

Missing most of the point of this pathetic case, the Chinese party-state, after putting an end to Li's saga, hit one nail on the head: "[I]n the scientifically advanced 1980s, seventy years after the end of the corrupt feudal empire, a scoundrel [used] such words as *huangdi* [emperor], *tianshu* [heavenly edict], and *shenxian* [supernatural spirit] to mislead. . . . Is this strange? Not so. Although we live in an advanced age, the influence of old ideas still remains."

Bizarrely, the one figure who links the Communist party-state emotionally with grassroots China is Mao Zedong. In the tradition of eclectic Chinese popular beliefs, Mao has been added to the pantheon

---

[46]Vermander, 2001, 11.
[47]Anagnost, 1985, 149; other quotes on the case from the same article, 150, 154, 156, 169.

of faith. In the late twentieth century, taxi drivers hung a portrait of Mao on the steering wheel to ward off accidents, policemen, and criminals. When devastating floods hit the Yangzi valley in 1991, farmers clutched Mao memorabilia, as Buddhists for centuries have clutched images or statues of Guan Yin, the Goddess of Mercy, to keep them safe and make them prosperous.

A self-described millionaire from Anhui Province wrote to me after reading a Chinese edition of my biography of Mao: "The more money I get, the more I feel nostalgia for Mao." A former factory manager in Tianjin wrote in gratitude: "After reading your *Mao*, I decided to give up my high, admired post, and do something 'useful.' I have become an entrepreneur." This a-political-life-after-death of Mao is a link with people's collective identity as Chinese, in the absence of emotional connection to the party-state. As the people become neo-Daoist, making money yet believing in the spirits, Jiang Zemin, Hu Jintao, and the ruling cluster of engineers become neo-Legalists, artfully controlling the neo-Daoist masses.

CONTEMPLATING CHINA'S twentieth-century quest for a new political form, Owen Lattimore asked: "How much of the ancient fabric will have to be destroyed? . . . How stable a modern structure can be set up on the ancient foundations?" This question is still in the process of being answered. More than Japan's co-prosperity dreams or Soviet communism, felt Lattimore, "it is the Westernizing of China's own ancient civilization that will in fact be decisive."[48] The years since the specialist on Inner Asia died in 1989 have made his opinion the more intriguing. China's most productive synergy during the past century was not the forced one attempted by Japan, or the Mao–Soviet partnership, but the current one with foreign capitalism.

Yet never in Chinese history has the political outcome of a Chinese–foreign synergy been generally expected. In particular, synergy with the West and its ideas and/or the maritime flank has been more

---

[48]Lattimore, 1962, 9.

rocky than synergy with Inner Asia. The Mongol and Manchu periods alone lasted a total of nearly 500 years. These dynasties involved a political takeover of the Chinese polity. The shorter synergies of the nineteenth and twentieth centuries, even the one with the Soviet Union, did not bring foreign occupation of the Chinese seat of power. Ideological borrowing, manipulation, joint ventures, pressure, injection of funds, may add up to a short-lived synergy.

Life in the World Trade Organization (WTO) could be a climactic test. A Great Wall between the Chinese polity and the forces playing on China from the synergy with foreign capital is impossible to maintain. Potentially, China and most of its trading partners will benefit from China's accession to the WTO. It will be difficult, however, for the Chinese party-state to follow the law of comparative advantage that underlies free trade. This is a law of economic rationality, whereas Beijing operates by political rationality.[49] Wrote a researcher in a free-wheeling southern Chinese newspaper in 2001: "Faced with globalization, the primary conflict is not with enterprises, it is with the government."[50] Will Beijing de-stress cotton, wheat, and sugar, all suggested by the law of comparative advantage? Encouraging fish ponds and flowers would make excellent sense for China. But with "politics in command," Beijing may shy away from the consequent extra unemployment of cotton, wheat, and sugar workers.

If Beijing takes the risk of substantial adherence to world trading rules, the illusory nature of the market in most of the Chinese economy will become clear. Revealed will be a maze of hidden subsidies, insider connections, double bookkeeping, fake stock markets, inflated statistics, and courts of law that bow a knee to the Communist Party. Shattered will be the myth that "the state shrank" in China under Deng and Jiang.

Regional disparities will grow with WTO membership. "Job losses in both agriculture and manufacturing," writes Nicholas Lardy, "have already and will likely continue to be relatively larger in the northwest

---

[49]Cabestan, 1992, 476.
[50]*Nanfang zhoumo,* Oct. 11, 2001.

while employment generation will likely continue to be most robust in the Yangzi and southeast coastal regions."[51] As sectors of agriculture suffer, tens of millions will join the "floating" population for which Beijing has no urban jobs, houses, or school places. Politically, this may be the greatest threat of life in the WTO, *if* Beijing implements most of the rules.

Hundreds of special interests, regional and sectoral, will also expect or demand help from interaction with world markets. A Guangdong newspaper in 2001 foresaw WTO entry as a solution to the troubles and losses of the Beijing underground train system! It saw state firms "no longer having a mountain to lean on," and having to give up the self-indulgence of "gorging from a large [public] pot."[52] A Chinese scholar visiting the United States predicted that WTO entry would "rescue Chinese pension funds." He declared: "We can use the skills of foreign firms to improve Chinese social services."[53] This is mostly wishful thinking.

Beijing, after an interval of careful compliance, will probably display the worst of two possible worlds. Absence of the rule of law will madden the WTO bureaucrats who seek to bring China into line with international practices. Yet "local developmentalism," as Zheng Yongnian calls the new statism of the post-Mao era, will also make adherence to WTO rules problematic.[54] Beijing will tell Geneva one thing, but Guangzhou or Chengdu may act in a way contrary to Beijing's assurances.

"By 2007," predicts economist Richard Cooper, "China will be in massive noncompliance with WTO rules. Beijing will be in the middle, between foreign complaints and Chinese provincial and local malfaisants."[55] Compliance with WTO rules would require the Chinese government to step back from control of the Chinese economy. But "small government" is impossible for a Leninist party-state. Even a political class that is highly intelligent, like China's, cannot escape the crunch the contradiction will produce.

---

[51]Lardy, 2002, 21.
[52]*Nanfang zhoumo*, Oct. 11, 2001, 7.
[53]Forum on China and the WTO at Kennedy School, Harvard University, Sept. 13, 2001.
[54]Zheng, 2000, 220.
[55]Richard Cooper, talk at Fairbank Center, Harvard University, Nov. 16, 2001.

FIVE SCENARIOS SUGGEST themselves for Chinese politics over the next two decades.

Scenario One sees a continuance of the neo-Dengism that marked Jiang Zemin's years. Beijing resists moves toward political pluralism, and China lives with the contradiction between politics and economics. The PRC remains united, and a lack of consistency and clear goals is not enough to uproot a regime that plays it safe, tells the Chinese people to "get rich," and encourages national pride. The world wonders how the devious Chinese Communists manage to avoid the fate of the Soviet Union. The United States worries that a China growing strong economically and remaining authoritarian will seek to replace America as Number One.

Under Scenario Two, a Beijing grown politically sclerotic weakens. China reaches the brink of regional fragmentation, as the prosperous south, together with restive Tibet and Xinjiang, seek more freedom from the center. The CCP still rules from the capital, but like the Beijing regime of the post-Yuan Shikai years, and the Nanjing regime from 1928, it does not actually control large sections of the country. China's international influence declines. Few countries worry about it dominating Asia, but many fear a massive departure of people from the PRC to safe havens on all sides.

Scenario Three sees the CCP regime subtly transformed, somewhat like South Korea and Taiwan in the 1980s, into a looser authoritarianism seemingly headed for a rough-and-ready democracy. Economic development and social diversification make possible a degree of political pluralism. Fewer political prisoners, newspapers that are more than an echo, professions with some autonomy, and tens of millions of people who are middle class and enjoy property rights. China has fewer headaches from critics at home and abroad.

Scenario Four is a gloomy one for the CCP. World Trade Organization entry eventually brings social and political consequences that the regime cannot handle. Economic growth continues, but at a lower level. The erosion of faith in communism, long in process, becomes total. The truth of the remark by one-time German Communist Willi Schlamm becomes widely accepted: "The problem with capitalism is capitalists; the problem with socialism is socialism." A previously quiescent populace mocks the CCP as a burnt-out case. A humble people finally say the emperor has no clothes. Quick crumbling of Communist rule occurs, similar to that in Moscow in 1991. A confusing array of semipolitical, apocalyptic, and province-level movements emerge. Individual CCP leaders pick themselves up from the floor, but in returning to the political struggle they re-dress as anti-Communist nationalists. In a puff of smoke, the Red Dynasty has gone.

Scenario Five sees surging argument in the CCP, as an economic downturn shrinks options, resulting in a split on philosophic grounds. The left holds fast to Leninism as a necessity for the unity of China. The right adheres to Marxism in word, but increasingly embraces social democracy. "[I]t is not clear," writes William McGurn, "that China's leaders fully comprehend where the market is taking them. If [Friedrich von] Hayek is right, it may be better that they don't."[56] The split comes because leftist leaders *do* realize that the market and Leninism are not compatible, and choose the Leninist system.

The dispute is protracted and the People's Liberation Army (PLA) steps in to settle it. The military, with an eye to protecting stability and its own budget and philosophy, backs the leftists, then withdraws to the barracks. The status quo ante resumes, in a mauled condition. None of the precrisis problems has been solved. As with the Tiananmen Square turning point of 1989, an old state has triumphed against a new society and economy. Guaranteed is a further reckoning not far ahead.

The above five scenarios are all less likely than the following two, each related in their first phase to Scenario Five.

Scenario Six also sees a tussle in the CCP, in the face of an economic slump, that defies resolution. The left holds fast to Leninism, while the reformers become social democrats. The leftists know the market and Leninism are not compatible, and wish to reverse course. Their opponents, for some years, in private, like some Czechs and Hungarians in the 1970s and 1980s, have viewed the reform process as ambiguous in its political destination. Now, they declare that the economic changes have destroyed the rationale for a Leninist political system.

---

[56]McGurn, 2000, 66.

The military steps in. In the end, however, the generals do not adjudicate between the two factions, but themselves occupy the vacuum as political bosses. The PLA hustles the leaders of both sides off the stage, declares military rule, and fascism arrives. The new government favors rural China, reduces international economic involvement, and cracks down on "unhealthy" cultural products and wealth illicitly gained. Urban strife punctuates the new regime's life.

Under this scenario, China succeeds in making Leninism and Marxism part company. This provides the foundation for a fascist period, an echo of Leninism's contribution to European fascism of the 1920s and 1930s, with nationalism forced into duty as a substitute for the departed Marxist faith. A fascist Beijing proves, *à la* Hitler and Mussolini, that repression and semicapitalism can coexist.

As Marxism fades in China, two points become clear. The Chinese revolution had relatively little to do with Marxism. Second, the idea that communism and fascism stand at opposite poles is a fallacy of Western intellectuals. James Gregor is nearer to the truth in identifying a "reactive nationalism," pitted against "real or fancied impostures of foreign penetration." Reactive nationalism is what produced the authoritarianism that made the twentieth century so violent. The revolutions and wars involved were *not between classes, but between nations.* This notion ties together Mussolini, Sun Yat-sen, Stalin, Mao, Hitler, Castro, and Deng. "Proletarian revolution" had very little to do with Communist totalitarianism.

It may be objected that the China of Deng and Jiang became substantially open to the international economy. But so, too, was the Italy of Mussolini. All these reactive, developmental states were searching for their place in a modern world of which, rightly or wrongly, they felt wary. Their leadership structure had a great deal in common. If the cult of Stalin was "mental illness," as post-Stalin Soviet Union apologists fancied, why have we seen the cult of personality also in Hitler, Castro, Mussolini, Mao, and others? What a rash of multicultural mental illness in high places! No, the cult of personality is part of the structure of autocracy.[57]

[57]Gregor, 2000, 201, 204, 219–220.

Scenario Seven begins the same way as the fifth and sixth, but ends differently. Argument over fundamental economic and political issues springs up in the CCP, resulting in a split on philosophic grounds. The left holds to Leninism while the right moves toward political pluralism. The open-ended reformers come out and say the economic changes have destroyed the rationale for a Leninist political system. As Beijing splits, local and regional interest groups, including farmers, southern businesspeople, and religious groups, express views, work the Internet, and raise demands. The interaction between elite struggle and interest-group articulation becomes crucial. As the crisis unfolds, there is also disputation over whether democracy is "Chinese," and over Tibet, Xinjiang, and Inner Mongolia. Eventually, in the face of apparent impasse, the military intervenes.

Led by the air force and navy, the PLA supports the putative social democrats. Hu Jintao, a Chinese Gorbachev, falls. He is crisply told that repairing the Communist system is not the order of business; its foundations are rotten. An evolution toward a new political system begins, with important non-Beijing input from farmers, private businesspeople, and religious groups. A "Chinese Yeltsin" appears. On national television he tears up his Communist Party membership card. In a relatively un-violent way, the Red Dynasty has come to an end. This is the best of our scenarios. A crunch occurs; there is a watershed beyond which the Leninist system does not exist. The party-state, never having permitted an opposition party to exist, finds opposition springing out *within* the CCP. Yet the political crisis brings no massive turmoil for society and the economy. A reasonable chance exists that after some time China will establish a democratic federation.

DESPITE STRONG GROUNDS for hope, the initial process of dismantling the CCP's monopoly on political power may be as confusing and indecisive as the dismantling of the monarchy was in 1911–1912. The center may weaken, at least for a while. Provincial politics are likely, once more, to be unleashed, with consequences that could muddy rather than clarify the national condition.[58] Politicians in the provinces may not turn out to have democratic instincts notably stronger than figures in Beijing, including would-be politicians in the military, who seek to map a post-Communist path. "Nobody has yet seriously proposed that the Chinese democrats all reside in the provinces," notes the historian Harald Bøckman.[59]

Any weakening of the center will bring farmers' concerns higher up the ladder of national attention. Rural interests, inevitably fractured among China's many diverse regions, will wield increased influence. Chinese nationalism, which boils down to an emotion of grievance against certain other nations and/or a sense of Chinese superiority, may play a major short-term role. A perceived initial setback to China resulting from CCP collapse could intensify reactive nationalism. Especially if Russia, Japan, or other nations should take advantage of Chinese short- or long-term weakness for their own commercial or territorial benefit.

Under several of my scenarios, the end of CCP rule may not mean China will be stable, free, or easy to deal with. I have argued that the calculated link between Leninism and the imperial tradition is the key to the nature of the Chinese state; Leninism piggybacks on a selectively salvaged autocratic tradition. But the loss of the CCP's monopoly of political power would not necessarily cancel the imperial remnants. Under the military fascism of Scenario Six, the imperial tradition may even be temporarily invigorated. "Because communism was always just an updated version of Chinese autocracy," writes Mosher with only slight exaggeration, "its death will leave these autocratic traditions intact."[60]

There are both subjective and objective reasons for the persistence of the imperial tradition. The CCP deliberately exploits values from the past. But the objective challenges of governance may also lead a future Chinese government to practices that recall the dynastic past. In addi-

[58]Young, 2000, 196.
[59]Bøckman, 1998, 334.
[60]Mosher, 2000, 75.

tion, a mentality of Chinese totalism is extant. Munro has shown that Mao's totalist way of thinking was "shared by his non-Communist predecessors and . . . after his death even among reform-minded dissidents."[61]

It would be futile, unnecessary, and unfortunate for tomorrow's China to reject everything from the public life and public philosophy of dynastic China. The past will complicate China's post-Communist steps, but it contains elements that can also enrich China's future. The Qing historian Helen Dunstan asks that Chinese "not . . . repudiate the pre-Opium War past, but . . . improve on it." She points to "unambiguously admirable features" of mid-Qing public ways, "from seriousness about the public interest to insistence on disciplined intellectual endeavor as a basis for good government."[62] Today's China stands in urgent need of such political values. Not intrinsic to democracy, they nevertheless may one day make the difference between a democracy that staggers and a democracy that works. Certain admirable strains of public life have been evident in the British polity in its evolution from monarchy through aristocracy to democracy, and the same could be true of a post-Communist China that stopped being ideological about its own past.

BEIJING'S INTERNATIONAL behavior will hinge on what happens, or doesn't happen, to the Chinese state. "Whether China will be a constructive partner or an emerging threat," writes the reformer-scholar Liu Junning, "will depend, to a very great extent, on the fate of liberalism in China: a liberal China will be a constructive partner; a nationalistic and authoritarian China will be an emerging threat."[63]

Can Americans do anything to influence China at its fork in the road? Washington can make a difference, but within limits. The political future of China is largely in the hands of the Chinese themselves. This was true when the Confucian monarchy tottered in the late nineteenth century and fell in 1912. Equally true when Mao's Communists

---

[61]Munro, 1996, 9.
[62]Dunstan, 1996, 104.
[63]Liu, 2000, 60.

and Chiang's Nationalists fought in the 1940s. It will again be true when Beijing reaches the threshold of a post-Communist future.

"Surely the goal of our foreign policy," writes William Kristol, "should be to help bring about the peaceful transformation of Beijing's dictatorship into a democracy like Taipei's."[64] But we could make a messy situation worse, with unforeseen consequences for the future. Our job is mainly to light the path. Chinese people currently like to learn from the West, but they do it their way, at their own pace.

The U.S. is the chief beacon of democracy and individual freedom in a world that recently has tipped toward democracy and free markets. This light on the hill influences the Chinese mind and pressures the Chinese Communist Party. We should speak up for American values, including federalism and individual rights, while stopping short of pushing solutions to China's domestic affairs. This requires a today-and-tomorrow perspective on Chinese politics: businesslike dealings with CCP Beijing, together with preparations for dealing with a different Beijing down the road. In the meantime, U.S. military power in East Asia is the key to preventing the new Chinese empire from taking the easy way out and substituting national glory for individual freedom.

LATTIMORE WAS substantially correct to sense that "the Westernizing of China's own ancient civilization" would be decisive in resolving Chinese dilemmas about tradition and modernity. Joseph Levenson showed how the twentieth-century revolutions changed Chinese perceptions of China's past. A philosophy assumed to be universal (the Confucian-flavored Chinese dynastic worldview) turned into a chapter of the history of one nation.[65] "[W]hen China ceased to be the world and became a nation, or struggled to become one," Levenson wrote, "Confucianism was provincial in that larger world that contained the Chinese nation."[66] In the course of the same revolutions, the CCP

---

[64] *Weekly Standard,* June 25, 2001.
[65] Levenson, 1968, Conclusion to each of the three volumes.
[66] Levenson, 1971, 5.

rejected, not only the Chinese past as "value," but also most of the West. The Chinese Communists distinguished two "Wests," liberal and Bolshevik, and chose the latter as the wave of the world's future. Here was a brand new universal that China could not only apply to its problems but also trumpet to the hungry villages of Africa and Latin America. The CCP put China's past in a gallery labeled "feudal." It declared the United States and the democratic West doomed to be buried by a new historical phase of socialism. The Communist stance, said Levenson, was "vengeance against the past and the West."[67]

The new China-led, antitraditional, left-wing cosmopolitanism crashed in ruins during the late Mao era. Maoism as a new way to be global ceased to appeal, not only in Paris and Jakarta and Havana, but within China itself. China in the 1960s and 1970s became doubly provincial; it denounced its own past and the "bourgeois" West. The Red Guards were just as "provincial," in Levenson's sense of the word, as the Westernized Chinese bourgeoisie whom they denounced as "provincial."

Deng and Jiang's China regained some poise by ceasing to reject the West and reclaiming some elements of China's past. But, in truth, China today is cosmopolitan only in a thin sense. The Communist political order has lost relation with China's own culture, and that political order has itself become sclerotic. New-new China has only its skyscrapers, export surplus, and missiles; not enough, in themselves, to redeem the twentieth-century false starts in seeking a postdynastic political order and public philosophy. The Internet, of itself, will not turn people into humanists, democrats, or cosmopolitans.

Mao's China, in Levenson's terms, turned Chinese philosophy into the specific history of China, preferring to put China on the side of a universal Marxist-Leninist history. Mao's revolution was fostered "in a cosmopolitan spirit—against the world to join the world, against [China's] past to keep it [China's], but past." Jiang's China gave up on Marxist cosmopolitanism and reclaimed some of China's past for itself. Unfortunately, Jiang and Deng, like Mao, chose from China's 3,000 years mostly myth and dictatorship.

---

[67]Levenson, 1971, 54.

The revolutionary China that saw "two Wests," liberal and Bolshevik, backed not only the wrong "West" but the wrong Chinese past. It has suited Deng, Jiang, and now Hu Jintao, hardly less than Mao, to clutch the Legalist autocratic Chinese past; Qin Shihuang was brought out of the museum to buttress the Four Absolutes. The humanist Confucian past remains untapped, except as a negative example. The pain of today's gap between China's politics and China's society is the price paid for false solutions to the problems of the past and the West. Culturally, Mao's China had no message for the world. Politically, today's China has no message for the world.

The leap from class-analysis nationalism to wealth-and-power nationalism has not landed China on cosmopolitan terrain. At the end of his life, Levenson wondered if China would remain a beached whale, or whether it would "join the world again on the cosmopolitan tide." Writing in the leftist period, Levenson thought the Cultural Revolution might do the job, but he hinted that a future Westernizing thrust might also do it.[68] Looking back, the contest was not even close. Western ways are more influential in China than they have been for decades. Yet, nationalism has been the one great constant from the late nineteenth century until the early twenty-first century. Almost by default, economic life, not culture or politics, is the centerpiece of today's Chinese cosmopolitanism.

———————

DERK BODDE, a University of Pennsylvania scholar of Chinese language and literature who was living in Beijing as the Communists closed in and took the city in the late 1940s, recorded an exchange with friends over Chinese and Western values. "Western civilization," he said of his own position, "despite all its harshness, and its stress on personal advancement, and despite the two wars with which it has laid waste the world within the space of forty years, still offers, it seems to me, the greatest hope for improvement, because of the place laboriously won in it for individual expression outside of prevailing orthodoxy. In

———————

[68]Levenson, 1971, 55.

other words, the very element of struggle which has loomed so darkly in our Western world, destructive though it often is, is what has given it its possibility for evolution and ultimate advancement."[69]

Later, on his return to the United States, in reviewing those words, Bodde felt he had to add a footnote. With East–West tension and nuclear weapons, he felt it harder to be as optimistic about the West as in 1948. Yet history took a further twist in the late twentieth century. The West did not decline, but reached a new peak. In the mid-1980s, some seventy countries and nearly two-thirds of the world's population lived under Communist or socialist governments. By the early 1990s, most communism and a good deal of socialism was dead or dying. Liberal ideas rooted in the West were in the ascendant.

China, the spectacular holdout, with North Korea and Cuba as *confrères*, seemed in a condition of great unreality. Its official positions often were untenable; the relation of its culture to its politics was hardly more resolved than in the last years of the Qing Dynasty. Yet even China was embracing values that some would call Western. An American walking the streets of China's cities does not sense a clash of civilizations. Politically, however, in 2003 China still has scarcely begun to align values of society and institutions of power. As a result, it has not shown that spiritual "advancement" for which Bodde saluted the West. It faces one more of its post-1911 political crises.

As the CCP divided Chinese history into two pasts, so two Chinese futures bid to inherit the twenty-first century. One sees a heavy-handed China with a siege mentality and a presumed mandate of history. A China that grows strong while remaining an imperial state. It threatens Taiwan, locks up democrats, makes a vassal of Myanmar (Burma), crusades against religion in Tibet, blocks Internet sites, and refuses to negotiate a settlement of disputed islands in the South China Sea. This repressive empire cannot be stable, comfortable with its own new socioeconomic vigour, or a friend to the United States or China's neighbors.

---

[69]Bodde, 1967, 53.

A second China would be a loosened-up China of (now) mostly younger people who are unmoved by the pretensions of the Communist regime, who focus on family, cultural, and economic life, rather than on the state. This China, I believe, will ultimately come into existence, ending the dream of a Chinese empire. China as a democratic federation could be a leading force in the world and our fruitful partner in Asia for decades. Recall that Chinese tradition offers visions other than autocracy, including the humanist strain of Confucianism, and autocracy's opposite, the Daoist idea of ruling by inaction. "A small state with few people" was one of Daoism's maxims. A leader "known to the people simply as existing" was another.[70] The *Daode jing*'s answer to the verbiage of the CCP would have been clear: "Those who have wisdom talk little," runs the classic of Daoism, "and those who talk much seldom have wisdom."[71]

Still, the Chinese have not found it easy to settle on political institutions. Rocky times may precede China becoming a democratic federation. The perverse strain of factionalism among the Chinese prodemocracy exiles is a warning sign. "For a thousand years we Chinese have struggled to survive," the veteran political writer Liu Binyan has said. "So we are incapable of abstract thinking for a higher cause that does not concern our own interests. . . . I think we have inherited our problems. They are in our blood."[72]

I do not believe a repressive China, however well-equipped with machines, missiles, and dollars, can play a dominant world role. The reason why today's Chinese state is ultimately not strong was stated by John Stuart Mill in 1859: "The worth of a State, in the long run," he wrote, "is the worth of the individuals composing it. . . . [A] State which dwarfs its men, in order that they may be more docile instruments in its hands even for beneficial purposes—will find that with small men no great thing can really be accomplished."[73] The PRC state indeed has dwarfed its people, if less so in its second half than its first half. Yet

---

[70]Dittmer and Kim, 1993, 41.
[71]*Daode jing,* zhang 56.
[72]Buruma, 2001, 23.
[73]Mill, 1929 (1859), 143–144.

individual human beings are the one truly creative force. The second China will eventually produce a modern democratic state. Such a state, infused with the actual wishes, wisdom, and heterogeneous strands of thought of the populace, will be worthy of Chinese civilization.

I must confess that the future is always more open than we prognosticators of China's future judge. China repeatedly eluded the limits set by the names its emperors and bureaucrats used to shape reality. Equally, it transcends the categories offered by past and present foreign mythmakers. Writes Andrew Nathan of China specialists: "[We] have found our quest to be toward an ever-receding horizon."[74] The elusiveness, I believe, stems from a gap between theory and practice in China's life, and from the lack of a clear boundary between the realm of China proper and the neighboring non-Chinese world. On both themes, I hope this book has shed a ray or two of light. Still, as the essence of China recedes and the definition of China remains blurred, the non-political China shines on. "My own experience in life," wrote senior Sinologist Richard Walker, "leads me to believe in the staying power of China, not necessarily as a nation-state or *guo* [nation] but as a way of life which will extend many of its contributions to *tian xia* [the worldwide realm]."[75]

---

[74]Hua, 2001, foreword, xiii.
[75]Walker, 1994, 9.

BIBLIOGRAPHY

This list includes books, chapters of books, and journal articles; in the footnotes they are cited by author, year, and page number. In the case of a newspaper or popular magazine (these are listed at the end of the Bibliography), or an extraneous source, the full citation is given in the footnote. For ancient Chinese books, which lack conventional publication information, a separate list appears after the alphabetized bibliography.

Almond, Gabriel. "The Return to the State," *American Political Science Review,* vol. 82, Sept. 1988.

Anagnost, Ann S. "The Beginning and End of an Emperor," *Modern China,* vol. 11, no. 2, April 1985.

Balazs, Etienne. *Chinese Civilization and Bureaucracy,* trans. by H. M. Wright. New Haven: Yale University Press, 1964.

Bao Ruo-Wang [Jean Pasqualini] and Rudolph Chelminski. *Prisoner of Mao.* New York: Penguin, 1976.

Barendse, R. J. *The Arabian Seas: The Indian Ocean World of the Seventeenth Century.* Armonk, N.Y.: Sharpe, 2001.

Barmé, Geremie. "Private Practice, Public Performance," *China Journal,* no. 35, Jan. 1996.

———. *Shades of Mao.* Armonk, N.Y.: Sharpe, 1996.

Barnett, A. Doak. *China's Far West: Four Decades of Change.* Boulder: Westview Press, 1993.

Beckwith, Christopher I. *The Tibetan Empire in Central Asia.* Princeton: Princeton University Press, 1987.

Becquelin, Nicolas, "Xinjiang in the Nineties," *China Journal,* no. 44, July 2000.

Bedeski, Robert E. *State-Building in Modern China: The Kuomintang in the Prewar Period*. Berkeley: Institute of East Asian Studies, University of California, 1981.

Benson, Linda. *The Ili Rebellion: The Moslem Challenge to Chinese Authority in Xinjiang, 1944–1949*. Armonk, N.Y.: Sharpe, 1990.

Benson, Linda, and Ingvar Svanberg. *China's Last Nomads: The History and Culture of China's Kazaks*. Armonk, N.Y.: Sharpe, 1998.

Bernstein, Richard, and Ross Munro. *The Coming Conflict with China*. New York: Knopf, 1997.

Bøckman, Harald. "China Deconstructs? The Future of the Chinese Empire-State in a Historical Perspective." In Kjeld Erik Brødsgaard and David Strand, eds., *Reconstructing Twentieth-Century China*. Oxford: Oxford University Press, 1998.

Bodde, Derk. *Peking Diary: 1948–1949, a Year of Revolution*. Greenwich, Conn.: Fawcett, 1967.

Bol, Peter. "Principles of Unity." Conference on Song Dynasty Statecraft in Thought and Action, Scottsdale, Ariz., 1986.

———. "Emperors Can Claim Antiquity Too—Huizong, the New Policies, and the Examinations." Conference on Huizong and the Culture of Northern Song China, Brown University, Dec. 2001.

Brady, Anne-Marie. "'Treat Insiders and Outsiders Differently': The Use and Control of Foreigners in the People's Republic of China," *China Quarterly*, no. 164, Dec. 2000.

Brødsgaard, Kjeld Erik. "Institutional Reform and the *Bianzhi* System in China," *China Quarterly*, no. 170, June 2002.

Brødsgaard, Kjeld Erik, and David Strand, eds. *Reconstructing Twentieth-Century China*. Oxford: Oxford University Press, 1998.

Buchheim, Hans. *Totalitarian Rule: Its Nature and Characteristics*, trans. by Ruth Hein. Middletown, Conn.: Wesleyan University Press, 1968.

Burles, Mark. *Chinese Policy Toward Russia and the Central Asian Republics*. Santa Monica, Calif.: Rand, 1999.

Burr, William, ed. *The Kissinger Transcripts: The Top Secret Talks with Beijing and Moscow*. New York: The New Press, 1998.

Buruma, Ian. *Bad Elements: Chinese Rebels from Los Angeles to Beijing*. New York: Random House, 2001.

Byington, Mark E. "Claiming the Koguryô Heritage: Territorial Issues in the Management of Koguryô Archaeological Sites in Northeast China." Paper at Society for East Asian Archaeology, Durham, England, July 2000.

Cabestan, Jean-Pierre. *L'administration Chinoise après Mao: Les Réformes de l'ère Deng Xiaoping et leurs Limites.* Paris: Éditions du Centre National de la Recherche Scientifique, 1992.

Cai Yongshun. "Between State and Peasant: Local Cadres and Statistical Reporting in Rural China," *China Quarterly,* no. 163, Sept. 2000.

Carpenter, Ted Galen, and James A. Dorn, eds. *China's Future: Constructive Partner or Emerging Threat?* Washington, D.C.: Cato Institute, 2000.

The Case of Peng Teh-huai, 1959–1968. Hong Kong: Union Research Institute, 1968.

Chang Chun-mai. *The Third Force in China.* New York: Bookman Associates, 1952.

Chang, Gordon. *The Coming Collapse of China.* New York: Random House, 2001.

Chang, K. C. "Chinese Archaeology Since 1949," *Journal of Asian Studies,* vol. 36, no. 4, Aug. 1977.

Chang Ya-chun. "Beijing's Maritime Rivalry with the U.S. and Japan," *Issues and Studies,* June 1998.

Ch'en Ta-tuan. "Investiture of Liu-Ch'iu Kings in the Ch'ing Period." In John K. Fairbank, ed., *The Chinese World Order: Traditional China's Foreign Policy.* Cambridge: Harvard University Press, 1968.

Chen Dunde. *Mao Zedong yu Nikeson zai 1972.* Beijing: Kunlun chubanshe, 1988.

Chen Fangming. *Zhimin di Taiwan: Zuoying zhengzhi yundong shilun.* Taipei: Maitian chuban gongsi, 1998.

Chen Jian. *China's Road to the Korean War.* New York: Columbia University Press, 1994.

Chen Qiyou, comp. *Lü shi chunqiu jiaoshi.* Shanghai: Xuelin chubanshe, 1984 (reprint).

Chen Qiyu. *Han Feizi zhishi,* 2 vols. Shanghai: 1958.

Chen Tsu-Lung. *La vie et les oeuvres de Wou-tchen.* Paris: Ecole Française d'Extrême-Orient, 1966.

Chesneaux, Jean. "Egalitarianism and Utopian Traditions in the East," *Diogenes,* no. 62, 1968.

Ch'i Hsi-sheng. *Nationalist China at War: Military Defeats and Political Collapse, 1937–45.* Ann Arbor: University of Michigan Press, 1982.

Chiang Kai-shek. *China's Destiny.* New York: Roy Publishers, 1947.

———. *Soviet Russia in China.* New York: Macmillan, 1970.

China's National Defense. Beijing: Information Office of the State Council, July 27, 1998.

Chou, Eric. *A Man Must Choose.* New York: Knopf, 1963.

———. *The Dragon and the Phoenix.* New York: Arbor House, 1971.

Chow Ching-wen. *Ten Years of Storm: The True Story of the Communist Regime in China.* New York: Holt, Rinehart and Winston, 1960.

Ch'u T'ung-Tsu. *Local Government in China Under the Ch'ing.* Cambridge: Harvard University Press, 1962.

Chubarov, Alexander. *The Fragile Empire: A History of Imperial Russia.* New York: Continuum, 1999.

Ciepley, David. "Why the State Was Dropped in the First Place," *Critical Review,* vol. 14, nos. 2–3, 2000.

Cohen, Myron. "Being Chinese: The Peripheralization of Traditional Identity," *Daedalus,* vol. 120, no. 2, Spring 1991.

Cohen, Paul. "The Post-Mao Reforms in Historical Perspective," *Journal of Asian Studies,* vol. 47, no. 3, Aug. 1988.

Cohen, Warren I. *East Asia at the Center: Four Thousand Years of Engagement with the World.* New York: Columbia University Press, 2001.

Courant, M. A. *L'Asie Centrale aux XVII et XVIIIe Siècles: Empire Kalmouk ou Empire Mantchou?* Lyon: A. Rey, 1912.

Creel, Herrlee G. *The Origins of Statecraft in China.* Chicago: University of Chicago Press, 1970.

Critical Review (New York). "Double Issue on State Autonomy," vol. 14, nos. 2–3, 2000.

Crossley, Pamela Kyle. *The Manchus.* Cambridge: Blackwell, 1997.

_____. *The Translucent Mirror: History and Identity in Qing Imperial Ideology.* Berkeley: University of California Press, 1999.

Dachao xinqi: Deng Xiaoping nanxun qianqian houhou. Beijing: Zhongguo guangbo dianshi chubanshe, 1992.

Davies, John Paton Jr. *Dragon by the Tail.* New York: Norton, 1972.

De Bary, Wm. Theodore. "The New Confucianism in Beijing," *The American Scholar,* vol. 64, no. 2, 1995.

De Beer, Gavin, ed. *Voltaire's British Visitors.* Geneva: Institut et Musée Voltaire, 1967.

Des Rotours, Robert. "Les Insignes en Deux Parties (fou) Sous la Dynastie des Tang (618–907)," *T'oung Pao* (Leiden), Livres 1–3, 1952.

Demieville, Paul. *Le Concile de Lhasa.* Paris: Imprimerie Nationale de France, 1952.

Deng Xiaoping. *Deng Xiaoping wenxuan,* 3 vols. Beijing: Renmin chubanshe, 1983–1993.

D'Entrèves, Alessandro. *The Notion of the State.* London: Oxford University Press, 1967.

Diamond, Jared M. *Guns, Germs, and Steel: The Fates of Human Societies.* New York: Norton, 1997.

Dickson, Bruce. *Democratization in China and Taiwan: The Adaptability of Leninist Parties.* New York: Oxford University Press, 1997.

Dittmer, Lowell, and Samuel Kim, eds. *China's Quest for National Identity.* Ithaca: Cornell University Press, 1993.

Doolin, Dennis J. *Territorial Claims in the Sino-Soviet Conflict.* Stanford: Hoover Institution, Stanford University, 1965.

Duara, Prasenjit. *Rescuing History from the Nation: Questioning Narratives of Modern China.* Stanford: Stanford University Press, 1995.

Dunstan, Helen. "The 'Autocratic Heritage' and China's Political Future: A View from a Qing Specialist," *East Asian History,* no. 12, Dec. 1996.

Eastman, Lloyd, et al. *The Nationalist Era in China, 1927–1949.* Cambridge: Cambridge University Press, 1991.

Eberhard, Wolfram. *Conquerors and Rulers: Social Forces in Medieval China.* Leiden: Brill, 1952.

_____. *China's Minorities: Yesterday and Today.* Belmont, Calif.: Wadsworth, 1982.

Elliott, Mark C. "The Limits of Tartary: Manchuria in Imperial and National Geographies," *Journal of Asian Studies,* vol. 59, no. 3, August 2000.

Elvin, Mark. *The Pattern of the Chinese Past.* Stanford: Stanford University Press, 1973.

Esherick, Joseph W. *Reform and Revolution in China: The 1911 Revolution in Hunan and Hubei.* Berkeley: University of California Press, 1976.

Fairbank, John K. "The Early Treaty System in the Chinese World Order." In John K. Fairbank, ed., *The Chinese World Order: Traditional China's Foreign Policy.* Cambridge: Harvard University Press, 1968.

_____. *The U.S. and China,* 4th ed. Cambridge: Harvard University Press, 1983.

Feng Chongyi. "Reluctant Withdrawal of Government and Restrained Development of Society," *China Perspectives,* no. 35, May-June 2001.

Feuerwerker, Albert. "Chinese History and the Foreign Relations of Contemporary China," *Annals of the American Academy of Political and Social Science,* vol. 402, July 1974.

Finer, S. E. *The History of Government from the Earliest Times,* 3 vols. Oxford: Oxford University Press, 1997.

Fitzgerald, C. P. *The Empress Wu.* Vancouver: University of British Columbia Press, 1968.

_____. *The Southern Expansion of the Chinese People.* New York: Praeger, 1972.

Fletcher, Joseph F. "China and Central Asia." In John K. Fairbank, ed., *The Chinese World Order: Traditional China's Foreign Policy.* Cambridge: Harvard University Press, 1968.

_____. "Ch'ing Inner Asia, c. 1800." In John K. Fairbank, ed., *The Cambridge History of China*, vol. 10, pt. 1. Cambridge: Cambridge University Press, 1978.

_____. *Studies on Chinese and Islamic Inner Asia*. Brookfield, Vt.: Variorum, 1995.

Forbes, A. D. W. *Warlords and Muslims in Chinese Central Asia*. Cambridge: Cambridge University Press, 1986.

Frank, Andre Gunder. *Re-Orient: Global Economy in the Asian Age*. Berkeley: University of California Press, 1998.

Franke, Wolfgang. "Historical Precedent or Accidental Repetition of Events?" In Françoise Aubin, ed., *Etudes Song: Sung Studies in Memorium Etienne Balazs*. The Hague: Mouton, 1976.

Fried, Morton H. "State: The Institution." In *International Encyclopedia of the Social Sciences*. New York: Macmillan, 1968.

Friedman, Edward. *National Identity and Democratic Prospects in Socialist China*. Armonk, N.Y.: Sharpe, 1995.

_____. "Does China Have the Cultural Preconditions for Democracy?" *Philosophy East and West*, vol. 49, no. 3, July 1999.

_____. "Globalization, Legitimacy, and Post-Communism in China: A Nationalist Potential for Democracy, Prosperity, and Peace." In Tien Hung-mao and Yun-han Chu, eds., *China Under Jiang Zemin*. Boulder: Lynne Rienner, 2000.

Fu Zhengyuan. *Autocratic Tradition and Chinese Politics*. Cambridge: Cambridge University Press, 1993.

Gao Xingjian. *Soul Mountain*, trans. by Mabel Lee. New York: HarperCollins, 2000.

Gernet, Jacques. "Introduction." In Stuart Schram, ed., *The Scope of State Power in China*. New York: St. Martin's Press, 1985.

Gibbon, Edward. *The Decline and Fall of the Roman Empire*, 3 vols. New York: Random House (The Modern Library), 1932.

Gladney, Dru C. *Muslim Chinese: Ethnic Nationalism in the People's Republic*. Cambridge: Council on East Asian Studies, Harvard University, 1991.

Goncharov, Sergei, John Lewis, and Litai Xue. *Uncertain Partners: Stalin, Mao, and the Korean War*. Stanford: Stanford University Press, 1993.

Goodman, David S. G. "In Search of China's New Middle Classes," *Asian Studies Review* (Australia), vol. 22, no. 1, March 1998.

Gregor, A. James. *A Place in the Sun: Marxism and Fascism in China's Long Revolution*. Boulder: Westview Press, 2000.

Grimm, Tilemann. "State and Power in Juxtaposition: An Assessment of Ming Despotism." In Stuart Schram, ed., *The Scope of State Power in China*. New York: St. Martin's Press, 1985.

Guang Pingzhang. "Dangdai gongzhu heqin kao," *Shixue nianbao* (Beijing), no. 2, 1935.

Guo Moruo, ed. *Zhongguo shigao*, 2 vols. Beijing: Renmin chubanshe, 1964.

Guo Sujian. *Post-Mao China: From Totalitarianism to Authoritarianism?* Westport, Conn.: Praeger, 2000.

Gurtov, Melvin. "The Foreign Ministry and Foreign Affairs During the Cultural Revolution," *China Quarterly,* no. 40, Oct.-Dec. 1969.

Ha Jin. *Waiting.* New York: Pantheon, 1999.

Hamilton, Gary G., ed. *Cosmopolitan Capitalists.* Seattle: University of Washington Press, 1999.

Han Minzhu, ed. *Cries for Democracy.* Princeton: Princeton University Press, 1990.

Han minzu xingcheng wenti taolunji. Beijing: Sanlian shudian, 1957.

Han Xiaorong. "Official Histories, Official Protests—China's Reaction to Japan's New History Textbook." Paper presented at Association for Asian Studies annual meeting, Washington, D.C., April 2002.

Hayek, Friedrich. *Studies in Philosophy, Politics, and Economics.* Chicago: University of Chicago Press, 1967.

———. *Denationalisation of Money: An Analysis of the Theory and Practice of Concurrent Currencies.* London: Institute of Economic Affairs, 1976.

He Luzhi, ed. *Guojia zhuyi gailun.* Shanghai: Zhongguo renwen yanjiusuo, 1948 (1929).

He Qinglian. *Zhongguo de xianjing.* Hong Kong: Mingjing chubanshe, 1997.

Hevi, Emmanuel. *An African Student in China.* London: Pall Mall Press, 1963.

Hilton, Isabel. *The Search for the Panchen Lama.* New York: Viking, 1999.

Ho Ping-ti. "The Significance of the Ch'ing Period in Chinese History," *Journal of Asian Studies,* vol. 26, no. 2, Feb. 1967.

Hoshino, Masahiro. "Neimenggu zizhiqu chengli zhi lishi kaocha," *Zhongguo bianjiang shidi yanjiu,* vol. 36, no. 2, June 2000.

Hostetler, Laura. *Qing Colonial Enterprise: Ethnography and Cartography in Early Modern China.* Chicago: University of Chicago Press, 2001.

Howe, Christopher. "Taiwan in the 20th Century: Model or Victim?" *China Quarterly,* no. 165, March 2001.

Hsiao, Frank S. T., and Lawrence Sullivan. "The Chinese Communist Party and the Status of Taiwan, 1928–1943," *Pacific Affairs,* vol. 52, no. 3, Fall 1979.

Hsiao Kung-ch'uan. *Rural China: Imperial Control in the Nineteenth Century.* Seattle: University of Washington Press, 1960.

———. *A History of Chinese Political Thought,* trans. by F. W. Mote. Princeton: Princeton University Press, 1979.

Hsu, Immanuel. *China's Entrance into the Family of Nations: The Diplomatic Phase, 1858–1880.* Cambridge: Harvard University Press, 1960.

———. "The Great Policy Debate in China, 1874: Maritime Defense vs. Frontier Defense," *Harvard Journal of Asiatic Studies,* vol. 24, 1964–1965.

———. *The Rise of Modern China,* 6th ed. New York: Oxford University Press, 1995.

Hua Shiping, ed. *Chinese Political Culture, 1989–2000.* Armonk, N.Y.: Sharpe, 2001.

Huang Chang-Ling. "Freedom, Rights, and Authority in Chen Duxiu's Thinking," *Issues and Studies,* vol. 36, no. 3, May–June 2000.

Huang Wufang. *Zhongguo dui Xianggang huifu xingshi zhuquan de juece licheng yu zhixing.* Hong Kong: Institute for East–West Studies, Baptist University, 1997.

Hucker, Charles O. *China's Imperial Past.* Stanford: Stanford University Press, 1975.

———. *The Ming Dynasty: Its Origins and Evolving Institutions.* Ann Arbor: Center for Chinese Studies, University of Michigan, 1978.

Huntington, Samuel. "The Erosion of American National Interests," *Foreign Affairs,* vol. 76, no. 5, Sept.-Oct. 1997.

Jeans, Roger B. *Democracy and Socialism in Republican China: The Politics of Zhang Junmai (Carsun Chang), 1906–1941.* Lanham, Md.: Rowman & Littlefield, 1997.

Jiang Junzhang. "Song Ziwen Mosike tanpan zuji," *Zhuanji wenxue,* vol. 54, no.2, 1989.

Johnston, Alastair Iain. *Cultural Realism: Strategic Culture and Grand Strategy in Chinese History.* Princeton: Princeton University Press, 1995.

Joint Publication Research Service (JPRS). *Translations on Communist China,* no. 128, Dec. 21, 1970 ("Talks and Writings of Chairman Mao"), JPRS 52029.

Jones, William C. "Second Ritholz Lecture, East Asian Legal Studies," Harvard University, April 26, 1999.

Kaup, Katherine Palmer. *Creating the Zhuang: Ethnic Politics in China.* Boulder: Lynne Rienner, 2000.

Khodarkovsky, Michael. *Russia's Steppe Frontier: The Making of the Colonial Empire, 1500–1800.* Bloomington: Indiana University Press, 2002.

Khrushchev, Nikita S. *Khrushchev Remembers: The Last Testament,* trans. by Strobe Talbott. Boston: Little, Brown, 1974.

Kim, Samuel. "Beijing's Foreign Policy in the Shadows of Tiananmen: The Challenge of Legitimation," *Issues and Studies,* vol. 27, no. 1, Jan. 1991.

Kirby, William C. "The Internationalization of China: Foreign Relations at Home and Abroad in the Republican Era," *China Quarterly*, no. 150, June 1997.

_____. "The Nationalist Regime and the Chinese Party-State, 1928–1958." In Merle Goldman and Andrew Gordon, eds., *Historical Perspectives on Contemporary East Asia*. Cambridge: Harvard University Press, 2000.

Krasner, Stephen. "Approaches to the State," *Comparative Politics*, vol. 16, no. 3, Jan. 1984.

Kristof, Nicholas D., and Sheryl Wudunn. *China Wakes: The Struggle for the Soul of a Rising Power*. New York: Times Books, 1994.

Kuhn, Philip A. *Origins of the Modern Chinese State*. Stanford: Stanford University Press, 2002.

Lam Lai Sing. *Mao Tse-Tung's Ch'i and the Chinese Political Economy*. Lewiston, N.Y.: E. Mellon Press, 2000.

Lam Truong Buu. "Intervention Versus Tribute in Sino-Vietnamese Relations, 1788–1790." In John K. Fairbank, ed., *The Chinese World Order: Traditional China's Foreign Policy*. Cambridge: Harvard University Press, 1968.

Landes, David. *The Wealth and Poverty of Nations: Why Some Are So Rich and Some So Poor*. New York: Norton, 1998.

Lardy, Nicholas. *China's Unfinished Economic Revolution*. Washington, D.C.: Brookings Institution, 1998.

_____. "The Challenge of Economic Reform and Social Stability." In Tien Hung-mao and Yun-han Chu, eds., *China Under Jiang Zemin*. Boulder: Lynne Rienner, 2000.

_____. "China's Economy After the World Trade Organization." Paper prepared for the 31st Sino-American Conference on Contemporary China, Taipei, June 2002.

Lattimore, Owen. *The Desert Road to Turkestan*. Boston: Little, Brown, 1929.

_____. *Inner Asian Frontiers of China*. Boston: Beacon Press, 1962.

Lee, Robert H. G. *The Manchurian Frontier in Ch'ing History*. Cambridge: Harvard University Press, 1970.

Levenson, Joseph. *Confucian China and Its Modern Fate*, 3 vols., combined edition. Berkeley: University of California Press, 1968.

_____. *Revolution and Cosmopolitanism: The Western Stage and the Chinese Stages*. Berkeley: University of California Press, 1971.

Lewis, Mark Edward. *Writing and Authority in Early China*. Albany: State University of New York Press, 1999.

Li Cheng and Lynn White. "The Fifteenth Central Committee of the Chinese Communist Party," *Asian Survey*, vol. 38, no. 3, March 1998.

Li Guoqiang. "Dui jiejue Nanshao cundao zhuquan zhengyi jige fang'an de jieshi," *Zhongguo bianjiang shidi yanjiu,* vol. 10, no. 3, Sept. 2000.

Li Hongfeng. *Deng Xiaoping xinshiqi zhongyao huodong jiyao.* Beijing: Huaqiao chubanshe, 1994.

Li Qiang. "'Xinli erchong quyu' yu Zhongguo de wenjuan diaocha," *Shehuixue yanjiu,* March 2000.

Li Shiyu. "Qing zhengfu dui Yunnan de guanli yu kongzhi," *Zhongguo bianjiang shidi yanjiu,* Dec. 2000.

Li Xueqin, ed. *Xia Shang Zhou duandai gongcheng, 1996–2000 nian jieduan cengguo baogao, jianben.* Beijing: Shijie tushu chuban gongsi, 2000.

Li Zhisui. *The Private Life of Chairman Mao.* New York: Random House, 1994.

Liao Kuang-Sheng. "Linkage Politics in China," *World Politics,* vol. 28, no. 4, July 1976.

Lieberthal, Kenneth, et al., eds. *Perspectives on Modern China: Four Anniversaries.* Armonk, N.Y.: Sharpe, 1991.

Link, Perry. "China: The Anaconda in the Chandelier," *New York Review of Books,* April 11, 2002.

Little, Daniel. "Rational-Choice Models and Asian Studies," *Journal of Asian Studies,* vol. 50, no. 1, Feb. 1991.

Liu Junning. "The Intellectual Turn: The Emergence of Liberalism in Contemporary China." In Ted Galen Carpenter and James A. Dorn, eds., *China's Future: Constructive Partner or Emerging Threat?* Washington, D.C.: Cato Institute, 2000.

Liu, Lawrence S. "New Identity, Old System and the Relevance of Law: Taiwan After Two Decades of the TRA." Paper delivered at the International Conference on United States–Taiwan Relations, Academia Sinica, Taipei, April 1999.

Loh, Robert. *Escape from Red China.* New York: Coward-McCann, 1962.

Lovelace, Leopoldo, Jr. "Is There a *Question of Taiwan* in International Law?" *Harvard Asia Quarterly,* vol. 4, no. 3, Summer 2000.

Lukacs, Georg. "Reflections on the Cult of Stalin," *Survey,* vol. 47, April 1963.

Luo Guanzhong. *Sanguo yanyi.* Taipei: Wenyuan shuju, 1970 (reprint).

Ma Yao. *Yunnan jianshi.* Kunming: Yunnan renmin chubanshe, 1987 (revised 1990).

Macartney, George. *An Embassy to China; Being the Journal Kept by Lord Macartney During his Embassy to the Emperor Ch'ien-lung, 1793–1794,* edited by J. L. Cranmer-Byng. Hamden, Conn.: Archon Books, 1963.

MacFarquhar, Roderick. *The Origins of the Cultural Revolution*, vol. 3: *The Coming of the Cataclysm, 1961–66*. Oxford: Oxford University Press, 1997.

Machiavelli, Niccolo. *The Prince*, trans. by Luigi Ricci. London: Oxford University Press, 1960.

Manac'h, Etienne M. *La Chine: Memoires d'Extrême Asie*. Paris: Fayard, 1980.

Mancall, Mark. "The Persistence of Tradition in Chinese Foreign Policy," *Annals of the American Academy of Political and Social Science*, vol. 349, Sept. 1963.

_____. "The Ch'ing Tribute System: An Interpretive Essay." In John K. Fairbank, ed., *The Chinese World Order: Traditional China's Foreign Policy*. Cambridge: Harvard University Press, 1968.

_____. *China at the Center: 300 Years of Foreign Policy*. New York: Free Press, 1984.

Mann, James. *About Face: A History of America's Curious Relationship with China from Nixon to Clinton*. New York: Knopf, 1999.

Mao Zedong. *Selected Works*, 5 vols. Beijing: Foreign Languages Press, 1961–1977.

_____. *Jianguo yilai Mao Zedong wengao*, 13 vols., covering 1949–1976. Beijing: Zhongyang wenxian chubanshe, 1987–1998.

Mao Zedong sixiang wansui, 3 vols. 1967; April 1967; 1969.

McDonald, Angus. "Mao Tse-tung and the Hunan Self-government Movement, 1920," *China Quarterly*, no. 68, Dec. 1976.

McGurn, William. "The Gang of Three: Mao, Jesus, and Hayek." In Ted Galen Carpenter and James A. Dorn, eds., *China's Future: Constructive Partner or Emerging Threat?* Washington, D.C.: Cato Institute, 2000.

Mei Yi-Pao, trans. *The Ethical and Political Works of Motse*. London: Probsthain, 1929.

Mill, John Stuart. *On Liberty*. London: Watts, 1929 (1859).

Miller, H. Lyman. "The Late Imperial Chinese State." In David Shambaugh, ed., *The Modern Chinese State*. Cambridge: Cambridge University Press, 2000.

Millward, James A. *Beyond the Pass: Economy, Ethnicity, and Empire in Qing Central Asia, 1759–1864*. Stanford: Stanford University Press, 1998.

Mosher, Steven W. *Hegemon: China's Plan to Dominate Asia and the World*. San Francisco: Encounter Books, 2000.

Mote, Frederick W., and Denis Twitchett, eds. *Cambridge History of China*, vol. 7: *Ming Dynasty*, part 1. Cambridge: Cambridge University Press, 1988.

Mou Fuli [Mote, Frederick W.] et al., eds. *Jianqiao Zhongguo Ming dai shi*. Beijing: Zhongguo shehui kexue chubanshe, 1992.

Munro, Donald J. *The Imperial Style of Inquiry in Twentieth-Century China: The Emergence of New Approaches.* Ann Arbor: Center for Chinese Studies, University of Michigan, 1996.

Munro, Ross. "Eavesdropping on the Chinese Military: Where It Expects War—Where It Doesn't," *Orbis,* vol. 38, no. 3, Summer 1994.

Nettl, J. P. "The State as a Conceptual Variable," *World Politics,* vol. 20, no. 4, July 1968.

Ng-Quinn, Michael. "National Identity in Premodern China: Formation and Role Enactment." In Lowell Dittmer and Samuel Kim, eds., *China's Quest for National Identity.* Ithaca: Cornell University Press, 1993.

Nivison, D. S. "The Three Dynasties Chronology Project: Two Approaches to Dating." Paper presented at Association for Asian Studies annual meeting, Washington, D.C., April 2002.

Nixon, Richard. *RN: The Memoirs of Richard Nixon,* 2 vols. New York: Warner, 1978.

Nordlinger, Eric A. *On the Autonomy of the Democratic State.* Cambridge: Harvard University Press, 1981.

Oksenberg, Michel. "China's Political System: Challenges of the Twenty-First Century," *China Journal,* no. 45, Jan. 2001.

Paine, S. C. M. *Imperial Rivals: China, Russia, and Their Disputed Frontier.* Armonk, N.Y.: Sharpe, 1996.

Parkinson, C. Northcote. *East and West.* Boston: Houghton Mifflin, 1963.

Patten, Chris. *East and West.* New York: Times Books, 1999.

Pei Minxin. "China's Governance Crisis," *Foreign Affairs,* vol. 81, no. 5, Sept.-Oct. 2002.

Pepper, Suzanne. *Civil War in China.* Berkeley: University of California Press, 1978.

———. "Elections, Political Change, and Basic Law Government: Hong Kong in Search of a Political Form," *China Quarterly,* no.162, June 2000.

Perdue, Peter C. "Boundaries, Maps, and Movement: Chinese, Russian, and Mongolian Empires in Early Modern Central Eurasia," *International History Review,* vol. 20, no. 2, June 1998.

———. "Culture, History, and Chinese Imperial Strategy: Legacies of the Qing Conquests." In Hans Van de Ven, ed., *Warfare in Chinese History.* Leiden: Brill, 2000.

Perelomov, L., and A. Martynov. *Imperial China: Foreign-Policy Conceptions and Methods,* trans. by Vic Schneierson. Moscow: Progress Publishers, 1983.

Perry, Elizabeth J. "Reinventing the Wheel? The Campaign Against Falungong," *Harvard China Review,* vol. 11, no. 1, Spring/Summer 2000.

Peyrefitte, Alain. *L'Empire Immobile ou Le Choc des Mondes*. Paris: Librarie Arthème Fayard, 1989.

Pillsbury, Michael. *China Debates the Future Security Environment*. Washington, D.C.: National Defense University Press, 2000.

Pomeranz, Kenneth. *The Great Divergence*. Princeton: Princeton University Press, 2000.

Pye, Lucian. *The Spirit of Chinese Politics*. Cambridge: MIT Press, 1968.

_____. "China: Erratic State, Frustrated Society," *Foreign Affairs*, vol. 69, no. 4, Fall 1990.

Qi Yunshi. *Huangchao fanbu yaolüe*. Hangzhou: Zhejiang shuju, 1884 (1846).

Qu Jianyi. *Zhongguo lidai nu zhengzhi jia*. Hong Kong: Shanghai shuju chubanjian, 1963.

Ratchnevsky, Paul. *Genghis Khan*. Oxford: Oxford University Press, 1991.

Rawski, Evelyn. *The Last Emperors: A Social History of Qing Imperial Institutions*. Berkeley: University of California Press, 1998.

Richardson, Hugh E. "Ming-si-lie and the Fish-Bag," *Bulletin of Tibetology*, vol. 3, no. 1, 1970.

_____. *High Peaks, Pure Earth*. London: Serindia, 1998.

Rodman, Peter. "Between Friendship and Rivalry." In Ted Galen Carpenter and James A Dorn, eds., *China's Future: Constructive Partner or Emerging Threat?* Washington, D.C.: Cato Institute, 2000.

Ropp, Paul S., ed. *Heritage of China: Contemporary Perspectives on Chinese Civilization*. Berkeley: University of California Press, 1990.

Ross, Robert. "The Geography of the Peace: East Asia in the Twenty-first Century," *International Security*, vol. 23, no. 4, Spring 1999.

Rossabi, Morris. "Two Ming Envoys in Inner Asia," *T'oung Pao* (Leiden), vol. 62, nos. 1–3, 1976.

Rossabi, Morris, ed. *China Among Equals: The Middle Kingdom and Its Neighbors, 10th–14th Centuries*. Berkeley: University of California Press, 1983.

Rozman. Gilbert, ed. *The Modernization of China*. New York: The Free Press, 1981.

Sabine, George. H. "State." In *Encyclopedia of the Social Sciences*. New York: Macmillan, 1930–1935.

Sage, Steven. *Ancient Sichuan and the Unification of China*. Albany: State University of New York Press, 1992.

Sakai, Robert K. "The Ryukyu (Liu-Ch'iu) Islands as a Fief of Satsuma." In John K. Fairbank, ed., *The Chinese World Order: Traditional China's Foreign Policy*. Cambridge: Harvard University Press, 1968.

Sautman, Barry. "Anti-black Racism in Post-Mao China," *China Quarterly*, no. 138, June 1994.

_____. "Peking Man and the Politics of Paleoanthropological Nationalism in China," *Journal of Asian Studies,* vol. 60, no. 1, Feb. 2001.

Sawyer, Ralph D. *The Tao of Spycraft.* Boulder: Westview Press, 1998.

Schafer, Edward H. *The Golden Peaches of Samarkand.* Berkeley: University of California Press, 1963.

Schram, Stuart. *Mao's Road to Power: Revolutionary Writings 1912–1949.* vol. 1: *The Pre-Marxist Period, 1912–1920.* Armonk, N.Y.: Sharpe, 1992.

Schram, Stuart, ed. *The Scope of State Power in China.* New York: St. Martin's Press, 1985.

Schrecker, John. *The Chinese Revolution in Historical Perspective.* New York: Greenwood, 1991.

Schwartz, Benjamin. "The Chinese Perception of World Order, Past and Present." In John K. Fairbank, ed., *The Chinese World Order: Traditional China's Foreign Policy.* Cambridge: Harvard University Press, 1968.

Segal, Gerald. "Does China Matter?" *Foreign Affairs,* Fall, Sept.-Oct. 1999.

Seton-Watson, Hugh. *Nations and States: An Enquiry into the Origins of Nations and the Politics of Nationalism.* Boulder: Westview Press, 1977.

Shakya, Tsering. *The Dragon in the Land of Snows.* New York: Penguin, 2000.

Shambaugh, David, ed. *The Modern Chinese State.* Cambridge: Cambridge University Press, 2000.

Shao Dongfang. "Controversy on the 'Modern Text' *Bamboo Annals* and Its Relation to Three Dynasties Chronology." Paper presented at Association for Asian Studies annual meeting, Washington, D.C., April 2002.

Shapiro, Judith. *Mao's War Against Nature: Politics and the Environment in Revolutionary China.* Cambridge: Cambridge University Press, 2001.

Shepherd, John Robert. *Statecraft and Political Economy on the Taiwan Frontier, 1600–1800.* Stanford: Stanford University Press, 1993.

Sheridan, Mary. "The Emulation of Heroes," *China Quarterly,* no. 33, Jan.-March, 1968.

Shi Zhe. *Zai lishi juren shenbian.* Beijing: Zhongyang wenxian chubanshe, 1991 (revised 1995).

Shijie lishi, 2 vols. Beijing: Renmin jiaoyu chubanshe, 1993.

Short, Philip. *Mao: A Life.* London: Hodder & Stoughton, 1999.

Smith, Anthony. *National Identity.* London: Penguin, 1991.

Smith, Paul J. *Taxing Heaven's Storehouse: Horses, Bureaucrats, and the Destruction of the Sichuan Tea Industry, 1074–1224.* Cambridge: Council on East Asian Studies, Harvard University, 1991.

Smith, Richard J. *China's Cultural Heritage: The Qing Dynasty 1644–1912,* 2nd ed. Boulder: Westview Press, 1994.

_____. *Chinese Maps: Images of "All Under Heaven."* New York: Oxford University Press, 1996.

_____. "Mapping China's World: Cultural Cartography in Late Imperial Times." In Yeh Wen-hsin, ed., *Landscape, Culture and Power in Chinese Society*. Berkeley: Institute of East Asian Studies, University of California, 1998.

Snow, Edgar. *Red Star Over China*. New York: Grove Press, 1961.

Solinger, Dorothy. "Globalization and the Paradox of Participation: The Chinese Case," *Global Governance*, vol. 7, 2001.

Song Ki-ho. "Open History, Open Nationalism," *Harvard Asia Pacific Review*, vol. 3, no. 1, Winter 1998–1999.

Steinfeld, Edward. *Forging Reform in China: The Fate of State-Owned Industry*. Cambridge: Cambridge University Press, 1998.

Sun Yat-sen. *The International Development of China*. New York: Putnam, 1922.

_____. *Xuanji*, 3 vols. Beijing: Renmin chubanshe, 1956.

Suzuki, Chusei. "China's Relations with Inner Asia." In John K. Fairbank, ed., *The Chinese World Order: Traditional China's Foreign Policy*. Cambridge: Harvard University Press, 1968.

Takeuchi, Minoru, ed. *Mao Zedong ji* (in Chinese), 2nd ed., 10 vols. Tokyo: Soshosa, 1983. Plus ten supplementary volumes (*Bujuan*), same publisher, 1983–1986.

Talmon, J. L. *The Origins of Totalitarian Democracy*. London: Secker & Warburg, 1952.

Tan Qixiang, ed. *Jianming Zhongguo lishi di tuji*. Beijing: Ditu chubanshe, 1996.

Tang Xiaobing. *Global Space and the National Discourse of Modernity: The Historical Thinking of Liang Qichao*. Stanford: Stanford University Press, 1996.

Teiwes, Frederick C., with Warren Sun. *China's Road to Disaster*. Armonk, N.Y.: Sharpe, 1999.

Terrill, Ross. "Trying to Make China Work," *Atlantic Monthly*, July 1983.

_____. *China in Our Time*. New York: Simon & Schuster, 1992.

_____. *Mao: A Biography*. Stanford: Stanford University Press, 1999.

Tian Xiaoxiu, ed. *Zhonghua minzu*. Beijing: Huaxia chubanshe, 1991.

Tien Hung-mao and Yun-han Chu, eds. *China Under Jiang Zemin*. Boulder: Lynne Rienner, 2000.

Tikhvinsky, S. L., and Perelomov, L., eds. *China and Her Neighbors from Ancient Times to the Middle Ages*. Moscow: Progress Publishers, 1981.

Ting, V. K. *How China Acquired Her Civilization*. Shanghai: China Institute of Pacific Relations, 1931.

Tsou Tang. *America's Failure in China, 1941–50*. Chicago: Chicago University Press, 1963.

Tu Cheng-sheng. Interview, *China Perspectives,* no. 15, Jan.-Feb. 1998.

Tu Wei-ming. "Cultural China: The Periphery as the Center," *Daedalus,* vol. 120, no. 2, 1991.

Unger, Jonathan, ed. *Using the Past to Serve the Present.* Armonk, N.Y.: Sharpe, 1993.

Van de Ven, Hans. "Recent Studies of Modern Chinese History," *Modern Asian Studies,* vol. 30, pt. 2, 1996.

Van de Ven, Hans, ed. *Warfare in Chinese History.* Leiden: Brill, 2000.

Vermander, Benoît. "Looking at China Through the Mirror of Falungong," *China Perspectives,* no. 35, May-June 2001.

Wade, Geoff. "The Southern Chinese Borders in History." In Grant Evans et al., eds. *Where China Meets Southeast Asia.* New York: St. Martin's Press, 2000.

Wagner, Rudolf. "Reading the Chairman Mao Memorial Hall in Beijing." In Susan Naquin and Chun-fan Yu, eds., *Pilgrims and Sacred Sites in China.* Berkeley: University of California Press, 1992.

Wakeman, Frederic. "Models of Historical Change: The Chinese State and Society, 1839–1989." In Kenneth Lieberthal et al., eds., *Perspectives on Modern China: Four Anniversaries.* Armonk, N.Y.: Sharpe, 1991.

Wakeman, Frederic, and Xi Wang, eds. *China's Quest for Modernization.* Berkeley: Institute of East Asian Studies, University of California, 1997.

Waldron, Arthur. *The Great Wall of China: From History to Myth.* Cambridge: Cambridge University Press, 1990.

_____. "Historical Pivot," *Free China Review* (Taipei), March 1991.

_____. *From War to Nationalism: China's Turning Point, 1924–1925.* Cambridge: Cambridge University Press, 1995.

_____. "China's Future: Implications for U.S. Interests." Summary remarks at seminar sponsored by National Intelligence Council and Library of Congress, Washington, D.C., Sept. 24, 1999.

_____. "The Life of Mao Zedong," *Orbis,* vol. 44, no. 4, Fall 2000.

Walker, Richard. "The Cultural Factor Still Counts," *American Journal of Chinese Studies,* vol. 2, no. 1, April 1994.

Wang, David. "The Xinjiang Question of the 1940s: The Story Behind the Sino-Soviet Treaty of August 1945," *Asian Studies Review* (Australia), July 1997.

_____. *Under the Soviet Shadow: The Yining Incident: Ethnic Conflicts and International Rivalry in Xinjiang, 1944–1949.* Hong Kong: Chinese University Press, 1999.

Wang Guanghao. *Chu wenhua yuan liu xin zheng.* Wuhan, China: Wuhan daxue chubanshe, 1988.

Wang Gungwu. "Early Ming Relations with Southeast Asia." In John K. Fairbank, ed., *The Chinese World Order: Traditional China's Foreign Policy*. Cambridge: Harvard University Press, 1968.

———. "The Rhetoric of a Lesser Empire: Early Sung Relations with Its Neighbors." In Morris Rossabi, ed., *China Among Equals: The Middle Kingdom and Its Neighbors, 10th–14th Centuries*. Berkeley: University of California Press, 1983.

———. "Chineseness: The Dilemmas of Place and Practice." In Gary Hamilton, ed., *Cosmopolitan Capitalists*. Seattle: University of Washington Press, 1999.

Wang Guowei. *Shuijing zhujiao*. Shanghai: Shanghai renmin chubanshe, 1984.

Wang Ruilai. "Lun Songdai xiangquan," *Lishi yanjiu*, no. 2, 1985.

Wang Shaoguang and Angang Hu. *The Chinese Economy in Crisis*. Armonk, N.Y.: Sharpe, 2001.

Watkins, Frederick H. "State: The Concept." In *International Encyclopedia of the Social Sciences*. New York: Macmillan, 1968.

Watson, Burton, trans. *Han Fei Tzu: Basic Writings*. New York: Columbia University Press, 1964.

Whitlam, Edward Gough. *The Whitlam Government, 1972–1975*. New York: Viking, 1985.

Wilkinson, Endymion. *Chinese History: A Manual,* revised and enlarged. Cambridge: Harvard University Asia Center for the Harvard–Yenching Institute, 2000.

Wills, John E., Jr. "Ch'ing Relations with the Dutch, 1662–1690." In John K. Fairbank, ed., *The Chinese World Order: Traditional China's Foreign Policy*. Cambridge: Harvard University Press, 1968.

Wittfogel, Karl A. "The Foundations and Stages of Chinese Economic History," *Zeits für Sozialforschung* (Paris), vol. 4, no. 1, 1935.

Wong, John. "China's Sharply Declining Fertility," *Issues and Studies,* May-June 2001.

Woodside, Alexander. "Emperors and the Chinese Political System." In Kenneth Lieberthal et al., eds., *Perspectives on Modern China: Four Anniversaries*. Armonk, N.Y.: Sharpe, 1991.

Wright, A. F, and D. C. Twitchett, eds. *Perspectives on the T'ang*. New Haven: Yale University Press, 1973.

Wright, Mary, ed. *China in Revolution: The First Phase, 1900–1913*. New Haven: Yale University Press, 1968.

Wu, Harry, and Carolyn Wakeman. *Bitter Winds: A Memoir of My Years in China's Gulag*. New York: Wiley, 1994.

Wu Xiuquan. *Huiyi yu huainian*. Beijing: Zhonggong zhongyang dangxiao chubanshe, 1991.

Xie Yizheng. *Song zhi waijiao*. Shanghai: Dadong shuju, 1935.

Xu Yuqi, ed. *Xinjiang sanqu geming shi*. Beijing: Minzu chubanshe, 1998.

Yan Jiaqi. *Quanli yu zhenli*. Beijing: Guangming ribao chubanshe, 1987.

———. *Lianbang Zhongguo gouxiang*. Hong Kong: Mingbao chubanshe, 1992.

Yang, Benjamin. *Deng: A Political Biography*. Armonk, N.Y.: Sharpe, 1998.

Yang, C. K. *The Chinese Family in the Communist Revolution*. Cambridge: MIT Press, 1959.

Yang Jianye. *Ma Yinchu zhuan*. Beijing: Zhongguo qingnian chubanshe, 1986.

Yang Lien-sheng. "Historical Notes on the Chinese World Order." In John K. Fairbank, ed., *The Chinese World Order: Traditional China's Foreign Policy*. Cambridge: Harvard University Press, 1968.

Yomano, Shelly. "Reintegration in China Under the Warlords, 1916–1927," *Republican China*, vol. 12, no. 2, April 1987.

Young, Ernest. "China in the Early Twentieth Century: Tasks for a New World." In Merle Goldman and Andrew Gordon, eds., *Historical Perspectives on Contemporary East Asia*. Cambridge: Harvard University Press, 2000.

Yu Jie. *Shuo, haishi bu shuo*. Beijing: Wenhua yishu chubanshe, 1999.

Zhang Bibo. "Guanyu lishishang minzu guishu yu bianyu wenti de zai sikao," *Zhongguo bianjiang shidi yanjiu*, vol. 36, no. 2, June 2000.

Zhang Bofeng and Li Zongyi, eds. *Beiyang junfa*. Wuhan: Wuhan chubanshe, 1990.

Zhang Boquan and Wei Cuncheng, eds. *Dongbei gudai minzu, kaogu, yu jiangyu*. Changchun: Jilin daxue chubanshe, 1998.

Zhang Weihua. *Lun Han Wudi*. Shanghai: Shanghai renmin chubanshe, 1957.

Zhao Shilin, ed. *Fang "zuo" beiwanglu*. Taiyuan: Shuhai chubanshe, 1992.

Zheng Yongnian. "Institutionalizing de Facto Federalism in Post-Deng China." In Tien Hung-mao and Yun-han Chu, eds., *China Under Jiang Zemin*. Boulder: Lynne Rienner, 2000.

Zhongguo falu nianjian. Beijing: Zhongguo falu nianjian she, various years.

Zhongguo lishi, 4 vols. Beijing: Renmin jiaoyu chubanshe, 1992–1995.

Zhou Enlai. *Zhou Enlai zhuanji*. Hong Kong: Zilian, 1971.

Note on Old Chinese Books

Citations are made from a number of ancient and medieval classics, histories, and other works that in many cases have no known author, were passed around in oral form before being written down, and for some time had no set title. Conventional publication details and numerical pagination for the most part are moot. Here I give a translation of the established titles of the work, the period of its compilation and/or the period covered by its contents, and details of an English translation if it exists (my own citations, however, are drawn from the Chinese original).

———

Cefu yuangui (Outstanding Models from the Storehouse of the Past); early 11th century; I used a reprint of the 1642 edition, Taipei: Xianggang Zhonghua shuju, 20 vols., 1960, 1967.

Chunqiu (Spring and Autumn Annals); covers the years 722–481 B.C.; an English version exists in James Legge, editor and trans., *The Chinese Classics,* 5 vols., Hong Kong: Hong Kong University Press, 1960 (1865), vol. 5.

Chunqiu fanlu (Commentary on the Spring and Autumn Annals); by Dong Zhongshu, 2nd century B.C.; covers the years 722–481 B.C.

Daode jing (Classic of Morality); attributed to Lao Zi and others; 5th–3rd centuries B.C.; in English as *The Classic of the Way and Virtue,* trans. by Richard John Lynn, New York: Columbia University Press, 1999.

Liji (Records of Ritual); Spring and Autumn era; in English as *Book of Rites,* trans. by James Legge, edited by Ch'u Chai and Winberg Chai, New Hyde Park, New York: University Books, 1967.

Lü shi chunqiu (Annals of Lü Buwei); 3rd century B.C.; trans. by John Knoblock and Jeffrey Riegel, Stanford: Stanford University Press, 2000.

Jiu Tangshu (History of the Tang—Old Version); comp. by Liu Xu and others, 10th century; covers the years 618–906.

Ming shilu (Veritable Records of the Ming); Ming Shi Zong shilu refers to the records of the reign of Emperor Shi Zong, 16th century, vols. 339–353 of the total work; likewise, Ming Ying Zong shilu refers to the section covering the reign of Emperor Ying Zong, 15th century, vols. 144–187.

Shangjun shu (Book of Lord Shang); 4th century B.C.; trans. by J. J. L. Duyvendak, as *The Book of Lord Shang: A Classic of the Chinese School of Law,* London: Probsthain, 1928.

Shiji (Records of the Historian); by Sima Qian (145–86 B.C.) and others; covers earliest times until 95 B.C.; part of the work is trans. by Burton Watson, *Records of the Grand Historian,* 3 vols., New York: Columbia University Press, 1993.

Song huiyao jigao (Collection of Important Documents of the Song); comp. by Xu Song (1781–1848); covers the years 960–1220.

Song shi (History of the Song); comp. by Toghto and others, 14th century; covers the period 960–1279.

Sui shu (History of the Sui); comp. by Wei Zheng and others, 7th century; covers the years 581–617.

Tang da zhaoling ji (Collected Edicts of the Tang); comp. by Song Minqiu, 11th century.

Xin Tangshu (History of the Tang—New Version); comp. by Ouyang Xiu, Song Qi, and others, 11th century; covers the years 618–906.

Zizhi tongjian (Comprehensive Mirror to Good Government); by Sima Guang (1019–1086) and others; covers 403 B.C. to A.D. 959.

Zuozhuan (The Tradition of Zuo); a commentary on the Chunqiu; 5th–2nd centuries B.C.; covers 805–453 B.C.; trans. into English in Legge, *The Chinese Classics,* vol. 5.

Items from the following newspapers and periodicals are cited in the notes:

The Australian's Review of Books, Sydney, monthly in English (now defunct).
Beijing Review, Beijing, weekly in English.
Boston Globe, Boston, daily in English.
China Daily, daily in English, Beijing.
China Focus, Princeton, N.J., monthly in English (now defunct).
China Rights Forum, New York, quarterly in English.
Christian Science Monitor, Boston, daily in English.
Far Eastern Economic Review, Hong Kong, weekly in English.
Guangjiaojing, Hong Kong, monthly in Chinese.
Guangming ribao, Beijing, daily in Chinese.
Heilongjiang ribao, Harbin, daily in Chinese.
International Herald Tribune, Paris, daily in English.
Jingbao, Hong Kong, daily in Chinese.
Kaifang, Hong Kong, monthly in Chinese.
Lianhe bao, Taiwan, daily in Chinese.
Los Angeles Times, Los Angeles, daily in English.
Mingbao, Hong Kong, daily in Chinese.
Nanfang zhoumou, Guangzhou, weekend edition of *Nanfang ribao,* daily in Chinese.

National Review, New York, biweekly in English.

New Republic, Washington, D.C., weekly in English.

New York Times, New York, daily in English.

Newsday, Long Island, N.Y., daily in English.

Renmin ribao, Beijing, daily in Chinese.

South China Morning Post, Hong Kong, daily in English.

Taipei Journal, Taiwan, weekly in English.

Taipei Review, Taiwan, monthly in English.

Taipei Times, Taiwan, daily in English.

Taipei Update, Taipei Economic and Cultural Representative Office (TECRO), Washington, D.C., monthly in English.

Wall Street Journal, New York, daily in English.

Washington Post, Washington, D.C., daily in English.

The Weekly Standard, Washington, D.C., weekly in English.

World View, New York, monthly in English (now defunct).

Xinhua she, Beijing, daily news bulletin in Chinese.

Zhengming, Hong Kong, monthly in Chinese.

Zhongguo fazhi bao, Beijing, daily in Chinese.

Zhongguo qingnian, Beijing, monthly in Chinese.

INDEX